THE
COMPLETE
GUIDE
TO THE
NAMES OF
GOD

THE
COMPLETE
GUIDE
TO THE
NAMES OF
GOD

**EVERYTHING YOU NEED TO KNOW ABOUT
THE FATHER, SON, AND HOLY SPIRIT**

GEORGE W. KNIGHT

BARBOUR BOOKS
An Imprint of Barbour Publishing, Inc.

Published by Barbour Books, an imprint of Barbour Publishing, Inc., 1810 Barbour Drive, Uhrichsville, Ohio 44683, www.barbourbooks.com

Our mission is to inspire the world with the life-changing message of the Bible.

Contents

Introduction

King Solomon of Israel (ruled about 970–930 BC) inherited the task of building the temple in Jerusalem from his father, David (2 Chronicles 6:7–11). Solomon and his subjects thought of this ornate sanctuary as a place where God's presence would dwell. But when he dedicated the temple, the king declared, "The heavens, even the highest heaven, cannot contain you. How much less this temple I have built!" (1 Kings 8:27 NIV).

Solomon was right. God is so much greater than the little human systems we build to place Him in a box. We should approach any study of His names and His characteristics with a strong dose of humility.

I have tried to strike this chord of reverence and humility in this book. It brings together one man's thinking on the major names of God in the Bible. These divine names—of God the Father, God the Son, and God the Holy Spirit—give insight into who God is and how He acts in the world.

Throughout the book you will also find related articles with timely information on the nature and work of God. These topics include people, places, and ideas that are especially associated with Him and His redemptive purpose for humankind.

I have been teaching the Bible to Sunday school groups for more than fifty years. We have spent many exciting hours discussing the subjects in this book. I hope the information you find here will kindle your appetite for even deeper study of the nature and purpose of the awesome God whom we serve.

GEORGE W. KNIGHT
HARTSELLE, ALABAMA

Moses, seated, is helped by his brother, Aaron, and a man named Hur during a battle against the Amalekites (see Exodus 17:8-13). Throughout his forty-year career as leader of God's people, Moses received Aaron's aid.

A

AARON

The Lord instituted the priesthood as a means of reconciliation between Himself and the people of the nation of Israel through Aaron. Aaron was consecrated to this task by his brother, Moses, upon specific instructions from God (see Exodus 29:9).

Aaron's sons and their sons after them were to succeed Aaron as priests for the Israelites (see Exodus 28:40–43). Their function was to make it possible for a holy God to accept the sinful Israelites by offering various sacrifices to atone for their sins (see Leviticus 16:30).

The priestly system established through Aaron was a distinct feature of Jewish worship for more than a thousand years. But Christians believe these earthly sacrificial practices were replaced by the atoning sacrifice of Jesus on the cross. Man's acceptance by the Lord is made possible by our faith in His Son as our Savior and Lord (see Ephesians 2:8–10). See also *High Priest*; *Priests*; *Sacrificial Offerings*.

ABBA, FATHER

This is the name with which Jesus the Son addressed God the Father in His agonizing prayer in the garden of Gethsemane: "Abba, Father, all things are possible unto thee; take away this cup from me: nevertheless not what I will, but what thou wilt" (Mark 14:36). *Abba* is an Aramaic word of affection for "Father," similar in meaning to "Papa" or "Daddy" in the English language.

The Jewish people generally avoided such affectionate terms for God. They thought of Him as an exalted and larger-than-life being who demanded respect. He was to be spoken of in hushed reverence rather than addressed as if He were a member of the family.

But it was appropriate for Jesus to address the Father as "Abba." As God's Son, He knew Him more intimately than anyone has ever known God. Jesus Himself declared, "As the Father knoweth me, even so know I the Father" (John 10:15).

Through Jesus' death on the cross, He made it possible for us to know God as a loving, forgiving Father. The apostle Paul declared, "And because ye are sons, God hath sent forth the spirit of his Son into your hearts, crying, Abba, Father" (Galatians 4:6). See also *Father*.

ABLUTION

See *Ceremonial Washing*.

ABRAHAM

Abraham was the first of the patriarchs of the Old Testament whose great faith earned him the honor of being called "the Friend of God" (James 2:23). Abraham is the only person in the Bible who is described in this fashion. He is considered the father of the nation of Israel, a people whom God blessed in a special way so they in turn could be a blessing to the rest of the world.

A native of Ur in southern Babylonia, Abraham married Sarah and moved with his family to Haran (see Genesis 11:28–31). Later he obeyed God's call to leave Haran and his father's household for a "land I will show you" (Genesis 12:1 NIV). God made a covenant with Abraham and promised to give the land of Canaan to his descendants (see Genesis 13:14–17).

Although Abraham and Sarah were childless at an advanced age, God promised Abraham a son (see Genesis 17:21). At Sarah's urging, Abraham fathered Ishmael by Sarah's servant, Hagar (see Genesis 16:1–4, 15). God changed the names of Abraham and Sarah from Abram and Sarai (see Genesis 17:5–16) and established circumcision as a sign of His covenant with the Israelites (see Genesis 17:23–27). The covenant was to be fulfilled through Isaac rather than Ishmael (see Genesis 17:20–21). Isaac was born in the couple's old age (see Genesis 21:1–4).

As a test of faith, God asked Abraham to sacrifice his son Isaac (see Genesis 22:1–13). Then God Himself intervened to save Isaac and again promised to bless Abraham for his unwavering faith (see Genesis 22:16–18).

Abraham died at 175 years of age and was buried beside Sarah near Hebron (see Genesis 25:7–10).

Abraham is considered a model of faith and righteousness for all believers (see Psalm 47:9). He is viewed as the spiritual father of all who share a like faith in Christ (see Galatians 3:6–9). In Matthew's genealogy of the Savior, Jesus' earthly lineage is traced back to Abraham (see Matthew 1:2). See also *Israelites*; *Son of Abraham*.

ACCEPTANCE BY THE LORD

See *Access to God*; *Impartiality of God*.

ACCESS TO GOD

In Old Testament times, access to God was limited for most people because He was viewed with such awe and reverence. God allowed Moses to commune with Him on Mount Sinai, but He would not permit the rest of the people to approach the mountain. "Put limits for the people around the mountain," He told Moses, "and tell them, 'Be careful that you do not approach the mountain or touch the foot of it. Whoever touches the mountain is to be put to death'" (Exodus 19:12 NIV).

But these restrictions changed with the coming of God's Son, Jesus, into the world. Through His atoning death and our faith in Him, we are given unlimited access to God and all His blessings. The writer of the book of Hebrews put it like this: "Let us therefore come boldly unto the throne of grace, that we may obtain mercy, and find grace to help in time of need" (Hebrews 4:16).

Although Jesus is exalted to the highest position as God's Son, He is still as approachable to us as a member of the family or a close friend. We can bring our needs boldly to Jesus and expect to be welcomed into His presence and assured of His grace. See also *Impartiality of God*; *Priesthood of Believers*.

ACCOMMODATION OF GOD

See *Divine Accommodation*.

ACCOUNTABILITY TO GOD

According to this biblical principle, all of us are answerable to our Creator, the one true God, for our words, thoughts, and actions (see Romans 14:12). As the sovereign Lord of the universe, God has the authority to set the standards for right and wrong and to hold people accountable when they fail to follow His commands.

Believers are especially subject to this requirement. The gifts and talents granted to us by the Lord are to be used in service to Him, the Church, and fellow believers (see 1 Peter 4:10). Jesus may have had this truth in mind when He told His followers, "From everyone who has been given much, much will be demanded" (Luke 12:48 NIV). See also *Discipleship*.

ACCUSER OF OUR BRETHREN

See *Satan*.

ADAM

After God created Adam as the first man, he was an upright and intelligent being—the first worker and the first husband (see Genesis 2:8–24). He received God's command, only to disobey it, along with Eve (see Genesis 3:6).

JESUS AS THE GATE

"Jesus said again, 'Very truly I tell you, I am the gate for the sheep. All who have come before me are thieves and robbers, but the sheep have not listened to them. I am the gate; whoever enters through me will be saved. They will come in and go out, and find pasture. The thief comes only to steal and kill and destroy; I have come that they may have life, and have it to the full'" (John 10:7–10 NIV).

Adam and his wife, Eve, react to God's order that they leave the Garden of Eden. The couple's sin marred the originally perfect world. . .and affected every human being to follow.

Their sin resulted in broken fellowship with the Creator and brought God's curse and eviction from the Garden of Eden (see Genesis 3:14–24).

As head of the human race, Adam introduced sin into the world. He represents the lost and dying condition of all unrepentant sinners (see Romans 5:12–19). But this problem was solved with the coming of Christ, who was called the "second Adam." See also *Fall of Man*; *Last Adam*.

ADONAI

This Hebrew word for God in the Old Testament is usually translated as "Lord" or "my Lord" in English translations of the Bible. The word implies God's lordship over the world, including humankind. As supreme master and Lord, God has the right and authority to rule as He pleases, to set the standards for right and wrong, and to tell us as His creatures how to live. See also *Elohim*; *Shaddai*; *Yahweh*.

> Adoption brings children into a new family, giving them all the rights and privileges of biologically born children. In the same way, God adopts those who accept Jesus into His family, with all the rights and privileges that implies.

ADOPTION

In a spiritual sense, adoption is the act of God's grace by which sinful people are justified by grace and brought into the family of God. The apostle Paul mentions this idea several times in his letters.

Paul was probably influenced by the practice of physical adoption in the Roman culture of his time. The person adopted by a Roman family was usually an adult who had to agree to come into the new family. Legally, he was in effect transformed by the adoption into a new person—an apt illustration of the Christian believer's conversion (see 2 Corinthians 5:17; Galatians 4:5). See also *Inheritance*; *Spirit of Adoption*.

RESULTS OF SPIRITUAL ADOPTION

- A desire for God's glory (see Matthew 5:16).
- Holiness and likeness to God (see 2 Corinthians 6:17–18).
- A forgiving spirit (see Matthew 5:44–45; 6:14).
- Confidence in God's provision (see Matthew 6:25–34).
- Love of peace (see Matthew 5:9).

ADORATION OF GOD

See *Worship of God*.

ADVENT

This word comes from a Latin term meaning "arrival." As used by Christians, it generally refers to the arrival of God's Son in the world.

When God's perfect justice must be met, Jesus Christ steps into the courtroom as advocate for those who believe in Him.

Jesus left the glories of heaven and took on the form of a man in order to reconcile the world to His heavenly Father.

The season known as Advent is celebrated in many churches during the four successive Sundays before Christmas. It is a time of prayer, fasting, and quiet contemplation about the meaning and significance of Jesus' birth.

The phrase "second Advent" is often used to refer to the second coming of Jesus. Just as He came to earth the first time, He will return to bring the world to its appointed end and fulfill His promises to those who belong to Him. "My Father's house has many rooms," He told His followers. "If that were not so, would I have told you that I am going there to prepare a place for you? And if I go and prepare a place for you, I will come back and take you to be with me that you also may be where I am" (John 14:2–3 NIV). See also *Annunciation*; *Christmas*; *Second Coming of Christ*.

ADVOCATE

One who pleads the cause of another before a court of law is an advocate, or in modern terms, a defense attorney. This word appears only once in the Bible, as a name or title of Christ: "If any man sin, we have an advocate with the Father, Jesus Christ the righteous" (1 John 2:1).

The Greek word rendered as "advocate" in this verse appears four times in John's Gospel (see John 14:16, 26; 15:26; 16:7). In these verses the word refers to the Holy Spirit, and it is translated as "Comforter" in the KJV.

All believers need an advocate because we fall into sin occasionally, in spite of all our efforts to resist temptation. Christ and the Holy Spirit serve as our defense attorneys, pleading our cause before God the Father and securing His forgiveness on our behalf. See also *Comforter*; *Counsellor*.

AGAPE

A Greek word for selfless love, *agape* is the type of love that God wants all believers to practice. Agape is primarily an act of the will rather than the emotions (see Romans 5:8). This love is the greatest and most enduring of all Christian virtues.

According to the apostle Paul's great discourse on agape love in 1 Corinthians 13, this love is long-suffering or patient, kind, unselfish, and generous; it is not vain or proud; it believes the best about people, giving them the benefit of the doubt when they are not on their best behavior. Such love is characteristic

of God, the author of love (see 1 John 4:7). See also *Love of God*.

Thomas H. Huxley (1825–1895) created the term *agnostic* to describe his own belief that ultimate reality was unknowable. He was known as "Darwin's Bulldog" for his strong support of the theory of evolution.

AGNOSTICISM

The word *agnostic* was first used by an English biologist, T. H. Huxley, in a speech in 1869. He coined the term from two Greek words, *a*, meaning "without," and *gnosis*, meaning "knowledge." Thus, agnosticism is the belief that humans are "without knowledge" of God. It is impossible, agnostics say, to know the truth about whether God does or does not exist. This emphasis on knowledge and its companion, reason, makes them skeptical about the concept of God and His relationship to the world.

By contrast, those who believe in God say that human knowledge and reason have their limits. Our faith tells us that God does exist, that He created the world, and that He has a benevolent concern for His world and its inhabitants. The writer of Hebrews put it like this: "Faith is the substance of things hoped for, the evidence of things not seen" (Hebrews 11:1).

People of faith also believe that we can know certain truths about God. We need look no further than His created order, the world of nature. The sun comes up every day on the timetable that He established when He brought the universe into existence. Or, if you want to get technical about it, the sun comes into view as the earth makes another turn on its axis. Indeed, "the heavens declare the glory of God; the skies proclaim the work of his hands" (Psalm 19:1 NIV). See also *Atheism*.

ALIVE FOR EVERMORE

The words "I am alive for evermore" (Revelation 1:18) are among the first that Jesus spoke to the apostle John when He revealed Himself to John on the isle of Patmos. This revelation occurred about fifty or sixty years after Jesus' death and resurrection. He assured John that He was not only alive but that He was "alive for evermore."

During His brief ministry of about three years, Jesus predicted His death and resurrection on more than one occasion (see Matthew 16:21; Mark 10:32–34; Luke 9:43–45). But even His disciples had a hard time believing this would happen.

Even after Jesus appeared to them in His resurrection body, they had doubts. He asked them to touch His hands and feet to show that He had flesh and bones and they were not seeing a ghost or a vision. He even ate a piece of fish and a honeycomb as they looked

on to prove that He had a physical body just like them (see Luke 24:37–43).

Since Jesus experienced a physical resurrection and is alive for evermore, we as believers have His assurance that death is not the end of life but a glorious new beginning. "I am the resurrection and the life," He declared. "The one who believes in me will live, even though they die; and whoever lives by believing in me will never die" (John 11:25–26 NIV). See also *Resurrection and the Life*.

ALLAH

This is the name of God in the religion known as Islam, the faith practiced by Muslims throughout the world. The term is derived from two Arabic words, *al* ("the") and *llah* ("God"). The central teaching of Islam (another Arabic word meaning "submission") is total devotion to Allah and submission to His divine commands.

Islam is one of three great monotheistic (belief in one supreme God) world religions. The other two are Judaism and Christianity. But Muslims reject the doctrine of the Trinity as held by Christians. They believe that Allah is the one true, omnipotent creator who reigns supreme in his world. To them, he is strictly undivided in either his nature or his essence. They echo this belief in their familiar confession, "There is no God but Allah, and Mohammed is his prophet." See also *Monotheism*.

ALL, AND IN ALL

Jesus was born into a divided world. Jews looked down on Gentiles. Greeks considered themselves superior in education and culture to the Jews. But the apostle Paul declared

A worshipper pauses before the name Allah, in Arabic script, on a wall in Turkey.

The fury of a thunderstorm reminds us of the awesome power of the almighty God.

in Colossians 3:11 that the coming of Jesus changed all that: "There is neither Greek nor Jew, circumcision nor uncircumcision, Barbarian, Scythian, bond nor free: but Christ is all, and in all." Jesus is the "All in All"—the great unifier—who brings all people together at the foot of the cross.

To those who know Jesus, worldly distinctions and social status are no longer important. The only thing that really matters is Christ. He is the sum and substance of life— the absolute and the center of our existence. Since He gave His all to purchase our salvation, our purpose in life is to bring honor and glory to Him. See also *Impartiality of God*; *Lord over All*.

ALLELUIA

This is the Greek form of the Hebrew word *Hallelujah*, meaning "praise the Lord." The word *alleluia* appears only four times in the King James Version, all of these in Revelation 19 (see vv. 1, 3, 4, and 6), in universal praise to God on His heavenly throne in the end time.

The Hebrew form of the word appears several times in the Psalms, but it is rendered in most English translations of the Bible as "praise the Lord" or "praise ye the Lord" (see, for example, Psalms 106:1; 148:1). This phrase appears as the first and last words of Psalm 146.

When we say "hallelujah," we declare in forceful words that the Lord is worthy of our highest praise because of His goodness, love, and mercy. See also *Worship of God*.

ALMIGHTY GOD

In Genesis 17:1 (NIV) the Lord identified Himself to Abraham as the "Almighty God"

and called on him to "walk before me faithfully and be blameless." God had already promised Abraham that He would make Abraham's descendants a great nation and give them a land of their own (see Genesis 12:1–3; 13:15–17). But Abraham had no son through whom this promise could be fulfilled. The Lord, by identifying Himself as the Almighty God, declared to Abraham that He had the power to make this happen.

The Hebrew words behind this compound name also express the idea of plenty. Some interpreters suggest that they may be rendered as "the All-Sufficient One" or "the All-Bountiful One." God not only has

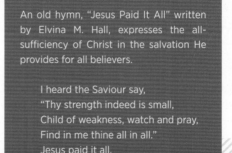

JESUS PAID IT ALL

An old hymn, "Jesus Paid It All" written by Elvina M. Hall, expresses the all-sufficiency of Christ in the salvation He provides for all believers.

I heard the Saviour say,
"Thy strength indeed is small,
Child of weakness, watch and pray,
Find in me thine all in all."
Jesus paid it all,
All to Him I owe;
Sin had left a crimson stain,
He washed it white as snow.

the power to bless His people, but He will do so abundantly. The apostle Paul declared that God is "able to do exceeding abundantly above all that we ask or think" (Ephesians 3:20).

Other titles of God that express basically the same idea as Almighty God are "Lord Almighty" (2 Corinthians 6:18), "Lord God Almighty" (Revelation 15:3), "Lord God omnipotent" (Revelation 19:6), "Mighty God"

(Jeremiah 32:18), "mighty One of Israel" (Isaiah 1:24), "mighty One of Jacob" (Isaiah 49:26), and "most mighty" (Psalm 45:3). All these names express the idea that the Lord is unlimited in His strength and power. The prophet Jeremiah expressed this truth dramatically when he said, "Ah, Sovereign LORD, you have made the heavens and the earth by your great power and outstretched arm. Nothing is too hard for you" (Jeremiah 32:17 NIV).

Jesus is also referred to as the Almighty in the book of Revelation (see Revelation 4:8; 16:7; 19:15). Revelation portrays the final victory of Jesus Christ over the forces of evil. As the Almighty, He is the Lord of the universe who was foretold in the Old Testament (see Revelation 12:5). He is also the source of the believer's new life with God the Father in the heavenly city (see Revelation 21:22; 22:1).

God as the Almighty has delegated all authority and power to His Son, who is also known as the Almighty. Using His unlimited power, He will bring the world to its conclusion in accordance with God's purpose. In his famous prophecy about the coming Messiah, Isaiah declared that Jesus would be called the "Mighty God" (Isaiah 9:6). He also referred to Him as the "Mighty One of Israel" (Isaiah 30:29) and the "Mighty One of Jacob" (Isaiah 60:16).

The hymn "Praise to the Lord, the Almighty" by Joachim Neander invites all people to worship this all-powerful Lord. Both God the Father and God the Son deserve our highest praise.

> Praise to the Lord, the Almighty, the King of creation!
> O my soul, praise Him, for He is thy health and salvation!
> All ye who hear,
> Now to His temple draw near;
> Join me in glad adoration!

See also *Breath of the Almighty*.

ALPHA AND OMEGA

In Revelation 22:13, Jesus said of Himself, "I am Alpha and Omega, the beginning and the end, the first and the last" (see also Revelation 1:8, 11; 21:6). The alpha and the omega were the first and last letters of the Greek alphabet—the language in which most of the New Testament was originally written. Thus this name is a poetic way of declaring that Jesus is the beginning and the end of all things. We might put it this way in modern terms: "Jesus is the *A* and *Z* of life and everything in between."

No letter stands before the alpha, and no letter follows the omega. This shows that Jesus defines truth and reality. All other gods that people worship are counterfeit deities. He encompasses everything and rejects all limitations.

Jesus also declared that He is the "first and the last" (Revelation 1:17; 2:8; 22:13)—a name that means basically the same thing as Alpha and Omega. As the First, He was present with God the Father before the creation (see John 1:2). As the Last, He will bring the world to its appointed end in the last days (see Revelation 22:10–13). See also *Beginning of the Creation of God*.

ALTAR

Offerings or sacrifices were placed on altars as an act of devotion to God. Some altars were probably nothing more than heaps of dirt or stones (see Exodus 20:24–25).

A "horned" altar, from around 800 BC, on display in the Israel Museum at Jerusalem.

Abraham built several altars that were probably of this type while moving around from place to place in the land of Canaan (see Genesis 12:8). But some altars were more ornate and permanent, like the one in the temple in Jerusalem built by King Solomon (see 2 Chronicles 4:1).

Physical altars were needed as long as people believed they had to bring literal offerings and sacrifices to God in order to secure His favor and acceptance. But the writer of Hebrews declared that we as believers "have an altar," referring to the sacrifice of God's Son, Jesus Christ (see Hebrews 13:10). He did away with the need for altars when He became the once-for-all sacrifice to atone for our sins. See also *Sacrificial Offerings*.

OUR LIVES ON THE ALTAR

In his hymn "Is Your All on the Altar?" Elisha A. Hoffman reminded all believers that yielding our lives to Christ is the sacrifice that He desires.

Oh, we never can know what the Lord will bestow
Of the blessings for which we have prayed.
Till our body and soul He doth fully control.
And our all on the altar is laid.
Is your all on the altar of sacrifice laid?
Your heart does the Spirit control?
You can only be blest and have peace and sweet rest,
As you yield Him your body and soul.

AMEN

Through the apostle John in the book of Revelation, Jesus delivered a special message for the church at Laodicea. By designating himself in this message as the "Amen" (Revelation 3:14), He claimed to be speaking a truthful, authoritative word for this church, one of the seven churches of Asia Minor.

The word *amen* has a rich biblical history. In the Old Testament, it was used to confirm an oath or consent to an agreement. For example, Nehemiah called on the people of his time not to cheat and defraud one another. The people responded with "amen" to pledge their agreement with Nehemiah's proposal (see Nehemiah 5:13).

Jesus often used the word *verily*—or *amen*—in His teachings to show that He was about to speak God's words of truth (see Matthew 16:28). Sometimes He repeated the word—"verily, verily"—to call special attention to what He was about to say or do. Here are just a few of His well-known phrases that He introduced with this word.

- "Verily. . .they have their reward" (referring to the hypocritical prayers of the Pharisees; see Matthew 6:5).
- "Verily. . .this poor widow hath cast more in" (describing the sacrificial gift of a poor woman who gave everything she had; see Mark 12:43).
- "Verily. . .no prophet is accepted in his own country" (lamenting His rejection by the people of His own hometown, Nazareth; see Luke 4:24).
- "Verily. . .except a man be born again, he cannot see the kingdom of God" (describing the new birth to Nicodemus; see John 3:3).

The Greek word behind "amen" is rendered as "I tell you the truth" (NIV) or "I assure you" (HCSB) by modern translations. The early church used "amen" to declare "let it be so" or "let it be true" at the close of prayers (see 2 Thessalonians 3:18), just as we do today.

Because Jesus is the great Amen, we can trust His words and His leadership. He is the sum and substance of truth (see John 14:6). He will never say or do anything that will cause us to stumble or go astray. He has promised that if we follow Him, we will know the truth, and this truth will make us free (see John 8:32). See also *Spirit of Truth; Truth.*

ANCESTOR WORSHIP

This is a form of primitive religion in which the living offered prayers or presented offerings to the spirits of their dead relatives. In some ancient cultures, this was done not out of reverence but from fear that the dead might return and take revenge on the living.

A form of ancestor worship may have been practiced by the Canaanites and other tribal enemies of the Israelites in Old Testament times. The Lord prohibited this practice among His people: "Do not cut your bodies for the dead or put tattoo marks on yourselves. I am the LORD" (Leviticus 19:28 NIV). See also *Idolatry.*

ANCESTRAL SIN

See *Original Sin.*

ANCIENT OF DAYS

This name of God is used only by the prophet Daniel (see Daniel 7:9, 13, 22; *Ancient One*, NRSV). He had a vision of four world empires that rose to great power and prominence, only to eventually fall and crumble into insignificance.

In contrast to the short shelf life of these world powers was One who had always existed and always would. Daniel's use of the imagery of old age in this description of God suggests His eternality. Unlike humans and worldly affairs, the Lord is not limited by time. Everything around us changes, but He remains the same. The only real security we have in this world is to place our trust in the Ancient of Days.

King of Old, a title used by the psalmist (see Psalm 74:12), expresses basically the same idea about God as Ancient of Days. In his hymn "Immortal, Invisible," Walter Chalmers Smith expressed exuberant praise for the Lord as the Ancient of Days.

> Immortal, invisible, God only wise,
> In light inaccessible hid from our eyes,
> Most blessed, most glorious, the Ancient
>   of Days,
> Almighty, victorious, Thy great name we
>   praise.

See also *Everlasting God*.

Moses removes his sandals as commanded by the Angel of the Lord, speaking through a burning bush. This ancient icon is in Saint Catherine's Monastery at the foot of Mount Sinai.

ANCIENT ONE

See *Ancient of Days*.

ANGEL OF HIS PRESENCE

In Isaiah 63:9, the prophet Isaiah described God's patience with His people. Although they sinned and rebelled against Him again and again, He never left them. Indeed, He provided the "Angel of His Presence" as their Savior and Redeemer.

Although angels are mentioned often throughout the Bible, this is the only place where the phrase "Angel of His Presence" occurs. This is probably a reference to Jesus Christ in His pre-earthly existence. There is no doubt that Jesus existed with God in His pre-incarnate state long before He was born into the world (see John 1:1–3). So He certainly could have served as God's agent of redemption with His people in the days before His earthly ministry.

This name of Jesus may explain the references to the mysterious Angel of the Lord in the Old Testament. This special agent was sent by God to communicate His message and to assure selected individuals of His presence. This messenger was clearly not the typical angel, but neither was He the Lord

Michael—an archangel, according to
Jude 9—battles the dragon, Satan,
as described in Revelation 12.

Himself. The best explanation is that this special messenger—the Angel of His Presence—was Jesus Christ. See also *Angels.*

APPEARANCES OF THE ANGEL OF THE LORD

- To Hagar (see Genesis 16:7–11).
- To Abraham (see Genesis 22:11–12).
- To Jacob (see Genesis 31:11).
- To Moses (see Exodus 3:1–2).
- To Joshua (see Joshua 5:14).
- To Gideon (see Judges 6:11–12).
- To the parents of Samson (see Judges 13:1–18).
- To the prophet Zechariah (see Zechariah 1:7–12).

ANGEL OF THE LORD

See *Angel of His Presence.*

ANGELS

These are heavenly beings who serve as God's messengers, encouragers, or helpers to human beings. Angels are created beings (see Psalm 148:2, 5). Thus they are subject to God's authority as their Creator (see 1 Peter 3:22) and are not to be worshiped (see Revelation 19:10).

The Bible mentions several different types of angels—(1) creatures known as cherubim and seraphim, (2) common angels, (3) archangels, and (4) the Angel of the Lord. Common angels served God by performing such duties as protecting His people (see Daniel 3:28), relieving human hunger and thirst (see Genesis 21:17–19), and praising His name (see Psalm 103:20–21). Angels of this class are apparently unlimited in number.

In one of his visions, the prophet Daniel saw "ten thousand times ten thousand" heavenly beings—probably angels—standing around the throne of God (see Daniel 7:10).

An archangel was a chief angel, or one next in rank above common angels. Archangels were apparently commissioned by the Lord to deliver messages of supreme importance to the world. Michael the archangel revealed to Daniel his famous prophecy about the end time (see Daniel 10:1–21). Another archangel, Gabriel, informed Mary that she would give birth to Jesus the Messiah (see Luke 1:26–33).

Some people believe that each of us is assigned his or her own personal guardian angel for protection, but this has no basis in scripture. Another popular view—that angels have wings—is also not stated specifically in most accounts of angels in the Bible. The one exception to this occurs in the prophet Isaiah's vision of God on His throne in the temple. Angelic creatures known as seraphim were flying around the throne while singing praises to God (see Isaiah 6:1–3). See also *Angel of His Presence.*

ANGER OF GOD

See *Wrath of God.*

ANIMISM

This word (pronounced AN uh MIZ um) comes from a Latin term, *anima*, meaning "soul" or "life." It refers to the belief among primitive tribal peoples that all of nature is inhabited by spirits, both good and evil. These spirits must be pleased by bringing them gifts or sacrifices or bowing down in worship in an attempt to gain their favor.

Animism is a form of idolatry. The one

true God is the Eternal Spirit who is separate and apart from His creation. He alone is worthy of our worship. See also *Idolatry*.

ANNUNCIATION

This announcement, by an angel to the virgin Mary, indicated she would give birth to the Messiah. Mary was troubled by the news. But the angel assured her that she was "highly favored" and had been especially selected by the Lord to be the earthly mother of the Messiah.

After this assurance from the angel, Mary declared, "I am the Lord's servant. . . . May your word to me be fulfilled" (Luke 1:38 NIV). She is one of the best examples in the Bible of humble servanthood and dedication to the Lord. See also *Mary*; *Virgin Birth of Jesus*.

ANOINTED ONE

Psalm 2 is a messianic psalm that predicts the coming of the Messiah. Rebellion against the Lord by the nations of the world is futile, the psalmist declared, because the Lord has appointed Christ, His Anointed (v. 2; *Anointed One*, NLT), as the King of the earth.

This name of Jesus ties into the anointing custom of the Old Testament. Priests and kings were anointed by having oil poured on their heads (see 1 Samuel 16:13). This ritual showed that a person had been especially chosen or set apart to perform the responsibilities of his office.

As God's Anointed One, Jesus Christ was set apart for His role as the divine Mediator and Redeemer. Through Him we find forgiveness for our sins and the abundant life that God intends for His people. In the New Testament, the Greek term *christos*, translated as "Christ," means "anointed" or "anointed one." The word always refers to the Messiah, God's Chosen One.

Just as Jesus has been anointed by His Father, He in turn has anointed us as believers for the task of declaring His message of hope in a desperate world. The apostle Paul put it like this: "We are therefore Christ's ambassadors, as though God were making his appeal through us. We implore you on Christ's behalf: Be reconciled to God" (2 Corinthians 5:20 NIV). See also *Messiah*; *One Chosen Out of the People*.

ANTHROPOMORPHISM

This pencil sketch detail from Michelangelo's famed Sistine Chapel painting *The Creation of Adam* shows "anthropomorphism"—giving a visible human hand to God, who is an unseen spirit.

This big word (pronounced an THROW puh MORF iz um) is a favorite term of theologians. It comes from two Greek words, *anthropos* ("man") and *morphe* ("form"). It means to think of God in human terms or to ascribe human characteristics to the Lord.

The biblical writers often described God like this, particularly in the Old Testament. For example, the prophet Isaiah declared, "The Lord's hand is not shortened, that it

The angel Gabriel delivers God's amazing message to a girl named Mary: She will conceive and give birth to God's Son, Jesus, the Savior of the world.

cannot save; neither his ear heavy, that it cannot hear" (Isaiah 59:1). God is an invisible, spirit being (see John 4:24), so it is doubtful that He has literal hands and ears. Isaiah was using these words metaphorically to express a profound truth about the Lord—His ability to hear and to save His people—in a way that we humans can understand.

In addition to ascribing hands and ears to God, the biblical writers also speak of His breath and mouth (see Psalm 33:6), eyes (see Isaiah 1:15), face (see 1 Peter 3:12), nose or nostrils (see Job 4:9), and wings (see Psalm 57:1). These images show us that God is more than an impersonal force or a figment of our imagination. He is a living, personal being who is involved in the lives of His people. See also *Anthropopathism*; *Imagery Used of God*.

ANTHROPOPATHISM

This theological term (pronounced an THROW poe PAHTH iz um) is similar to *anthropomorphism* (see above)—but with this slight difference: to speak of God in anthropopathic terms is to ascribe to Him human feelings and emotions.

For example, the writers of the Bible describe the Lord as being grieved by sin (see Genesis 6:6), remembering His covenant with Abraham (see Exodus 2:24), having reason (see Isaiah 1:18) and understanding (see Psalm 147:5), laughing (see Psalm 59:8), and being jealous (see Deuteronomy 5:9). Some theologians see these descriptions as metaphorical, insisting that God is not subject to such feelings. This freedom from emotions is known as the impassibility of God.

We as believers know that God cares for His people. He demonstrated this again and again in His dealings with His special people, the Israelites. But does God experience emotions like we as humans do? This question is a little harder to answer than whether He has literal arms and eyes. What we can know for certain is that He is a God of love. The Bible tells us that it was love that motivated Him to send His Son, Jesus, into the world to save us from our sins (see John 3:16). See also *Anthropomorphism*; *Imagery Used of God*; *Jealousy of God*.

ANTICHRIST

This false prophet and evil being opposes everything that Jesus Christ represents, thus his name, *anti* (or "opposed to") *Christ*. The term appears only in the writings of the apostle John (see 1 John 2:18, 22; 4:3; 2 John 7; and Revelation chapters 13, 14, 19, and 20) in the New Testament. The apostle Paul never uses the name Antichrist in his writings, but he does describe his work, referring to him in one passage as the "man of sin" (2 Thessalonians 2:3; *man of lawlessness*, NIV).

Deception is the main work of the Antichrist. This is also true of Satan, another evil being who will be allied with the Antichrist in the end time (see Revelation 13:4). Before the return of Christ, the Antichrist will appear to wage war against Christ and His people (see Revelation 13:6–8). But he will be defeated by Christ and cast into a lake of fire (see Revelation 19:20; 20:10). See also *Satan*.

APOSTASY

This is a falling away from the truth or renunciation of one's faith in Christ (see Hebrews 3:12). Apostasy is caused by Satan (see Luke 22:31–32) and influenced by false teachers (see 2 Timothy 4:3–4). Professed believers may fall away because of persecution (see Matthew 13:21) or love of worldly

Judas Iscariot betrays Jesus with a kiss, becoming an "apostate"—one who falls away from Christ.

things (see 2 Timothy 4:10). Apostasy will not occur if believers are grounded in the truth (see Ephesians 4:13–16) and depend on God's protective armor (see Ephesians 6:10–18). See also *Backsliding*.

APOSTLE

Jesus selected twelve disciples, or apostles (see Mark 3:14; 6:30), to learn from Him and to carry on His work after He finished His earthly ministry. But in Hebrews 3:1 He Himself is called the "Apostle." This is the only place in the Bible where this name of Jesus occurs.

The basic meaning of the word *apostle* is a person sent on a special mission with delegated authority and power. Jesus sent out the Twelve to teach and heal, and He gave them the ability to succeed in this mission (see Mark 6:7–13). They continued this teaching and healing ministry even after His resurrection and ascension to the Father (see Acts 2:38–43).

But Jesus Himself was the ultimate Apostle. Under the authority of His Father, He came into the world on a mission of love and grace. This mission wasn't an easy assignment. He was opposed by the religious establishment of His time. Some people who saw His miracles tried to turn Him into a military deliverer. Even His own "sent ones," the apostles, were slow to understand who He was and what He was about.

But as the author of Hebrews expressed, Jesus was "faithful to him that appointed him" (Hebrews 3:2). He did not falter in the mission on which He was sent. From the cross He declared triumphantly, "It is finished" (John 19:30). His provision for our salvation was a done deal, and the Good News about His death and resurrection—the Gospel—rolls on across the ages. See also *Great Commission of Jesus*.

APOSTLES' CREED

See *Creeds of the Church*.

APOSTOLIC BENEDICTION

See *Benediction*.

ARCHANGEL

See *Angels*.

ARIANISM

This heretical teaching in the early history of the church rejected the divinity of Christ. It originated with Arius (about AD 250–336), a priest of the church in the city of Alexandria, Egypt. He taught that Christ as God's Son did not always exist, but was created by—and therefore distinct from and inferior to—God the Father.

This false teaching gained many adherents throughout the Roman Empire. The Roman emperor Constantine the Great called church leaders together at the Council of Nicaea in AD 325 to deal with the issue. They responded by issuing the Nicene Creed, a document that reaffirmed Jesus' divinity as well as His humanity.

Throughout Christian history a few groups have either followed Arius's teachings outright or placed little emphasis on the divinity of Christ while emphasizing His humanity. But the orthodox teaching of the church is that Jesus as God's Son was fully human and fully divine and equal to God the Father in every respect. See also *Creeds of the Church*; *Docetism*; *Gnosticism*.

THE BEAT GOES ON

In her hymn "I Love to Tell the Story," Katherine Hankey reminds us that Jesus' work as the Apostle goes on through His followers as we tell others about His love and grace.

I love to tell the story of unseen things above,
Of Jesus and His glory, of Jesus and His love:
I love to tell the story because I know 'tis true;
It satisfies my longing as nothing else can do.
I love to tell the story, 'twill be my theme in glory
To tell the old, old story of Jesus and His love.

ARMAGEDDON

The final conflict between God and the forces of evil—and God's ultimate victory—will take place at this site (see Revelation 16:16). The word means "mountain of Megiddo." The site is named for the ancient fortress city of Megiddo, which overlooked a valley known as the Plain of Jezreel.

A major trade route linking Egypt in the south to Syria in the north passed through this valley. Thus, the country that occupied Megiddo had a distinct commercial and military advantage over other nations in the ancient world. Many important battles have been fought for control of this city and the territory through which this ancient highway passed. King Josiah of Judah (ruled about 640–609 BC) was killed at Megiddo in a battle with the Egyptians (see 2 Kings 23:29).

Farm fields and fishponds checkerboard the modern Jezreel valley, believed by many to be the location of the final battle between God and Satan in the book of Revelation.

Megiddo's association with many decisive battles in ancient times may explain why the apostle John spoke of the battle of Armageddon in the book of Revelation. See also *Eschatology*.

ARM OF GOD

This figurative expression symbolizes God's awesome power. Since God is Spirit (see John 4:24), He does not have a physical body. But to speak of His strength in human terms seemed to be the best way for the biblical writers to portray God's ability to deliver and protect His people.

THE LORD'S POWERFUL ARM

- "Do you have an arm like God's, and can your voice thunder like his?" (Job 40:9 NIV).
- "With your mighty arm you redeemed your people" (Psalm 77:15 NIV).
- "With your strong arm you scattered your enemies" (Psalm 89:10 NIV).

This phrase is most often used in the Old Testament to refer to God's deliverance of the Israelites from slavery in Egypt. The psalmist put it like this: The Lord brought them out "with a strong hand, and with a stretched out arm" (Psalm 136:12).

The prophet Isaiah also declared that God had "made bare his holy arm" (Isaiah 52:10) before all the nations. To bare the arm was to pull back one's robe—or roll up the sleeves, in modern terminology—and get ready for action. This was Isaiah's way of saying that God was getting ready to reveal His strength in a new way—by sending His Messiah as a spiritual deliverer for the world. See also *Anthropomorphism*; *Imagery Used of God*.

ASCENSION OF CHRIST

Luke, the author of both the Gospel of Luke and the book of Acts, gives an account of the ascension of Jesus in these writings (see Luke 24:51; Acts 1:9–11). This event occurred forty days after His resurrection (see Acts 1:3). He spent this time with His disciples, preparing them for carrying on His work after His return to God the Father.

Jesus made it clear that He was not leaving His followers alone; the Holy Spirit would come upon them in great power, strengthening them for the task of proclaiming the Gospel "in Jerusalem, and in all Judea and Samaria, and to the ends of the earth" (Acts 1:8 NIV).

Jesus' ascension marked the beginning of His intercession at the right hand of God for all believers (see Romans 8:34). His physical departure was also the occasion for a renewal of His promise that we will see Him again at His return. After Jesus disappeared from sight into a cloud, two angels appeared and stood by His disciples. "This same Jesus, who has been taken from you into heaven," they told these believers, "will come back in the same way you have seen him go into heaven" (Acts 1:11 NIV). We can rest assured that just as Jesus ascended into heaven in bodily form, so He will return to earth at His second coming.

ASEITY OF GOD

See *Self-Existence of God.*

ASSURANCE OF GOD

The dictionary defines assurance as "freedom from doubt and uncertainty." When used in a spiritual sense, this word refers to the believer's total confidence in God's promises. His greatest promise is that the death and resurrection of His Son, Jesus, has atoned for our sin. Our eternal destiny is assured when we place our faith in Christ and His sacrifice on our behalf (see John 10:28–30).

The Bible tells us we can be assured that God will answer our prayers if we offer them in His name and in accordance with His will (see 1 John 5:14–15). We are also assured of peace with God through Christ (see Romans 5:1), of God's comfort in our afflictions (see Psalm 3:6), of our adoption as God's children (see Ephesians 1:4–5), of God's presence when facing death (see Psalm 23:6), and of our bodily resurrection at Christ's return (see Philippians 3:21). See also *Promises of God.*

In a fresco from a Viennese church, Jesus rises toward heaven (the Ascension) while His awed disciples watch.

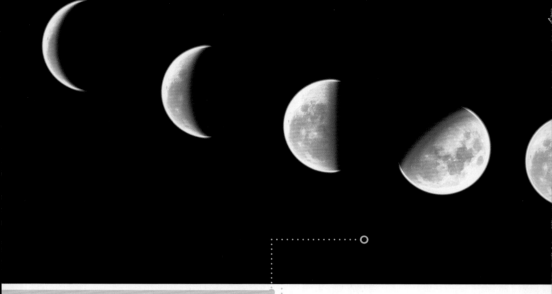

Phases of the moon. The moon, sun, stars, and other heavenly bodies—set in the sky by God on the fourth day of creation (Genesis 1:14–19)—are used by some to try to predict the future.

ASTROLOGY

This is the practice of studying the stars and other heavenly bodies in an attempt to predict the future. The prophet Isaiah described the practitioners of this art as "stargazers" (Isaiah 47:13). Astrologers are also mentioned several times in the book of Daniel (see 1:20; 2:2, 27; 4:7; 5:7, 11, 15). The prophet Daniel served in the court of the king of Babylon. These references in the prophet's book show that astrology was a prominent feature of Babylonian culture.

Daniel did not have to gaze at the stars to see into the future. He received his prophecies through direct revelation from the Lord in the form of dreams and visions (see Daniel 7:1; 8:1; 9:21–23). On several occasions he was able to interpret a dream of the king of Babylon when the king's own magicians failed to do so (see, for example, Daniel 5:15–17).

One modern form of astrology is the daily horoscope. It predicts how a person's day will go, depending on the astral sign under which he was born. Checking your daily destiny is okay, as long as you remember that this is just something that's fun to do. The bottom line is that only God knows the future. Whatever happens today, tomorrow, or a year from now is in His powerful hands. See also *Moon*; *Stars*; *Sun*.

ATHANASIAN CREED

See *Creeds of the Church*.

ATHEISM

In contrast to agnosticism, atheism is the outright denial of the existence of God. This is implied in the term's origination

from two Greek words, *a* ("without") and *theos* ("God").

Atheism has always existed, but it seemed to gain momentum and greater influence in Europe during the French Revolution in the 1700s. In modern times, several Communist countries adopted an anti-God stance and outlawed all forms of religious practice. But state-sanctioned atheism has declined considerably since the fall of the Berlin Wall in 1989.

Atheistic organizations throughout the world today seem to be more zealous in spreading their views than ever before. They are no longer content to keep their views to themselves but seem determined to combat the influence of religion in society. This crusading approach is often referred to as the New Atheism.

The Bible's view of atheism is terse and pointed: "The fool says in his heart, 'There is no God'" (Psalm 14:1 NIV). See also *Agnosticism*.

ATONEMENT

God and man are reconciled through sacrifices made to the Lord. In Old Testament times, such reconciliation was accomplished through animal sacrifices that symbolized the people's repentance.

The Jewish holy day on which atonement was made for all Israel was known as the day of atonement (see Leviticus 16:29–30; 23:27). Preceded by special Sabbaths and fasting (see Leviticus 23:24), this event recognized the people's inability to make atonement for themselves (see Hebrews 10:1–10). On this day the Jewish high priest first made atonement for himself and then the sins of the people by sprinkling the blood of a sacrificial animal on the altar (see Leviticus 16:12–15). The scapegoat, representing the sins of the people, was released into the wilderness to symbolize their pardon (see Leviticus 16:22–23).

True reconciliation with God is made possible by Christ's atoning death and resurrection (see Romans 5:10). God's righteousness

A Nubian ibex photographed near the Dead Sea at En-gedi. God told the high priest Aaron to symbolically place the Israelites' sin on a "scapegoat. . .used for making atonement by sending it into the wilderness" (Leviticus 16:10 NIV).

is imparted through Christ's sacrifice (see 2 Corinthians 5:20). His atonement is the foundation for peace among all people (see Ephesians 2:13–16). All who are redeemed through their acceptance by faith of the sacrifice of Christ are called as ministers of reconciliation (see 2 Corinthians 5:18–21). See also *Reconciliation; Sacrificial Offerings; Scapegoat.*

ATTRIBUTES OF GOD

The characteristics of the Lord, as revealed in the Bible, tell us what He is like. The listing of His attributes varies from few to many, depending on one's subjective judgment. But the following list includes His major characteristics that have been cited by theologians for many years. See articles on these individual attributes throughout this book.

> *Eternity of God*
> *Faithfulness of God*
> *Freedom of God*
> *Goodness of God*
> *Grace of God*
> *Holiness of God*
> *Immanence and Transcendence of God*
> *Immutability of God*
> *Impartiality of God*
> *Justice of God*
> *Longsuffering of God*
> *Love of God*
> *Mercy of God*
> *Omnipotence of God*
> *Omnipresence of God*
> *Omniscience of God*
> *Righteousness of God*
> *Self-Existence of God*
> *Self-Sufficiency of God*
> *Sovereignty of God*
> *Truthfulness of God*
> *Wisdom of God*

AUTHOR AND FINISHER OF OUR FAITH

Jesus is called "author" in two verses in the King James Version, both of them in the book of Hebrews (see 5:9; 12:2). In one modern translation, He is also called the "author of salvation" (Hebrews 2:10 NASB). An author is someone who creates. Jesus is the author of our faith or our salvation in that He has provided us with the only flawless example of what the life of faith is like. The NRSV expresses this idea by calling Him the "pioneer" of our faith. He blazed the trail for all others who seek to follow His example.

But Jesus not only started the journey of faith. In Hebrews 12:2 He is also called the "finisher" of our faith (*perfecter*, NRSV). He brought our faith to completion. He did not stop until He guaranteed our final redemption, making it possible for us to enjoy eternal life with Him in heaven. The writer of Hebrews expressed it like this: He "endured the cross, despising the shame, and is set down at the right hand of the throne of God" (Hebrews 12:2). See also *Faithful.*

AUTHORITY OF GOD

Chapter 40 of the book of Isaiah is one of the strongest affirmations of God's authority in the Bible. The prophet declared, "Before him all the nations are as nothing; they are regarded by him as worthless and less than nothing" (v. 17 NIV).

In the ancient world, powerful nations like Assyria and Babylonia boasted of their power over the weaker countries of Isaiah's time. But the prophet knew that God's power is absolute and unconditional. He rules over earthly governments, the physical world, the tides of history, and daily events in the lives of ordinary people.

Law enforcement officials practice delegated authority—but God's authority is absolute and intrinsic to His nature.

THE AUTHORITY OF CHRIST REVEALED

- He forgives sins (see Colossians 1:14).
- He gives His life and brings it back again (see John 10:17–18).
- He has the keys to eternal life (see John 17:2).

God's authority is intrinsic, not borrowed or delegated. It does not come to Him from some source outside Himself. His power is an essential element of His nature as the supreme Creator and ruler of the universe. The apostle Paul observed, "There is no authority except that which God has established" (Romans 13:1 NIV). All authority is derived from the Lord and is secondary to His power (see John 19:11).

Since Jesus is God's Son and has existed from eternity, He has the same intrinsic authority as God the Father (see John 10:25–30).

When He taught the people, He did not quote from some noted rabbi or philosopher but spoke the words of truth on His own authority. This amazed the common people, "for he taught them as one having authority, and not as the scribes" (Matthew 7:29). See also *Almighty God*; *Sovereignty of God*.

B

BAAL

A major pagan god of the Canaanites, Baal worship was associated with immorality (see Hosea 9:10) and child sacrifice (see Jeremiah 19:5)—pagan rituals considered especially offensive to the one true God of the Israelites.

Stone carvings discovered by archaeologists show Baal holding a bolt of lightning. This probably shows that he was thought to bring the rain, which caused crops to grow. Baal is also shown in other carvings as a mating bull—another fertility symbol.

After settling in Canaan, some of the Israelites were influenced by their pagan neighbors to worship this false god. During the days of King Ahab of Israel, one of his wives, Jezebel, actually promoted Baal worship throughout the land. With King Ahab looking on, the prophet Elijah won a decisive victory over the prophets of Baal in a dramatic contest on Mount Carmel (see 1 Kings 18:20–39). This proved that the one true God of the Israelites was superior to this pagan deity. See also *Idolatry.*

BABE

Luke 2:16 is one of the most familiar and beloved verses in the Bible: "They [shepherds] came with haste, and found Mary, and Joseph, and the babe lying in a manger."

This verse brings to mind the Christmas plays that are presented every year at Christmastime. We see shepherds in bath robes with towels around their heads. Mary and Joseph kneel beside a rough feeding trough that some member of the church has

Born helpless, as every other member of His human creation, Jesus grew up like other children as well: "And Jesus increased in wisdom and stature, and in favour with God and man" (Luke 2:52).

hammered together. Inside the trough is a doll—or a baby if a newborn is available and the parents can be persuaded to lend him for the occasion—representing the baby Jesus. Even though we have seen it all before, we still get a little misty-eyed when we stand at the conclusion of the play and sing "Joy to the World."

The wonder of Christmas is that Jesus came into the world like any newborn of the ancient world. He was a helpless baby who cried when he was hungry and uncomfortable. He had to be fed, burped, and changed. He probably got His days and nights mixed up like any baby, causing Mary and Joseph to wonder if they would ever get a good night's sleep.

It's natural for us to wonder why God would choose this way to send His Son into the world. He could have arrived as a king to the blast of trumpets. He could have dazzled the crowds by riding into town as a triumphant general at the head of a massive army. But perhaps God wanted His Son to experience the helplessness of a little baby so He could sympathize with us in our sin and weakness. Going through the stages of life like all people do, He could participate fully in the humanity of those He came to serve.

The writer of the book of Hebrews expressed it like this: "For we do not have a high priest who is unable to empathize with our weaknesses, but we have one who has been tempted in every way, just as we are—yet he did not sin" (Hebrews 4:15 NIV). See also *Incarnation of Christ*.

BACKSLIDING

A believer who sins and grows negligent in his devotion to God is considered a "backslider." The causes of backsliding include spiritual apathy (see 2 Peter 1:9), persecution because of one's faith (see Matthew 13:20–21), and love of material things (see 1 Timothy 6:10). The sin of backsliding separates the offender from God's blessings (see Isaiah 59:2). But confession and repentance will bring God's forgiveness (see 1 John 1:9).

After his sin of adultery, David prayed, "Create in me a clean heart, O God; and renew a right spirit within me" (Psalm 51:10). Although the consequences of his sin followed him for the rest of his life, David was restored to a right relationship with the Lord. See also *Apostasy*.

BAPTISM

The rite of baptism signifies a believer's cleansing from sin through Christ's atoning death. John the Baptist baptized converts to signify their repentance (see Matthew 3:6–8). In the New Testament church, Gentiles who received the Holy Spirit were promptly baptized (see Acts 10:44–48). Christian baptism memorializes the death, burial, and resurrection of Christ (see Romans 6:3–5). For the believer, baptism is a testimony of faith and a pledge to "walk in newness of life" with Jesus Christ (see Romans 6:4–11). See also *Baptism of Jesus*.

A KING IN A STABLE

After His birth in a stable in Bethlehem, the baby Jesus was placed in a manger, a feeding trough for livestock. This manger may have been hewn out of rock. Stone mangers about three feet long, eighteen inches wide, and two feet deep have been discovered in the ruins of King Ahab's stables at the ancient city of Megiddo.

The "swaddling clothes" in which Jesus was wrapped after His birth were strips of cloth that were wound tightly around a newborn's body to restrict movement. This custom is also mentioned in Ezekiel 16:4.

The inns or public lodging places of Bible times were nothing like our modern motels. They were little more than primitive shelters or camping sites near a well where people and their animals could bed down for the night. Travelers were expected to provide their own bedding, food, and cooking utensils.

The inn at Bethlehem had no lodging spaces left when Mary and Joseph arrived in town. But they were allowed to sleep in the adjoining stables where the animals of travelers were kept.

John baptizes Jesus in a seventeenth-century painting by Bartolomé Esteban Murillo.

BAPTISM OF JESUS

Many believers have questions about the baptism of Jesus by John the Baptist—an event recorded by three of the Gospels (see Matthew 3:13–17; Mark 1:9–11; Luke 3:21–22). Since Jesus was God's Son and therefore had no sin, why did He have to be baptized?

In Jesus' case, baptism was not a mandatory requirement but a voluntary act. When John objected to Jesus' request to be baptized, He replied, "It is proper for us to do this to fulfill all righteousness" (Matthew 3:15 NIV).

These words, "to fulfill all righteousness," meant that Jesus was identifying Himself with the ministry of John the Baptist, His forerunner. Jesus would continue the emphasis on repentance and baptism that John had begun. His baptism was also an act of identification with sinful humankind whom God the Father had sent Him to save. This act declared to all people, "I am committed to doing whatever it takes to deliver you from sin and bring you into God's kingdom." See also *Baptism*.

BEATITUDES

Jesus made pronouncements of blessing, known as the Beatitudes, at the beginning of His Sermon on the Mount (see Matthew 5:1–11). God's special blessings or rewards are promised to those who recognize their spiritual need (see v. 3); those who mourn (see v. 4); those who are humble (see v. 5), obedient (see v. 6), merciful (see v. 7), and pure in heart (see v. 8); those who practice peacemaking (see v. 9); and those who are persecuted for Jesus' sake (see vv. 10–11). See also *Sermon on the Mount*.

BEELZEBUB

See *Satan*.

BEGINNING AND THE END

See *Alpha and Omega*.

A spiral galaxy in deep space shows God's creative intelligence and power. According to John 1:3, the "creation of God" came through Jesus Christ.

BEGINNING OF THE CREATION OF GOD

The affirmation of Revelation 3:14 is that Jesus has always been. In this verse He is called the "beginning of the creation of God." Before He was born into the world in human form, He existed with God the Father. The Nicene Creed, a famous statement of faith formulated by the church in AD 325, puts it like this: "I believe in one Lord, Jesus Christ . . .born of the Father before all ages."

Not only has Jesus existed eternally; the Bible affirms that He participated with God in the creation. On the sixth day of creation,

JESUS AS CREATOR BEFORE THE BEGINNING

- "In the beginning was the Word, and the Word was with God, and the Word was God. The same was in the beginning with God. All things were made by him; and without him was not any thing made that was made" (John 1:1–3).
- "For by him were all things created, that are in heaven, and that are in earth. . . . And he is before all things, and by him all things consist" (Colossians 1:16–17).

the Lord declared, "Let us make man in *our* image, after *our* likeness" (Genesis 1:26, emphasis added). The plural "our" probably refers to God in His three trinitarian modes of existence: God the Father, God the Son, and God the Holy Spirit.

Two key passages from the New Testament also teach that Jesus Christ is eternal and that He was involved with God the Father in the creation of the world (see sidebar). See also *Creator*; *Word*.

BEGOTTEN SON

See *Only Begotten Son.*

BELIAL

See *Satan*.

BELIEF

See *Faith*.

BELOVED SON

Matthew 3:16–17 describes what happened when Jesus was baptized by John the Baptist at the beginning of His public ministry. The heavens opened, the Holy Spirit settled on Jesus, and God identified Him clearly as His beloved Son who brought Him joy: "This is my beloved Son, in whom I am well pleased" (v. 17). God was pleased with Jesus because He had waited patiently on God's timing until He was about thirty years old (see Luke 3:23). Now He was ready to begin the work for which He had been sent into the world.

God repeated His words about being pleased with His Son near the end of Jesus' public ministry following His transfiguration (see Matthew 17:1–5). His words on this occasion showed He pleased with what His beloved Son had accomplished. Only Jesus' death and resurrection to follow could top the divine work He had already done.

Because Jesus was God's beloved Son, we as believers are also known as His beloved (see Romans 1:7; Ephesians 1:6). We hold a special place in His heart because we have been cleansed by His blood and are committed to the work of His everlasting kingdom. See also *Son of God*.

BENEDICTION

A benediction is a short, formalized statement, prayer, or pronouncement of God's blessing. The first biblical benediction was issued by the Lord to the creatures He had brought into being. He blessed them and told them, "Be fruitful, and multiply, and fill the waters in the seas, and let fowl multiply in the earth" (Genesis 1:22).

Several different benedictions appear throughout the Bible, including Jacob's blessing upon his sons (see Genesis 49), Joshua's upon Caleb (see Joshua 14:13), King Solomon's upon the people at the dedication of the temple (see 2 Chronicles 6:3), and Simeon's upon the baby Jesus and His parents (see Luke 2:34).

The best known biblical benediction is probably the one pronounced by the apostle Paul upon the believers at Corinth: "May the grace of the Lord Jesus Christ, and the love of God, and the fellowship of the Holy Spirit be with you all" (2 Corinthians 13:14 NIV). Known as the Apostolic Benediction, it is often quoted by the minister at the conclusion of a worship service. See also *Blessing*.

BETHLEHEM

Jesus was born in the village of Bethlehem in fulfillment of an ancient prophecy that this would be the birthplace of the Messiah (see Micah 5:2–5).

Bethlehem was in the hill country of Judah about six miles south of Jerusalem. Luke's Gospel tells us that Jesus' earthly parents, who were expecting a child, traveled from their home in Nazareth to this little town to be counted in a census that had been ordered by the Roman emperor. Here Jesus was born in a stable, with an animal's feeding trough for His crib, because "there was no room for them in the inn" (Luke 2:7).

The traditional place of Jesus' birth has been preserved inside an ancient church known as the Church of the Nativity. Here in a cave under the huge building, visitors are shown a spot marked by a star that is reputed to be the very site where God's Son, the Savior of the world, was born.

Bethlehem was called the "city of David" because King David of Israel tended sheep in this area when he was just a boy (see 1 Samuel 17:15; Luke 2:4). The town, the church, and the birth cave are must-see sites for modern Christian pilgrims who visit the Holy Land. See also *Babe*.

The tower of the Church of the Nativity rises above modern-day Bethlehem. Tradition says the church was built over a cave that was the birthplace of Jesus.

BIBLE

Perhaps the best definition and description of the Bible is found in the Bible itself: "The grass withers and the flowers fall, but the word of the Lord endures forever" (1 Peter 1:24–25 NIV).

Most writings end up on the ash heap of history within a few generations. But the Bible is different. About two thousand years after the Bible took its final form with the writing of the New Testament books, God's Word is still speaking to His world. Such staying power cannot be explained in human terms. God brought the Bible into being, and He has preserved it across the centuries as a guide for human belief and behavior.

The word *Bible* comes from the Greek word *biblos*, which means "book." In a sense, the Bible is one unified book. God speaks with one voice throughout His book, calling us to accept His offer of eternal life and to follow His commands. But the Bible is also made up of individual books—thirty-nine in the Old Testament and twenty-seven in the New Testament. These books were written under God's inspiration by many different authors over a period of many centuries.

The relationship between God, His message, and the people whom He used to bring us the Bible is demonstrated by the Lord and His servant Moses in the Old Testament: "Then the LORD said to Moses, 'Write down these words, for in accordance with these words I have made a covenant with you and with Israel.' Moses was there with the LORD forty days and forty nights without eating bread or drinking water. And he wrote on the tablets the words of the covenant—the Ten Commandments" (Exodus 34:27–28 NIV).

God could have dropped the Ten Commandments from heaven in a display of wonder and magic. But instead He chose to work through a man, inspiring the words and letting Moses write them down for His people. This same principle is seen in the New Testament. The apostle Peter wrote about the prophecies of the Bible, "Prophecy never had its origin in the human will, but prophets, though human, spoke from God as they were carried along by the Holy Spirit" (2 Peter 1:21 NIV). God spoke—of this there is no doubt—but He used human agents to record and preserve His message in the Bible.

The main reason why God has given us the Bible is to tell us how to live. It is an authoritative, dependable guide to the conduct and character that God desires in His people. His Word will never lead us down the wrong path. The psalmist put it in these beautiful words: "Thy word is a lamp unto my feet, and a light unto my path" (Psalm 119:105). See also *Inspiration of the Bible*.

THE STAYING POWER OF THE BIBLE

Skeptics try to undermine the authority of the Bible by claiming it is outdated and irrelevant in our modern, scientific age. But John Clifford, a British pastor in the 1800s, took the opposite view in this inspiring poem.

I paused last eve before the blacksmith's door,
And heard the anvil ring, the vespers chime.
And looking in, I saw upon the floor old hammers,
Worn with beating years of time.
"How many anvils have you had," said I,
"To wear and batter all these hammers so?"
"Just one," he answered. Then with twinkling eye:
"The anvil wears the hammers out, you know."
And so, I thought, the anvil of God's Word
For ages skeptics' blows have beat upon,
But though the noise of falling blows was heard,
The anvil is unchanged; the hammers gone.

BIRTH OF JESUS

See *Annunciation*; *Babe*; *Virgin Birth of Jesus*.

BISHOP OF YOUR SOULS

This name of Jesus appears only once in the Bible: "For ye were as sheep going astray; but are now returned unto the Shepherd and Bishop of your souls" (1 Peter 2:25). The word *bishop* refers to a person who oversees, supervises, or watches over the welfare of others. Thus, this name is translated by modern translations as "Guardian of your souls" (NRSV) or "Overseer of your souls" (NIV).

Notice the mention of "sheep" and "Shepherd" in connection with this name in 1 Peter. Sheep were helpless animals who often wandered away from the flock. They needed a shepherd—a guardian or overseer—to watch over them and keep them out of danger. The shepherd or bishop is a good image for leaders, particularly church leaders. The terms *bishop* and *elder* are often used interchangeably in the Bible to designate those who are responsible for leading God's flock, or the Church (see Acts 14:23; 1 Timothy 3:1).

It's good to know that we as wandering sheep have someone to watch over us. The Bishop of Our Souls is on the job, and He will keep us safe. See also *Good Shepherd*; *Guide unto Death*.

BLACK MAGIC

See *Magic and Divination*.

BLASPHEMY

Engaging in disrespectful acts such as cursing or slandering that show contempt and lack of reverence toward God is considered blasphemy. In Old Testament times, blaspheming God was a serious crime that was punishable by death (see Leviticus 24:15–16).

Queen Jezebel of Israel used this law for her own evil purposes. She had Naboth

executed under a charge of blasphemy. Then she claimed his vineyard for her husband, King Ahab (see 1 Kings 21:10–13). But God did not overlook this criminal act against His rule of justice. Jezebel was tossed to her death from her palace window when Ahab's reign came to an end (see 2 Kings 9:33).

A shepherd in traditional garb watches his flock in Israel. First Peter 2:25 connects the terms *shepherd* and *bishop* in the person of Jesus Christ.

Showing disrespect toward God and His commands is a serious matter. In the New Testament, the apostle Paul cautioned believers against any behavior that could be considered blasphemous (see 1 Timothy 6:1). See also *Reverence for God*.

BLASPHEMY AGAINST THE HOLY SPIRIT

See *Unpardonable Sin*.

BLESSED AND ONLY POTENTATE

In 1 Timothy 6:15 the apostle Paul heaped up three names of Jesus in a row, each showing His unlimited power. Jesus, the apostle declared, is the "blessed and only Potentate," the King of kings, and the Lord of lords. The titles King of kings and Lord of lords appear elsewhere in the Bible (see Revelation 17:14; 19:16), but this is the only place where Jesus is called the blessed and only Potentate.

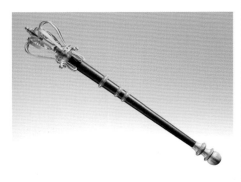

The scepter is a symbol of a king's power. The writer of Hebrews describes God the Father saying to Jesus Christ, "Thy throne, O God, is forever and ever: a sceptre of righteousness is the sceptre of thy kingdom" (1:8).

The word *potentate* comes from the Latin word *potent*, which means "power." A potentate was a king, monarch, or ruler with total power over his subjects. He shared his power with no one, and no earthly council could question his judgment or veto his decisions.

But Jesus is a Potentate of a different type—a spiritual ruler who will triumph over all the forces of evil when He judges the world at His second coming. He is the "blessed" Potentate. Chosen and blessed by God, He has been given ultimate power and authority. He is the "only" Potentate—the sole ruler who has the right to reign over the new creation that God will bring into being in the end time. See also *Almighty God*; *Omnipotence of God*; *Sovereignty of God*.

BLESSING

This is the act of wishing or declaring God's favor upon others. One of the best examples of this in the Bible is the long blessing that the patriarch Jacob invoked upon his twelve sons (see Genesis 49:1–28).

In Old Testament times, a blessing was apparently thought to carry great power. Jacob schemed to have his father, Isaac, bless him instead of his older brother, Esau (see Genesis 27:22–23). Once this blessing was given, it could not be changed or transferred to someone else (see Genesis 27:30–35).

In a spiritual sense, God is the source of all blessing, and He desires to bless all people (see Genesis 12:3). His blessing in Old Testament times was dependent on a person's obedience to His commands (see Deuteronomy 11:26–28). Since the coming of His Son, Jesus, into the world, His most abundant blessing is granted to those who confess Christ as Savior and Lord. He blesses us continually as His people by forgiving our sins (see Romans 4:7–8) and giving us eternal life (see Romans 6:23). See also *Benediction*.

BLOOD

The blood that circulates throughout the bodies of people and animals is the fluid that keeps us alive. Without this oxygen-enriched liquid that is pumped by the heart, we would die within a few minutes.

Because blood is the essence of life, God declared in Old Testament times that the bloody sacrifice of an animal on an altar was needed to show His forgiveness of human sin. He told the Israelites: "For the life of a creature is in the blood, and I have given it to you to make atonement for yourselves on the altar; it is the blood that makes atonement for one's life" (Leviticus 17:11 NIV).

In the New Testament, the phrase "the blood of Christ" refers to the sacrificial death of Jesus on the cross. His sacrificial blood is the agent of redemption for believers (see Hebrews 9:12–14). Christ Himself declared that His own blood would seal the new covenant with His followers (see Mark 14:24). His sacrifice for us is memorialized in our observance of the Lord's Supper (see 1 Corinthians 10:16). Nothing perishable or material can save; only Christ's precious blood has the power to redeem (see 1 Peter 1:18–19). See also *Atonement*; *Redemption*.

BODY OF CHRIST

The term "body of Christ" is a symbolic expression for the Church, the organization that continues the work of Christ in the world. The apostle Paul declared that Christ as God's Son was the head of the Church, and he described the Church as Christ's body (see Colossians 1:24). The risen Christ dwells in

His body and presides over the Church (see Ephesians 1:19–23). Christ assigns spiritual gifts to His body to accomplish His work and bring believers to maturity (see Ephesians 4:11–13). Members of the body are to care for one another (see 1 Corinthians 12:25–27). See also *Church*; *Head of the Church*.

BOOK OF LIFE

Those persons who will enjoy full fellowship with the Lord in heaven in the end time are referred to symbolically, according to the apostle Paul, as those whose names will be written in the book of life (see Philippians 4:3).

The concept of a book of life may have originated with Moses. He prayed that God would erase his name from His book instead of wiping out the Israelites because of their worship of the golden calf in the wilderness (see Exodus 32:32). At the final judgment those whose names are written in the Lamb's book of life will dwell with God in the New Jerusalem (see Revelation 21:27). See also *Last Judgment*.

BORN AGAIN

See *New Birth*.

BORN OF GOD

See *Regeneration*.

BOWING

In Bible times bowing before another person was a gesture of honor and respect. One extreme form of this custom was getting down on the knees, lowering the head, and then placing the head on the ground. This form of bowing was demonstrated by Abraham when he welcomed three strangers to his tent: "He hurried from the entrance of his tent to meet them and bowed low to the ground" (Genesis 18:2 NIV). A more extreme form of this custom may have been falling facedown before the person to whom respect was being paid (see 1 Chronicles 29:20).

The custom of bowing was a natural way for biblical writers to describe the respect and honor that humans should show the Lord. The psalmist declared, "Come, let us bow down in worship, let us kneel before the LORD our Maker" (Psalm 95:6 NIV).

This biblical practice of bowing before the Lord has extended into modern times. Many of us never think about it, but when we bow our heads in prayer, we are showing reverence and respect toward the one supreme God to whom we owe our lives. See also *Prayer*; *Reverence for God*.

BOW BEFORE THE SUPREME GOD

- "They all praised the LORD. . .prostrating themselves before the LORD and the king" (1 Chronicles 29:20 NIV).
- "Before me [God] every knee will bow; by me every tongue will swear" (Isaiah 45:23 NIV).
- "At the name of Jesus every knee should bow. . .and every tongue acknowledge that Jesus Christ is Lord, to the glory of God the Father" (Philippians 2:10–11 NIV).

BRANCH OF RIGHTEOUSNESS

The prophet Jeremiah predicted in many passages throughout his book that God's judgment would fall on the nation of Judah because of their sin and rebellion against the Lord. But in Jeremiah 33:15, he looked beyond that time of destruction to the day when God would send the Messiah. He would be known as the "Branch of Righteousness" who would rule over God's people with love and mercy.

The Messiah would be like a new shoot or limb that sprang from a dead tree trunk. God had promised King David centuries before Jeremiah's time that a descendant of David would always rule over His people (see 2 Samuel 7:12–16). This promise was fulfilled in Jesus Christ. He was the new Davidic king in a spiritual sense who came to redeem the world from its bondage to sin and the powers of darkness. See also *Righteous*; *Righteous Servant*.

BREAD

John 6 might be called the "bread chapter" of the New Testament. It begins with Jesus' miracle of multiplying five small loaves of bread and two fish to feed a large crowd of hungry people (see John 6:2–13). It continues across seventy-one verses as He talks with the crowds and the religious leaders about the spiritual bread that He came to provide for the world.

In this long chapter, Jesus uses four different names for Himself that involve the imagery of bread: Bread from Heaven (see v. 32), Bread of God (see v. 33), Bread of Life (see v. 35), and Living Bread (see v. 51).

Jesus probably used these names for Himself because bread made from wheat or barley was the staple food of His day. The common people could identify with this comparison. Bread was also closely identified with some of the major events from Israel's history. When the Israelites left Egypt in the Exodus, they baked their bread without leaven because they didn't have time to wait for the bread to rise (see Exodus 12:30–34). They commemorated this event in future years with a religious festival known as the Feast of Unleavened Bread (see Exodus 13:3–10). The Lord also kept His people alive in

A fresh shoot emerges from an old trunk—much like the "Branch of Righteousness," Jesus Christ, arising from the nation of Israel.

BREAD FOR THE HUNGRY

In her hymn "Break Thou the Bread of Life," Mary A. Lathbury expressed the deep desire of all believers for fellowship with Christ, the Living Bread.

> Break Thou the bread of life, dear Lord, to me,
> As Thou didst break the loaves beside the sea;
> Beyond the sacred page I seek Thee, Lord;
> My spirit pants for Thee, O living God.

the wilderness after the Exodus by providing manna, a bread substitute, for them to eat (see Numbers 11:6–9).

Just as God provided food in the wilderness, He also provides spiritual sustenance for His people today. Jesus is the Bread from Heaven that was sent by God Himself. As the Living Bread and the Bread of Life, He provides eternal life for those who claim Him as their Lord and Savior. "This is the bread that came down from heaven," Jesus declared. "Your ancestors ate manna, and died, but whoever feeds on this bread will live forever" (John 6:58 NIV). See also *Passover and Feast of Unleavened Bread*.

God prepares to breathe life into Adam, whom the Lord had formed from the dust of the ground. The 1795 painting is by William Blake.

BREATH OF GOD

This is a symbolic phrase, known as an anthropomorphism, that portrays God in human terms. With these words, He is pictured by the biblical writers as a living being who has the power to give life to others (see Psalm 33:6). This is a dramatic contrast to lifeless pagan gods, who have neither life in themselves nor the power to bring life into being.

When God created Adam from the dust of the earth, He brought him to life by "breath[ing] into his nostrils the breath of life" (Genesis 2:7). His breath demonstrates His power and creative ability (see 2 Samuel 22:14–16). See also *Anthropomorphism*; *Breath of the Almighty*; *Imagery Used of God*.

BREATH OF THE ALMIGHTY

This name of the Holy Spirit (see Job 33:4) comes from the long speech that the young man Elihu addressed to Job. He spoke after Job's three friends—Eliphaz, Bildad, and Zophar (Job 2:11)—had ended their speeches.

Elihu stated that he owed his life to the "breath of the Almighty." This is a reference to God's creation of the first man in the Garden of Eden. It was God's own breath that brought Adam to life (see Genesis 2:7). Even today, our ability to breathe life-giving oxygen into our lungs is evidence of God's care of the physical world through the agency of His Spirit.

The Holy Spirit, or the Breath of God, also energizes believers in a spiritual sense. Just before His ascension to His Father, Jesus empowered His followers for the task of carrying on His work by breathing on them and charging them to "receive the Holy Spirit" (John 20:22 NIV). This is the same life-giving Spirit that enables believers in our time to witness to others about God's transforming power.

In his hymn "Breathe on Me," Edwin Hatch expressed the prayer of every believer for divine power from the Father through His Spirit.

> Holy Spirit, breathe on me,
> Fill me with power divine;
> Kindle a flame of love and zeal
> Within this heart of mine.
> Breathe on me, breathe on me,

A bridegroom promises to love, protect, and provide for his bride—much like Jesus does for His bride, the Church.

Holy Spirit, breathe on me;
Take thou my heart, cleanse every part,
Holy Spirit, breathe on me.

See also *Breath of God*; *Wind*.

BRIDEGROOM

The followers of John the Baptist asked Jesus why He and His disciples did not participate in the ritual of fasting. Jesus asked them, "How can the guests of the bridegroom mourn while he is with them?" Then He went on to tell them, "The time will come when the bridegroom will be taken from them; then they will fast" (Matthew 9:15 NIV). Jesus' answer picked up imagery from a Jewish wedding, with Jesus referring to Himself as the Bridegroom and His disciples as the wedding guests.

It was not appropriate, Jesus said, for His disciples to fast or mourn while He as the Bridegroom was physically present with them. They should save their fasting for the time when He would be taken up to heaven by God the Father after His death and resurrection.

We are accustomed to thinking of Jesus as the King, Redeemer, or Savior. But Bridegroom? This name strikes us as a little strange. What did He mean when He applied this name to Himself?

One possibility is that He used this name to identify closely with God the Father, who referred to Himself as the Husband of His people (see Jeremiah 31:31–32). Jesus as the Bridegroom will provide for His followers, just as a human bridegroom assumes responsibility for taking care of his wife and children.

Another possibility is that Jesus was looking ahead to the birth of the Church, which is spoken of symbolically as His bride (see Revelation 21:9). The apostle Paul pointed out that just as "the husband is the head of the wife," so "Christ is the head of the Church" (Ephesians 5:23). Jesus loved the Church so much that He gave His life for it (see Ephesians 5:25). Every single member of His kingdom has experienced this sacrificial love.

On second thought, maybe Bridegroom is not such a strange name for Jesus after all.

See also *Husband.*

BRIGHT AND MORNING STAR

The "morning star" shines brightly alongside a crescent moon. Scripture uses the imagery of the morning star to describe Jesus Christ.

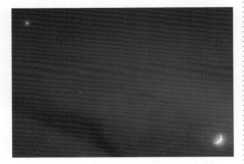

One of the last names of Jesus mentioned in the Bible appears in the final chapter of the last book of the Bible—Revelation 22:16. How appropriate that in this verse He should call Himself the "bright and morning star," a name associated with a heavenly body and its light.

The people of ancient times did not know as much about stars, planets, and heavenly bodies as we know today. To them the last star to disappear in the eastern sky as the sun began to rise was known as the morning star. Scholars and astronomers of modern times have identified this "star" as the planet Venus, Earth's closest neighbor. Because of its closeness, Venus is the third brightest object in the sky, outshone only by the sun and the moon.

When the light from all the other stars disappeared in the early morning, this star twinkled on, signaling the beginning of a new day. The birth of Jesus also marked the beginning of a new day. This truth should bring joy to our hearts. What better way to greet the dawning of each new day than to breathe a prayer of thanks to God for sending His Bright and Morning Star into the world.

Another name of Christ that means basically the same thing as Bright and Morning Star is Day Star (see 2 Peter 1:19). See also *Star Out of Jacob.*

BRIGHTNESS OF GOD'S GLORY

The Old Testament contains many references to God's glory, referring to His excellence and majesty. But the writer of Hebrews said, in effect, "You don't know divine glory until you experience the glory that appears in Jesus Christ." He referred to Him as the "brightness of [God's] glory" (Hebrews 1:3; *radiance of God's glory*, NIV; *reflection of God's glory*, NRSV). In God's Son, Jesus, the glory of God appeared as it had never been seen before.

As God's Son, Jesus shared in the Father's glory or His divine nature. He was born into the world by supernatural conception in the womb of Mary (see Luke 1:34–35). His teachings and His miracles were performed under God's authority, causing people to exclaim, "We have never seen anything like

JESUS AND HIS GLORY

- "The Word was made flesh, and dwelt among us, (and we beheld his glory)" (John 1:14).
- "Father, I will that they also, whom thou has given me [Jesus' disciples], be with me where I am; that they may behold my glory" (John 17:24).
- "God. . .hath shined in our hearts, to give the light of the knowledge of the glory of God in the face of Jesus Christ" (2 Corinthians 4:6).

this!" (Mark 2:12 NIV). His glorious resurrection demonstrated His power over the forces of evil and death.

But the greatest demonstration of Jesus' glory is reserved for the future. In the end time at His return, the apostle Paul declared, every knee will bow and every tongue will confess that "Jesus Christ is Lord, to the glory of God the Father" (Philippians 2:10–11).

Another title of Jesus that expresses basically the same idea as Brightness of God's Glory is Lord of Glory (see James 2:1). See also *Father of Glory*; *Spirit of Glory*.

BUCKLER

The psalmist called the Lord "a buckler to all those that trust in him" (Psalm 18:30). A buckler was a small shield that warriors wore on their arms. It was a defensive weapon that protected them from the thrusts of swords and spears in hand-to-hand combat. To the psalmist the Lord was like a buckler because He shielded him from the harsh words and savage attacks of his enemies.

According to the writer of Proverbs, God is also "a buckler to them that walk uprightly"

These medieval style bucklers protected their holders from the sword thrusts that left the many scratches on their surfaces. In a similar way, God protects His people.

(Proverbs 2:7). God promises protection for His people if we trust in Him and follow His commands. See also *Shield*.

BURNING BUSH

The shepherd Moses became aware of God's presence through a flaming shrub on Mount Horeb, or Sinai (see Exodus 3:2–4). The mysterious plant burned but was not consumed. As it glowed, God expressed compassion for His captive people and called Moses to return to Egypt to deliver them from bondage.

This phenomenon is known as a theophany, or a visible appearance of God. According to some interpreters, the bush may have symbolized that Israel's "fiery trial" of slavery under the Egyptians was about to come to an end through God's intervention on their behalf. See also *Fire*; *Moses*; *Theophany*.

C

CAESAREA PHILIPPI

This city at the foot of Mount Hermon in northern Palestine is where Peter confessed Jesus as the Messiah (see Matthew 16:13–16). Many rumors about Jesus and who He claimed to be had been circulating throughout the country. Jesus asked His disciples who they thought He was.

Peter spoke for all the other disciples when He answered, "You are the Messiah, the Son of the living God" (Matthew 16:16 NIV). This confession has a special meaning because of the background of the city of Caesarea Philippi. In Old Testament times, it was a place where the pagan god Baal was worshiped by the Canaanites. During the time of Jesus, the city may have contained a temple devoted to worship of the Roman emperor.

In contrast to these dead, impotent gods of the past, Peter declared that Jesus was the Son of the *living* God. He was alive and active on behalf of His people, as Jesus demonstrated through His healing and teaching ministry. See also *Son of God*.

CALLING OF GOD

See *Divine Calling*.

CALVARY

Just outside the city walls of Jerusalem is a hill called Calvary where some people believe Jesus was crucified (see Luke 23:33). The word comes from a Latin word that means "skull," thus "place of the skull." The Aramaic form of this word is *Golgotha* (see Mark 15:22).

Two separate places in Jerusalem claim to be the exact spot where Jesus was crucified. The site with the longest tradition behind it is located inside the Church of the Holy Sepulchre, an ancient, massive church within the walls of Jerusalem's Old City. This church is the successor to several others that have been built over this sacred spot since about AD 335.

The second place, known as Gordon's Calvary, sits on a rocky, skull-shaped hill outside the walls of the Old City. It has been accepted by many believers as the authentic site of the crucifixion since its discovery in the 1800s.

Perhaps the best approach to Calvary is to focus on the significance of what happened here rather than the exact place where it occurred. "It is Jesus that people must believe in, not His sepulcher," one Holy Land

The skull-shaped mass of Calvary looms behind Jesus in a dramatic eighteenth-century painting by Italian artist Giovanni Battista Tiepolo.

traveler declared. "It is not on Golgotha that we must look for salvation, but to the precious blood of the Lamb of God." See also *Cross*; *Crucifixion of Christ*.

CANAAN

God promised the territory between the Mediterranean Sea and the Jordan River, called Canaan, to Abraham and his descendants (see Genesis 13:15–17). Several centuries passed before this promise was fulfilled. Even then, the land had to be taken from the Canaanites, a warlike people who had inhabited the land long before Abraham's time (see Genesis 12:6).

The task of conquering Canaan fell to Joshua, who succeeded Moses as leader of the people. A gifted commander, Joshua served as a model of faithfulness to the Lord for the rest of the Israelites (see Joshua 24:25–27). See also *Israelites*; *Palestine*.

CAPERNAUM

This city on the northwestern shore of the Sea of Galilee served as the headquarters for Jesus during His Galilean ministry. Capernaum had no special features that set it apart from all the other villages in the region of Galilee. So why did Jesus decide to settle here? Perhaps because this was the place where at least five of His twelve disciples lived. The fishermen brothers, Peter and Andrew and James and John, worked on Lake Galilee near Capernaum (see Matthew 4:18–22), and Matthew was a tax collector in the town (see Luke 5:27–32).

Peter had a house at Capernaum where Jesus healed Peter's mother-in-law of a fever

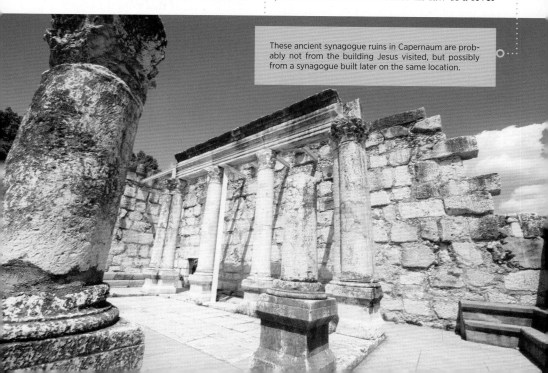

These ancient synagogue ruins in Capernaum are probably not from the building Jesus visited, but possibly from a synagogue built later on the same location.

soon after He arrived in the village (see Matthew 8:14–15). This house may have been the place where Jesus lived while He ministered among the people of this area.

This healing at Capernaum was just the first of many that Jesus performed here. Some of His most important teachings and healings occurred in or near this little town. But in spite of all these good works, the people were generally unresponsive to His message. He condemned the town for its unbelief, along with other nearby villages (see Luke 10:15). See also *Galilee*.

CAPTAIN OF SALVATION

Hebrews 2:10 is the only place in the Bible where Jesus is called the "captain of salvation." The Greek word behind "captain" in this verse is rendered as "author" in Hebrews 12:2 (see *Author and Finisher of Our Faith*).

FOLLOWING THE LORD'S LEADERSHIP

God the Father and His Son, Jesus Christ, are trustworthy leaders who will lead us in the right paths. This sentiment was expressed beautifully by Joseph H. Gilmore in his hymn "He Leadeth Me! O Blessed Thought!"

He leadeth me! O blessed thought!
O words with heav'nly comfort fraught!
Whate'er I do, where'er I be,
Still 'tis God's hand that leadeth me!
He leadeth me, He leadeth me,
By His own hand He leadeth me:
His faithful follower I would be,
For by His hand He leadeth me.

Other meanings of this word are "prince" and "leader."

In what sense is Jesus the captain or leader of salvation? For one thing, this verse goes on to say that He was made "perfect through sufferings." A genuine leader does not ask his followers to do something that he is not willing to do himself. He sets the example for those whom he leads. This is what Jesus did when He died on the cross for us. We as believers will never suffer more by following Him than He did to make it possible for us to be cleansed of our sins.

A leader also guides, encourages, inspires, and motivates the people in his charge. We can rest assured that we are in good hands when we follow our Captain of Salvation. See also *God of My Salvation*.

CAPTAIN OF THE HOST OF THE LORD

This is the name by which a mysterious messenger of the Lord identified Himself to Joshua as the Israelites prepared to enter Canaan (see Joshua 5:14). The best explanation of this verse is that the messenger was the Angel of the Lord, also called the "angel of his presence" in Isaiah 63:9.

In the third century AD, the scholar Origen identified this messenger as Jesus Christ in a pre-incarnate appearance. This approach to the passage has been followed by many modern Bible students. One strong argument for this interpretation is that Joshua bowed down and worshiped this messenger. This indicates that He was a divine being of high stature, not just a messenger of a lower angelic order.

This name of Jesus uses military imagery. The NIV and NRSV render it as "commander of the army of the LORD." After Moses died, Joshua became the new leader of Israel. He faced the daunting task of leading Israel against the Canaanites and claiming the land of promise for God's people. The appearance of the Captain of the Host of the Lord assured Joshua that he would be successful in this campaign. This would happen not because of their military might but because God would go before them into battle. See also *Angel of His Presence*; *Lord of Hosts*.

CARPENTER

Soon after launching His public ministry, Jesus paid a visit to His hometown of Nazareth. Mark 6:3 describes the skeptical response to His teachings by the people who had known Him for many years. To them He was nothing but "the carpenter," a skilled tradesman who had grown up in their midst and who was nothing special.

This is the only place in the Bible where this name is applied to Jesus. The people of His hometown used it in a derogatory way, but it is actually a name of honor and dignity. Jesus probably learned the skill of carpentry from His earthly father, Joseph. He must have worked at this trade for at least fifteen or twenty years before He began His public ministry at about thirty years of age (see Luke 3:23).

The word *carpenter* in our society applies generally to a skilled workman who constructs buildings. But in New Testament times, this occupation was more likely what we know today as woodworking. Jesus probably worked with Joseph in a woodworking shop, making and repairing furniture and tools for the citizens of Nazareth.

As the Carpenter of Nazareth who worked with His hands, Jesus dignified labor and identified with the common people of His day. He spoke in language they could understand, driving home His teachings with parables drawn from everyday life. No wonder "the common people heard him gladly" (Mark 12:37).

In Matthew's Gospel, the skeptical people of Nazareth referred to Jesus not as the Carpenter but as the "carpenter's son" (Matthew 13:55).

Young Jesus holds a candle for his father, Joseph, who drills a hole in a block of wood. Both men are identified in scripture as carpenters.

CARPENTER'S SON

See *Carpenter*.

CEREAL OFFERING

See *Sacrificial Offerings*.

CEREMONIAL WASHING

In Old Testament times, the Lord demanded that priests who offered sacrifices at the altar should be ritually clean. So He told Moses when He instituted the priesthood, "Bring Aaron and his sons to the entrance to the tent of meeting, and wash them with water" (Exodus 29:4 NIV).

Eventually this concern for ceremonial cleanliness included all the people. A person could be defiled, or made unclean, by many different actions, such as giving birth to a child, having sexual intercourse, or touching a dead body. But cleanliness could be restored by going through rituals of purification.

By New Testament times, these outward rituals had become more important than the inner spiritual reality they were meant to signify. This is why the Pharisees criticized Jesus and His disciples on one occasion for failing to perform a ritualistic washing of their hands before they ate. But Jesus declared, "Nothing outside a person can defile them by going into them. Rather, it is what comes out of a person that defiles them" (Mark 7:15 NIV). Only the blood of Jesus Christ can wash away sin. The old hymn expresses it well: "What can wash away my sin? Nothing but the blood of Jesus."

Washing as a religious ritual is sometimes referred to as ablution. See also *Purification*.

CHANGELESSNESS OF GOD

See *Immutability of God*.

CHARMER

See *Magic and Divination*.

CHERUBIM

Winged creatures called cherubim, perhaps an order of angels, functioned to praise God and glorify His name. God revealed His message to the prophet Ezekiel in a series of visions in which cherubim played a prominent role (see Ezekiel 10:7; 11:22; 41:20).

The cherubim that Ezekiel saw were similar to the seraphim that appeared in the prophet Isaiah's vision of God on His throne (see Isaiah 6:1–2). These seraphim were vocal in their praise of God. "Holy, holy, holy, is the LORD of hosts," they cried. "The whole earth is full of his glory" (Isaiah 6:3). See also *Angels*.

CHIEF CORNERSTONE

In Ephesians 2:19–20, the apostle Paul assured the believers in the church at Ephesus that they were recipients of God's grace. Their faith in Christ had brought them into God's kingdom since He was the "chief corner stone" on which this kingdom was built.

Jesus as the Cornerstone of our faith is one of the most important images of Christ in the Bible. It is rooted in a famous messianic passage that was written several centuries before Jesus was born. In Psalm 118:22, the psalmist declared, "The stone which the builders refused is become the head stone of the corner."

Jesus identified with this messianic passage during the final days of His ministry. He knew that He would be rejected as the Messiah and executed by the religious leaders of His nation. So he told them: "Did ye never read in the scriptures, The stone which the builders rejected, the same is become the head of the corner: this is the Lord's doing, and it is marvellous in our eyes? Therefore . . .the kingdom of God shall be taken from you, and given to a nation bringing forth the fruits thereof" (Matthew 21:42–43).

Jesus was referring to the non-Jewish or Gentile nations that would accept Him as Lord and Savior. This is exactly what happened as the Gospel was proclaimed throughout the Roman world after His death and resurrection. The leader of this movement was a Jewish zealot and persecutor of the Church—the apostle Paul—who was gloriously converted to Christianity and transformed into the "apostle to the Gentiles" (see Acts 9:15).

In the stone buildings of Bible times, a cornerstone was used to hold two opposing rows of stones together at the point where they came together in a corner. Jesus as the Chief Cornerstone is the force on which our faith is based. Though He may be rejected by the nonbelieving world, He is our hope in this life and the life to come.

In a famous prophecy about the coming Messiah, Isaiah also referred to Jesus as the "precious corner stone" and the "tried stone" (Isaiah 28:16). See also *Gentiles*; *Head of the Corner*.

CHIEF SHEPHERD

See *Good Shepherd*.

CHILDHOOD OF JESUS

See *Child Jesus*.

CHILD JESUS

Luke 2:43 refers to God the Son as "the child Jesus." This verse is part of the only account we have in the Gospels about the childhood of Jesus. According to Luke 2:41–52, Jesus made a trip to Jerusalem with His parents to observe the Passover festival when He was twelve years old. Joseph and Mary were traveling with a group back to Nazareth when they discovered that the boy Jesus was missing.

OUR PRIVILEGES AS GOD'S CHILDREN

- "To those who believed in his name, he gave the right to become children of God—children born not of natural descent, nor of human decision or a husband's will, but born of God" (John 1:12–13 NIV).
- "Do everything without grumbling or arguing, so that you may become blameless and pure, 'children of God without fault in a warped and crooked generation'" (Philippians 2:14–15 NIV).
- "Now we are children of God, and what we will be has not yet been made known. But we know that when Christ appears, we shall be like him, for we shall see him as he is" (1 John 3:2 NIV).

He had "tarried behind" in Jerusalem.

They returned quickly to the Holy City, where they discovered Jesus in the temple among the Jewish teachers and scholars. These learned men were experts in the Old Testament law. After expounding on the law in a temple service, they invited any interested persons to meet with them for further discussion. Everyone was amazed at Jesus' religious insights at such a young age.

This account tells us that Jesus even as a child was aware of His special mission as the Son of God. When His mother scolded Him for staying behind in Jerusalem and causing her and Joseph such anxiety, He replied, "Why were you searching for me? . . . Didn't you know I had to be in my Father's house?" (Luke 2:49 NIV).

This account in Luke goes on to report that Jesus did return to Nazareth with His earthly parents and that He "increased in wisdom and stature, and in favour with God and man" (Luke 2:52). In other words, He grew up like any typical Jewish boy of the first century and was subject to His parents during His childhood. He did not launch His public ministry until He was about thirty years old (see Luke 3:23). As the Child

Jesus, He went through all the normal stages of life—from birth, to infancy, to childhood, to adulthood. He is a Savior who can identify with us in all our human experiences.

In Peter's remarks to the Jewish Sanhedrin after healing a lame man near the temple, he referred to Jesus as the "holy child Jesus" (see Acts 4:27, 30). See also *Babe*.

CHILDREN OF GOD

The classic passage on this theological truth occurs in the writings of the apostle Paul. "For as many as are led by the Spirit of God, they are the sons of God," Paul declared. "The Spirit itself beareth witness with our spirit, that we are the children of God" (Romans 8:14, 16). We as believers become God's children by placing our faith in His Son, Jesus Christ. Through the ministry of the Holy Spirit, we enjoy a special relationship with God the Father.

Paul went on in this passage from Romans to compare the method by which we become God's children to the process of adoption (see Romans 8:17–18). When a couple adopts a child into their family, they do so out of love. In the same way, we come into God's family not because we deserve His favor but because of His love and grace: "This is love: not that we loved God, but that he loved us and sent his Son as an atoning sacrifice for our sins" (1 John 4:10 NIV). See also *Adoption*; *Spirit of Adoption*.

CHILDREN OF ISRAEL

See *Israelites*.

CHOSEN OF GOD

This is the name that the religious leaders and the scoffing crowd assigned to Jesus as He was dying on the cross (see Luke 23:35). The irony is that the name they used in ridicule—the "chosen of God"—was a perfect description of Him and the mission from His Father that brought Him into the world.

For generations the Jewish people had looked for a Messiah sent from God who would serve as a deliverer for His people. Jesus was that Chosen One, but He was not the type of champion they expected Him to be. He came not as a military conqueror but as a spiritual Savior who died to deliver people from their sin. His work as the Chosen One of God continues to this day as He calls people to take up their cross and follow Him (see Matthew 16:24).

Jesus was the Chosen of God in a special sense. But He followed in the tradition of many people in the Bible who were said to be chosen of God. These included the descendants of Jacob, or the Israelites (see 1 Chronicles 16:13), King Solomon (see 1 Chronicles 29:1), Moses (see Psalm 106:23), Zerubbabel (see Haggai 2:23), the apostle Paul (see Acts 9:15), and all believers (see 1 Peter 2:9). See also *Anointed One*; *Messiah*; *One Chosen Out of the People*.

CHOSEN ONE

See *Elect*; *One Chosen Out of the People*.

CHOSEN PEOPLE

See *Israelites*.

A mosaic of Jesus Christ from Istanbul, Turkey.

CHRIST

Chapter 16 of Matthew's Gospel contains an account of Peter's recognition and confession of Jesus as the Messiah. In one verse in this chapter, Peter declared openly, "Thou art the

Christ, the Son of the living God" (v. 16). But just four verses later, Jesus instructed His disciples that "they should tell no man that he was Jesus the Christ" (Matthew 16:20).

Notice the use of the article *the* ("the Christ") in both these verses. The English word *Christ* comes from the Greek word *christos*, which means "anointed." Thus Peter was declaring that Jesus was the Anointed One, a special agent who had been sent into the world under divine appointment by God Himself. He was the Son of God, the Messiah, the great deliverer for whom the Jewish people had been looking for many years.

Jesus commended Peter for his recognition of Him as God's Anointed One. But why did He want His identity as the Messiah to be kept a secret?

He probably charged His disciples to keep quiet about His messiahship because the Jewish people expected their Messiah to be a military and political champion. They thought He would rally the people, raise an army, deliver their nation from Roman tyranny, and restore Israel to its glory days.

Jesus could not live up to these expectations because He was a Messiah in a spiritual sense. He had been sent to teach about the kingdom of God, to heal the sick, and to deliver the people from their sin. He would eventually reveal Himself as the Messiah (see Luke 22:70–71), but only after He had completed the spiritual mission on which He had been sent.

Jesus is called Christ (the Messiah or the Anointed One) hundreds of times throughout the New Testament. Often this name or title is grouped with other names. For example, Jesus Christ (see John 1:17) actually means "Jesus the Anointed One" or "Jesus the Messiah." Christ of God (see Luke 9:20) means "the Anointed One of God." The name Christ Jesus appears often in the epistles, especially in those written by the apostle Paul (see Romans 3:24; 1 Corinthians 1:2). This reversal of the two names places emphasis on the messiahship of God's Son.

Because Jesus was the Anointed One of God, we as His followers are also commissioned to continue His work in the world. The apostle Paul said, "It is God who strengthens us, with you, in Christ, and has anointed us" (2 Corinthians 1:21 HCSB). See also *Anointed One*.

CHRIST CRUCIFIED

This name of Jesus appears only once in the Bible. The apostle Paul declared to the Corinthian believers, "We preach Christ crucified, unto the Jews a stumblingblock, and unto the Greeks foolishness" (1 Corinthians 1:23). Since the name or title "Christ" means "the

A NAME TO CARRY PROUDLY

The name or title "Christ" is carried by all Christians—those who belong to Him. This name appears only three times in the New Testament. According to the book of Acts, it was first applied to the believers in the church at Antioch (see Acts 11:26). An unbeliever, King Agrippa, used it when he told the apostle Paul, "Almost thou persuadest me to be a Christian" (see Acts 26:28). And the apostle Peter encouraged the persecuted believers to whom he wrote with these words: "Yet if any man suffer as a Christian, let him not be ashamed; but let him glorify God on this behalf" (1 Peter 4:16).

This sixteenth-century painting makes little attempt to sanitize the bloody reality of Jesus' crucifixion. The illustration is by the German painter and engraver Albrecht Altdorfer.

Anointed One" or "the Messiah," the literal meaning of this name is "the Messiah Crucified."

In Jewish tradition, the coming Messiah was to be a powerful leader who would defeat all their enemies and rule over a restored Israel in splendor and glory. That this Messiah would die on a Roman cross like a common criminal was something they found totally unacceptable—a "stumblingblock" that prevented them from accepting Jesus as the Messiah.

A crucified Savior who died in our place to set us free from bondage to sin is still a foreign concept to many people. Like the rich young ruler, they want to know "what good thing" (Matthew 19:16) they must do in order to be assured of eternal life. But there is nothing we can do that will buy us God's favor. We must accept by faith the provision that God has already made for our salvation through the death of His Son.

The apostle Paul put it like this: "For by grace are ye saved through faith; and that

At the very first Christmas, shepherds arrive to worship the baby Jesus in a Bethlehem-area stable.

not of yourselves: it is the gift of God: not of works, lest any man should boast" (Ephesians 2:8–9). See also *Cross*; *Crucifixion of Christ*.

CHRIST JESUS OUR LORD

Romans 8:38–39 is one of the most inspiring passages in all the writings of the apostle Paul: "For I am persuaded, that neither death, nor life, nor angels, nor principalities, nor powers, nor things present, nor things to come, nor height, nor depth, nor any other creature, shall be able to separate us from the love of God, which is in Christ Jesus our Lord." Generations of believers have claimed its promise that no force on earth or heaven is strong enough to break the grip of God's love on their lives.

This passage is also unusual because Paul strung together three separate names or titles of Jesus—Christ, Jesus, and Lord—to express this truth in such a powerful way. Christ means "the Anointed One" or "the Messiah" (see *Christ*). Jesus was His personal name, which means "God is salvation" (see Luke 1:31; 2:21). The title Lord expresses His unlimited dominion and power, a characteristic that Jesus shares with God His Father.

With Paul, we can declare that Christ Jesus our Lord walks with us through every experience of life, and His love will never let us go.

Other variations on this name are Lord and Saviour Jesus Christ (see 2 Peter 3:18), Lord Christ (see Colossians 3:24), and Lord Jesus Christ Our Saviour (see Titus 1:4). See also *Anointed One*.

CHRISTMAS

This is the day on which Christians around the world celebrate the birth of Jesus—His coming into the world in human form. The official name of this celebration in the calendar of the church year is the Feast of the Nativity of Christ.

There is no evidence for the observance of this feast in the early years of the church. December 25th was adopted as the date for this celebration by the Roman Catholic Church some time before AD 336. This day in December had been associated previously with a pagan Roman holiday that paid homage to the sun.

The exact time and date of Jesus' birth is not as important as the fact that He did come in accordance with God's plan. The apostle Paul put it like this: "But when the fullness of the time was come, God sent forth his Son, made of a woman, made under the law, to redeem them that were under the law, that we might receive the adoption of sons" (Galatians 4:4–5). See also *Babe*; *Incarnation of Christ*.

CHRISTOLOGY

The field of study within Christian theology that focuses on the nature and person of Jesus Christ is known as Christology (Greek *Christos* + *logia* or "knowledge"). Included in this study are such topics as how Jesus the Son is related to God the Father and God the Holy Spirit, Jesus' teachings and miracles in the Gospels, His characteristics and attributes, His role in salvation, and the promise of His second coming. See also *Theology*.

CHURCH

A local body of believers assembled for Christian worship (see Acts 15:4) as well as all the redeemed of the ages who belong to Christ (see Ephesians 5:27) are known as the

Church. The word *church* is a translation of a Greek term that means "an assembly." The mission of the Church is to continue the work of Christ in the world.

Although Jesus anticipated the Church, it did not begin in a formal way until the dramatic outpouring of the Holy Spirit upon His followers on the day of Pentecost (see Acts 2:1–6). Jesus commissioned all believers to carry out His orders to tell others the good news about His life, death, and resurrection (see Matthew 28:18–20). The book of Acts tells how this good news spread throughout the Roman world of the first Christian century.

Christ is head of His body, the Church. He alone is worthy of this position because of His redeeming work and lordship (see Colossians 3:15–17). See also *Body of Christ*; *Head of the Church*.

CIRCUMCISION

This ritual signified the covenant between God and His people, the Israelites. It was performed by removing the loose foreskin of the male sex organ. This practice probably began with Abraham, who was instructed by the Lord to circumcise every male child in his household (see Genesis 17:11).

Over time, the Jewish people came to think of circumcision as a sign of their racial superiority. They referred to the Gentiles, or non-Jews, as "the uncircumcised" (see Ezekiel 32:27). This insult implied that people of other nationalities were not worthy of God's love.

This prideful attitude caused a problem in the early church. Many believers in the years after the ascension of Jesus were converts from Judaism. Some of them believed Gentiles had to undergo the rite of circumcision before they were genuinely converted and worthy of acceptance by other believers (see Acts 15:1). In a meeting called to discuss this issue, church leaders decided that this ritual was not a requirement for salvation (see Acts 15:22–29). This opened the door for full acceptance of Gentiles into the fellowship of the church. From that point on, missionary work among non-Jews resulted in explosive growth in the early church.

The apostle Paul was particularly effective in his preaching among Gentiles. In his first letter to the Christians at Corinth, he declared, "Circumcision is nothing and uncircumcision is nothing. Keeping God's commands is what counts" (1 Corinthians

NOW HEAR THIS

In three other places in his writings, Paul repeated his statement that circumcision was not required for Gentile converts to the Christian faith. In essence, he was saying, "In case you missed this the first time, let me tell you again."

- "In Christ Jesus neither circumcision nor uncircumcision has any value. The only thing that counts is faith expressing itself through love" (Galatians 5:6 NIV).
- "Neither circumcision nor uncircumcision means anything; what counts is the new creation" (Galatians 6:15 NIV).
- "Here there is no Gentile or Jew, circumcised or uncircumcised, barbarian, Scythian, slave or free, but Christ is all, and is in all" (Colossians 3:11 NIV).

7:19 NIV). God's old covenant with Israel, symbolized by circumcision, has been replaced by His new covenant with all who place their faith in Jesus Christ as Savior and Lord. See also *Gentiles*; *Impartiality of God*.

CLEAN AND UNCLEAN

See *Ceremonial Washing*; *Purification*.

CLOUD

Clouds are often associated in the Bible with God's presence and His protection of His people. For example, when Moses received God's law on Mount Sinai, God appeared to him in a cloud (see Exodus 24:16). The Lord also used a mysterious cloud to keep the Egyptian army from overtaking the Israelites in the wilderness (see Exodus 14:19–20).

Clouds are also mentioned in connection with the ministry of Jesus in the New Testament. When Jesus was transfigured before His disciples, God the Father spoke from a cloud to show His satisfaction with the work of His Son (see Matthew 17:5). At His second coming, Christ will come in "the clouds of heaven" (Matthew 24:30). See also *Pillar of Fire and Cloud*.

COMFORTER

After Jesus told His disciples that His death was drawing near, He went on to assure them: "I will pray the Father, and he shall give you another Comforter, that he may abide with you for ever" (John 14:16). He would no longer be with them in a physical sense, but He was not leaving them alone. He would send a "Comforter," the Holy

A dramatic cloud formation glows with the sunset. Clouds appear throughout scripture in various connections with God.

Spirit, to fill the void caused by His return to the Father in heaven after His resurrection.

Notice that Jesus referred to the Holy Spirit as "another" Comforter. The Greek word He used means "another of the same kind." This implies that Jesus Himself was the other or first Comforter of His disciples; He was sending another like Himself to serve as His stand-in. So close and personal would be the presence of the Holy Spirit that it would seem as if He had never left.

The Greek word behind Comforter is *parakletos*, meaning "one called alongside." This is the same word translated as "Advocate," one of the names of Jesus (see 1 John 2:1). In addition to "Comforter" and "Advocate" as rendered by the King James Version, this word is translated as "Counselor," "Companion," "Guide," "Helper," "Instructor," or "Teacher" by other English versions of the Bible.

When Jesus promised that the Comforter would come "alongside" us, He meant that the Holy Spirit will help us in our times of need. If we are lost and stumbling, He will serve as our Guide. If we are discouraged, He will lift us up. If we are confused, He will bring wisdom and understanding. If we are mired in grief, He will sustain us with His presence. The Comforter will be there for us when we need Him most. See also *Advocate*; *Holy Spirit*.

COMMANDER

See *Leader and Commander*.

COMMANDER OF THE ARMY OF THE LORD

See *Captain of the Host of the Lord*.

COMMANDMENTS, TEN

See *Ten Commandments*.

COMMISSION

See *Great Commission of Jesus*; *Missions*.

Japanese officials lead a condemned man to his punishment in a sketch from the 1860s.

COMMUNION

See *Lord's Supper*.

COMPASSION OF GOD

See *Love of God*; *Mercy of God*.

COMPREHENSION OF GOD

See *Divine Accommodation*.

CONDEMNATION

To condemn someone, according to the dictionary, is to declare him or her guilty of a crime and deserving of punishment. In a spiritual sense, condemnation is what all people deserve because of their sin against God and their failure to live up to His standards.

But God the Father had a plan to help us avoid His condemnation. He sent His own Son, Jesus Christ, to bear the penalty of our sin through His death on the cross. This bought our justification—the very opposite of condemnation. Jesus Himself said, "God did not send His Son into the world to condemn the world, but to save the world through him" (John 3:17 NIV). See also *Imputed Righteousness*; *Justification*.

CONFESSION

The word *confess* appears many times throughout the Bible. It means to admit, own up to, or take responsibility for one's sin and to turn to God for healing and forgiveness.

One of the strongest confessions in the Bible is David's admission to God of his sin with Bathsheba. "Against you, you only, have I sinned," he prayed, "and done what is evil in your sight" (Psalm 51:4 NIV). David did not blame anyone else or the circumstances for his wrongdoing. This honesty and openness before the Lord led to his forgiveness and restoration.

Confession is an important word, and it belongs in every believer's vocabulary. See also *Prayer*; *Worship of God*.

CONFESSION BY THE NUMBERS

1. Confess our sins to God: "I said, 'I will confess my transgressions to the Lord.' And you forgave the guilt of my sin" (Psalm 32:5 NIV).
2. Confess our faith in Jesus: "Whoever publicly acknowledges me before others, the Son of Man will also acknowledge before the angels of God" (Luke 12:8 NIV).
3. Confess our faults to others: "Confess your sins to each other and pray for each other so that you may be healed" (James 5:16 NIV).

CONSCIENCE

When making moral decisions, many people use the principle "Let your conscience be your guide." They believe their intuitive sense of right and wrong will always lead them to do the right thing.

But the apostle Paul had a different view on this matter. He warned Titus, his associate in ministry, against false teachers, pointing out that even the conscience can be overwhelmed by sin. "To those who are corrupted and do not believe, nothing is pure," he told Titus. "In fact, both their minds and consciences are corrupted" (Titus 1:15 NIV). Paul knew that the conscience is a poor guide for moral behavior. As a part of man's fallen sinful nature, it has been infected and hopelessly flawed by sin.

The conscience is also subjective. It is

affected by many different human circumstances that vary from person to person. For example, all of us are taught important values and principles of behavior by our parents while we are growing up. These rules become a part of us that we cannot break without violating our conscience.

This is well and good as long as we have been taught the right values. But what about children who grow up in homes where stealing is acceptable? They can go on stealing for the rest of their lives without a protest from their conscience.

The conscience, like every other part of human nature, needs to be redeemed from its fallen condition. This comes about only through the saving power of Jesus Christ (see 2 Corinthians 5:17–18). See also *Fall of Man*; *Sin*.

CONSECRATION

This is the act of dedicating or setting apart someone or something for God's exclusive use. In the Old Testament, Aaron and his sons were set apart to serve as priests for the rest of the Israelites (see Leviticus 8:12–13). The firstborn of livestock and the firstfruits of the agricultural harvest were also dedicated to the Lord (see Exodus 13:2; 23:19).

In the New Testament, Jesus Christ is the best example of the concept of consecration (see John 17:19). The writer of Hebrews declared, "He sacrificed for [our] sins once for all when he offered himself" (Hebrews 7:27 NIV). Just as Christ gave Himself for us, we as

believers are expected to give our lives in service to Him and others (see Romans 12:1). See also *Sanctification*.

CONSOLATION OF ISRAEL

A few weeks after Jesus was born, Joseph and Mary took Him to the temple in Jerusalem to dedicate Him to the Lord. A man named Simeon was moved by the Holy Spirit to come to the temple while they were there. He immediately recognized the young Jesus as the Messiah who had been sent as the "consolation of Israel" (Luke 2:25).

The word *consolation* means "comfort" or "relief." God had promised in the Old Testament that He would send His Messiah to His people someday. Simeon was convinced that he would not die before he had seen this promise fulfilled (see Luke 2:26). God apparently showed him by divine revelation that the baby Jesus was the Promised One whom the nation of Israel had been looking for.

But this good news had a dark side. Simeon told Mary and Joseph that many people would accept their Son as the Messiah, but many would not (see Luke 2:34). He also revealed to Mary that "a sword will pierce your own soul too" (Luke 2:35 NIV)—a prediction of His future crucifixion.

Today, as then, Jesus' birth was a good-news/bad-news scenario—good news for those who accepted His messiahship and bad news for those who refused to believe He had been sent by God the Father. Our task as believers is to help others find the consolation

SIMEON'S PRAYER IN THE TEMPLE

"Sovereign Lord, as you have promised, you may now dismiss your servant in peace. For my eyes have seen your salvation, which you have prepared in the sight of all nations: a light for revelation to the Gentiles, and the glory of your people Israel" (Luke 2:29–32 NIV).

that Jesus can bring into their lives. See also *God of All Comfort.*

CONSULTER WITH FAMILIAR SPIRITS

See *Magic and Divination.*

CONSUMING FIRE

This name of God appears in Hebrews 12:28–29: "Let us have grace, whereby we may serve God acceptably with reverence and godly fear: for our God is a consuming fire." God is often associated with fire in the Bible. Sometimes fire symbolizes His guidance and protection. For example, He spoke to Moses from a burning bush (see Exodus 3:2). He guided the Israelites through the wilderness at night by a pillar of fire (see Exodus 13:21).

But this verse shows that fire is also a symbol of God's wrath. To those who are disrespectful or disobedient, He is a searing flame of judgment. People must decide for themselves whether the Lord will be a guiding light or a consuming fire in their lives. See also *Fire*; *Wrath of God.*

CONVERSION

This is the general term for the entire process by which a person is transformed from a state of sin into a "new person" who desires to please the Lord. The conversion experience varies from person to person. The apostle Paul was converted suddenly and dramatically in his encounter with the living Lord on the road to Damascus (see Acts 9:1–8). But other conversions, such as that of Lydia the businesswoman, are more gradual and subdued in nature (see Acts 16:14–15). See also *New Birth*; *Regeneration.*

Moses meets God face-to-face through the fiery branches of a burning bush.

CONVICTION

When a person is under conviction, they become aware of their sin and their need to turn to God for forgiveness and salvation. Conviction is one of the works of the Holy Spirit (see John 16:7–11).

One of the strongest statements of conviction in the Bible was expressed by David in a prayer after his sin of adultery with Bathsheba. "For I know my transgressions, and my sin is always before me. Against you, you only, have I sinned and done what is evil in your sight; so you are right in your verdict and justified when you judge" (Psalm 51:3–4 NIV).

David confessed his wrongdoing and was restored to a right relationship with the Lord. This is the result that God desires when He brings us under conviction. See also *Holy Spirit*; *Repentance.*

CORNERSTONE

See *Chief Cornerstone*; *Head of the Corner*.

COUNCIL

See *Sanhedrin*.

COUNCIL OF NICAEA

See *Creeds of the Church*.

COUNSELLOR

One of the most familiar messianic prophecies in the Bible occurs in Isaiah 9:6: "His name shall be called Wonderful, Counsellor, The mighty God, The everlasting Father, The Prince of Peace." This verse is especially quoted at Christmastime when we gather with other believers to celebrate the birth of Christ.

Most modern translations of this verse drop the comma between "Wonderful" and "Counselor" and render this name as "Wonderful Counselor." But no matter how many words are included in the name, Counselor is one of the most significant titles of Jesus in the Bible.

The word *counsel* refers to guidance, advice, or instruction. The Bible is filled with models of good counsel, bad counsel, and

English separatists sign the Mayflower Compact, a covenant binding the signers to develop and submit to the laws of the colony they would build in North America. In a similar way, God and the ancient Israelites agreed to work together in the development of a special biblical nation—though the people often failed to keep their part of the bargain.

counselors who fall into both these categories.

For example, Daniel provided wise counsel to Arioch, an aide to King Nebuchadnezzar of Babylon, when the king issued an order to have all his wise men put to death (see Daniel 2:10–16). But King Rehoboam of Judah rejected the wise counsel of the older leaders of the nation and listened to the foolish counsel of his young associates (see 1 Kings 12:8). This led to the rebellion of the northern tribes and the division of the united kingdom of Solomon into two separate nations (see 1 Kings 12:16–19).

We can depend on Jesus, our wise Counsellor, to always provide us with good instruction. He guides us with grace and righteousness. He will never give us bad advice that would cause us to go astray. See also *Spirit of Counsel and Might*.

COVENANT

A covenant is an agreement or contract between two people or two groups. In the Bible, the word is filled with theological meaning. It refers to the agreement between God and His people, the Israelites. God promised to bless the nation of Israel in a special way if they would honor Him and obey His commands. This promise began with Abraham and his descendants (see Genesis 12:1–3). It was renewed or restated on several occasions throughout the history of the Jewish nation (see Exodus 2:24; Judges 2:1).

But the Israelites broke their part of the agreement again and again. They gave in to the temptation to worship false gods. They failed to follow God's demand for honesty and justice in their dealings with others. Their failure brought on the need for a new covenant. This agreement was based on God's mercy and grace rather than keeping the law (see

Jeremiah 31:31–33). Through His sacrificial death, Jesus became the Mediator of this new covenant, bringing salvation and eternal life to all who trust in Him (see Hebrews 10:12–17). See also *Covenant of the People*; *Messenger of the Covenant*; *New Covenant*.

COVENANT, NEW

See *New Covenant*.

COVENANT OF THE PEOPLE

The forty-second chapter of Isaiah is one of the famous Servant Songs of his book. This Servant is Jesus, the Messiah, who will bring salvation to all people. In verse 6 of this chapter, the prophet referred to the Messiah as a "covenant of the people." He will do more than establish a new covenant of God with the people; He *is* the new covenant. Through Him and His death and resurrection, God provides the means by which people can have unbroken fellowship with the Lord of the universe. He is the only Mediator that people need between man and God. See also *New Covenant*.

STANDING ON THE SOLID ROCK

"The Solid Rock," a hymn by Edward Mote, declares that the blood of Jesus seals the new covenant between God and His people.

His oath, His covenant, His blood
Support me in the whelming flood;
When all around my soul gives way,
He then is all my hope and stay.
On Christ, the solid Rock, I stand;
All other ground is sinking sand,
All other ground is sinking sand.

Scuba divers investigate one part of God's creation—a coral reef. God created a vast collection of sea creatures—scientists estimate there may be up to one million species in the waters of the earth.

COVETOUSNESS

See *Greed.*

CREATION

The word *creation* refers to the actions of God through which He brought the physical world into being. God existed before the world, and He produced the universe from nothing (see Genesis 1:1–2). This insight opposed the typical view of the pagan peoples of Old Testament times. They thought that matter was eternal and that it had no beginning at a specific point in time. But the Bible declares that only God is eternal; the physical world owes its existence to Him.

From the first chapter of the Bible, we learn several important truths about God's creation of the world and its inhabitants.

1. He created the world from nothing; He is the ultimate cause of all that exists (see Genesis 1:1).

2. The creation was accomplished in orderly fashion, in six successive days (see Genesis 1:3–31).

3. Man is the crown of God's creation (see Genesis 1:26–27).

4. The Lord has given humans the responsibility to take care of His world (see Genesis 1:28).

Another truth about God's creation is that He is still involved in it. As the Lord of creation, He has placed within the universe certain natural laws that keep it running in orderly fashion. The prophet Jeremiah observed, "When he thunders, the waters in the heavens roar; he makes clouds rise from the ends of the earth. He sends lightning with the rain and brings out the wind from his storehouses" (Jeremiah 10:13 NIV).

For centuries scientists and Bible students alike have puzzled over the six days of creation mentioned in the Bible (see Exodus 31:17). Were these literal, twenty-four-hour days? Or was the writer of Genesis speaking metaphorically, using "day" in the sense of eons of time? Bible interpreters have come down on both sides of this issue.

Since God is all-powerful and answerable to no one, He could have used either method to bring the world into being. The mention of "evening and morning" in the Genesis account seems to support the literal day theory. On the other hand, God's way of reckoning time may be different than the measurement we humans use. The apostle Peter declared, "With the Lord a day is like a thousand years, and a thousand years are like a day" (2 Peter 3:8 NIV). See also *Creator.*

CREATOR

The prophet Isaiah referred to God by this name in one of his famous passages. The prophet was amazed that the people of Judah had rejected the one true God and were worshiping false gods instead. The "Creator" had brought the universe into being by the power of His word (see Hebrews 11:3). These pagan idols were weak and puny by comparison. "Do you not know?" the prophet asked. "Have you not heard? The LORD is the everlasting God, the Creator of the ends of the earth. He will not grow tired or weary, and his understanding no one can fathom" (Isaiah 40:28 NIV).

Not only did God make all things; He is the sovereign ruler of His creation (see Colossians 1:15–16). Isaiah reminds us that He alone is worthy of our loyalty and worship. See also *Almighty God*; *Beginning of the Creation of God*; *Maker.*

A symbol of Israel—the Star of David—outside the synagogue of Budapest, Hungary. The Old Testament is largely the story of the nation that God specially created and maintained.

CREATOR OF ISRAEL

Through the prophet Isaiah, the Lord made it clear why the Israelites existed: "I am the LORD, your Holy One, the creator of Israel" (Isaiah 43:15). The nation had been created by God Himself to serve as His agent of redemption to the rest of the world. This had been revealed centuries before Isaiah's time when the Lord told Abraham, "I will make you into a great nation. . .and all peoples on earth will be blessed through you" (Genesis 12:2–3 NIV).

But over and over again, the Israelites forgot the reason for their existence. They thought they deserved God's special blessing because of their cultural traditions and moral superiority. They had to be reminded constantly of the purpose of the One who was the "creator of Israel."

God, through His Son, Jesus Christ, is still in the business of creating a special kingdom of people for Himself. It's known as the Church. But our purpose is not to celebrate our favored status as believers. We should be about the task of helping others come to know Him as Lord and Savior.

Other names of God in the Bible that use the imagery of "Israel" are "God of Israel" (Matthew 15:31), "Holy One of Israel" (Psalm 78:41), "hope of Israel" (Jeremiah 14:8), "judge of Israel" (Micah 5:1), "light of Israel" (Isaiah 10:17), "Lord God of Israel" (1 Kings 8:23), "Redeemer of Israel" (Isaiah 49:7), "Rock of Israel" (2 Samuel 23:3), "stone of Israel" (Genesis 49:24), and "Strength of Israel" (1 Samuel 15:29). See also *King of Israel*.

CREEDS OF THE CHURCH

The word *creed* comes from the Latin term *credo*, which means "I believe." Thus, the creeds of the church are those formalized statements of faith held by believers in God the Father, God the Son, and God the Holy

THE NICENE CREED

I believe in one God the Father Almighty, Maker of heaven and earth, and of all things visible and invisible.

And I believe in one Lord, Jesus Christ, the only-begotten Son of God, born of the Father before all ages. God of God, Light of Light, true God of true God; begotten, not made, of one substance with the Father. By whom all things were made. Who for us and for our salvation came down from heaven.

And He became flesh by the Holy Spirit of the Virgin Mary and was made man. He was also crucified for us, suffered under Pontius Pilate, and was buried. And on the third day He rose again, according to the scriptures. He ascended into heaven and sits at the right hand of the Father. He will come again in glory to judge the living and the dead. And of His kingdom there will be no end.

And I believe in the Holy Spirit, the Lord and Giver of life, who proceeds from the Father and the Son. Who together with the Father and the Son is adored and glorified, and who spoke through the prophets. And one holy, Catholic [universal], and Apostolic Church. I confess one baptism for the forgiveness of sins. And I await the resurrection of the dead. And the life of the world to come. Amen.

Spirit. The earliest known such confession in the history of the church was the Apostles' Creed, written probably about AD 100. It served as the foundation of most other statements of faith developed in later years.

Two other historical confessions of faith are the Nicene Creed and the Athanasian Creed. The Nicene statement was adopted by the church at the Council of Nicaea in AD 325. This council was called to deal with a heresy known as Arianism, which denied the divinity of Christ. As you would expect, the Nicene Creed contains strong statements affirming the divinity of Jesus.

The Athanasian Creed, named for a church father known as Athanasius (about AD 293–373), originated in Europe about AD 400. Its focus was the doctrine of the Trinity and the bodily incarnation of Christ. See also *Arianism*; *Doctrine*; *Trinity*.

CROSS

Jesus was put to death by the Roman authorities on a cross, a wooden stake with a crossbeam. This was a common form of capital punishment in New Testament times. Attached to the cross with nails or leather thongs, the victim generally suffered for two or three days before dying from exposure, exhaustion, and the loss of body fluids. But Jesus died after only six hours on the cross

(see John 19:30–33).

The sacrificial death of Jesus on the cross freed believers from the power of sin (see Romans 6:6–11) and sealed their reconciliation to God (see 2 Corinthians 5:19). The cross is a symbol of God's love, His power to save, and His continuing work of redemption through the church (see 1 Corinthians 1:17–18). See also *Calvary*; *Crucifixion of Christ*.

CROWN

Kings and queens wear ornamental headdresses called crowns as a symbol of power and authority (see 2 Kings 11:12). The word is also used symbolically for righteous behavior befitting a believer. The apostle Paul said about this crown: "There is laid up for me a crown of righteousness, which the Lord, the righteous judge, shall give me at that day" (2 Timothy 4:8). This crown of righteousness has three dimensions.

First, we are made righteous or justified by Christ when we accept Him as Lord and Savior (see Romans 4:6). Second, we grow in Christ's righteousness through a lifetime of commitment to Him (see 1 Peter 2:24). Finally, Christ perfects His righteousness in us when we enter heaven. This final dimension of righteousness is what Paul was referring to in this verse. See also *Crown of Glory/Diadem of Beauty*.

OTHER CROWNS

- The believer's hope in Christ is a "crown of rejoicing" (1 Thessalonians 2:19).
- Eternal life for believers is an "incorruptible crown"—one that will never lose its luster (see 1 Corinthians 9:25).
- All people who claim Christ as their personal Savior will receive a "crown of glory" (1 Peter 5:4).

CROWN OF GLORY/DIADEM OF BEAUTY

Isaiah 28:5 predicts that Israel's sin will cause it to be overrun by an enemy nation. But God has a special "residue" or remnant of people who will avoid His judgment because of their faithfulness to Him: "In that day shall the LORD of hosts be for a crown of glory, and for a diadem of beauty, unto the residue of his

Jesus' cross may be one of the most common symbols throughout the entire world—and with good reason.

people." God will be like a crown to these obedient ones. They will share in His character—His holiness, righteousness, and justice.

God will also reward this obedient remnant by giving them a Diadem of Beauty. A diadem was a band around the head of a king that symbolized his royal authority. We as believers wear a "diadem" of sorts—our salvation.

This shows to the world that we belong to the Lord and that He has commissioned us to serve as His witnesses in the world. See also *Crown*; *King of Glory*; *Spirit of Glory*.

Roman soldiers nail Jesus to the cross while Jewish officials watch.

CRUCIFIXION OF CHRIST

None of the Gospels go into detail about the crucifixion of Jesus. They didn't have to. The people of New Testament times knew all about this cruel form of capital punishment and the pain and suffering it inflicted.

The victim's wrists were nailed to a horizontal crossbeam; then it was raised into position and attached to a stake fixed firmly in the ground. Sometimes the feet were crossed and nailed to the stake. Without any support for the body except the nails through the feet and wrists, the victim slumped forward on the cross. This put pressure on the heart and lungs, making breathing difficult. A slow, painful death usually occurred after two or three days from a combination of shock, fatigue, asphyxiation, and loss of blood.

Sometimes the victim's legs were broken with a club as an act of mercy to hasten death. This was not necessary in Jesus' case because He died after only a few hours on the cross (see Matthew 27:45–50). The Gospel of John declares that this was a fulfillment of the Old Testament prophecy, "A bone of him shall not be broken" (John 19:36; see Psalm 34:20).

To the Jewish people, crucifixion was a despicable and dishonorable way to die (see Galatians 3:13). But Jesus turned the cross into a symbol of hope and a badge of honor and self-sacrifice (see Philippians 2:5–8). See also *Christ Crucified*; *Cross*.

CURTAIN OF THE TEMPLE

See *Veil of the Temple*.

Deep underground, darkness can almost be felt—as God described the miraculous darkness He sent on Egypt as the ninth of ten plagues (Exodus 10:21). Even worse, though, is the spiritual darkness of rejecting God.

D

DANCING

Exuberant praise of the Lord often took the form of dancing, particularly in Old Testament times. For example, Moses' sister Miriam and other Israelite women danced and sang to the Lord to celebrate His deliverance of the people from the pursuing Egyptian army (see Exodus 15:20). King David also "danced before the LORD with all his might" when the ark of the covenant was relocated to the city of Jerusalem (see 2 Samuel 6:14).

Dancing as a form of praise before the Lord was usually accompanied by the playing of musical instruments. The psalmist encouraged the worshippers of his time to praise the Lord "in the dance: let them sing praises unto him with the timbrel and harp" (Psalm 149:3).

The very opposite of dancing—reverent silence—is often appropriate in worship (see Habakkuk 2:20). But sometimes our lively, energetic praise seems to be the only appropriate way to express our thanks for the Lord's abundant blessings. See also *Worship of God.*

King David dances before the ark of God in a painting from a church in Florence, Italy. David's dancing was so energetic, his wife complained (see 2 Samuel 6).

DARKNESS

Darkness is literally the absence of light. But the word is usually used in a symbolic way in the Bible. For example, sin is a form of darkness that causes people to defy God's will (see Job 24:13–17). In the Old Testament, Sheol—the realm of the dead—was a place of darkness (see Job 38:17).

But the worst form of darkness is unbelief. Those who refuse to acknowledge Jesus as God's Son and accept Him in faith are groping in the darkness (see John 12:35).

Turning away from this light leaves a person in a permanent state of darkness (see John 3:19–20).

Jesus referred to the Pharisees as "blind guides" (Matthew 23:24). Not only were they in the dark about the truth themselves; they led other people through their influence to remain in the dark. This form of spiritual blindness was criticized severely by Jesus. He accused them of shutting people out of the kingdom of God. "You yourselves do not enter," He told them, "nor will you let those enter who are trying to" (Matthew 23:13 NIV). See also *Light.*

DAVID

David was the popular king of Judah described by the Lord as "a man after mine own heart" (see 1 Samuel 13:14; Acts 13:22) and an earthly ancestor of the promised Messiah, Jesus Christ (see Luke 3:31). A descendant of the tribe of Judah, he was a native of Bethlehem (see 1 Samuel 17:12), a city often referred to as the "city of David" (Luke 2:11).

In fulfillment of Old Testament prophecy (see Micah 5:2), Jesus was born in Bethlehem. In the New Testament, Jesus was often called the "son of David" (see Matthew 20:30). See also *Root and Offspring of David; Son of David*.

DAY OF ATONEMENT

See *Atonement; Scapegoat*.

DAY OF THE LORD

This phrase is usually interpreted as a period in the end time when God will bring His purpose for man and the world to fulfillment. This will be a day of judgment for the rebellious and sinful (see Jeremiah 46:10) and a time of deliverance for the godly (see Joel 2:28–32). Any time—whether now or in the distant future—when the Lord acts, intervening in history for the purpose of deliverance and judgment, may also be described as the "day of the Lord" (Isaiah 13:6). See also *Last Judgment*.

DAYSMAN

In the Old Testament book named for him, the patriarch Job often complained that God was punishing him without cause. He was convinced that he had done nothing to deserve his suffering. To make matters worse, according to Job, God was all-powerful and he was a weak human being. He had no right to question God. So he longed in Job 9:33 for a "daysman" (*umpire*, NASB, NRSV)—a referee, mediator, or impartial judge—who could speak to God on his behalf.

Job's desire for someone to represent him before God the Father was eventually fulfilled with the coming of Jesus Christ into the world. As the God-man, He is fully human and fully divine. He communicates directly with the Father, since He is God's Son. But He identifies with humankind in our frailty because He came to earth in human form. As Job expressed it in 9:33, Jesus is able to "lay his hand upon us both"—God and man.

It's difficult for us to comprehend how Jesus could be both human and divine at the same time. But just because we don't understand it doesn't mean it isn't true. Here's how the apostle Paul expressed this great truth: "Let this mind be in you, which was also in Christ Jesus: who, being in the form of God, thought it not robbery to be equal with God: but made himself of no reputation, and took upon him the form of a servant, and was made in the likeness of men; and being

found in fashion as a man, he humbled himself, and became obedient unto death, even the death of the cross" (Philippians 2:5–8). See also *Incarnation of Christ*; *Mediator*.

A "daysman"—called an *umpire* by some Bible translations—comes between two sides to mediate a dispute. Jesus Christ, both human and divine, serves as the perfect daysman on our behalf.

DAYS OF CREATION

See *Creation*.

DAYSPRING FROM ON HIGH

Luke 1:78 is part of the passage in the Gospel of Luke known as the "Benedictus" (see Luke 1:68–79). This passage consists of a prayer uttered by Zacharias, father of John the Baptist, after John was born. An angel had revealed to Zacharias even before John's birth that his son would be the forerunner of

THE DEATH OF DEATH

"O death, where is thy sting? O grave, where is thy victory? The sting of death is sin; and the strength of sin is the law. But thanks be to God, which giveth us the victory through our Lord Jesus Christ" (1 Corinthians 15:55–57).

the Messiah. In this prayer Zacharias praised God for sending the Messiah, Jesus, whom he called the "dayspring from on high."

The English word *dayspring* comes from a Greek word that means "a rising up." It is generally used to describe the rising of the sun in the morning and the appearance of stars in the night sky. Thus Zacharias thought of Jesus the Messiah as a bright light that God was preparing to send into a dark world. The phrase "on high" reveals the origin of this Daystar. Jesus did not come into the world on His own as a "Lone Ranger" agent. He was on a mission of redemption from God the Father.

The prophet Malachi used a similar name for Jesus in his prophecy about the coming Messiah. He called Him the "Sun of righteousness" who would "arise with healing in his wings" (Malachi 4:2). See also *Sun*.

DAY STAR

See *Bright and Morning Star*.

DEATH

Death is the price humans pay for their sin and rebellion against God. But in His mercy, God provides salvation and eternal life for believers through the atoning death of Jesus Christ (see Romans 6:23). The Bible also speaks of "second death" (see Revelation 20:6). This is eternal separation from God—the fate of unbelievers. The psalmist asked, "Who can live and not see death?" (Psalm 89:48 NIV). That's a good question for all of us to think about as we ponder our eternal destiny after this earthly life comes to an end. See also *Lord of the Dead and Living; Second Death*.

DECALOGUE

See *Ten Commandments*.

DECEITFUL SPIRITS

See *Demons*.

DECEIVER

See *Satan*.

DEFILEMENT

See *Ceremonial Washing*.

DELIVERER

The name Deliverer is applied to both God the Father and God the Son in the Bible. In the Old Testament, the psalmist David often spoke of God as His Deliverer: "O God: thou art my help and my deliverer" (Psalm 70:5). Perhaps this was one of David's favorite divine names because he had experienced God as Deliverer many times throughout his life (see Psalms 18:2; 40:17; 2 Samuel 22:2).

For example, David escaped several attempts by King Saul to kill him (see 1 Samuel 18:10–11; 19:11–12; 23:24–28). Before facing the Philistine giant Goliath, this shepherd boy who eventually became the king of Israel declared, "The LORD that delivered me out of the paw of the lion, and out of the paw of the bear, he will deliver me out of the hand of this Philistine" (1 Samuel 17:37). David prevailed over the giant because of his faith in the divine Deliverer.

In Romans 11:26 in the New Testament, the apostle Paul referred to Jesus as his Deliverer by quoting a messianic psalm from the Old Testament: "There shall come out of Sion the Deliverer." Sion (*Zion*, NIV) is another name for the city of Jerusalem.

This is an unusual reference to the Messiah, since Jesus was born in Bethlehem, not Jerusalem. But Jesus was crucified and resurrected in Jerusalem. This is also the place where the church was born on the day of Pentecost (see Acts 2:1–41) following Jesus' ascension to God the Father. These facts are probably what Paul had in mind when he declared that Jesus as our Deliverer came out of Jerusalem.

The great work that Jesus performs as our Deliverer is rescue from sin. He sets us free from the guilt that accompanies our sin and separates us from God (see Isaiah 59:2). He delivers us from the power of Satan, who tempts us constantly to fall back into sin (see Ephesians 6:11–13). And He will deliver us from a world filled with sin when He returns to claim us as His own. See also *Saviour*.

DEMONIC POSSESSION

Evil spirits can invade and control people. During His earthly ministry, Jesus healed several persons of this malady. Some interpreters claim demonic possession was nothing more than a form of mental illness. But this problem cannot be explained away so easily.

Demons sometimes caused physical ailments, including blindness (see Matthew 12:22), deafness (see Mark 9:25), and deformities of the body (see Luke 13:10–17).

Rescue workers assist a person in need. In a similar way, God delivers His people from their troubles.

JESUS' POWER OVER DEMONS

- He healed many people who were "possessed with devils" (see Matthew 4:24).
- He cast demons out of a wild man who lived among the tombs (see Mark 5:1–20).
- He healed a demon-possessed man who could not speak (see Matthew 9:32–33).
- He healed a man with demons who was blind and deaf (see Matthew 12:22).
- He cast a demon out of a boy who suffered from epileptic seizures (see Luke 9:37–42).

But not all the illnesses that Jesus healed were caused by demons. The Gospels draw a clear distinction between normal illness and demon possession (see Matthew 4:24; Luke 6:17–18).

Some of the Pharisees of Jesus' time claimed they had the power to cast evil spirits out of people (see Matthew 12:27). But they used magical incantations and elaborate rituals in their healing efforts. Jesus simply ordered evil spirits to come out of people. This showed His mastery over Satan and his evil forces (see Mark 1:25). See also *Demons*.

DEMONS

Evil beings who are allied with Satan in opposition to God and His work in the world are known as demons. In the Old Testament, King Saul was afflicted with an "evil spirit" that caused him to develop jealousy toward David. This jealousy was so strong that he tried to kill David on several occasions (see 1 Samuel 18:10–11; 19:9–10; 23:8). In the New Testament, Jesus confronted demons who had taken over people. But He proved His superiority to these evil beings by casting them out.

Demons are also referred to in the Bible as "evil spirits," "unclean spirits," and "deceitful spirits." Their work of evil is a reality in our fallen world (see Matthew 13:36–49). But

Demons lead souls to perdition in a cathedral sculpture.

Satan and all his agents of corruption will be defeated by Christ in the end time (see Revelation 20:10). See also *Demonic Possession; Satan*.

DESCENT INTO PRISON BY JESUS

First Peter 3:19–20 is the only place in the Bible where Jesus' mysterious descent into prison is mentioned. The apostle Peter wrote that Jesus was "made alive in the spiritual realm. In that state he also went and made a proclamation to the spirits in prison" (1 Peter 3:18–19 HCSB).

Interpreters have puzzled over this passage for centuries and come up with many different views on what it means. The most logical explanation is that it refers to the time between Jesus' death and resurrection. Before appearing to His followers in His resurrection body, He descended in the spirit into Sheol, the underworld or realm of the dead, to proclaim His final victory over evil through His death on the cross.

Notice He did not offer these "spirits" a chance to repent and be released from their prison. The Bible is clear that no opportunity

for salvation exists after a person's earthly life comes to an end. Perhaps the apostle Peter was simply telling us that Jesus' victory over the grave should be announced from the depths of the earth to the heights of heaven. See also *Sheol*.

DESIRE OF ALL NATIONS

The prophet Haggai delivered an inspiring message from the Lord to the Jewish exiles who had returned to Jerusalem after their exile to a foreign land: "I will shake all nations, and the desire of all nations shall come: and I will fill this house with glory" (Haggai 2:7). The prophet challenged the people to get busy at the task of rebuilding the Jewish temple that had been destroyed about eighty years before by the invading Babylonian army. The temple is apparently the "house" referred to in this verse.

But Haggai's words looked beyond his time to the distant future when Israel's Messiah would become the "desire of all nations." At His return in glory in the end time, all nations will pay Him homage and recognize His universal rule throughout the earth.

Jesus is not only the desire of believers; He is the hope of the entire world. As the apostle Paul declared, "At the name of Jesus every knee should bow. . .and every tongue acknowledge that Jesus Christ is Lord, to the glory of God the Father" (Philippians 2:10–11 NIV).

In his hymn "Jesus Shall Reign Where'er the Sun," Isaac Watts expressed his sentiments about the universal rule of Christ in the end time.

Jesus shall reign where'er the sun
Does his successive journeys run;
His kingdom spread from shore to shore,
Till moons shall wax and wane no more.

See also *Ensign for the Nations*; *Gentiles*.

DEVIL

See *Satan*.

DIADEM OF BEAUTY

See *Crown of Glory/Diadem of Beauty*.

DISCIPLESHIP

Disciples of Jesus claim Him as Savior and Lord and honor Him by the way they live. The first disciples of Jesus set the standard for discipleship when they answered His call to follow Him and to learn from His teachings. The basic meaning of the word *disciple* is "learner" or "pupil."

Salvation and discipleship are two related parts of the process of conversion. There's nothing we can do to earn our salvation. But genuine saving faith automatically launches a believer on a lifetime of growth and learning under the Lord's leadership. To truly follow Jesus, we sometimes have to deny our natural inclinations and the standards of the world. "Whoever wants to be my disciple," He said, "must deny themselves and take up their cross daily and follow me" (Luke 9:23 NIV).

One interesting metaphor for discipleship in the Bible is "walking" or "walking with God." In the Old Testament, Enoch—an ancestor of Noah—is described as a righteous man who "walked with God" (Genesis 5:24). The apostle Paul called on the Galatian Christians to "walk in the Spirit" (Galatians 5:16). Walking is something that most of us do every day. Thus, to walk with the Lord under the banner of discipleship is to honor Him in the routine activities of everyday life. See also *Accountability to God*; *Fruit of the Spirit*.

DISCIPLINE

See *Self-Control*.

DISOBEDIENCE

See *Sin*.

DIVINATION

See *Magic and Divination*.

DIVINE ACCOMMODATION

Accommodating people do not insist on doing things their own way but adapt or adjust their behavior to the needs of others. When used of God, the word *accommodation* means that the Lord—the infinite being who is beyond our realm of experience—has adjusted Himself to our limitations and made Himself known in ways that we humans can understand.

The ultimate example of His accommodation is the coming of His Son, Jesus, to earth in human form. As the Gospel of John expresses it, "The Word was made flesh, and dwelt among us" (John 1:14). It's easy for us to understand that God has love and compassion for His creatures when we see that Jesus practiced these traits when He walked among us during His earthly ministry. See also *Incarnation of Christ*; *Revelation of God*.

DIVINE CALLING

Does God call people to special service in His kingdom? The answer is a definite yes if we take the Bible seriously. It contains several examples of His call of specific individuals to kingdom ministry.

Perhaps the best example of His special calling is the prophet Jeremiah. "Before I formed you in the womb I knew you," He told Jeremiah. "Before you were born I set you apart; I appointed you as a prophet to the nations" (Jeremiah 1:4–5 NIV). Even before the prophet was born, God's hand was on Jeremiah. He selected him to serve as His spokesman to the nation of Judah. Jeremiah labored at this task for more than forty years, calling on the people to turn away from idolatry back to worship of the one true God.

But God's call is not just to those who serve Him in vocational ministry. Every believer is called to service in His kingdom.

This is sometimes referred to as God's universal call. He calls us first to salvation (see 1 Thessalonians 2:12). This leads to our involvement in His ministry to others. Our purpose as believers is to "declare the praises of him who called [us] out of darkness into his wonderful light" (1 Peter 2:9 NIV). See also *Priesthood of Believers*.

DIVINE ELECTION

The doctrine of election deals with God's selection of specific groups or individuals on whom He confers His favor. In the Old Testament, He selected the Israelites to be His special people. God did not choose them because they deserved this great honor. It was because He loved them and was determined to keep the covenant He had made with their ancestor Abraham (see Deuteronomy 7:6–8).

In a Sunday school illustration from the early twentieth century, young Samuel hears God calling him in the night (see 1 Samuel 3).

In the New Testament, the apostle Paul enlarged this concept of election to include all people who were included in God's plan of salvation. The apostle told the believers at Thessalonica that he gave thanks for them because God from the beginning had chosen them "to be saved through the sanctifying work of the Spirit and through belief in the truth" (2 Thessalonians 2:13 NIV).

Did Paul mean that God from eternity elects certain people to be saved, regardless of their personal response to His grace? This is hard to square with the concept of human free will. God created humans with the freedom to choose. We have a say in whether or not we will follow His will and obey His commands. Otherwise, we would be mere puppets whose strings are being manipulated by the hands of the divine will.

So the concept of divine election cannot mean that God selects certain people to be saved and everyone else is written out of His plan. The apostle Paul also had this to say in another of his New Testament letters: "God our Savior. . .wants all people to be saved and to come to a knowledge of the truth" (1 Timothy 2:3–4 NIV). The elect are those who accept this generous invitation from the Lord. See also *Predestination*.

DOCETISM

This word (pronounced DOE suh TIZ um) comes from a Greek word, *dokein*, that means "to seem." It refers to the belief that Jesus was not really a man but only seemed to be. This idea has been promoted by some fringe groups throughout the history of Christianity.

Docetism is the exact opposite of Arianism, which rejects the divinity of Christ. Docetists emphasize Jesus' divine nature so strongly that they rule out any possibility

of His being human. An early advocate of Docetism was Cerinthus (lived c. AD 100), an opponent of the apostle John at Ephesus. In opposition to Cerinthus and others who denied the humanity of Jesus, John declared: "Every spirit that confesseth that Jesus Christ is come in the flesh is of God: and every spirit that confesseth not that Jesus Christ is come in the flesh is not of God" (1 John 4:2–3).

Docetic teachings were rejected at the Council of Nicaea, a gathering of church leaders, in AD 325. The orthodox position of the church is that Jesus was both fully human and fully divine. See also *Arianism*; *Creeds of the Church; Gnosticism*.

Like a compass pointing the way through the forest, good doctrine is God's way of leading us to eternal life.

DOCTRINE

A system of religious beliefs that is considered authoritative and thus worthy of passing on to other generations is known as doctrine. The major doctrines of the Christian faith are

A French beach collects garbage washed up by Atlantic Ocean waves. The pollution of the earth can be traced back to sin's pollution of the human race.

those about God the Father, God the Son, and God the Holy Spirit. Other doctrines that fit under these main headings include the doctrines of man, salvation, and the church. These doctrinal insights have been revealed to human authors by the Lord and recorded in the Bible for our edification and instruction.

The writings of the apostle Paul show that false doctrine was a problem in the early church. He cautioned against false teachers (see Ephesians 4:14) and encouraged believers to stay true to the authentic teachings of Jesus and the Bible (see 1 Timothy 6:3–4). See also *Creeds of the Church*.

DOMINION OF MAN

After He created the world, God assigned the responsibility for ruling over the earth to people (see Genesis 1:26–28). This command set humankind apart from the other living creatures that God had created. Humankind alone was charged with the care of the physical world—a duty that involved accountability to the Creator Himself.

The state of the natural world today shows that humans have done a poor job of fulfilling this responsibility. The worldwide environmental crisis can be laid at the feet of human greed, selfishness, and carelessness. See also *Creation*; *Humankind*.

DOOR

In the Gospel of John, Jesus declared to His followers, "I am the door: by me if any man enter in, he shall be saved, and shall go in and out, and find pasture" (John 10:9). This is one of several "I Am" statements of Jesus in the Gospel of John. A door is an opening or entryway into a building or a shelter. Jesus made it clear by affirming that He was the

"door" (*gate*, NIV), that He was the only way to salvation and eternal life.

In His Sermon on the Mount, Jesus also addressed this topic by talking about two gates (see Matthew 7:13–14). The broad gate, representing the way of the world, was so wide that people could drift through it without any conscious thought about what they were doing. But the narrow gate, representing Jesus and His teachings, required commitment and sacrifice from those who wanted to enter this way and follow Him.

Maybe you have heard people say, "It doesn't matter what you believe as long as you're sincere," or "All religions are basically the same; they just take us to heaven by different paths." Don't you believe it. Jesus declared, "I am the way, the truth, and the life: no man cometh unto the Father, but by me" (John 14:6). See also *Good Shepherd*.

OTHER "I AM" STATEMENTS OF JESUS

- "I am the bread of life" (John 6:35).
- "I am the light of the world" (John 8:12).
- "I am the door of the sheep" (John 10:7).
- "I am the good shepherd" (John 10:11, 14).
- "I am the resurrection, and the life" (John 11:25).
- "I am the true vine" (John 15:1).

DOOR OF THE SHEEP

See *Good Shepherd*.

DOXOLOGY

This is a short hymn of praise to God or a declaration of His power and glory. The word itself is not in the Bible, but the concept appears throughout the scriptures.

One of the best-known biblical doxologies is the praise sung to the Lord by angels after Jesus was born in Bethlehem (see Luke 2:14). The hymn based on this passage is "Angels We Have Heard on High." Its familiar refrain is "Gloria in excelsis Deo," a Latin phrase meaning "Glory to God in the Highest." See also *Song*.

A stained-glass window depicts music-making angels praising God at the birth of Jesus.

DREAMS AND VISIONS

In the Bible, God often used dreams and visions to make His will known. The difference between these two forms of revelation is that dreams came to people in their sleep, while visions occurred to people during their waking hours. Elihu, one of Job's friends, was convinced that God speaks through dreams and visions. "God does speak. . .in a dream," he declared, "in a vision of the night, when deep sleep falls on people as they slumber in their beds" (Job 33:14–16 NIV).

Joseph, Daniel, Isaiah, and Paul were among the biblical personalities who received messages from the Lord through dreams and visions. Joseph distinguished himself in Egypt by interpreting dreams for the pharaoh and his officers (see Genesis 40–41). Daniel interpreted King Nebuchadnezzar's dream that he would fall from power (see Daniel 4:18–27). Isaiah received his call as a prophet through a vision of the Lord in all His majesty, sitting on a throne (see Isaiah 6:1–10). Paul's missionary thrust into Europe began with his vision of a man from Macedonia appealing for help (see Acts 16:9–10).

Does God still reveal His will to people through dreams and visions? It is certainly possible, but not as probable as it was in Bible times. Today we have the Bible and the Holy Spirit as sources of His guidance and revelation. See also *Revelation of God*.

DRINK OFFERING

See *Sacrificial Offerings*.

DUST

God created Adam, the first man, from dust (see Genesis 2:7). One of the great truths of this verse is that humankind comes from the dirt of the earth, a common element that God had already created. He was not spun off from God Himself. Thus, he cannot claim to have any spark of divinity in his nature.

We owe our existence to God—not the other way around. In his speech to the philosophers at Athens, the apostle Paul expressed it like this: "He [God] is not served by human hands, as if he needed anything. Rather, he himself gives everyone life and breath and everything else. . . . 'For in him we live and move and have our being'" (Acts 17:25, 28 NIV). See also *Humankind*.

DWELLING PLACE

The psalm where this divine name occurs may be the oldest in the entire book of Psalms, since it is attributed to Moses. During the years when the Israelites wandered in the wilderness, Moses prayed to God, "LORD, you have been our dwelling place throughout all generations" (Psalm 90:1 NIV).

It's interesting that Moses would call God their dwelling place at a time when the Israelites did not have permanent houses. They lived in tents that they moved from place to place (see Numbers 9:17; Joshua 3:14). In spite of their less-than-ideal living arrangements, they still thought of God as their ultimate Dwelling Place. His presence followed them wherever they moved, and His faithfulness continued from one generation to the next.

God is still a Dwelling Place for His people. Whether we live in a mobile home or a mansion, we find in Him all the joys and comforts of home. See also *Refuge*.

NEXT PAGE

Bedouin tents in the Sahara Desert are reminiscent of the mobile, impermanent dwelling places of the early Israelites. But wherever they are, God's people have a perfect dwelling place in Him.

"Earthrise," as photographed from the moon by astronauts of the Apollo 17 mission. This view was unknown to humans until the late 1960s—but entirely familiar to God, who created "the heavens and the earth" (Genesis 1:1).

E

EARNEST

In the King James Version the word *earnest* is used by the apostle Paul (see 2 Corinthians 1:22; 5:5; Ephesians 1:14). It is rendered by most modern versions as "guarantee." Paul's point is that the Holy Spirit who lives in believers is our guarantee that we will receive our full inheritance—eternal life—from the Lord in the end time. See also *Promises of God*.

EARS OF GOD

This biblical metaphor expresses confidence in the ability of the Lord to hear and respond to the needs of His people. After being delivered from the wrath of King Saul, David proclaimed, "In my distress I called upon the Lord. . .and my cry did enter into his ears" (2 Samuel 22:7).

The psalmist also contrasted God's ability to hear and respond with the passivity of lifeless idols: "They have ears, but they hear not" (Psalm 115:6). See also *Anthropomorphism*; *Imagery Used of God*.

EARTH

In the Bible both God and man have a close relationship with the earth. God created the earth (see Genesis 1:1), then created man to be its caretaker (see Genesis 1:26–30). But God continues to hold the deed to the earth, since He brought it into being. "The earth is the Lord's, and the fullness thereof," the psalmist declared, "the world, and they that dwell therein" (Psalm 24:1).

The earth as we know it will not last forever. Jesus predicted that "the earth shall pass away" (Matthew 24:35). In the end time, God will bring the material earth to its appointed end when it is transformed into a "new earth" (see 2 Peter 3:13; Revelation 21:1). See also *God of the Whole Earth*; *Judge of All the Earth*.

Mary Magdalene, Mary the mother of James, and Salome find an angel, but no Jesus, in the tomb the Sunday morning after the crucifixion (see Mark 16). The day of Christ's resurrection day is celebrated as "Easter."

EASTER

On this religious holiday Christians celebrate the resurrection of Jesus Christ. Easter falls on a Sunday near the end of the church year. Its more formal title is the Feast of the Resurrection of Christ.

The celebration of the death and resurrection of Jesus probably began at an early time in Christian history. But it was not given official church sanction until AD 325 at the Council of Nicaea. The date adopted for its observance was the first Sunday after the first full moon following the beginning of spring. This is why the date for Easter varies from year to year. It may fall on any Sunday from the middle of March to late April.

The word *Easter* appears once in the King James Bible (see Acts 12:4). But this is a mistranslation of the Greek word *Pascha*. The NIV renders it correctly as "Passover." See also *Resurrection of Christ*.

EDEN

See *Garden of Eden*.

EL

See *Elohim*.

ELECT

Isaiah 42:1 is a verse from one of the Servant Songs in the book of Isaiah. In this verse the prophet used the name Elect (*Chosen One*, NIV) to describe the relationship of Jesus to God the Father. God elected or chose to send His Son, Jesus, into the world on a mission of redemption.

The concept of election is one of the richest theological themes in the Bible. It means simply God's gracious calling of people to participate in His work and to become part of His kingdom.

God elected the nation of Israel to become a special recipient of His grace and to serve as a channel of His blessing to the rest of the world (see Genesis 12:1–3). When Israel failed at this task, He elected to send His own Son to serve as His agent of grace and salvation.

God is still in the election business. The Church of Jesus Christ is the channel through which He continues His work. We as believers are His elect, and we work under the authority of Jesus as the supreme Elect One. We are called to bear witness for Him in a dark and unbelieving world. See also *Divine Election; One Chosen Out of the People*.

ELECTION

See *Divine Election*.

ELIJAH

Jesus compared John the Baptist to this fiery Old Testament prophet (see Matthew 17:10–13). Jesus made this comparison immediately after His transfiguration before three of His disciples. At this event Moses and Elijah appeared and talked with Jesus (see Mark 9:2–8).

The Jews referred to their scriptures as "the law and the prophets," with Moses the lawgiver symbolizing the law and Elijah as a representative of the prophets. Thus, the appearance of these two Old Testament personalities suggested that the scriptures were being fulfilled in the life and ministry of Jesus.

Elijah was known in Old Testament times as a great miracle worker. He had been taken up into heaven in a whirlwind without experiencing death (see 2 Kings 2:11). Some Jews believed Elijah would come back to earth and continue his ministry of miracles. This is probably why some people thought Jesus Himself was Elijah (see Matthew 16:14). His miracles and mighty works reminded them of this bold Old Testament prophet. See also *Transfiguration of Jesus*.

One of two Bible characters who never died (Enoch is the other, from Genesis 5:23), Elijah is taken directly to heaven in a flaming chariot, while fellow prophet Elisha looks on. Centuries later, Elijah would reappear at the transfiguration of Jesus.

ELOHIM

A Hebrew word for God, this name does not appear in the Bible. It is usually translated simply as "God" or "Lord" in English versions of the Bible. The word conveys the concept of the one supreme being of the universe who is the only true God.

The singular form of this word is the Hebrew term *el*. Sometimes "el" is added to a term to form a compound word referring to God. For example, Bethel (Beth-el)—a city where the ark of the covenant was kept for a time—means "house of God" (see Judges 20:26–27; 21:19). See also *Shaddai*; *Yahweh*.

EMMANUEL

See *Immanuel*.

ENCHANTER

See *Magic and Divination*.

END OF THE LAW

The apostle Paul declared that "Christ is the end of the law for righteousness to every one that believeth" (Romans 10:4). This is the only place in the Bible where Jesus is referred to by this name. The NIV clarifies the meaning of this verse by stating that He is the end of the law, "so that there may be righteousness

An ensign—the American flag—flies from the USS *Bowfin* submarine at Pearl Harbor, Hawaii. The prophet Isaiah said the coming Messiah would set up an "ensign for the nations" (Isaiah 11:12), serving as a rallying point for His followers.

for everyone who believes." This name of Jesus has a double meaning.

First, Jesus is the End of the Law because He did everything required by the Old

JESUS, THE BELIEVER, AND THE LAW

- "Sin shall not have dominion over you: for ye are not under the law, but under grace" (Romans 6:14).
- "We have believed in Jesus Christ, that we might be justified by the faith of Christ, and not by the works of the law" (Galatians 2:16).
- "The law made nothing perfect, but the bringing in of a better hope did; by the which we draw nigh unto God" (Hebrews 7:19).

Testament law to become a righteous person. He lived a sinless life and obeyed all of God's commandments, although He was tempted to do wrong, like any person in a human body (see Luke 4:1–13; Hebrews 4:15).

Second, Jesus is the End of the Law because He brought an end to law-keeping as the way for people to find justification in God's sight. Belief in Him as Lord and Savior is the only way to deal with sin and eliminate the separation that exists between God and man.

Some things outlive their usefulness and ought to be brought to an end or transformed into something better. We should rejoice that Jesus as the End of the Law offers all believers a glorious new beginning. See also *Law of Moses*.

ENSIGN FOR THE NATIONS

The eleventh chapter of Isaiah is one of the most pronounced messianic passages in the book. In verse 12 from this chapter, Isaiah portrayed the coming Messiah as an "ensign," or banner, not only for the Jewish people but for all nations of the world (*signal for the nations*, NRSV).

The prophet probably had in mind a battle flag under which warriors of Bible times fought. An army was distinguished from its enemies and from the fighting units of its allies by the banner under which it marched. Their flag was visible to all members of the unit, and it served as a rallying point for the army during the heat of battle.

As the Ensign for the Nations, Jesus calls on all believers to fall in step behind Him and spread the good news of the Gospel throughout the world. His Great Commission (see Matthew 28:19–20) is our call to action. The hymn "Onward, Christian Soldiers" by Sabine Baring-Gould is a stirring call to arms for all who belong to the army of the Lord.

Onward, Christian soldiers, marching as to war,
With the cross of Jesus going on before!
Christ, the royal Master, leads against the foe;
Forward into battle, see His banner go!
Onward, Christian soldiers, marching as to war,
With the cross of Jesus going on before!

See also *Great Commission of Jesus; Desire of All Nations*.

Jesus sits in judgment of the world in a sixteenth-century fresco.

ESCHATOLOGY

The biblical doctrine of last things is known as eschatology. The term (pronounced ESS kuh TAHL uh gee) comes from two Greek words, *eschatos* ("last") and *logos* ("word").

Thus, this doctrine focuses on all matters relating to the end time: the second coming of Jesus, the final judgment, heaven and hell, and the nature of human existence in the afterlife. See also *Heaven*; *Hell*; *Last Judgment*; *Second Coming of Christ*.

ETERNAL LIFE

Jesus is described as the provider of eternal life in several places in the New Testament. For example:

- "The gift of God is eternal life through Jesus Christ our Lord" (Romans 6:23).
- "This is the promise that he hath promised us, even eternal life" (1 John 2:25).
- "Looking for the mercy of our Lord Jesus Christ unto eternal life" (Jude 21).

But 1 John 5:20 is the only verse in the Bible where Jesus Himself is given the name "eternal life." John said, "We are in him that is true, even in his Son Jesus Christ. This is the true God, and eternal life." The apostle John was probably thinking about the resurrection of Jesus, His ascension to the Father, and His declaration, "I am alive for evermore" (Revelation 1:18).

Jesus tasted death like all mortal human beings. But He was gloriously raised and restored to His place of honor with God the Father in heaven. As the perfect model of eternal life, He promises that all who place their trust in Him will live forever. The apostle Paul put it like this: "As in Adam all die, even so in Christ shall all be made alive" (1 Corinthians 15:22). See also *Resurrection and the Life*.

ETERNAL PUNISHMENT

See *Hell*.

ETERNAL SPIRIT

The Gospels make it clear that the Holy Spirit guided and empowered Jesus throughout His public ministry. For example, He was led by the Spirit into the region of Galilee, where He began to teach and heal (see Luke 4:14–15). He cast demons out of people "by the spirit of God" (Matthew 12:28). And Hebrews 9:14 shows that the Holy Spirit—described in this verse as the "eternal spirit"—gave Jesus the determination and strength to offer His life as a sacrifice to atone for our sins.

This is the only place in the Bible where the phrase "eternal spirit" appears. It clearly identifies the Holy Spirit as a divine being. Only the three Persons of the Trinity—Father, Son, and Holy Spirit—are eternal. Everything else is created matter.

The eternality of the Holy Spirit is evident in the very first book of the Bible. As God began to mold and shape the universe, "the spirit of God moved upon the face of the waters" (Genesis 1:2). Thus, the Spirit of God existed with God before time began and participated with Him in the creation of the

THE CREATIVE WORK OF GOD'S SPIRIT

- "The Spirit of God has made me; the breath of the Almighty gives me life" (Job 33:4 NIV).
- "By the word of the LORD the heavens were made, their starry host by the breath of his mouth" (Psalm 33:6 NIV).
- "When you send your Spirit, they are created, and you renew the face of the ground" (Psalm 104:30 NIV).

world. The Bible makes it clear that Jesus was also involved with His Father in the creation (see John 1:1–3). So creation was an activity in which all three Persons of the Trinity played an active role. See also *Trinity*.

ETERNITY OF GOD

Two good synonyms for the word *eternity* are "endless" and "timeless." Thus, when we speak of the eternity of God, we mean that He has always existed and that He stands outside the bounds of time. The first four words of the Bible express this truth: "In the beginning God" (Genesis 1:1). Before the earth was, God existed; and before time began, God was.

Our finite minds have a hard time grasping this truth. Our journey through life has taught us that everything has a cause. We have seen it proven time after time that everything has a beginning and an end. But God is on a different level than our human experience. The psalmist tried to grasp this truth and express it in words, but this is the best he could do: "Before the mountains were born or you brought forth the whole world, from everlasting to everlasting you are God" (Psalm 90:2 NIV).

One of the most interesting passages in the Bible that reflects God's eternal existence is the account of God's encounter with Moses in the burning bush. When Moses asked God to give him His name, He replied, "I AM THAT I AM" (Exodus 3:14). This divine name is based on a Hebrew version of the English verb "to be." What God was telling Moses was something like this: "I was who I was; I am who I am; I will be who I will be." He was saying to Moses, "I existed long before you were born, and I will continue to be around long after you are dead. I am the Eternal One."

All of us have said at one time or another, "Nothing lasts forever." That's true of most things. But God is the ultimate exception. He alone is worthy of our worship and devotion. See also *Time and God*.

EUCHARIST

See *Lord's Supper*.

Adam sleeps as God puts the finishing touches on Eve, in a colorful stained-glass window from Strasbourg, France.

EVE

The name, meaning "life," was given by Adam to his wife as the mother of the human race (see Genesis 3:20). Fashioned from one of Adam's ribs, she was created to serve as his helpmate and companion (see Genesis 2:18–23).

Because of her sin and rebellion, Eve was to experience pain and sorrow, especially in connection with the birth of children (see Genesis 3:16).

Eve is mentioned in the New Testament by the apostle Paul, who noted, "The serpent deceived Eve by his cunning" (2 Corinthians 11:3 HCSB; see also 1 Timothy 2:12–14). She is an example of how easily a person can succumb to temptation and fall into sin. See also *Adam*; *Fall of Man*.

EVERLASTING FATHER

We are accustomed to making the distinction between God and Jesus by referring to God as the Father and to Jesus as the Son. But in a famous messianic passage from Isaiah, the prophet seems to blur these neat lines by referring to Jesus as the Father—the "everlasting Father": "Unto us a child is born . . .and his name shall be called Wonderful, Counsellor, The mighty God, The everlasting Father" (Isaiah 9:6).

This name of Jesus focuses attention on the dilemma we face as believers in trying to explain the Trinity, or God's existence in three different modes or essences—Father, Son, and Holy Spirit. Just where does the God mode stop and where do the Son and Spirit essences begin?

Some people explain the Trinity by using the analogy of water. We know that water is one substance, but it can exist in three different forms—liquid, ice, and vapor. In the same way, so this analogy goes, God exists in the three different modes known as the Trinity—one substance in three different forms.

Rather than resorting to analogies like this, we are better off if we admit that there is no neat and easy way to explain the Trinity. This concept is filled with mystery that defies logical explanation. But this doesn't mean it isn't true.

So, was Jesus God's Son? Yes. Was Jesus also God, the Everlasting Father, as Isaiah declared? Yes. This doesn't make sense to our scientific, analytical minds, but faith in God's Word comes to our rescue. We believe that Jesus was separate from God but one with Him at the same time because He Himself declared: "I and my Father are one" (John 10:30). See also *Trinity*.

EVERLASTING GOD

Abraham had moved from place to place for several years in the land of Canaan, the territory that God had promised to his descendants (see Genesis 12:1–5). Finally he decided to make a site known as Beersheba the center of the territory where he would graze his flocks and herds. Here he dug a well and planted a grove of trees to mark the site as his settling-down place.

At Beersheba it was appropriate that Abraham should call on the name of the "everlasting God" (Genesis 21:33). He was the One without beginning and end who would never cease to be. He would guide Abraham into the future and fulfill His promise that Abraham's offspring would eventually populate this entire region.

God kept His promise, but it took awhile.

THINGS ABOUT GOD THAT ARE EVERLASTING

- His mercy (see Psalm 100:5).
- His salvation (see Isaiah 45:17).
- His covenant (see Isaiah 61:8).
- His love (see Jeremiah 31:3).
- His kingdom (see Daniel 7:27).

It was more than five centuries after Abraham's time before the Israelites conquered this land and made it their own. We should remember that the Everlasting God does not watch the clock like we humans do. He acts in accordance with His own sense of time. See also *Ancient of Days*.

EVERLASTING KING

See *King Eternal, Immortal, Invisible*.

EVERLASTING LIGHT

In Isaiah 60:19 the prophet looked ahead to the end time when Christ will dwell with His people in heaven, or the New Jerusalem. There will be no need for the sun or moon in that time because Jesus will serve as the "everlasting light" for His people. This is the only place in the Bible where this name of Jesus appears.

The apostle John in the book of Revelation picked up on this prophecy, repeating Isaiah's declaration that no light would be needed in heaven except the light that Jesus will provide (see Revelation 21:23; 22:5).

It's difficult for earthbound human beings to realize that any light source could replace the sun. This hot, life-giving, luminous body has provided most of the light we have enjoyed throughout our lives. But scientists tell us that the sun is not immortal. They predict it will burn out in about five billion years.

Jesus, however, is the Everlasting Light. When the sun grows dark and disappears from the sky, His reign will continue, and we as believers will be with him in this New Jerusalem. See also *Light of Israel*; *Light of the World*.

EVIL

Skeptics often pose the problem of evil in the world to deny the existence of God. Their reasoning goes like this: (1) if God is all-loving and all-powerful, He would not allow evil in His world; (2) but we see evil all around us;

Wreckage from an April 2011 tornado near St. Louis, Missouri. Many question whether such destructive and "evil" events disprove a loving, all-powerful God.

(3) therefore, there is no such thing as God.

It's a clever piece of logic, but it fails to take into account one important part of the equation—the free will of man. The Lord did not create us as robots who had no choice but to follow His commands. He gave us the ability to reason, make decisions, and choose our own path—even if that path leads us away from Him.

This is the message of the fall of man in the Garden of Eden. Sin and evil came into the world when Adam and Eve disobeyed God's direct order and ate the forbidden fruit (see Genesis 3:6). This pattern of sin and rebellion, repeated in every generation since their time, is behind most of the evil and suffering that we see everywhere today.

But what about tragic events such as natural disasters that cannot be attributed to human actions? The all-powerful God could prevent floods and hurricanes that kill thousands of innocent people every year, so why doesn't He?

This question is not so easily answered. The best we can do is to admit the limit of our understanding. It is unrealistic to expect a simplistic answer for every bad thing that happens in the world. It is enough for us to declare that nothing on this earth escapes the notice of the Lord. What seems to be a tragic and meaningless event when it happens may eventually be shaped into an essential part of His eternal purpose. See also *Free Will of Man*; *Satan*; *Sin*.

EVIL ONE

See *Satan*.

EVIL SPIRITS

See *Demons*.

EXODUS FROM EGYPT

After more than four hundred years as slaves in Egypt (see Exodus 12:40–41), the Israelites were finally given their freedom. The series of signs and wonders by which the Lord brought this to pass is known as the Exodus. The word means "going out" or "a road out." The Exodus brought to fulfillment God's promise to Abraham many years before (see Genesis 12:1–3) that his descendants would become His chosen people with a land of their own.

The leader of this massive "going out" from Egypt was Moses, a man uniquely qualified for this difficult task. Although born an Israelite, he was reared in the court of the Egyptian king. He knew how to stand before the pharaoh and plead the cause of his enslaved people. Moses also spent many years as a shepherd in the desert —the very land the Israelites had to cross while traveling to Canaan. His knowledge of life in this remote territory enhanced his leadership skills as God's chosen leader.

Some of the most spectacular miracles recorded in the Bible occurred during the Exodus. These included God's call of Moses through a burning bush (see Exodus 3:2–3), the ten plagues that God sent to convince the pharaoh to let the people go (see Exodus 7:14–12:30), the drowning of the Egyptian army at the Red Sea (see Exodus 14:29–31), and the feeding of the people in the wilderness with a mysterious substance known as manna (see Exodus 16:15).

No wonder the Exodus was celebrated by future generations of Israelites as the defining moment of their history (see Psalm 136:10–16). It was a time when a collection of powerless slaves faced off against the world's greatest superpower—and won. The Israelites always remembered that it was the Lord who had evened the odds. See also *Passover and Feast of Unleavened Bread*.

The famed pyramids of Giza in Egypt, a common symbol for the north African nation. Under Moses, God's people—the Israelites—left four centuries of slavery in Egypt for their promised land of Canaan.

EXPIATION

See *Propitiation for Our Sins.*

EXPRESS IMAGE OF GOD

This name for Jesus occurs at the beginning of the book of Hebrews. The writer declared that Jesus is the climax of God's revelation of Himself to humans. In the past He had communicated to His people through the prophets, but now He has "spoken unto us by His Son" (Hebrews 1:2), who is the "express image" of God (see Hebrews 1:3).

The Greek word behind "express image" referred in New Testament times to engravings in wood, impressions in clay, or stamped images on coins. The imagery of this verse implies that Jesus was an exact duplicate of His Father in His attitudes, character, and actions. Physical features are not included in this resemblance, since God

is a spirit being (see John 4:24).

This name tells us that Christ perfectly represents God His Father. If we want to know what God is like, we should examine the life and ministry of His Son.

Have you ever heard someone say, "That boy is just like his father"? Sometimes this pronouncement can cause embarrassment for a father because of his son's bad behavior. But God was always pleased with the actions of His Son (see Luke 3:22).

Other names of Jesus that express essentially the same meaning as Express Image of God are "image of God" (2 Corinthians 4:4) and "image of the invisible God" (Colossians 1:15). See also *Invisibility of God.*

EYES OF GOD

The phrase "eyes of God" appears often throughout the Old Testament. It is a metaphor that expresses His awareness of everything that happens in the world and in the lives of its inhabitants. The writer of Proverbs observed, "The eyes of the LORD are everywhere, keeping watch on the wicked and the good" (Proverbs 15:3 NIV).

Nothing that we do escapes the observation of the Lord. He knows every act of every single day of our lives (see Job 34:21). He even sees into our innermost thoughts and the secret places of the heart (see Psalm 94:11; Luke 5:22). This truth should motivate us to make our lives an open book that is dedicated to Him and His service. This must have been the type of life that Noah lived. The Bible describes him as a righteous man who "found favor in the eyes of the LORD" (Genesis 6:8 NIV). See also *Anthropomorphism*; *God Who Sees*.

This familiar image, from the back of the United States' one-dollar bill, shows the all-seeing "eye of Providence" looking over the new nation founded in 1776, represented by the unfinished pyramid.

SEEN BY THE LORD'S EYES

- The haughty: "You save the humble, but your eyes are on the haughty to bring them low" (2 Samuel 22:28 NIV).
- The nations: "His eyes watch the nations—let not the rebellious rise up against him" (Psalm 66:7 NIV).
- The righteous: "The eyes of the LORD are on the righteous, and his ears are attentive to their cry" (Psalm 34:15 NIV).

EYEWITNESS

See *Faithful and True Witness*.

F

FACE OF GOD

The expressions "God's face" and "face of the Lord" are two of the richest metaphors in the Bible. The biblical writers used them to refer to God's presence. For example, the psalmist—when feeling that God had abandoned him—lamented to the Lord, "How long will you hide your face from me?" (Psalm 13:1 NIV).

God is such an awesome being that we as humans could not survive a full dose of His presence. This is why He often appeared to people in the Bible in such objects as a burning bush (see Exodus 3:2–3) or a quiet voice (see 1 Kings 19:12). Moses asked the Lord to reveal Himself to him in all His glory. But the Lord replied, "You cannot see my face, for no one may see me and live" (Exodus 33:20 NIV). God did agree to show Moses a veiled version of His glory by covering him with His hand as He passed by. Then He told Moses, "I will remove my hand and you will see my back; but my face must not be seen" (Exodus 33:23 NIV).

This strange passage expresses the theological truth that God is beyond our human

Three jumpers show faith in their parachutes by leaping off a tall building in Shanghai, China. Faith in God is a similar trust, the conscious belief that He is what His Word says and will do what He has promised.

comprehension. We can have some sense of His presence, but we are unable to experience Him in His full glory. What we know and sense about Him just barely scratches the surface of who He really is.

But a day is coming when our earthly limitations will be no more. We as believers whose names are written in the Lamb's book of life will be able to experience God's presence in His full glory. The apostle John described this as a time when God will be seated on His throne in heaven and we as His servants "will see his face" (Revelation 22:4 NIV). See also *Anthropomorphism*; *Divine Accommodation*.

FAITH

The dictionary defines *faith* as "firm belief in something for which there is no proof." However, Christian faith is not founded merely on "blind" belief. The writer of Hebrews expands on this by emphasizing the spiritual dimension of faith: "Now faith is the substance of things hoped for, the evidence of things not seen" (Hebrews 11:1).

Biblical faith involves two related ideas—a total reliance on Christ for salvation and commitment to His lordship over our lives. The apostle Paul declared that our faith in Christ is the sole basis of our salvation. It does not depend on doing good works or keeping the rules of a strict moral code (see Ephesians 2:8–9). See also *Spirit of Faith*.

FAITHFUL

A faithful person is one who is deeply committed to a cause or purpose. This is a perfect description of the earthly life and ministry of Jesus. No wonder the apostle Paul applied the name "Faithful" to Him in 1 Thessalonians 5:24: "Faithful is he that calleth you, who also will do it."

Throughout His brief earthly ministry, Jesus refused to be turned aside from His mission as the Messiah sent by the Father to bring people into His kingdom of grace. He resisted Satan's temptation at the beginning of His ministry to become a "bread Messiah" and dazzle the crowds with death-defying stunts (see Matthew 4:1–11). He did not become the military conqueror or political hero that the Jewish people thought the Messiah should be. While on the cross, He did not try to save Himself, although He could have done so. He chose instead to die for our sins (see Luke 23:35). He was faithful to His mission as the Suffering Servant to the very end.

He who was faithful in His earthly existence continues to be the Faithful One to those who follow Him. We as believers have His promise that we will enjoy eternal life with Him in heaven. As the apostle Paul declared, "He who began a good work in you will carry it on to completion until the day of Christ Jesus" (Philippians 1:6 NIV). See also *Author and Finisher of Our Faith*; *Faithfulness*.

JESUS CHRIST, THE FAITHFUL ONE

- "If we confess our sins, he is faithful and just and will forgive us our sins and purify us from all unrighteousness" (1 John 1:9 NIV).
- "The Lord is faithful, and he will strengthen you and protect you from the evil one" (2 Thessalonians 3:3 NIV).
- "God is faithful, who has called you into fellowship with his Son, Jesus Christ our Lord" (1 Corinthians 1:9 NIV).

FAITHFUL AND TRUE

Near the end of the book of Revelation, the apostle John saw Jesus in a vision: "I saw heaven opened, and behold a white horse; and he that sat upon him was called Faithful and True, and in righteousness he doth judge and make war" (Revelation 19:11). The white horse on which Christ was seated symbolized His triumph over all His enemies. As the "Faithful and True," he was coming to earth in judgment against all forms of unrighteousness and injustice.

This verse contains images that are similar to the portrayal of God as the divine judge in the Old Testament (see *Judge*). For example, the psalmist looked forward to the time when God would judge the earth. He would "judge the world with righteousness, and the

Witnesses in a courtroom swear to tell "the whole truth and nothing but the truth." In scripture, Jesus is called both the "faithful and true witness" (Revelation 3:14) and "the truth" (John 14:6).

people with his truth" (Psalm 96:13). Since God is the standard of truth, He has the right to set the standards by which the world will be judged.

In this verse from Revelation, God has delegated His authority to judge the world to His Son. He is faithful to God's promise of judgment, and He is the True One who will judge by God's standard of ultimate truth.

As believers, we recognize that truth does not always win out in an unjust and unrighteous world. But the final work of judgment belongs to God and His Son—the Faithful and True. See also *Faithful*.

FAITHFUL AND TRUE WITNESS

Witness is one of those words used again and again by the apostle John in his writings—the Gospel of John, his three epistles, and the book of Revelation. It occurs about seventy times in these five writings. In Revelation 3:14 John applied this word to Jesus, calling Him the "faithful and true witness."

A witness is a person who gives testimony to others about something he has seen, felt, or experienced. The best modern example of a witness is a person who is summoned by the justice system to present testimony in a legal proceeding such as a trial. The task of such a witness is to tell the court what he or she knows from personal experience that is relevant to the case under investigation.

The witness that Jesus bore about God grew out of His personal experience. He is the only person who has ever seen God the Father. Thus He knows God like no one has ever known Him. He came into the world to show that His Father is a merciful God who relates to His people in love and grace. Jesus showed by dying on the cross just how much God the Father and God the Son love us.

Those of us who are transformed by God's love are also charged to give testimony about His love to others (see Luke 24:45–48). Jesus told His disciples, "This gospel of the kingdom will be preached in the whole world as a testimony to all nations" (Matthew 24:14 NIV). This witnessing work continues in our time through the Church and individual believers. If you know Jesus as Lord and Savior, you have no choice in the matter—you are automatically in the witnessing business. See also *Faithful and True*.

FAITHFUL CREATOR

The apostle Peter wrote his first epistle to believers who were undergoing persecution because of their commitment to Christ. Peter encouraged them to place their hope in their Faithful Creator, Jesus, and to "continue to do good" (1 Peter 4:19 NIV). This is the only place in the Bible where Jesus is called by this name.

Jesus as participant in the physical creation with God the Father is described in other New Testament passages (see John 1:1–3; Colossians 1:16). But the emphasis of this verse from 1 Peter is on His role as spiritual Creator. According to the apostle Paul, we become "new creatures" (2 Corinthians 5:17) when we accept Christ as Savior. As our Faithful Creator, Jesus not only gives us a new nature; He also keeps us from falling back into sin, and He leads us toward the goal of eternal life with Him in heaven.

All believers can affirm with the apostle Paul, "The Lord will rescue me from every evil attack and will bring me safely to his heavenly kingdom" (2 Timothy 4:18 NIV). See also *Beginning of the Creation of God*; *Creator*.

FAITHFULNESS

Faithful people are those who are loyal to other people or the values on which they base their lives. Other characteristics of a person like this are dependability and stability. Believers are called on to be faithful to their promise to live for the Lord (see 1 Timothy 3:11; Revelation 2:10).

Human beings are weak and subject to temptation. Even the stablest among us may waver in our faithfulness to our friends, our values, or the Lord. But the Lord always lives up to His commitments (see Psalm 89:1–2). The word *faithful* appears in several of the names by which God the Father and God the

Son are known in the Bible. See also *Faithful and True*; *Faithful and True Witness*; *Faithful Creator*.

FAITHFULNESS OF GOD

See *Faithful*; *Faithful and True Witness*; *Faithful Creator*.

FALLEN ANGELS

See *Lucifer*.

FALL OF MAN

Adam and Eve's transition from obeying God to rebelling against Him is called the fall of man. It is often referred to simply as "the fall." The account of the fall is found in the second and third chapters of Genesis.

After creating Adam and Eve—the first man and woman—God placed them in a perfect place known as the Garden of Eden (see Genesis 2:8–9). He graciously provided everything they needed to sustain life in this lush paradise. But He told them clearly not

The fall of man in sculpture: Eve bites into the forbidden fruit while handing more fruit to her husband, Adam, as the serpent—in this case, half woman—looks on. The statuary decorates the Notre Dame Cathedral in Paris, France.

to eat from one specific tree—the tree of the knowledge of good and evil (see Genesis 2:16–17). This tree represented God's sovereignty and His authority to place limits on human behavior.

Another important element in this biblical account is human freedom. Although God is sovereign, He created humans with free will—the ability to choose whether to obey God or to follow our own desires. This is where Satan with his devious scheme known as temptation entered the picture. He approached Eve in the form of a serpent and convinced her that God didn't really mean what He said. She in turn persuaded Adam to go against the clear instructions of the Lord. Both ate fruit from the forbidden tree (see Genesis 3:1–6). This act of rebellion is a perfect picture of our sinful nature. The essence of sin is human pride that refuses to conform to the divine will and insists on going its own way.

Because of their disobedience of God, Adam and Eve were expelled from the Garden of Eden and the perfect environment they had enjoyed (see Genesis 3:22–24). Other consequences of their sin were the introduction of pain and death into the world (see Genesis 3:16–19).

This original rebellion of Adam and Eve is a model of the sin that affects the entire human race. As the apostle Paul put it, "All have sinned, and come short of the glory of God" (Romans 3:23). But God has not left us without hope in our sinful condition. He has provided for our redemption through the atoning sacrifice of His Son, Jesus Christ. He is known as the Last Adam, who corrected the sin problem caused by the first Adam. See also *Adam; Humankind; Last Adam.*

FALSE WORSHIP

See *Idolatry.*

FAMILY OF GOD

See *Adoption; Children of God.*

FASTING

Going without food and drink for a time in order to center one's attention on God is known as fasting. Jesus fasted for forty days during His time of temptation in the wilderness before He launched His public ministry (see Matthew 4:2).

The people of the prophet Isaiah's time went without food and water, but their fasting had no spiritual substance or meaning. While denying their physical appetites, they were guilty of exploiting the poor and other forms of injustice. The prophet told them, "On the day of your fasting, you do as you please and exploit all your workers. . . . Is not this the kind of fasting I have chosen: to loose the chains of injustice and untie the cords of the yoke, to set the oppressed free?" (Isaiah 58:3, 6 NIV).

Isaiah's message is that religious formalism is no substitute for compassionate actions toward others. We honor God with our pure hearts and deeds of mercy, not elaborate rituals and empty creeds. See also *Hypocrisy.*

FATHER

The prophet Isaiah prayed, "You, LORD, are our father. We are the clay, you are the potter; we are all the work of your hand" (Isaiah 64:8 NIV). He realized that God had a role in shaping His people, just as earthly fathers participate in the creative process of bringing children into the world.

This is one of the few places in the Old Testament where God is referred to as "Father" (see Deuteronomy 32:6; Psalm 89:26; Isaiah 63:16; Malachi 2:10). By contrast, Father as a name for God occurs often in the New Testament, particularly on the lips of Jesus (see Matthew 26:39; Luke 23:34; John 17:1).

People of Old Testament times generally did not think of God in fatherly terms. To them He was an all-powerful being who stood above and beyond the relationships and events of everyday life. It took Jesus to show us that God is a loving Father: "For God so loved the world, that he gave his only begotten Son, that whosoever believeth in him should not perish, but have everlasting life" (John 3:16). See also *Abba, Father*.

FATHER OF GLORY

The apostle Paul assured the believers at Ephesus that he was praying to the Father on their behalf. He prayed "that the God of our Lord Jesus Christ, the Father of glory, may give unto you the spirit of wisdom and revelation in the knowledge of him" (Ephesians 1:17). This is the only place in the Bible where God is called the Father of Glory.

The word *glory* appears many times throughout the Bible, usually in reference to God's splendor, moral beauty, and perfection. At times His glory was revealed visibly, as in the tabernacle and temple after they were built (see Exodus 40:34; 1 Kings 8:11). The prophet Isaiah declared of the Lord, "The whole earth is full of his glory" (Isaiah 6:3). Or, to put it another way, the beauty and majesty of the physical world give evidence of God's presence in His creation.

God the Father is also referred to in the Old Testament as the "crown of glory" (Isaiah 28:5). In New Testament times Stephen, in his long speech before his persecutors, also referred to the Lord as the "God of glory" (Acts 7:2). See also *Spirit of Glory*.

FATHER OF LIES

See *Satan*.

FATHER OF LIGHTS

One of the most interesting names of God appears in the book of James in the New Testament: "Every good gift and every perfect gift is from above, and cometh down from the Father of lights, with whom is no

Good fathers are strong, protective, and loving—everything the Bible portrays God the Father as being.

Demonstrations of God's Glory

- To Moses on Mount Sinai when God revealed His plan for the tabernacle (see Exodus 24:16–17).
- To the world at the coming of the Messiah (see Isaiah 40:4–5; 60:1).
- To the prophet Ezekiel as he ministered among Jewish exiles in Babylon (see Ezekiel 3:22–23).
- To the shepherds at the announcement of the birth of Jesus (see Luke 2:9).

variableness, neither shadow of turning" (James 1:17). By referring to God as the "Father of lights," James probably had in mind the creation account in the book of Genesis. On the fourth day of creation, God created the sun, moon, and stars and "set them in the vault of the sky to give light on the earth" (Genesis 1:17 NIV).

The people of many ancient cultures thought of the heavenly bodies as gods. But James declared that they were created things, brought into being by the one true God of the universe. Only the Father of Lights is

An ultraviolet view of the neighboring galaxy M31 in the constellation Andromeda, as photographed by NASA's Swift satellite. God is the "Father of lights," according to James 1:17.

worthy of worship.

This God who created the light-giving bodies of the heavens is also dependable and trustworthy. As the New International Version translates this verse from James, He "does not change, like shifting shadows." His presence is an unwavering light that guides His people throughout this life and beyond. See also *Light of Israel*; *Light of the World*; *Sun*.

FATHER OF MERCIES

This is one of the apostle Paul's names for God that appears in only one verse in the Bible: "Blessed be God, even the Father of our Lord Jesus Christ, the Father of mercies, and the God of all comfort" (2 Corinthians 1:3). He used this name for God in his prayer for the believers in the church he founded at Corinth.

God is the "Father of mercies" because He has mercy on His people. If He withheld His mercy and grace and gave us exactly what we deserved, we would be destitute and lost, hopelessly trapped by our sin and rebellion. But His love and patience won't let us go. He keeps calling us back into His presence by extending His mercy and forgiveness.

Since God is the originator—or Father—of mercies, He expects His people to show this attribute of His character to others. Jesus declared, "Be ye therefore merciful, as your Father also is merciful" (Luke 6:36). See also *Mercy of God*.

FATHER OF OUR LORD JESUS CHRIST

In Colossians 1:3 the apostle Paul prayed for the Colossian believers. "We give thanks to God and the Father of our Lord Jesus Christ," he said, "praying always for you." This name of God—"Father of our Lord Jesus Christ"—draws attention to the miraculous birth of Jesus the Son. He did not have a human father but was miraculously conceived in the womb of Mary by God the Father, acting through the Holy Spirit (see Luke 1:34–35).

Jesus was sent by God to fulfill the Father's work of redemption in the world. Jesus stated when He was only twelve years old that this was His divine mission (see Luke 2:48–49). His declaration from the cross, "It is finished" (John 19:30), shows that He accomplished the purpose for which He was sent—our salvation.

FATHER OF OUR SPIRITS

Hebrews 12:9 is one of those places in the Bible where the addition of one word makes all the difference in its meaning. Rather than "Father of spirits" as it reads in the King James Version, the New Living Translation renders this name of God as "Father of our spirits." This rendering makes it clear that the writer of Hebrews was contrasting physical fathers ("fathers of our flesh") with God as our Father in a spiritual sense.

God the Father looks down as the angel Gabriel makes the important announcement to Mary: She will bear God's Son, Jesus Christ.

GOD IS PLEASED WITH HIS SON

- "A voice came from heaven: 'You are my Son, whom I love; with you I am well pleased'" (Mark 1:11 NIV).
- "God was pleased to have all his fullness dwell in him" (Colossians 1:19 NIV).
- "He received honor and glory from God the Father when the voice came to him from the Majestic Glory, saying, 'This is my Son, whom I love; with him I am well pleased'" (2 Peter 1:17 NIV).

Earthly fathers discipline their children and teach them right from wrong and respect for others. God, our spiritual Father, teaches us to obey Him as the ultimate authority, to follow His commands, and to present our lives as living sacrifices for His honor and glory. The next verse in the NLT puts it like this: "Our earthly fathers disciplined us for a few years, doing the best they knew how. But God's discipline is always good for us, so that we might share in his holiness" (Hebrews 12:10 NLT).

FEAR OF GOD

See *Reverence for God*; *Spirit of Knowledge and the Fear of the Lord*.

FEAST OF UNLEAVENED BREAD

See *Passover and Feast of Unleavened Bread*.

FELLOWSHIP WITH GOD

See *Imputed Righteousness*.

FINAL JUDGMENT

See *Last Judgment*.

FINGER OF GOD

This biblical metaphor expresses God's awesome power. After the third plague that God sent on the Egyptians—swarms of gnats—the pharaoh's magicians declared, "This is the finger of God" (Exodus 8:19 NIV). They were saying, in effect, "If God can do this much damage with one finger, we shudder to think about what He'll do next." They found out with the tenth plague, when God caused the death of all the firstborn people and animals among the Egyptians (see Exodus 12:29).

Michelangelo's classic image of the creation of Adam, from the ceiling of Rome's Sistine Chapel, depicts the "finger of God" in a literal manner.

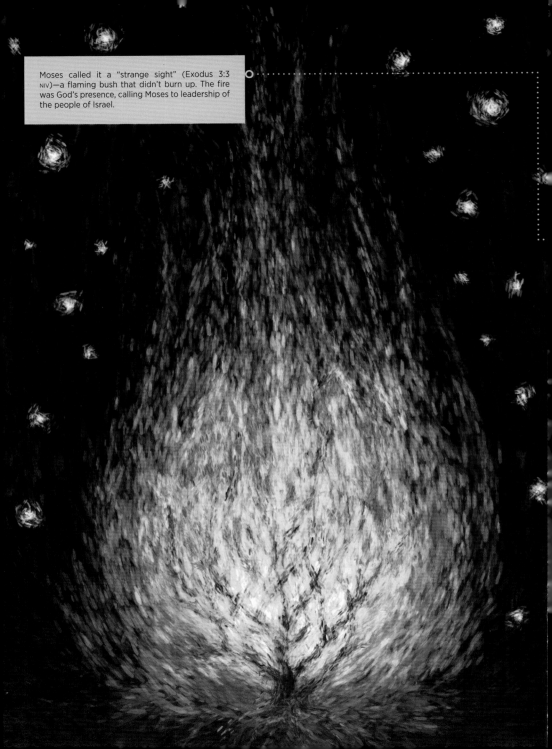

Moses called it a "strange sight" (Exodus 3:3 NIV)—a flaming bush that didn't burn up. The fire was God's presence, calling Moses to leadership of the people of Israel.

God, of course, does not have literal fingers. But He does have power that is superior to all the magic tricks of all the wizards of the world. See also *Anthropomorphism*; *Imagery Used of God*.

FINISHER OF OUR FAITH

See *Author and Finisher of Our Faith*.

FIRE

Fire is often associated in the Bible with God's presence and power. God spoke to Moses from a flaming bush (see Exodus 3:2–12). God placed a pillar of fire behind the Israelites to protect them from the pursuing Egyptian army (see Exodus 14:19–24). Some sacrificial animals were consumed by fire to symbolize the Lord's acceptance of these offerings from the people (see 1 Kings 18:38).

Sometimes fire is an apt illustration of a person's determination to serve the Lord. The prophet Jeremiah was tempted to quit his unpopular preaching to the wayward people of Judah. But God's call and the divine message that consumed his life always gave him the motivation to go on. "If I say, 'I will not mention his word or speak anymore in his name,'" the prophet declared, "his word is in my heart like a fire, a fire shut up in my bones. I am weary of holding it in; indeed, I cannot" (Jeremiah 20:9 NIV). See also *Pillar of Fire and Cloud*; *Refiner's Fire*; *Wall of Fire*.

FIRST AND LAST

See *Alpha and Omega*.

FIRSTBEGOTTEN

Hebrews 1:6 makes an interesting reference to God and Christ: "When he bringeth in the firstbegotten into the world, he saith, And let all the angels of God worship him." The word *he* here refers to God the Father, and *firstbegotten* refers to His Son, Jesus Christ. But since Jesus has existed from eternity with the Father, how could He be the firstborn or "firstbegotten into the world"?

"Firstbegotten" in this context refers to Jesus' incarnation, or His appearance in human flesh. True, He has existed with the Father from the beginning. But there was a specific point in time when He was conceived by the Holy Spirit in Mary's womb and then born nine months later like any human infant (see Luke 1:35; 2:7). This is one sense in which the name Firstbegotten is applied to Jesus.

RIGHTS AND RESPONSIBILITIES OF THE FIRSTBORN

Jesus as the Firstbegotten or Firstborn picks up on a key term that appears often throughout the Old Testament. The firstborn offspring of both humans and animals were considered special blessings of God, and they were to be devoted to Him (see Exodus 13:2). The firstborn son in a Jewish family inherited a larger share of the family property than the other sons, but he also assumed responsibility for taking care of the family after his father's death.

As the Firstborn, Jesus is exalted as head of the Church, but He is also responsible for its welfare. All believers should rejoice that the Church rests in such capable hands.

The word also refers to rank or order. To say that Jesus is God's Firstbegotten is to declare that He ranks above all other earthly or divine beings except God Himself. This verse from Hebrews makes the point that Jesus is higher than all of God's angels, because they are told to bow down and worship Him. Similar names of Jesus that express the idea of His preeminence and superiority are "firstborn" (Psalm 89:27), "firstborn among many brethren" (Romans 8:29), and "firstborn of every creature" (Colossians 1:15).

As God's Firstbegotten or Firstborn, Jesus is worthy of our honor and praise. The apostle Peter declared that all believers should glorify Jesus Christ, "to whom be praise and dominion for ever and ever" (1 Peter 4:11). See also *Only Begotten Son.*

FIRSTBORN AMONG MANY BRETHREN

See *Firstbegotten.*

In the Old Testament, the first portion of the Israelites' harvest was devoted to God. New Testament writers used the concept to describe Jesus' resurrection as the first of many others to follow.

FIRSTBORN FROM THE DEAD

The apostle Paul applied this name to Jesus in his description of Jesus as head of the Church in his epistle to the Colossian believers (see Colossians 1:18). "Firstborn from the dead" expresses basically the same meaning as the name "first begotten of the dead" in the book of Revelation (see Revelation 1:5).

This name obviously refers to Jesus' resurrection from the dead. But in what sense was He the Firstborn from the Dead? Jesus was not the first person in the Bible to be brought back to life following physical death. The prophet Elisha raised the son of a family in Shunem back to life (see 2 Kings 4:18–37). Jesus Himself raised three people from the dead: the daughter of Jairus (see Matthew 9:18–26), the son of a widow in the village of Nain (see Luke 7:11–15), and His friend Lazarus (see John 11:38–44).

But all these resurrections were temporary stays of death. These resurrected people eventually died again. Jesus rose from the grave, never to die again. He was the first person to overcome death and to appear in a glorified body (see Luke 24:36–39). He also rose as the head of a new creation, the Church. As the Firstborn from the Dead, He has the authority and power to provide bodily resurrection and eternal life for all who commit their lives to Him (see 1 Corinthians 15:12–26). See also *Resurrection and the Life*; *Resurrection of Christ*.

FIRSTBORN OF EVERY CREATURE

See *Firstbegotten*.

FIRST DAY OF THE WEEK

See *Lord's Day*.

FIRSTFRUITS

References to Jesus as the "firstfruits" occur in the apostle Paul's famous passage about the resurrection of Jesus and His promise of a similar resurrection for all believers (see 1 Corinthians 15:12–57). In verse 20 the apostle declared, "Now is Christ risen from the dead, and become the firstfruits of them that slept."

Some people in the church at Corinth apparently were teaching that the resurrection was spiritual, not physical, in nature, or that the resurrection had already happened. They may have even been denying the resurrection altogether, since Paul scolded, "How can some of you say that there is no resurrection of the dead?" (1 Corinthians 15:12 NIV).

Paul based his argument for the physical resurrection of Jesus on the fact that He had been seen by His disciples as well as many other believers during the days after He rose from the dead (see 1 Corinthians 15:3–7). He was the "firstfruits" of the resurrection, or the model that had blazed the trail for others.

The Jewish people thought of the firstfruits, or the first of their crops to be gathered, as God's harvest. These were presented as offerings to God on the day of the firstfruits, a part of the celebration of the harvest festival known as Pentecost (see Numbers 28:26; 2 Chronicles 31:5).

To Paul, Jesus in His resurrection was the Firstfruits of a spiritual harvest known as eternal life. Believers were the rest of the harvest that would be gathered in at the appointed time. Just as Jesus had been raised from the dead to reign with His Father in glory, so their bodies would be "raised incorruptible" (1 Corinthians 15:52) at His second coming, and they would live with Him forever in heaven. See also *Resurrection of Christ*.

FLESH

The apostle John claimed that in Jesus, "the Word was made flesh, and dwelt among us, (and we beheld his glory, the glory as of the only begotten of the Father,) full of grace and truth" (John 1:14). This bold affirmation of the apostle John in his Gospel is the strongest declaration in the New Testament about the humanity of Jesus. It carries the authority of an eyewitness.

John knew that Jesus existed in the flesh because he had lived and worked with Him. As one of His disciples, he had walked with Him along the dusty roads of Palestine, watched His interaction with people, and learned from His teachings across a period of about three years. Certainly, John must have been impressed by Jesus' miracles and His claim to be the divine Son of God. But he was also convinced that Jesus was an authentic human being, just like him.

John's personal association with Jesus in the flesh was a valuable asset to the church in his later years. False teachers began to teach that Jesus did not exist in human form and that He only seemed to be a man. John rejected this heresy with these strong words: "Every spirit that confesseth that Jesus Christ is come in the flesh is of God: and every spirit that confesseth not that Jesus Christ is come in the flesh is not of God" (1 John 4:2–3).

We find it hard to understand how Jesus could be both divine and human in the same body. But this is the clear affirmation of the New Testament. And the church has upheld this doctrine for almost two thousand years, although it is ridiculed by the world. Even the apostle Paul admitted it was a deep mystery, but he accepted it in faith. "And most certainly, the mystery of godliness is great," he said. "He was manifested in the flesh, vindicated in the Spirit, seen by angels, preached among the nations, believed on in the world, taken up in glory" (1 Timothy 3:16 HCSB).

Other names of Jesus that emphasize the human side of His nature are "man ap-

proved of God" (Acts 2:22) and "man Christ Jesus" (1 Timothy 2:5). See also *Incarnation of Christ.*

FOOTSTOOL

A footstool was a piece of furniture, similar to a modern ottoman, on which a person rested his feet while in a seated position. To treat a person as a footstool was to bring him into total subjection to one's power and authority. The word is used as a metaphor in the Bible to portray God's power (see Psalm 110:1).

Sometimes the word is used in the same sense as "feet." The psalmist issued a call to worship by telling the people, "We will go into [the Lord's] tabernacles: we will worship at his footstool" (Psalm 132:7).

FORBEARANCE OF GOD

See *Longsuffering of God.*

FOREKNOWLEDGE OF GOD

This attribute of the Lord refers to His knowledge of the future. The psalmist expressed this truth perfectly when he prayed, "Before a word is on my tongue you, LORD, know it completely" (Psalm 139:4 NIV). Nothing that happens in this world is a surprise to God. He knows our deeds even before we do them and our words even before they drop from our lips.

Although God knows the events of the future, this does not mean that He causes them to happen. He has given man free will and the right to choose whether to follow God's will or his own selfish desires. Our poor choices often lead to disastrous results in our fallen world.

EVIDENCES OF JESUS' EXISTENCE IN THE FLESH

- His fatigue (see Mark 4:38).
- His amazement (see Mark 6:6).
- His disappointment (see Mark 8:12).
- His displeasure (see Mark 10:14).
- His anger (see Mark 11:15–17).
- His sorrow (see Mark 14:34).

Earth is Jesus' footstool in this Austrian church painting of the last judgment.

The ability to see into the future is a power that belongs only to the Lord of the universe. He warned His people against listening to wizards or fortune tellers who claimed to be able to read the future (see Deuteronomy 18:10–11). See also *Omniscience of God.*

FOREORDAINED BEFORE THE FOUNDATION OF THE WORLD

First Peter 1:20 is the only place in the Bible where Jesus is referred to as the One "foreordained before the foundation of the world." This name echoes the words of the apostle Peter on the day of Pentecost when three thousand people became believers in Christ (see Acts 2:41). In his sermon on that occasion, Peter told the crowd that Jesus had been sent into the world by the "deliberate plan" of God (see Acts 2:23 NIV).

The word *foreordained* shows that Jesus was especially chosen by God the Father for the redemptive mission on which He was sent. His coming to earth was no accident; it was part of God's plan. The phrase "before the foundation of the world" tells us that Jesus had existed with God the Father from the beginning (see John 1:1–3). Even before He created the world, God had designated His Son as the agent of salvation for all humankind.

This is difficult for us earthbound humans to understand. But aren't you glad that God didn't wait until we had perfect understanding before He sent Jesus to deliver us from the bondage of sin?

Another name of Jesus similar in meaning to Foreordained before the Foundation of the World is "man whom [God] ordained" (Acts 17:31). See also *One Chosen Out of the People.*

FORERUNNER

A forerunner is an "out-front" agent, the lead person on a team. He goes ahead on a scouting mission to spot possible dangers and prepare the way for others who will follow. Two good examples of forerunners in the Bible are the twelve spies sent by Moses to investigate the land of Canaan (see Numbers 13:1–3) and the forerunner of Jesus, John the Baptist (see Mark 1:1–8).

But the ultimate "forerunner," according to the author of Hebrews, was Jesus Christ (see Hebrews 6:20). He came to prepare the way so we could become citizens of God's

The Gospel writer Mark paraphrases Malachi 3:1 ("I will send my messenger, who will prepare the way before me") in describing the ministry of John the Baptist, a forerunner of Jesus Christ.

kingdom. Following His death and resurrection, He returned to His Father in heaven (see Acts 1:9). Here He has prepared a place for us. We as believers have His word that we will live there with Him forever. "If I go and prepare a place for you," He promised, "I will come back, and take you to be with me that you also may be where I am" (John 14:3 NIV). See also *Author and Finisher of Our Faith*; *John the Baptist*.

FORGIVENESS

To be forgiven is to be excused by other persons for the wrongs we have committed against them. In a biblical sense, forgiveness refers to God's pardon of our sin and rebellion against Him.

Human sin deserves the Lord's punishment because it violates His holiness and His high moral standards (see Romans 1:18–22). In Old Testament times, God accepted an animal sacrifice as a way for people to pay for their sins and receive His forgiveness (see Leviticus 17:11, 14). But in the New Testament, Christ became the Mediator between God and man. God the Father delegated to Him the authority to forgive sins (see Matthew 1:21). Through His death on the cross, He became the once-for-all sacrifice that became the basis for our forgiveness.

Since believers have been forgiven freely through Christ's sacrifice, we are expected to be generous in our forgiveness of others. This was a major theme of the teachings of Jesus (see Mark 11:25–26; Luke 6:37). See also *Remission of Sins*.

FORTRESS

In Jeremiah 16:19 the prophet portrayed the Lord as his "fortress." A fortress was any heavily guarded or fortified place that provided protection from enemy attacks. In Bible times, a defensive wall around a city with its reinforced towers and gates was considered the ultimate fortress.

Jeremiah's unpopular message that Judah would fall to its enemies subjected him to ridicule, imprisonment, and charges of treason. At the beginning of the prophet's ministry, God promised that He would make him "a fortified city, an iron pillar and a bronze wall to stand against the whole land" (Jeremiah 1:18 NIV). The Lord had made good on His promise.

Like Jeremiah, all of us need a fortress at times. This advice from Peter can help us hang in there when troubles seem to fall from the sky like the spring rain: "Cast all your anxiety on him because he cares for you" (1 Peter 5:7 NIV).

The hymn "A Mighty Fortress Is Our God" was written by Martin Luther during

FORGIVENESS IN THE WRITINGS OF PAUL

- "Blessed are those whose transgressions are forgiven, whose sins are covered" (Romans 4:7 NIV).
- "Be kind and compassionate to one another, forgiving each other, just as in Christ God forgave you" (Ephesians 4:32 NIV).
- "When you were dead in your sins. . .God made you alive with Christ. He forgave us all our sins" (Colossians 2:13 NIV).

the turbulent years of the Protestant Reformation in the 1500s. His faith in God in spite of the threats against his life has inspired generations of believers.

> A mighty fortress is our God,
> A bulwark never failing;
> Our helper He, amid the flood
> Of mortal ills prevailing.
> Let goods and kindred go,
> This mortal life also;
> The body they may kill:
> God's truth abideth still,
> His kingdom is forever.

See also *Hiding Place; Refuge; Strong Tower.*

The ancient Israeli fortress of Masada, in the Judean desert. In AD 73, its height provided Jewish rebels temporary protection against the Roman army—until legionnaires build a giant ramp to the top of the hill. Upon breaking through, the Romans found that the Jews had committed mass suicide rather than accept capture.

FOUNDATION

In his first letter to the believers at Corinth, the apostle Paul dealt with divisions in the church (see 1 Corinthians 1:10–15). The people were following four different authority figures—Paul, Apollos, Cephas, and Christ. Paul made it clear that the one foundation on which they should be basing their faith was Jesus Christ: "No one can lay any foundation other than the one already laid, which is Jesus Christ" (1 Corinthians 3:11 NIV).

Jesus Himself addressed this issue during His earthly ministry. In the parable of the two foundations, He described two men who built houses on two different sites (see Matthew 7:24–27). The house built on sand collapsed in the first storm that came up. But the second house held firm in violent weather because "it was founded upon a rock" (v. 25).

The message of this parable is that almost any foundation will do when the weather is good. But only a faith based on the solid Foundation known as Jesus Christ can withstand the

gales and floods of life.

Several centuries before Jesus was born, the prophet Isaiah looked ahead to the coming of the Messiah and referred to Him as the "sure foundation" (Isaiah 28:16). The old hymn "How Firm a Foundation" by George Keith assures believers they can rely on Jesus Christ and the promise of His abiding presence.

> How firm a foundation, ye saints of the
>   Lord,
> Is laid for your faith in His excellent Word!
> What more can He say than to you He hath
>   said,
> To you who for refuge to Jesus have fled?

FOUNTAIN

The prophet Zechariah looked forward to the day when the nations of Israel and Judah would be restored to moral purity. They were worshiping false gods. The Lord would provide a fountain in which they could be cleansed of their sin (see Zechariah 13:1). This passage has been interpreted as a reference to Jesus Christ. He is the "Fountain" whose blood provides cleansing from sin. This Fountain is available to everyone—nobles as well as commoners, poor as well as wealthy.

The word *fountain* in the Bible generally refers to a spring or some source of fresh water, such as a well or a free-flowing stream. This type of water was preferable to standing water that was stored in cisterns. The prophet Isaiah used this image of a fountain in referring to God (see *Fountain of Living Waters*).

As the Fountain of salvation, Jesus invites us to drink freely of the living water that He provides. "Whosoever drinketh of the water that I shall give him shall never thirst," He told the woman at the well. "The water that I shall give him shall be in him a well of water springing up into everlasting life" (John 4:14). See also *Fountain of Living Waters.*

Israel's En-gedi oasis, where David hid from the murderous King Saul. En-gedi's flowing spring was like "water of life" compared to muddy, stagnant waters.

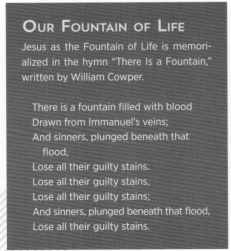

OUR FOUNTAIN OF LIFE

Jesus as the Fountain of Life is memorialized in the hymn "There Is a Fountain," written by William Cowper.

> There is a fountain filled with blood
> Drawn from Immanuel's veins;
> And sinners, plunged beneath that
>   flood,
> Lose all their guilty stains.
> Lose all their guilty stains,
> Lose all their guilty stains;
> And sinners, plunged beneath that flood,
> Lose all their guilty stains.

(F)

FOUNTAIN OF LIVING WATERS

The prophet Jeremiah was called by the Lord to condemn the people of Judah for their idolatry. In one of his most famous passages, the prophet declared this message on behalf of the Lord: "My people have committed two evils; they have forsaken me the fountain of living waters, and hewed them out cisterns, broken cisterns, that can hold no water" (Jeremiah 2:13).

God found it hard to believe that they had rejected the waters of a flowing spring—or worship of the one true God. Instead they chose to drink stagnant water from a broken cistern—or to worship the pagan gods of surrounding nations that were untrustworthy and powerless.

This situation is not unique to Jeremiah's time. When we allow anything besides the Lord to take first place in our lives, it's like drinking contaminated water from a muddy pond. God wants only the best for us. He gives water in abundance from "the fountain of the water of life" to all who will come and drink (see Revelation 21:6). See also *Fountain*.

FREEDOM OF GOD

This attribute of God means that He is not bound by time, space, distance, or any of our ideas about who He is and what He should be doing in the world. He is absolutely free, able to act in accordance with His divine will and purpose. The apostle Paul told the learned philosophers at Athens, "Human hands can't serve [God's] needs—for he has no needs" (Acts 17:25 NLT). See also *Self-Existence of God*.

FREE SPIRIT

David's prayer for forgiveness in Psalm 51 is one of the most eloquent prayers in the Bible. He had plotted the murder of Uriah, the husband of Bathsheba, to cover up his sin of adultery that had resulted in her pregnancy (see 2 Samuel 11:1–17). David's great sin had separated him from God. He prayed for the restoration of this relationship ("a right spirit," v. 10) through a movement of God's Spirit, which he described as God's "free spirit" (v. 12; *willing spirit*, NIV).

The Holy Spirit of God might be described as "free" in two distinct senses:

He is free because His presence is offered freely by God the Father to those who accept His Son, Jesus, as Savior and Lord. We can't buy God's grace and forgiveness (see Acts 8:18–20; Ephesians 2:8). But He offers it willingly to those who repent of their sins and commit themselves to His lordship over their lives.

The Holy Spirit is also free in the sense that He is not bound by our expectations. God is sovereign; He does not have to wait for our permission before He acts in His world. Sometimes His actions take us by surprise. For example, it took a while for the early church to realize that the Gospel was meant for all people, not just the Jews. The famous vision of the apostle Peter on the roof of Simon the tanner convinced him that he "should not call any man common or unclean" (Acts 10:28).

This insight came to Peter from the Holy Spirit, who brought many Gentiles to saving faith in Jesus Christ. The work of God's Free Spirit is evident throughout the book of Acts. So powerful is the Spirit's work in this New Testament book that it is often called "The Acts of the Holy Spirit" rather than "The Acts of the Apostles."

This is how Jesus described the work of the Holy Spirit as God's Free Spirit to Nicodemus: "The wind blows wherever it pleases. You hear its sound, but you cannot tell where it comes from or where it is going. So it is with everyone born of the Spirit" (John 3:8 NIV).

We as believers should be grateful that God's Free Spirit is not limited by time or circumstances. He kept on working until He convicted us of our sin, drove us to our knees in repentance, and brought us into God's kingdom. See also *Self-Existence of God*.

FREE WILL OF MAN

The phrase "free will of man" does not appear in the Bible. But the concept is at the heart of Christian theology.

Perhaps the best way to grasp the idea of human free will is to contrast it with divine sovereignty. God is all-powerful (sovereign), so He can do whatever He desires. But in His wisdom He has chosen not to force us to do His bidding. He created us with free will—the right and ability to decide whether to obey His commands or to ignore His instructions.

Does human free will somehow negate God's purpose in sending His Son into the world? Not at all. Just as in Jesus' time, some people will believe in Him and some will not (see Acts 17:32–34). God wants all people to become a part of His kingdom, but only those who choose to accept Him through the exercise of their faith—their own free will—will be saved (see Ephesians 2:8). See also *Divine Election*; *Predestination*.

FRIEND OF PUBLICANS AND SINNERS

Jesus condemned the Pharisees, who were criticizing Him for associating with people whom they considered the outcasts of society. "The Son of man came eating and drinking," he told them, "and they say, Behold a man gluttonous, and a winebibber [*Here is*

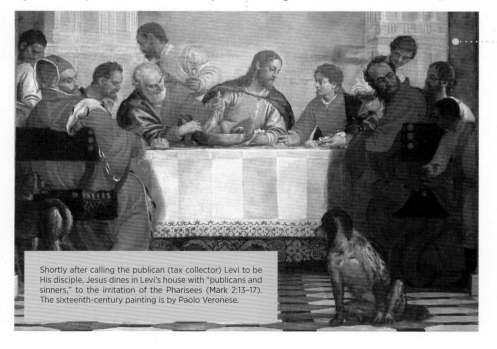

Shortly after calling the publican (tax collector) Levi to be His disciple, Jesus dines in Levi's house with "publicans and sinners," to the irritation of the Pharisees (Mark 2:13–17). The sixteenth-century painting is by Paolo Veronese.

a glutton and a drunkard, NIV], a friend of publicans and sinners" (Matthew 11:19).

Jesus took their criticism as a compliment. He had been sent into the world to become the Savior of sinners. On one occasion He told the scribes and Pharisees, "It is not the healthy who need a doctor, but the sick. I have not come to call the righteous, but sinners" (Mark 2:17 NIV).

In addition to befriending all sinners, Jesus was also a special friend to His disciples—the twelve ordinary men whom He trained to carry on His work after His earthly ministry came to an end. In His long farewell address to them in the Gospel of John, He told them, "I no longer call you servants, because a servant does not know his master's business. Instead, I have called you friends, for everything that I learned from my Father I have made known to you" (John 15:15 NIV).

Most of us get to know a lot of people during our lifetimes—teachers, neighbors, fellow church members, work associates. But few of these become true friends. In this select group whom we consider friends, one

stands out above all others—our Lord Jesus Christ. He is the Friend who made the ultimate sacrifice on our behalf. "Greater love has no one than this," He declared, "to lay down one's life for one's friends" (John 15:13 NIV). See also *Publicans*.

FRUIT OF THE SPIRIT

Attitudes and actions that characterize the believer whose life is under the control of the Holy Spirit are known as the fruit of the Spirit. The apostle Paul listed nine of these results of the Spirit's work in his famous passage from Galatians: "The fruit of the Spirit is love, joy, peace, forbearance, kindness, goodness, faithfulness, gentleness, and self-control" (Galatians 5:22–23 NIV).

This list causes most believers to cringe a little because we know we don't always demonstrate these qualities of righteousness. Falling short of God's standard shouldn't burden us with guilt. But it should convince us that Christian maturity is a goal for which we should be striving every day of our lives. See also *Discipleship*; *Holy Spirit of God*.

FULLERS' SOAP

The third chapter of Malachi, the last chapter in the Old Testament, contains an unusual name for the coming Messiah. The prophet declared that he would be like "a refiner's fire, and like fullers' soap" (Malachi 3:2; *launderer's soap*, NIV). The Jewish people expected Him to be a conquering hero. But the prophet Malachi declared that He would come in judgment against the sinful nation of Israel.

A fuller, or launderer, made his living by washing and dyeing clothes or cloth. Soap as we know it did not exist in Bible times, so the fuller used a strong alkaline substance to get

---

JESUS OUR FRIEND

"Jesus Is All the World to Me," a hymn by Will L. Thompson, focuses on the neverfailing friendship of Jesus for all believers.

Jesus is all the world to me,
My life, my joy, my all;
He is my strength from day to day,
Without Him I would fall:
When I am sad, to Him I go
No other one can cheer me so;
When I am sad
He makes me glad,
He's my friend.

clothes clean. It was made from a plant that was reduced to ashes to form potash or lye.

The name Fullers' Soap emphasizes the judgment side of Jesus' ministry. He will return to earth in judgment against those who refuse to accept Him as Lord and Savior (see 2 Corinthians 5:10). See also *Last Judgment.*

The "fruit of the Spirit" shows itself in our loving, patient, gentle interactions with other people—whether we serve in a caregiving role or not.

G

GABRIEL

See *Angels*.

GALILEE

This territory of northern Palestine is where Jesus spent most of His earthly ministry. This region had many people of Gentile, or non-Jewish, descent. It was often referred to as "Galilee of the Gentiles" (Matthew 4:15). Thus, Jesus' years in Galilee signified that His ministry was intended for all people and all nations,

This image of the modern city of Tiberias indicates much of what Galilee is famous for—hills, greenery, and the Sea of Galilee.

not just the Jewish people of the land of Israel.

Within the territory of Galilee was a beautiful little lake known as the Sea of Galilee. Jesus called two sets of brothers—Peter and Andrew, James and John—to leave their vocation as fishermen on this lake and become His disciples (see Mark 1:16–20). The city of Capernaum, situated on the shore of this lake, served as His headquarters (see Matthew 4:13). He taught and healed many people in the surrounding countryside.

Toward the end of His ministry in Galilee, Jesus left this territory and "set his face to go to Jerusalem" (Luke 9:51). This was Luke's way of telling us that Jesus knew it was time for His purpose to be fulfilled. He did so by sacrificing Himself for our redemption on a cross in the religious capital of the Jewish world. After His resurrection, Jesus did return to Galilee for a time. The Gospel of John tells us that He met some of His disciples on the shore of Lake Galilee. Here he gave them convincing proof that He had been raised from the dead (see John 21:10–12). See also *Nazareth*.

GARDEN OF EDEN

The Lord created a fruitful garden specifically as the home for Adam and Eve, the first man and woman in the Bible. The four rivers of Eden, including the Euphrates, suggest that it may have been located in Mesopotamia, the land between the Tigris and Euphrates Rivers. Because of their sin and rebellion against God, Adam and Eve were expelled from the garden (see Genesis 3:22–25). See also *Fall of Man*.

Adam and Eve are tiny figures in the expansive, beautiful Garden of Eden, in an early nineteenth-century painting by the American artist Thomas Cole.

GARDEN OF GETHSEMANE

On the night of His betrayal and arrest, Jesus prayed in this garden on the Mount of Olives outside Jerusalem. Here he faced the temptation to reject His divine mission as the Savior of the world and to avoid the suffering of the cross. But He was strengthened through prayer to God the Father to declare, "Not my will, but yours be done" (Luke 22:42 NIV).

A church known as the Church of All Nations occupies the site of the Garden of Gethsemane today. In a small garden in the church courtyard, ancient olive trees with twisted trunks remind visitors of the agony that Jesus endured on this fateful night before His crucifixion. The garden and church are two of the most-visited sites on modern Holy Land tours. See also *Mount of Olives*.

GATE

See *Door*.

GEHENNA

This is the Greek word (pronounced geh HEN uh) for the valley of Hinnom, which was a deep ravine south of the city of Jerusalem. This valley was used as a garbage dump by the residents of the city of Jerusalem. This dump's bad smell, rotting rubbish, and smoldering fires became a graphic symbol of woe and desolation and thus a reminder of hell itself. Each time the word appears in the New Testament, it is translated as "hell" (see Matthew 5:22; James 3:6). See also *Hell*.

GENERAL REVELATION

See *Revelation of God*.

GENTILES

God considered the Israelites His special people. He chose them to serve as a light to the other nations of the world (see Genesis 12:1–3). But over time the Jews forgot this responsibility and focused instead on their special racial status. They came to view anyone not born a Jew as inferior to them. Their name for these second-class citizens was "Gentiles." This term meant simply "non-Jew."

A smoldering garbage dump near the Indian city of Sithalapakkam hints at the biblical Gehenna, translated "hell."

Jesus struck a blow at this prideful attitude. During a visit to His hometown, Nazareth, He reminded the townspeople that two Gentiles in the Old Testament—Naaman the Syrian and the widow of Zarephath—had been blessed by God (see Luke 4:25–27). This showed that He had always loved Gentiles as well as Jews. The citizens of Nazareth were so angered by these remarks that they tried to throw Him off a cliff outside the city (see Luke 4:28–30).

Jesus followed up these words about Gentiles by ministering to them on several occasions. He healed the daughter of a Gentile woman (see Mark 7:25–30). He restored to health a demon-tormented man who lived among the tombs in Gentile territory (see Luke 8:26–39). He made it clear in His Great Commission that the Gospel was not restricted to the Jewish people. It was to be proclaimed to "all nations" (see Matthew 28:19–20).

In spite of Jesus' inclusive attitude toward non-Jews, the church struggled in its early years to accept Gentiles as fully worthy of the Gospel. Then God sent the apostle Peter a vision of clean and unclean animals to show him that no race was impure in His eyes (see Acts 10:9–15). This slow-to-learn leader of the church got the message. He told Cornelius, a Gentile to whom he witnessed following this vision, "I now realize how true it is that God does not show favoritism but accepts from every nation the one who fears him and does what is right" (Acts 10:34–35 NIV).

From that point on, the Gospel broke out of the narrow confines of Judaism and spread throughout the Roman world. Leading this advance was a former Jewish zealot named Paul. After his dramatic conversion on the Damascus Road, he became known as the "apostle to the Gentiles." In the book of Romans, he gave a concise statement of his motivation for witnessing to the Gentile world. "Is God the God of Jews only?" he asked. "Is

Wise men from the east ("magi") worship and give gold, frankincense, and myrrh to the young Jesus, as described in Matthew 2. But the gifts given to Christ were nothing compared to the "gift of God" Jesus is to all people.

he not the God of Gentiles too? Yes, of Gentiles too" (Romans 3:29 NIV).

Wherever we see the word *Gentile* in the Bible today, we might read it as "all the people of all the world." No single nationality or ethnic group has an exclusive claim on God's love. See also *Impartiality of God.*

GETHSEMANE

See *Garden of Gethsemane.*

GIFT OF GOD

Jesus used this name for Himself in His conversation with the woman at the well outside the village of Sychar (see John 4:5–26). While talking with her, He made it clear that He was the "gift of God" who had been sent into the world by God the Father as His agent of salvation (see v. 10).

The dictionary defines a gift as "something voluntarily transferred by one person to another without compensation." This is a fancy way of saying that a gift is something a person gives us without expecting anything in return. Speaking in spiritual terms, we might add the element of grace to this definition: God through His Son gave us a gift that we could never earn and certainly did not deserve.

Some earthly gifts are better than others. Most of us have received gifts that we couldn't use or had to be returned to the store because they were the wrong size or the wrong color. But not so with God's gift of His Son. We needed this gift more than anything in the world, it was selected with great care, and it was given in love. This familiar verse from the Gospel of John says it all: "For God so loved the world, that he gave his only begotten Son, that whosoever believeth in him should not perish, but have everlasting life" (John 3:16).

Another name of God that means essentially the same thing as Gift of God is "unspeakable gift" (2 Corinthians 9:15).

GLORIFY GOD

In the Bible to "glorify God" is to worship the Lord. We as humans have nothing to present to Him that could add to His glory. But He does desire our thanksgiving and praise. So the psalmist declared, "I will praise you, Lord my God, with all my heart; I will glorify your name forever" (Psalm 86:12 NIV). See also *Worship of God.*

GLORY OF GOD

When the Bible speaks of God's glory, it refers to His splendor, honor, and moral perfection. One of the greatest demonstrations of His glory overwhelmed the shepherds on the night of Jesus' birth: "An angel of the Lord appeared to them, and the glory of the Lord shone around them, and they were terrified" (Luke 2:9 NIV).

GOD'S GREATEST GIFT

- "The wages of sin is death; but the gift of God is eternal life through Jesus Christ our Lord" (Romans 6:23).
- "By grace are ye saved through faith; and that not of yourselves: it is the gift of God: not of works, lest any man should boast" (Ephesians 2:8–9).

The brilliant flames of a space shuttle launch hint at the bright "glory of God" as described in the Bible.

God's glory continued to abide with Jesus throughout His earthly ministry. At His transfiguration before His disciples, God's glory was so intense that His face and clothes glowed with God's presence (see Luke 9:29–32). In the end time, all believers will share in God's glory (see Colossians 3:4). See also *Father of Glory*; *King of Glory*; *Transfiguration of Jesus*.

An old French *encyclopedia*, from a Latin term indicating a course of general education. Gnostics believed that advanced knowledge was the key to salvation.

GLORY OF ISRAEL

When He was a baby, Jesus was taken by His parents to the temple in Jerusalem for a dedication ceremony. A man named Simeon happened to be in the temple that very day. He recognized the infant Jesus as the Messiah whom God had sent into the world. God revealed to Simeon that Jesus would grow up to become the "glory of Israel" (Luke 2:32).

As God's chosen people, the nation of Israel was charged with the responsibility of leading other nations to come to know and worship the one true God. Jesus was born into the world as a Jew and a native of Israel. In this sense, He was the glory of Israel, showing that God had not given up on His promise to bless the entire world through Abraham and his descendants (see Genesis 12:1–3).

The tragedy is that Jesus was rejected by His own people. They were tripped up by their expectations of a Messiah who would restore Israel to its golden days as a political power. But God's purpose was not turned aside by their refusal to accept Him and His spiritual mission. The glory of one nation, Israel, went on to become a light to the Gentiles, as Simeon predicted. At His return He will become the Glorified One among all the peoples of the world (see Philippians 2:11). See also *Consolation of Israel*.

GNOSTICISM

This system of belief (pronounced NAHS tuh SIZ um) in the early history of Christianity emphasized the divinity of Christ to the exclusion of His humanity. The Gnostics believed that all matter, including the human body, was evil. Thus, they denied the incarnation of Jesus, claiming that God would never send His Son to earth in the form of a man.

These Gnostic beliefs were refuted by the apostle John in his New Testament letters. He insisted that Jesus was human as well as divine because he, as one of His disciples, had seen Him in the flesh with his own eyes (see 1 John 1:1–2). "Every spirit that acknowledges that Jesus Christ has come in the flesh is from God," John declared, "but every spirit that does not acknowledge Jesus is not from God" (1 John 4:2–3 NIV).

The term *Gnosticism* comes from *gnosis*, a Greek word meaning "knowledge." The Gnostics believed knowledge was the way to salvation. They engaged in bizarre rituals of instruction designed to give them the knowledge that would bring them into God's presence. The apostle Paul warned the believers at Colossae about falling for such religious humbuggery: "See to it that no one takes you captive through hollow and deceptive philosophy, which depends on human tradition and the elemental spiritual forces of this world rather than on Christ" (Colossians 2:8 NIV). See also *Docetism*.

GOD (Name of Jesus)

Chapter 20 of the Gospel of John describes an appearance of Jesus to His disciples after His resurrection. He had revealed Himself to them a few days before at a time when Thomas was not present. Thomas had declared that he would not believe Jesus was alive unless he could see Him with his own eyes.

When Thomas finally saw the resurrected Lord, he not only believed but he acknowledged Him as God in the flesh. He said to Jesus, "My Lord and my God" (John 20:28). This is one of the clearest statements of the divinity of Jesus and His oneness with the Father in all the New Testament.

Thomas, like all the other disciples of Jesus, had lived and worked with Him for about three years. They had walked with Him among the people, observing His miracles and listening to His teachings on the kingdom of God. But they were slow to understand that Jesus was actually God come to earth in human form. Theologians call this the doctrine of incarnation, a word that derives from the Latin term *in carne*, meaning "in flesh."

As the God-man, Jesus is both the all-powerful Father for whom nothing is impossible and the man of sorrows who can sympathize with us in our human weakness. He is the all-sufficient Savior.

Other names of Jesus that express His divinity and oneness with the Father are "God blessed for ever" (Romans 9:5), "God manifest in the flesh" (1 Timothy 3:16), "God our Saviour" (1 Timothy 2:3), and "true God" (see 1 John 5:20). See also *God-Man; Incarnation of Christ*.

GODHEAD

This word appears only three times in the King James Bible—Acts 17:29, Romans 1:20, and Colossians 2:9. It refers to God in His divine essence, as opposed to His existence as the three Persons of the Trinity—God the Father, God the Son, and God the Holy Spirit. The term has essentially the same meaning as "Godhood." Thus, just as manhood is that quality that makes a man a man, so Godhead/Godhood refers to those realities that make God, God. See also *Attributes of God*.

GODLESSNESS

This style of life deliberately ignores God and His commands. The godless have no fear of God's judgment, they engage in idolatry, and they try to influence others to do the same (see Romans 1:25, 32). The apostle Paul said of such people: "They invent ways of doing evil. . .they have no understanding, no fidelity,

---

JESUS' ONENESS WITH GOD THE FATHER

- "In the beginning was the Word, and the Word was with God, and the Word was God" (John 1:1).
- "I and my Father are one" (John 10:30).
- "He that hath seen me hath seen the Father" (John 14:9).

no love, no mercy" (Romans 1:30–31 NIV). The exact opposite of godlessness is godliness. See also *Godliness.*

GODLINESS

Godly characteristics of believers—holy living and respect for God—set them apart from the unconverted. The word appears only in the New Testament in the writings of the apostle Paul and the apostle Peter.

Paul encouraged Timothy, his young colleague in ministry, to seek godliness (see 1 Timothy 6:11). He pointed out that this quality in a believer, especially a minister such as Timothy, was greater than material riches (see 1 Timothy 6:6). The apostle Peter also called on believers to add godliness to all the other Christian virtues that would make them effective witnesses in a sinful world (see 2 Peter 1:6–7). See also *Righteousness of God.*

GOD-MAN

This word is often used of Jesus because of His unique nature. He is the divine Son of God. But He came to earth as a man born in the flesh. He experienced all the things that are common to the human race (see Hebrews 4:15). He was both fully human and fully divine.

This is a difficult concept for the human mind to grasp. But the God-man nature of Jesus has always been affirmed by the church as an essential element of the Christian faith. The apostle Paul summed it up like this: "When the set time had fully come, God sent his Son, born of a woman, born under the law, to redeem those under the law, that we might receive adoption to sonship" (Galatians 4:4–5 NIV). See also *Flesh; Incarnation of Christ.*

GOD MANIFEST IN THE FLESH

See *Flesh.*

GOD OF ABRAHAM, ISAAC, AND JACOB

God used this name for Himself when He called Moses to lead the Israelites out of slavery in Egypt (see Exodus 3:15). The Lord assured Moses that He had promised the land of Canaan to Abraham and his descendants many years before. He had not changed; He was the same God who would finally lead the Israelites to take this land and make it their own.

This promise had been made originally to Abraham, then renewed with Abraham's son Isaac, and then renewed again with Isaac's son Jacob. In Moses' time this promise had been all but forgotten. The Israelites had

Two of the Bible's great patriarchs—elderly Isaac and his son Jacob—appear in a seventeenth-century painting by Govert Flinck. God made a promise (or covenant) to Isaac's father, Abraham, which He reiterated to succeeding generations.

been in Egypt for more than four hundred years, suffering as slaves for part of that time (see Exodus 12:40).

The message of this divine name is that God keeps His promises. Their fulfillment may take awhile, but He will make good on what He says He will do for His people. See also *Son of Abraham*.

GOD OF ALL COMFORT

In 2 Corinthians 1:3 the apostle Paul declared, "Blessed be God, even the Father of our Lord Jesus Christ, the Father of mercies, and the God of all comfort." The context of this verse makes it clear that the apostle Paul was thinking of the sufferings that believers endure when he spoke of the Lord as the "God of all comfort." We as Christians are often ridiculed by the world for our beliefs and the stands we take. But our persecution should not lead us to despair. God's comforting presence will enable us to remain joyful and optimistic in spite of our hurt (see James 1:2).

Because we know and feel God's comfort, we are expected to channel this comfort to others. Paul stated in the next verse of this passage that we should "comfort those in any trouble with the comfort we ourselves

OUR COMFORT IN THE LORD

- "Your rod and your staff, they comfort me" (Psalm 23:4 NIV).
- "I [God] will give them comfort and joy instead of sorrow" (Jeremiah 31:13 NIV).
- "Blessed are those who mourn, for they will be comforted" (Matthew 5:4 NIV).

receive from God" (2 Corinthians 1:4 NIV). See also *Consolation of Israel*.

GOD OF GLORY

See *Father of Glory*.

GOD OF GODS

King Nebuchadnezzar of Babylon had a disturbing dream about a huge statue. None of his pagan priests or magicians could interpret the dream. But the prophet Daniel told him what the dream meant after declaring that it would be revealed to him by the one true God.

This pagan king was so impressed by this interpretation of his dream that he declared Daniel's God to be the "God of gods" (Daniel 2:47)—or the God above all the other deities in the kingdom of Babylon. This was a shocking admission, since the Babylonians had a god for every need and purpose—war, fertility, science, literature, etc. This type of worship was typical of all the pagan nations during Bible times.

As believers, we know that God is capable of mighty acts. But sometimes He amazes even unbelievers with His awesome deeds. See also *Almighty God*; *God of the Whole Earth*.

GOD OF HEAVEN

Nehemiah 1:4 describes the reaction of Nehemiah when he heard disturbing news about the Jewish exiles who had returned to their homeland. The Persian king had allowed them to return to rebuild the city of Jerusalem. But the work was at a standstill, and the Jews were being persecuted by their enemies.

Nehemiah's name for God in this verse—"God of heaven"—appears several times in his book (see Nehemiah 1:5; 2:4, 20) as well as the book of Ezra (see Ezra 5:12; 6:9–10; 7:21, 23). These two books describe the bleak conditions of God's people after the exile. They had lived for almost seventy years as captives of the pagan nations of Babylon and Persia. They had to start life all over again when they were finally allowed to return to their homeland.

Perhaps the Israelites had a hard time seeing God at work among them during these turbulent times. But Ezra and Nehemiah assured them that God was still in His heaven and had not forsaken His people.

When you feel lonely and forgotten, try addressing a prayer to the God of heaven—the One who has an unobstructed view of everything that is happening on the earth. This should assure you that He is watching over you. See also *Lord from Heaven.*

GOD OF JACOB

See *Mighty One of Jacob.*

GOD OF MY SALVATION

The prophet Habakkuk proclaimed his trust in the Lord during a time of trouble in the land: "Although the fig tree shall not blossom, neither shall fruit be in the vines; the labour of the olive shall fail, and the fields shall yield no meat; the flock shall be cut off from the fold, and there shall be no herd in the stalls: Yet I will rejoice in the LORD, I will joy in the God of my salvation" (Habakkuk 3:17–18).

The "Cyrus Cylinder," covered with text regarding the Persian king who allowed exiled Jews to return to Jerusalem. In Ezra 1:2 (NIV), Cyrus said, "The LORD, the God of heaven. . .has appointed me to build a temple for him at Jerusalem."

This passage from a little-known prophet is one of the most beautiful in the Bible. It is filled with agricultural imagery from the prophet's time, including crop failures and the loss of livestock. But Habakkuk's faith allowed him to see beyond the troubles of the moment to the deeper reality that the "God of my salvation" was in charge. He would not let him down.

Rephrased in modern terms, Habakkuk's sentiments might read something like this: "Although the grocery money is gone, energy prices are going through the ceiling, our mortgage payment just jumped by four hundred dollars a month, and I don't know where the next meal is coming from, I will rejoice in the Lord and continue to trust in the God of my salvation." See also *Captain of Salvation*; *Horn of Salvation*.

OUR FAITHFUL GOD

God's faithfulness to His people is celebrated in the hymn "Great Is Thy Faithfulness," written by Thomas O. Chisholm.

Great is Thy faithfulness, O God my
    Father,
There is no shadow of turning with Thee;
Thou changest not, Thy compassions,
    they fail not;
As Thou hast been Thou forever wilt be.
Great is Thy faithfulness! Great is Thy
    faithfulness!
Morning by morning new mercies I see;
All I have needed Thy hand hath
    provided;
Great is Thy faithfulness, Lord, unto me!

GOD OF PEACE

The author of the epistle to the Hebrews brought his book to a close with a request for the blessings of the "God of peace" to rest upon His people: "Now the God of peace, that brought again from the dead our Lord Jesus . . .through the blood of the everlasting covenant, make you perfect in every good work to do his will, working in you that which is wellpleasing in his sight, through Jesus Christ; to whom be glory for ever and ever. Amen" (Hebrews 13:20–21). This is one of the most beautiful benedictions in the Bible.

Some people think of peace as the absence of conflict. But peace according to the New Testament is the inner tranquility of those who have placed their trust in Jesus Christ and have been reconciled to God because their sins have been forgiven.

The Lord is the God of peace because He sent His own Son to make it possible for us to experience this sense of well-being. This is how the apostle Paul expressed it: "Therefore, since we have been justified through faith, we have peace with God through our Lord Jesus Christ" (Romans 5:1 NIV). See also *Lord Is Peace*; *Lord of Peace*.

GOD OF THE WHOLE EARTH

This name of God from the prophet Isaiah emphasizes His unlimited jurisdiction (see Isaiah 54:5). There is no place on earth that His authority does not reach. This idea is just the opposite of the view of most pagan nations of Bible times. They believed their gods were local or regional in scope. These deities existed to serve their needs and protect them from their enemies, so their authority as gods did not extend beyond their national borders.

This is why Naaman, a Syrian military

commander, wanted to carry dirt from Israel back to his country after he was healed by the prophet Elisha in Israelite territory (see 2 Kings 5:17). He thought this miracle-working God was a regional god whose power he could transfer to his own people.

The Lord's presence doesn't have to be carried back and forth from one country to another. He already exists in every place—the supreme God over all the world. The psalmist declared, "The earth is the LORD's, and the fulness thereof; the world, and they that dwell therein" (Psalm 24:1).

Other earth-related names of God in the Bible are "Judge of all the earth" (Genesis 18:25), "King over all the earth" (Psalm 47:2), "LORD of all the earth" (Joshua 3:13), "LORD of the whole earth" (Micah 4:13), "most high over all the earth" (Psalm 83:18), and "possessor of heaven and earth" (Genesis 14:19). See also *King of Kings*.

GOD OF THIS AGE

See *Satan*.

GOD'S RIGHT HAND

See *Man of God's Right Hand*.

GOD WHO SEES

Sarah's servant, Hagar, called the Lord the "God who sees" when the angel of the Lord appeared to her in the wilderness (see Genesis 16:13 NIV). After conceiving a child by Abraham, she had been driven away by Sarah, Abraham's wife. The Lord assured Hagar that He was aware of her plight, and He would bless her and others through the life of her unborn child.

After she gave birth to a son, she named

him Ishmael, meaning "God hears." Hagar's experience shows us that the Lord is not a distant and detached God who refuses to get involved in our lives. He sees our needs, hears our prayers, and comes to our aid in our times of trouble. See also *Eyes of God*.

The angel of the Lord assures Hagar that God has seen her plight in the wilderness. Confident that she and her son, Ishmael, will live, she calls the Lord "the God who sees."

GOD WILL PROVIDE

Abraham called God by this name and assigned it to the site where he was told to sacrifice his son Isaac as a burnt offering to the Lord. In the King James Version, the Hebrew compound word *Jehovah-jireh* is spoken by Hagar (see Genesis 22:14). Other versions render the meaning of this word as "God will provide" or "the LORD will provide."

When Abraham raised a knife to take Isaac's life, God stopped him. Then Abraham noticed a ram that had been trapped in a nearby thicket. He offered this ram as a sacrifice instead of Isaac. It was clear to him

that God had provided this ram for this purpose. God still delights in providing for His people. He will meet our needs through His love and grace.

GOD WITH US

See *Immanuel*.

GOLGOTHA

See *Calvary*.

GOOD FRIDAY

The Friday before Easter Sunday when Christians focus their attention on the death of Christ is known as Good Friday. Jesus was crucified and placed in a tomb on Friday, then resurrected on the following Sunday. This Friday is called "good" because of the salvation that He provided for all believers through His death. See also *Crucifixion of Christ*; *Easter*.

GOOD MASTER

The account of Jesus' encounter with a young man who was seeking eternal life appears in all three Synoptic Gospels—Matthew, Mark, and Luke. Matthew tells us that he was young (see Matthew 19:22). Mark reveals that he was rich (see Mark 10:22). Luke informs us that he was a ruler (see Luke 18:18). Thus, he is known to Bible students as the "rich young ruler."

This young man called Jesus "Good Master" and bowed before Him (see Mark 10:17). This shows that he was respectful toward Jesus and recognized Him as a teacher of some authority. But Jesus gently corrected him for calling Him "good." "There is none good but

On Good Friday 2012, a woman prays along the Via Dolorosa (the "Way of Sorrows"), Jesus' supposed route to the cross through Jerusalem.

one," He replied, "that is, God" (Mark 10:18).

Why did Jesus resist this name? Perhaps He saw "good" as meaningless flattery. Or this may have been His way of testing the young man's commitment to God the Father, who held the keys to eternal life—the very thing he was seeking. He wanted to know what he could *do* to have eternal life. Jesus made it clear that this is a gift that God bestows on those who follow His commands.

The message of this account is that flattery gets us nowhere with God. He grants His grace to those who commit to follow Him in absolute obedience. The rich young ruler was more committed to his riches than he was to following the Lord. This kept him from finding the eternal life that he sought. See also *Master*.

GOODNESS OF GOD

We don't hear the word *goodness* very often today, except as an expression of shock or surprise: "Oh my goodness!" But the word appears often in the Bible, mostly in reference to the kind and loving deeds of the Lord. Goodness is one of the essential elements, or attributes, of the divine character. We might express it like this: God is good and He showers good things upon His people. Some people refer to this divine attribute as the omni-benevolence of God.

Psalm 107 refers to God's goodness so many times that it might be called the "Goodness Psalm" of the Bible. This expression appears five times as a refrain throughout the psalm: "Oh that men would praise the LORD for his goodness" (see vv. 8, 9, 15, 21, 31). The NIV renders the Hebrew word for God's goodness in this passage as His "unfailing love."

The call to prayer issued by the psalmist is well taken. Not a day should pass without our taking the time to thank the Lord for His goodness. See also *Good Spirit*.

GOOD NEWS

See *Gospel*.

GOOD SHEPHERD

In John 10:1–16 Jesus compared His followers to sheep and identified Himself as the Shepherd who leads His flock. "I am the good shepherd," He told them. "The good shepherd lays down his life for the sheep" (v. 11 NIV).

In the Old Testament, God is also known by this name (see *Shepherd*). Sheep were helpless animals that had no natural defenses against predators such as wolves and lions. They would wander away from the flock and find themselves in danger unless they were watched constantly. They had to be led from one grassy area to another to find new sources of food and water. Sheep needed a vigilant leader—a shepherd—to provide all these resources.

But Jesus is more than just another

OTHER DESCRIPTIONS OF GOD'S GOODNESS

- "My people shall be satisfied with my goodness, saith the LORD" (Jeremiah 31:14).
- "How great is [God's] goodness" (Zechariah 9:17).
- "Your goodness is as a morning cloud" (Hosea 6:4).

Jesus as the "Good Shepherd" is a favorite theme for stained glass windows in churches around the world.

shepherd. He is the *Good* Shepherd. The "good" in His name shows that He was deliberately contrasting Himself with the religious leaders of Israel—the scribes and Pharisees—who were leading the people astray. They were like "hirelings" (John 10:12), or hired hands who were paid to do a job but had no personal interest in the sheep they were leading. But Jesus is different.

- He knows His sheep personally and calls them by name (see John 10:3).
- He doesn't drive His sheep; He guides them by showing the way (see John 10:4).
- He is the door of the sheepfold that offers shelter and safety for His sheep (see John 10:9).
- Unlike hired shepherds, He is willing to put His own life on the line for His sheep (see John 10:11).
- He loves His sheep (see John 10:14).

Other names of Jesus that use the imagery of a shepherd are "chief Shepherd" (1 Peter 5:4), "door of the sheep" (John 10:7), "great shepherd of the sheep" (Hebrews 13:20), and "Shepherd of your souls" (1 Peter 2:25).

Some people might consider it an insult if we referred to them as sheep. But believers don't mind, since we as God's sheep are in the care of the Good Shepherd.

In her hymn "Savior, Like a Shepherd Lead Us," Dorothy A. Thrupp prayed for the tender leadership of the Good Shepherd.

Savior, like a shepherd lead us,
Much we need Thy tender care;
In Thy pleasant pastures feed us,
For our use Thy folds prepare.
Blessed Jesus, blessed Jesus,
Thou hast bought us, Thine we are,

Blessed Jesus, blessed Jesus,
Thou hast bought us, Thine we are.

See also *Bishop of Your Souls.*

GOOD SPIRIT

Nehemiah 9:20 describes the provision of God for the Israelites in the wilderness after their release from slavery in Egypt: "You gave your good Spirit to instruct them. You did not withhold your manna from their mouths, and you gave them water for their thirst" (NIV). These words were spoken by Levites in Nehemiah's time who led the people to renew the covenant with God the Father. They described the Holy Spirit as God's "good Spirit."

Since the very essence of God is goodness, He showered His people with goodness during their perilous years of wandering in the wilderness. He led them by His presence in a cloud and fire, encouraged them with His promise of a land of their own, and instructed them in how to live through the laws that He delivered to Moses. Through His good Spirit, God provided many good things for His people.

God is still the God of goodness who provides abundantly for believers through His Spirit. He expects us to exemplify this spirit of goodness to others. The apostle Paul told the believers at Rome: "I. . .am persuaded of you, my brethren, that ye also are full of goodness, filled with all knowledge, able also to admonish one another" (Romans 15:14). See also *Goodness of God.*

GOOD WORKS

The acts and deeds of believers done in the Lord's service that bring honor and glory to God are known as good works. The Bible is clear that works and deeds do not save a person. The apostle Paul declared, "By grace are ye saved through faith; and that not of yourselves: it is the gift of God: not of works, lest any man should boast" (Ephesians 2:8–9).

But the Bible is just as insistent that good works flow naturally from a life that has been transformed by God's grace. Paul went on to say in verse 10 of this same passage from Ephesians: "We are God's handiwork, created in Christ Jesus to do good works, which God prepared in advance for us to do" (Ephesians 2:10 NIV).

Christ was an example for us in good works (see John 10:32). We as believers show by our good works—visiting the sick, feeding the hungry, witnessing to the lost, comforting the bereaved—that God is alive and active in our lives (see John 14:12). See also *Discipleship.*

GOSPEL

The Greek word behind "Gospel" in the New Testament means "good news." That's exactly what the Gospel is—the glorious good news of salvation that God the Father has provided through His Son, Jesus Christ.

Jesus is more than a *messenger* of the good news. He Himself *is* the good news.

In Asheville, North Carolina, volunteers construct a Habitat for Humanity house to benefit a low-income family. The Bible teaches that good works should flow out of our relationship with Jesus Christ.

God's good news to all people existed in Jesus' life, His teachings, His atoning death, and His resurrection. This Gospel continues to impact the world today through the work of the Holy Spirit in and through the Church. All believers are called to share this good news with others. See also *Church*; *Great Commission of Jesus*.

GOVERNOR

The word *governor* appears often in the Bible as a designation for a ruler over a nation or a section of a nation. For example, Jacob's son Joseph was made a governor in Egypt (see Genesis 42:6), and Nehemiah held this position for a time in the nation of Judah (see Nehemiah 12:26). Both God the Father and God the Son are referred to as "governor" in the Bible.

In the Old Testament, the psalmist said of God, "The kingdom is the LORD's: and he is the governor among the nations" (Psalm 22:28). Earthly rulers sometimes abuse their authority, but the Lord rules over the nations and His people with righteousness and justice (see Nehemiah 9:32–33; Exodus 9:27).

In the New Testament, the name governor is applied to Jesus in connection with His birth. When He was born in Bethlehem, wise men came from a far country to find Him after a strange star appeared in the eastern sky. They stopped in Jerusalem to find out where this new ruler had been born. The Jewish scholars of Jerusalem quoted from the prophet Micah to tell these wise men that this governor, or civil official, was supposed to be born in Bethlehem (see Micah 5:2; Matthew 2:6).

The world into which Jesus was born knew all about governors. These officials were sent by Rome to rule over the provinces —territories similar to states—of the Roman Empire. A provincial governor was responsible for collecting taxes for the Roman treasury, keeping the peace, and administering the rule of Rome in the territory to which he was assigned. Three Roman governors are mentioned in the New Testament: Cyrenius (see Luke 2:2), Pontius Pilate (see Matthew 27:2), and Felix (see Acts 23:24).

But Jesus is a governor of a different type. He was sent as a spiritual ruler to guide and direct His people in the ways of the Lord. He rules by love and not by force. As believers, our lives should reflect more of His rule every day as we grow in our commitment to Him and His teachings.

Governors of states and nations come and go, but Jesus' rule over His followers is eternal. As the prophet Isaiah declared, "Of the greatness of his government and peace there will be no end" (Isaiah 9:7 NIV).

In other passages about the Messiah's rulership, Jesus is called a "leader and commander" (Isaiah 55:4) and a "ruler in Israel" (Micah 5:2).

GRACE IN THE WRITINGS OF PAUL

- "Where sin increased, grace increased all the more" (Romans 5:20 NIV).
- "By the grace of God I am what I am" (1 Corinthians 15:10 NIV).
- "It is by grace you have been saved" (Ephesians 2:8 NIV).
- "Let your conversation be always full of grace" (Colossians 4:6 NIV).

GRACE OF GOD

Some Bible interpreters think of grace only as an attribute of God—an essential element of His character. While that is true, an additional way to think of His grace is to see it as an action that He takes on behalf of His people.

In the Old Testament, for example, the Lord through His grace made the Israelites His special people and delivered them from Egyptian bondage. He did this not because the Israelites deserved such treatment but because of His love for them. He showed them favor in spite of their unworthiness (see Deuteronomy 7:7–8). In essence, that's what God's grace is—His unmerited favor shown to sinful and undeserving human beings. His grace is a gift. There's absolutely nothing we can do to earn it.

A distinct word for God's grace and love in the Old Testament is "lovingkindness." It's almost as if the writers of the Old Testament had to put two words together to show the depth of God's love and kindness toward His people. This word appears twenty-one times throughout the Psalms. The psalmist prayed, "O continue thy lovingkindness unto them that know thee; and thy righteousness to the upright in heart" (Psalm 36:10).

The ultimate expression of God's grace was His gift of His Son, Jesus, to the world. Christ was the beneficiary of the grace of His Father (see Luke 2:40). But He was also the ultimate model of grace, bringing it to sinful people for their salvation (see Titus 2:11).

God's grace is one of the major themes in the writings of the apostle Paul. Perhaps he could write so eloquently about grace because he had experienced it so dramatically in his own life. In the early years of the church, Paul persecuted the followers of Christ. Then he was dramatically converted on the road to Damascus (see Acts 9:1–6).

Saul, a persecutor of Christians, is knocked to the ground by a bright light from heaven—and converted, by God's grace, into a powerful preacher of Christ. The early seventeenth-century painting is by the Italian master Caravaggio.

God's grace turned Paul's life around and transformed him into a zealous missionary for the Gospel (see 1 Corinthians 15:9–10). In all his writings, Paul made it clear that God's grace is at the heart of the Christian life (see Ephesians 4:7).

The apostle John, writer of the book of Revelation in the New Testament, also knew about God's grace because of his personal relationship with God's Son, Jesus. How appropriate that John should end this final book of the New Testament with a benediction of grace: "The grace of the Lord Jesus be with God's people" (Revelation 22:21 NIV). See also *Spirit of Grace and Supplications*.

GRAIN OFFERING

See *Sacrificial Offerings.*

GRAVEN IMAGE

Images of false gods were often made from wood or stone and set up in a prominent place as objects of worship (see Exodus 20:4). The prophets warned God's people against such false worship (see Isaiah 44:9–10; Hosea 11:2). The psalmist declared that confusion reigned in the minds of "all they that serve graven images, that boast themselves of idols" (Psalm 97:7). Most modern translations render these words as "idol." See also *Idolatry.*

GREAT COMMISSION OF JESUS

Jesus left no doubt about what His followers were supposed to do after He ascended back to heaven. He summed it up in a few words known as His Great Commission: "Go and make disciples of all nations, baptizing them in the name of the Father and of the Son and of the Holy Spirit, and teaching them to obey everything I have commanded you. And surely I am with you always, to the very end of the age" (Matthew 28:19–20 NIV).

Jesus' command in Matthew's Gospel is probably familiar to most Bible students. But two of the other Gospels as well as the book of Acts contain this Great Commission in slightly different wording.

Mark: "Go into all the world and preach the gospel to all creation" (16:15 NIV).

Luke: "Repentance for the forgiveness of sins will be preached in his [Jesus'] name to all nations, beginning at Jerusalem. You are witnesses of these things" (24:47–48 NIV).

Acts: "You will receive power when the Holy Spirit comes on you; and you will be my witnesses in Jerusalem, and in all Judea and

David Livingstone (1813–1873) left his home in Scotland to explore and evangelize the "Dark Continent" of Africa. He was following Jesus' "Great Commission"—though the making of disciples can occur across the street as well as around the world.

Samaria, and to the ends of the earth" (1:8 NIV).

This command from Jesus is often referred to as the "marching orders" of the Church. His followers were not to be a club of like-minded people idling away their time in trivial pursuits. He expected the Church to be a living, moving, aggressive force that spread His message of love and grace throughout the entire world.

This involved stepping outside their familiar surroundings ("go"), witnessing to total strangers ("all nations"), bringing people into God's kingdom ("make disciples," "baptizing"), and nurturing them into effective followers of the Savior ("teaching them to obey everything I have commanded you"). In essence, this directive of Jesus is a brief summary of the mission of the Church.

The book of Acts in the New Testament shows how the Church bought into this mission and penetrated the known world of the first century with the good news of the Gospel. Paul and Silas were two early Christian missionaries who carried this good news throughout the Roman world. When they preached in the city of Thessalonica, Jewish zealots tried to incite the crowds against them by shouting, "These men who have caused trouble all over the world have now come here" (Acts 17:6 NIV). Their rabble-rousing cry was actually the greatest tribute they could have paid to the life-changing power of the Gospel.

Jesus' marching orders to His Church are still in effect. Jesus assured us that His presence through the Holy Spirit will strengthen us for the task to which He has called us. See also *Church*; *Missions*.

GREATER THAN JONAH/ GREATER THAN SOLOMON

In Matthew 12:41–42 Jesus condemned the scribes and Pharisees for their unbelief. Although they had seen Him perform many miracles, they were biased against Him and His teachings. They kept asking Him to perform more spectacular signs. Jesus used two case studies from the Old Testament to make a point about their hopeless skepticism.

First, Jesus asked them to think about the citizens of the pagan city of Nineveh. They had repented at the reluctant preaching of the prophet Jonah (see Jonah 3:5). The repentance of these pagan Ninevites was a judgment against Jesus' generation. Jesus was "greater than Jonah" would ever be, but still the scribes and Pharisees refused to accept Him or His message.

Then Jesus reminded them of the queen

of Sheba and drew a contrast between her and their attitude. She had to travel many miles to learn from King Solomon (see 1 Kings 10:1). By contrast, Jesus stood among the Jewish religious leaders as a willing and accessible teacher. She was eager to learn from Solomon, but the religious leaders were hardened in their attitude toward Jesus. The queen's eagerness to learn also stood in judgment against Jesus' generation because they had rejected the teachings of the One who was "greater than Solomon."

The minds of the scribes and Pharisees were like concrete—permanently set. For generations they had been expecting God to send the Messiah into the world. But when He stood among them, they didn't recognize Him. They were trapped by their expectations of what the Messiah would be like.

Jesus always has been and always will be a "greater than" personality. His grace exceeds our understanding. He always has more truths to teach us than we are willing to accept. He has prepared a place for us in heaven that is more glorious than we can imagine. This means that we as believers need open and teachable minds. Hold on for the ride; God is not finished with us yet.

GREAT HIGH PRIEST

The worship rituals of Old Testament times were presided over by the priesthood. Priests offered various types of sacrifices on behalf of the people to atone for their sins. This name of Jesus from the book of Hebrews picks up on this priestly imagery: "Seeing then that we have a great high priest, that is passed into the heavens, Jesus the Son of God, let us hold fast our profession" (Hebrews 4:14).

At the top of the priestly hierarchy stood the high priest. His responsibility as head of

A fresco of Israel's first high priest, Aaron, from a church in Vienna, Austria. Jesus is the last and "great" high priest.

the priesthood was to see that all the priestly functions were carried out appropriately (see 2 Chronicles 19:11). Below him were the priests, who performed sacrificial rituals at the altar. On the lower end of the priesthood were the Levites, who performed menial jobs as assistants to the priests, doing such chores as preparing animals for sacrifice, cleaning sacrificial vessels, and taking care of the tabernacle and the temple.

In this verse from Hebrews, the writer adds another level to this priesthood hierarchy by referring to Jesus as the "great high priest." He stands above even the high priest of Israel because He laid down His own life as the perfect sacrifice for sin.

The book of Hebrews might be called the "priestly book of the New Testament." It is filled with references to Jesus as our priest or our high priest. In modern terms, a priest is usually understood as a religious leader who intercedes between God and man on behalf of sinful people. As believers, we need no human intermediary to represent us before God. We can come directly into His presence through "one mediator between God and man, the man Christ Jesus" (1 Timothy 2:5).

Other priestly names of Jesus that express basically the same idea as great high priest are "high priest for ever" (Hebrews 6:20), "High Priest of our profession" (Hebrews 3:1), "merciful and faithful high priest" (Hebrews 2:17), and "priest for ever" (Hebrews 7:17). See also *High Priest*; *High Priest after the Order of Melchisedec*.

GREAT PROPHET

Luke 7:16 describes the reaction of the people of Nain when Jesus brought back to life the son of a widow of that town: "They were all filled with awe and praised God. 'A great prophet has appeared among us,' they said" (NIV). Perhaps they were comparing Jesus to Elijah, the famous prophet of Old Testament times, who also brought back from the dead the son of a poor widow (see 1 Kings 17:17–24).

Their reaction was similar to that of the people whom Jesus fed when He multiplied five loaves and two fish to feed more than five thousand people. They declared, "Surely this is the Prophet who is to come into the world" (John 6:14 NIV). They were referring to a promise God had made to Moses many centuries before that a prophet similar to Moses would one day appear among His people (see Deuteronomy 18:18). Jesus was

ᵒ EARTHLY PRIESTS COMPARED TO JESUS' PRIESTHOOD

HUMAN PRIESTS	JESUS OUR PRIEST
Became priests through human succession (see Hebrews 5:1).	Appointed a priest by God (see Hebrews 5:5, 10).
Required to offer sacrifice for their own sin (see Hebrews 7:27–28).	Had no sin (see Hebrews 4:15).
Animal blood could not take away sin (see Hebrews 10:1–4).	Offered His own blood as atonement for human sin (see Hebrews 9:12).
Subject to death (see Hebrews 7:23).	Has an eternal priesthood; lives forever (see Hebrews 7:24–25).

this promised Prophet.

Jesus was the ultimate Prophet in a long line of prophets whom God had sent to His people, the Israelites, across many centuries. The classic definition of a prophet in the Jewish tradition is that he should declare God's message to His people, and he should foretell the future. Jesus fit this definition perfectly.

As the master teacher, He expounded God's timeless truth to people as they had never been taught before. He taught about the kingdom of God and how people could become citizens of this heavenly realm. He also drew back the curtain to reveal the end time, encouraging people to get ready for the time when God would bring the world to its appointed conclusion.

A true prophet must be committed to declaring God's truth, no matter how his message is received. He accepts the fact that he will never be the most popular person in town. It was no different with Jesus. Some of the saddest words He ever uttered were spoken after He was rejected by the people of His own hometown: "A prophet is not without honor except in his own town and in his own home" (Matthew 13:57 NIV).

Other names of Jesus that emphasize His role as Prophet are "prophet mighty in deed and word" (Luke 24:19) and "prophet of Nazareth of Galilee" (Matthew 21:11). See also *Spirit of Prophecy.*

GREAT SHEPHERD OF THE SHEEP

See *Good Shepherd.*

GREAT TRIBULATION

There will be a short time of intense suffering and distress in the end time (see Revelation 7:14). This event will fulfill the predictions of the prophet Daniel (see Daniel 7–12). It will be a time of evil caused by false Christs and false prophets when natural disasters strike the earth (see Mark 13:8, 22).

Students of the Bible disagree on whether this event will precede or follow Christ's millennial reign or come before the ushering in of the new heavens and new earth. See also *Millennium; Rapture; Second Coming of Christ.*

GREAT WHITE THRONE JUDGMENT

See *Last Judgment.*

GREED

Excessive desire for material things is known as greed. This sin is referred to as "covetousness" in the King James Version. It is distinctly prohibited by the Ten Commandments (see Exodus 20:17).

One of the most blatant examples of greed in the Old Testament is King Ahab's desire for a vineyard that belonged to a man named Naboth. The king plotted with his wife, Jezebel, to have Naboth killed so he could take possession of the vineyard (see 1 Kings 21:7–16). But God was not blind to Ahab's greed. He made it clear that the king would pay for his crime (see 1 Kings 21:17–22). Ahab was eventually killed by a stray arrow in a battle with the Syrians (see 1 Kings 22:33–40).

Jesus also warned against the sin of greed. "Watch out!" He told His followers. "Be on guard against all greed because one's life is not in the abundance of his possessions" (Luke 12:15 NIV).

GUARANTEE

See *Earnest.*

GUARDIAN OF YOUR SOULS

See *Bishop of Your Souls.*

GUIDE UNTO DEATH

The unknown author of Psalm 48 made the same declaration that David did when he wrote the Twenty-Third Psalm. God will abide with us and continue to lead us, even through the experience of death itself: "God is our God for ever and ever: he will be our guide even unto death" (Psalm 48:14). David expressed the same thought in these words: "Yea, though I walk through the valley of the shadow of death, I will fear no evil: for thou art with me" (Psalm 23:4).

The prophet Jeremiah spoke of God as "the guide of my youth" (Jeremiah 3:4). It is comforting to know that whether our lives are just beginning or coming to an end, we can trust God as our never-failing guide. See also *Bishop of Your Souls; Lord of the Dead and Living.*

GUILT OFFERING

See *Sacrificial Offerings.*

Results of an earthquake that struck Christchurch, New Zealand, in March 2011. The Bible says earthquakes will be part of the "great tribulation" at the end of time.

The prophet Jeremiah described God as a potter whose hands formed, shaped, and reshaped clay into the form "as seemed best to him" (Jeremiah 18:4 NIV).

H

HADES

This Greek word (pronounced HAY deez) refers to the grave or the realm of the dead. Hades is the Greek equivalent of the Hebrew term *sheol*, meaning the place where the spirits of people went when they died.

Hades is sometimes used in the New Testament as a synonym for *hell*. This is how Jesus used it in the parable of the rich man and Lazarus. He described the rich man as "in torment" in Hades (see Luke 16:23 NIV). This is a clear reference to the eternal punishment of hell that awaits all nonbelievers. See also *Hell; Sheol.*

HALLELUJAH

See *Alleluia.*

HANDS OF GOD

This biblical expression is a metaphor for the Lord's great power and His mighty acts on behalf of His people. It refers frequently to His work of creation, as in these words of the psalmist: "In the beginning you laid the foundations of the earth, and the heavens are the work of your hands" (Psalm 102:25 NIV). Sometimes the hand of God is a metaphor for His guidance and protection of His people (see Psalm 63:8).

The biblical writers often described God with flesh-and-blood features to make Him more understandable to human beings. To say that God works with His hands also shows His ability to take action, as opposed to the weakness and inactivity of dumb idols. The prophet Isaiah described the false gods of his time as nothing but idle and listless "wood and stone, fashioned by human hands" (Isaiah 37:19 NIV). See also *Anthropomorphism; Imagery Used of God.*

Some have suggested Thutmosis III as the hard-hearted pharaoh of the Exodus. This statue is on display in Egypt's Luxor Museum.

HARDNESS OF HEART

To harden one's heart is to become stubborn in opposition to the clear will and purpose of God. In the Old Testament, the Egyptian king, or pharaoh, hardened his heart several times. He was opposed to God's command through Moses to release the Israelites from slavery.

The entire Exodus account shows an interesting interplay between God's sovereignty and Pharaoh's free will. When God called Moses to lead the people out of slavery, He told him that He would harden the king's heart (see Exodus 4:21). Then the hardening of his heart is described in three different ways in the following chapters of Exodus:

1. The king's heart became hard (see Exodus 7:14).
2. The king hardened his heart (see Exodus 8:15).
3. God hardened the king's heart (see Exodus 10:1).

What the Bible is telling us in these verses is that God knew in advance that the Egyptian king would resist God's determination to free the Israelites. But for God to *know* in advance what would happen does not mean that He *caused* it to happen. The king was free to make his own response to God's will and was responsible for his own stubborn resistance. See also *Free Will of Man*.

HARP

This stringed musical instrument was often associated with worship of the Lord in Old Testament times. The harp is mentioned more times than any other musical instrument in the Bible (see 1 Samuel 16:16, 23; Psalm 147:7). The Hebrew word for "harp" is also rendered as "lyre" in some modern translations.

The harp was an ancient instrument (see Genesis 4:21), probably dating back to as early as 2700 BC. Similar to the modern harp with its many strings, it varied throughout biblical history in size and design. See also *Music*; *Worship of God*.

Ripened wheat awaits the harvest. Jesus used this familiar imagery to describe the gathering of souls into God's kingdom.

HARVEST

The time for gathering crops after the growing season came to an end was a joyous occasion in Bible times. The harvest was celebrated with thanksgiving to the Lord and a harvest festival known as Pentecost (see Isaiah 9:3; Exodus 23:16).

BEWARE OF HARDNESS OF HEART

- "Do not be hardhearted or tightfisted toward [the poor]" (Deuteronomy 15:7 NIV).
- "Whoever hardens their heart falls into trouble" (Proverbs 28:14 NIV).
- "Today, if you hear his voice, do not harden your hearts as you did in the rebellion" (Hebrews 3:15 NIV).

King David contemplates God while strumming a harp, in a seventeenth-century painting by Gerard van Honthorst.

Jesus referred to a spiritual harvest that was needed to bring people into the kingdom of God. "The harvest is plentiful," He declared, "but the workers are few" (Matthew 9:37 NIV). The need for this harvest still exists, and the need for workers is greater still. All believers should be involved in the Savior's harvesting work. See also *Lord of the Harvest*; *Pentecost*.

HEAD OF ALL PRINCIPALITY AND POWER

In Colossians 2:9–10 the apostle Paul dealt with a false teaching in the church at Colossae. Some people were claiming that Jesus was a member of an order of angels, thus a created being like all other things created by God. Paul declared that Jesus was actually the "head of all principality and power," or a non-created being who was above all heavenly beings, with the exception of God Himself. And even in His relationship to God, Jesus reflected "all the fulness of the Godhead" (v. 9).

Just as Jesus is supreme in the heavens, He also exercises dominion over all the earth. This truth should drive us to our knees in worship and praise. In her hymn "Praise Him! Praise Him!" this is how Fanny J. Crosby expressed it:

> Praise Him! Praise Him! Jesus our
>   blessed Redeemer!
> Sing, O Earth, His wonderful love
>   proclaim!
> Hail Him! Hail Him! highest archangels
>   in glory;
> Strength and honor give to His holy
>   name!

Whether a massive stone cathedral or a tiny country meeting place, church buildings house the true "Church"—believers in Jesus who form His "body" in the world. Christ Himself is the "head of the church."

Other names of Jesus that express His supreme headship are "head of every man" (1 Corinthians 11:3) and "head over all things" (Ephesians 1:22).

HEAD OF EVERY MAN

See *Head of All Principality and Power*.

HEAD OF THE CHURCH

Jesus is called the "head of the church" in Ephesians 5:23 and Colossians 1:18. There is little doubt that Jesus had the Church in mind from the very beginning of His ministry.

The first evidence of His commitment to the Church was His selection of twelve disciples to join Him in ministry. The word *disciple* means "learner"—and that's exactly what they were. They learned from Jesus—who He was, the mission on which He had been sent, the characteristics of citizens of the kingdom of God, and God's love for all people,

Gentiles included. Jesus trained these common, ordinary men to carry on His work after His earthly ministry came to an end.

Jesus also spoke openly about the Church several times. On one occasion he told Peter, "Upon this rock I will build my church" (Matthew 16:18). Peter had just declared his belief that Jesus was the long-awaited Messiah and "the Son of the living God" (Matthew 16:16). Jesus was saying that His Church would be built on confessions of faith just like the one Peter had made. The Church would consist of people who accepted Jesus as Savior and Lord and committed themselves to His work of redemption in the world.

Other clues about Jesus' commitment to the Church appear in the Gospel of John. He promised His disciples that He would send the Holy Spirit to comfort and guide them after He returned to God the Father (see John 14:16–18). He sealed this promise some time later with a fervent prayer on their behalf. He asked God to protect His disciples and keep them committed to the mission for which He had trained them. "As you sent me into the world," He prayed, "I have sent them into the world" (John 17:18 NIV).

The Church is still the key element in Jesus' strategy to bring the world into the kingdom of God. He is the Head of the Church, and we as believers make up the body. A body without a head is useless, but a body joined to a head becomes a living, breathing, working organism. There's no limit to what it can accomplish for the cause of Christ. See also *Church*; *Head of the Corner*.

JESUS' LOVE FOR HIS CHURCH

If Jesus loved the Church enough to die for it, believers should love it too. This is the message of "I Love Thy Kingdom, Lord," a hymn by Timothy Dwight.

I love Thy kingdom, Lord,
The house of Thine abode,
The Church our blessed Redeemer saved
With His own precious blood.
For her my tears shall fall;
For her my prayers ascend;
To her my cares and toils be given
Till toils and cares shall end.

HEAD OF THE CORNER

When the religious leaders of Jesus' day questioned His authority, He quoted Psalm 118:22–23: "Did ye never read in the scriptures,

The stone which the builders rejected, the same is become the head of the corner: this is the Lord's doing, and it is marvellous in our eyes?" (Matthew 21:42). This was a passage that they probably knew well. His point was that He was destined to be rejected by them as the Messiah.

But He, the rejected stone, would become the centerpiece of a new building that would include all people who accepted Him as Savior and Lord. This building would be the Church, a fresh, new organism that would be born out of the ashes of the old religious order based on the Jewish law.

The apostle Peter also quoted this same verse from the Psalms (see 1 Peter 2:7). Peter went on to say that Jesus, the rejected stone, was also a stone of stumbling and a rock of offense (see 1 Peter 2:8) to those people who thought the Messiah would be a powerful political and military leader. It was unthinkable to them that He would come as a spiritual deliverer who would suffer and die on the cross. See also *Chief Cornerstone*.

HEAD OVER ALL THINGS

See *Head of All Principality and Power*.

HEALER

See *Lord Who Heals*; *Physician*.

The heart is called a "vital organ" because of its importance to the body. In Bible times, *heart* indicated even more than it does today—encompassing the entire personality.

HEART

In the Bible the heart is much more than the body's central organ that circulates blood and keeps a person alive. The heart is the center of a person's existence, wisdom, and skills. With the heart a person thinks, understands, remembers, and makes decisions. One's personality and true character are symbolized by the heart.

The Bible declares that God does not judge a person by his outer appearance but by his heart, or inner motives and secret thoughts (see 1 Samuel 16:7). For this reason David prayed after his sin of adultery with Bathsheba, "Create in me a clean heart, O God; and renew a right spirit within me" (Psalm 51:10).

God is still concerned about the human heart. It can lead us to believe in His Son, Jesus, and experience His presence in our lives (see Ephesians 3:17–19).

No one knows exactly where heaven is or what it will be like. But the Bible is clear that entry to heaven is through faith in Jesus Christ.

HEAVEN

The doctrine of heaven is a favorite target of skeptics, unbelievers, and humanistic philosophers. One intellectual freethinker asked, "Can you imagine anything more idiotic than the Christian idea of heaven? What kind of deity is it that would be capable of creating angels and men to sing his praises day and night for eternity?"

His criticism is misguided, of course. But too many Christians are guilty of fuzzy thinking when it comes to the concept of heaven. We get so hung up on the figurative language of the book of Revelation that we turn heaven into a palatial retirement home where angels stand ready to serve us at our beck and call. Heaven is such a glorious place that words are inadequate to describe it. So biblical writers often reverted

to metaphorical language to try to describe its realities. We must probe behind these figures of speech to find an authentic, Bible-based doctrine of heaven.

The first great affirmation of scripture is that heaven is a place where we will enjoy everlasting fellowship with God (see Revelation 21:3). While the place known as heaven is beautiful (see Revelation 21:18–21), our greatest joy will come from being in the Lord's presence.

The Bible affirms that our heavenly existence will have the qualities or attributes of God's nature: holiness (see Revelation 21:27), immortality (see Revelation 21:4), love (see 1 Corinthians 13:13), joy (see Revelation 19:6–7), and moral perfection (see 1 John 3:2).

In our heavenly home, we will also be reunited with our born-again relatives and friends from whom we have been separated by death. This biblical insight comes from the apostle Paul: "The Lord himself will come down from heaven. . .and the dead in Christ will rise first. After that, we who are still alive and are left will be caught up together with them in the clouds to meet the Lord in the air. And so we will be with the Lord forever" (1 Thessalonians 4:16–17 NIV).

Finally, the Bible affirms that heaven will be a place filled with activities performed in the Lord's service (see Revelation 22:3). Worship of the Lord will be one of these activities. So we will not be forced to idle our time away in a hammock, suspended between two clouds and wishing for something to do. See also *God of Heaven*; *Lord from Heaven*.

OUR WELCOME INTO HEAVEN

Henry Van Dyke, an American author of the early 1900s, wrote the following essay, "Gone from My Sight," to express what heaven meant to him.

I am standing upon the seashore. A ship at my side spreads her white sails to the morning breeze and starts for the blue ocean. She is an object of beauty and strength. I stand and watch her until she hangs like a speck of white cloud just where the sea and sky come to mingle with each other.

Then someone at my side says, "There, she is gone."

"Gone where."

Gone from my sight, that is all. She is just as large in mast and hull as she was when she left my side, and she is just as able to bear her load of freight to her destined port.

Her diminished size is in me, not in her. And just at the moment when someone at my side says, "There, she is gone," there are other eyes watching her coming, and other voices ready to take up the glad shout, "Here she comes!"

And that is what it means to leave this earthly life and be welcomed into our heavenly home.

HEAVENLY CITY

See *New Jerusalem*.

HEAVENS, NEW

See *New Heavens and New Earth*.

HEAVE OFFERING

See *Sacrificial Offerings*.

HEBREW PEOPLE

See *Israelites*.

HEIR OF ALL THINGS

The dictionary defines an heir as "one who receives or is entitled to receive some endowment or quality from a parent or predecessor." Most heirs receive only a small amount of property or cash that their parents have managed to accumulate during a lifetime of working and saving. But the writer of Hebrews declared that Jesus was the "heir of all things," and these were granted to Him by none other than God the Father (see Hebrews 1:1–2).

The heirship of Jesus is both material and spiritual. He participated with God in the creation of the world (see John 1:3), so God has granted Him ownership and dominion over the universe. In the spiritual sense, He sets the terms by which all people will be judged for their sins. Then He Himself became the means by which people could be made righteous in God's sight. This was accomplished through His death on the cross.

The great thing about Jesus' spiritual heirship is that He shares His inheritance with us. As the apostle Paul expressed it, we are "joint-heirs with Christ" (Romans 8:17) because He lives eternally with the Father and He has made it possible for us to enjoy eternal life with Him. See also *Inheritance*.

HELL

This is the place of eternal punishment reserved for those people who refuse to accept Jesus Christ as Lord and Savior. The idea of hell developed across a period of several centuries. The closest thing to the concept in the Old Testament was a place known as *sheol*, the shadowy underworld where people went when they died. And nowhere in the Old Testament are suffering and punishment mentioned in connection with sheol.

But this changed dramatically in the New Testament. Here we find graphic descriptions of the lot of the lost who will find themselves in hell after the final judgment. They will be subjected to eternal and terrible

A large group of heirs gathers to hear the reading of the will, in an early nineteenth-century painting by David Wilkie. The Bible describes Jesus as "heir of all things" and His followers as "joint-heirs."

pain. Their suffering is summed up in such phrases as "the fire is not quenched" (Mark 9:46, 48), "weeping and gnashing of teeth" (Matthew 8:12), and "outer darkness" (Matthew 22:13).

Some people are so disturbed by the Bible's descriptions of hell that they refuse to take them literally. Their idea of hell is a place of separation from God in a state of meaningless existence. They believe the suffering of hell described in the Bible is figurative language in overkill mode designed to warn us of the dangers of living a godless life.

But the Bible's graphic language about hell cannot be dismissed so easily. Jesus warned us that the body and the soul can be cast into hell (see Matthew 10:28). If hell is simply symbolic language for a meaningless existence apart from God, how can a physical body be thrown into something that is nothing but a metaphor?

The bottom line is this: Whether hell is literal or figurative, it is best to avoid it. The writer of Hebrews declared, "It is a dreadful thing to fall into the hands of the living God" (Hebrews 10:31 NIV). See also *Last Judgment*; *Sheol*; *Wrath of God*.

HELPER

See *Comforter*; *Holy Spirit*.

HERODIANS

This influential Jewish group joined forces with the Pharisees against Jesus (see Mark 3:6). This was a strange alliance, since the Pharisees and Herodians were natural enemies. The Herodians were favorable toward Greek customs and Roman law. But the Pharisees hated everything about foreign culture and wanted to establish a purely Jewish way of life.

The Pharisees and the Herodians also joined forces on another occasion in an attempt to trap Jesus on the issue of paying taxes to the Roman government. But Jesus was not fooled by their tricks, and He refused to be boxed in by their question. "Give back to Caesar what is Caesar's," He replied, "and to God what is God's" (Mark 12:17 NIV). See also *Pharisees*; *Sadducees*.

HIDING PLACE

In Psalm 32:7 (NIV) the psalmist David said to God, "You are my hiding place; you will protect me from trouble and surround me with songs of deliverance." During his early years, David had to flee for his life because the jealous King Saul was trying to kill him. Once he hid in a cave, and he later wrote about this experience in one of his psalms (see 1 Samuel 22:1; title of Psalm 142).

The problem with a physical hiding place is that it can't last forever. David eventually had to come out of his cave for food and water. But he found the Lord to be his ultimate hiding place. There's no safer place for any of us to be than under the protective hand of a loving, benevolent God. See also *Fortress*; *Refuge*.

HIGH PLACE

Pagan worshippers bowed down before images of their false gods on hilltops or mountaintops. They believed these elevated sites would put them closer to their gods and increase their chances of being heard. God made it clear that He would judge the Israelites if they adopted these practices of their pagan neighbors (see Leviticus 26:30). See also *Idolatry*.

HIGH PRIEST

The chief priest or head of the priesthood in the Jewish religious system was known as the high priest. This office was filled by succession of the oldest son of each generation through the lineage of Aaron, Israel's first high priest (see Exodus 28). In a spiritual sense, Jesus fills this office because He laid down His life as a "living sacrifice" on our behalf (see Hebrews 9:26). After His arrest, Jesus was put on trial before the Jewish Sanhedrin, presided over by Caiaphas the high priest. See also *Great High Priest*; *High Priest after the Order of Melchisedec*.

HIGH PRIEST AFTER THE ORDER OF MELCHISEDEC

This name of Jesus in Hebrews 5:9–10 refers to one of the most mysterious personalities of the Bible. Melchisedec was the king of Salem—an ancient name for Jerusalem—and a priest of the most high God. He appeared to Abraham and his servants after they defeated several kings who had carried Abraham's nephew, Lot, away as a captive.

When Abraham returned from battle with the spoils of war they had taken from these kings, Melchisedec met him, blessed him, and gave him and his hungry men bread and wine to eat. In return, Abraham presented Melchisedec with a tithe—one-tenth of the spoils of war they had taken from these kings (see Genesis 14:12–20).

The author of Hebrews called Jesus a "high priest after the order of Melchisedec" because Melchisedec did not become a priest by virtue of his birth. He was not a descendant of Aaron, the first high priest of Israel through whose family line all succeeding priests of Israel emerged.

Just like Melchisedec, Jesus did not

The Jewish high priest stands before the ark of the covenant (the golden, angel-topped chest in background), wearing a golden breastplate with twelve precious stones representing the tribes of Israel.

inherit His priestly responsibilities. He was appointed to this role by God the Father. His priesthood is eternal, without beginning or end, and thus superior to the priests and the sacrificial system of the Old Testament (see Hebrews 7:16, 24). See also *Great High Priest*.

HIGH PRIEST FOR EVER

See *Great High Priest*.

Jesus finishes His high priestly prayer as Peter, James, and John slumber—and Jewish officials approach to arrest Him. The painting, by Hans Holbein the Younger, dates to the 1520s.

HIGH PRIESTLY PRAYER OF JESUS

John 17 contains the longest recorded prayer of Jesus in the Gospels. It is often called His "high priestly" prayer because He assumed the role of the high priest in making intercession for the people and offering a sacrifice on their behalf. Soon He would make the ultimate sacrifice for them—His own atoning death on the cross.

In this prayer, Jesus prayed for Himself (see vv. 1–5), His disciples (see vv. 6–19), and all future believers (see vv. 20–26). He also reviewed His life and ministry, rejoiced in His experiences with His followers, and looked forward to the unity and love that God and the redeemed will share in eternity. See also *Great High Priest*.

HIGH PRIEST OF OUR PROFESSION

See *Great High Priest*.

HIGH TOWER

See *Strong Tower*.

HOLINESS OF GOD

Holiness is one of the key attributes, or qualities, of God's character. Over and over again throughout the Bible, He reminds His people, "I the Lord your God am holy" (Leviticus 19:2). Many biblical writers, as they meditated on the Lord's nature and how He revealed Himself to them, came to the same conclusion about God's moral perfection—

GOD'S INCOMPARABLE HOLINESS

- "Who among the gods is like you, Lord? . . . majestic in holiness" (Exodus 15:11 NIV).
- "God is seated on his holy throne" (Psalm 47:8 NIV).
- "The sovereign Lord has sworn by his holiness" (Amos 4:2 NIV).
- "God disciplines us for our good, in order that we may share in his holiness" (Hebrews 12:10 NIV).

The Holy Ghost (called "Holy Spirit" in more modern translations of the Bible) descended on Jesus "like a dove" (Luke 3:22) at His baptism.

His holiness. The psalmist declared, "The LORD is righteous in all his ways, and holy in all his works" (Psalm 145:17). When Hannah learned that she would finally give birth to a child, she exclaimed in her prayer of thanks, "There is no one holy like the LORD" (1 Samuel 2:2 NIV).

The Hebrew word behind "holiness" means "separation" or "setting apart." Thus, God's holiness indicates that He is totally unlike humans or any other part of His creation. As the very essence of righteousness, He is incapable of any wrongdoing. He is on a different plane than anything that is impure, sinful, or morally imperfect.

It's not possible for weak and sinful human beings to attain the level of holiness that belongs to the three Persons of the Trinity— Father, Son, and Holy Spirit. But the Bible does affirm that believers should be growing toward this ideal (see 1 Peter 1:15). See also *Holy One.*

HOLY CHILD JESUS

See *Child Jesus.*

HOLY COMMUNION

See *Lord's Supper.*

HOLY GHOST

The farewell speech of the apostle Paul to the elders of the church at Ephesus is one of many places in the King James Version of the Bible where the Holy Spirit is referred to as the "Holy Ghost" (see Acts 20:28).

When the KJV was first published in England in 1611, *ghost* was a word that meant the spirit, or immaterial part of a person, in contrast to the physical or visible body. In modern times the word *ghost* refers to the shadowy, supernatural appearance of a dead person. All modern translations render the KJV's "Holy Ghost" as "Holy Spirit."

HOLY OF HOLIES

The sacred inner sanctuary of the temple and tabernacle associated with the presence of God was known as the holy of holies. This place was considered so sacred by the Israelites that only the high priest could enter it. Even he could go in only one day a year on the day of atonement, when he made a special sacrifice for the sins of the people (see Hebrews 9:2–3, 7). Some modern translations render this term as "holy place." See also *Tabernacle*; *Temple*.

HOLY ONE

The divine name Holy One is one of the few in the Bible that is applied to all three Persons of the Trinity—God the Father, God the Son, and God the Holy Spirit.

Name of God. The Lord told the prophet Isaiah, "I am the LORD, your Holy One" (Isaiah 43:15). This verse shows one of the Lord's most distinctive attributes—His holiness. The Hebrew word behind "holy" expresses the idea of separation. Thus He is separated from or exalted above all earthly things. We as humans are limited in our abilities and are subject to sin and death. But He is totally different and separate in His nature. He is perfect in His moral excellence.

The holiness of God is one of the major themes of the prophet Isaiah. At the beginning of his ministry he had a vision of God in the temple. He was sitting on His throne, and winged seraphim, or angelic messengers, were singing His praises: "Holy, holy, holy, is the LORD of hosts: the whole earth is full of his glory" (Isaiah 6:3).

This vision of the Holy One made Isaiah aware of his sin and unworthiness. But God seared his lips with a hot coal carried by one of these seraphim. This symbolized God's purging of the prophet's sin (see Isaiah 6:5). God's holiness and our sin are just as pronounced as they were in Isaiah's time, and His forgiveness is still our only hope.

Name of Jesus. In Paul's famous sermon in the book of Acts on the day of Pentecost, he called Jesus the "Holy One" (Acts 3:14). Peter contrasted the righteousness of Jesus with the unrighteousness of Barabbas, a criminal whom the crowd released instead of Jesus on the day of His crucifixion (see Matthew 27:15–26).

Jesus can be called by this name because He is the only sinless person who ever lived.

HOLY TO THE THIRD DEGREE

The repetition of the word *holy* in Isaiah 6:3 is reflected in the hymn "Holy, Holy, Holy" by Reginald Heber. The threefold repetition emphasizes this attribute of God's character.

Holy, holy, holy! tho' the darkness hide
    Thee,
Tho' the eye of sinful man Thy glory may
    not see;
Only Thou art holy; there is none beside
    Thee;
Perfect in power, in love, and purity.

Perfect in holiness before He was born, He resisted sin throughout His entire life because of His close relationship with God the Father.

We as believers will never achieve complete holiness in this life. We will always struggle with temptation and our sinful human nature. But we ought to be becoming more and more like Jesus in this important dimension of the Christian life. The apostle Peter admonishes us, "Just as he who called you is holy, so be holy in all you do" (1 Peter 1:15 NIV).

Name of the Holy Spirit. The apostle John made it clear in 1 John 2:20 that the specific role of the Holy Spirit as the Holy One was to safeguard believers from erroneous thinking about the nature of Jesus. Some false teachers in John's time were claiming that Jesus was the divine Son of God but denying that He had come to earth in human form. To them He only seemed to be human. In his second epistle, the apostle John also declared that Jesus was both fully human and fully divine (see 2 John 7).

John also pointed out that the Holy One anointed or filled believers with the truth about Jesus. They knew "all things" (see 1 John 2:20)—or the only thing they really needed to know—about Jesus and His nature as the God-man who came into the world as the mediator between God and man. See also *Holiness of God.*

HOLY ONE OF JACOB

See *Mighty One of Jacob.*

HOLY PLACE

See *Holy of Holies.*

The Holy Spirit descends upon Jesus "like a dove" (Matthew 3:16) immediately upon the Lord's baptism by John. The Holy Spirit would also appear in biblical times as flames of fire (Acts 2).

HOLY SPIRIT

The Holy Spirit is the third Person of the Trinity. The Old Testament contains glimpses and promises of the Holy Spirit (see Genesis 1:2; 6:3; Zechariah 4:6). The Spirit rested on Jesus from His birth (see Luke 1:35). But the full manifestation of the Spirit's power occurred at Pentecost after Jesus' resurrection and ascension to the Father (see Acts 2:1–21). The special branch of theology that focuses on the Holy Spirit is called pneumatology, from the Greek word *pneuma*, meaning "wind" or "breath."

Jesus promised He would send the Holy Spirit as a comforter, helper, and advocate in His absence (see John 14:16; 1 John 2:1). The Spirit would glorify the Son (see John 16:14), empower believers (see John 14:12–27), and convict unbelievers of sin and coming judgment (see John 16:8–11). Another function of the Holy Spirit is to inspire the scriptures, thus providing guidance and direction to believers.

Several different names are applied to the Holy Spirit throughout the Bible. See the following individual articles in this book for a complete picture of the nature and work of this third Person of the Trinity:

Breath of the Almighty
Comforter
Eternal Spirit
Free Spirit
Good Spirit
Holy One
Holy Spirit of God
Holy Spirit of Promise
New Spirit
Power of the Highest
Seven Spirits
Spirit of Adoption
Spirit of Christ
Spirit of Counsel and Might
Spirit of Faith
Spirit of Glory
Spirit of God
Spirit of Grace and Supplications
Spirit of Judgment/Spirit of Burning
Spirit of Knowledge and the Fear of the Lord
Spirit of Life
Spirit of Prophecy
Spirit of Truth
Spirit of Wisdom and Revelation

HOLY SPIRIT OF GOD

The apostle Paul cautioned the believers at Ephesus, "Do not grieve the Holy Spirit of God, with whom you were sealed for the day of redemption" (Ephesians 4:30 NIV). This verse emphasizes several important truths about the Holy Spirit.

It is clear from this verse that the Holy Spirit can be grieved or pained by the sinful actions of believers. This shows that the Holy Spirit is not a vague, ethereal force but a person. Only a person can experience emotions like grief and sorrow. Thus, we should speak of the Spirit not as "it" but as "He." He is as much a person as God the Father and Jesus the Son.

This verse also emphasizes the "sealing" work of the Holy Spirit. A seal symbolizes ownership and security. The seal of the Holy Spirit upon us as believers marks us as God's property until the day of our total and final redemption in the end time (see Romans 8:23).

If some actions by believers grieve the Holy Spirit, it follows that certain acts and attitudes bring Him joy and pleasure. These include the fruit of the Spirit in the apostle Paul's famous list in Galatians 5:22–23 (see sidebar). Paul contrasted these positive attributes with works of the flesh that he listed in Galatians 5:19–21. The fruit that we bear

---

PAUL'S LIST OF THE FRUIT OF THE SPIRIT (GALATIANS 5:22–23)

• Love	• Goodness
• Joy	• Faith
• Peace	• Meekness
• Longsuffering	• Temperance
• Gentleness	

as believers should issue from the influence of the divine Spirit in our lives rather than our fleshly human nature. See also *Fruit of the Spirit*.

A wax seal on a letter. Seals both identified the letter's sender and protected its contents—similar to the Holy Spirit's role in the lives of Christians.

HOLY SPIRIT OF PROMISE

Ephesians 1:13 is the only place in the Bible where the Holy Spirit is called by this name. The apostle Paul used it in his long greeting to the church at Ephesus—the congregation that he founded and where he spent more than two years (see Acts 19:1–12). Paul wanted these Ephesian believers to realize what a treasure they had received in the "Holy Spirit of promise."

This is an appropriate name for the Spirit because of the revelation given to the prophet Joel about six hundred years before Paul's time. God promised through Joel that He would pour out His Spirit "upon all flesh

. . .and also upon the servants and upon the handmaids in those days will I pour out my spirit" (Joel 2:28–29).

God's Spirit was active among God's people in Old Testament times, but the Spirit seemed to be given only to select leaders for accomplishing specific tasks (see *Spirit That Was upon Moses*). God's promise through Joel was that in the future He would place His Spirit as a constant presence in all His people.

During Jesus' earthly ministry, He renewed this promise of God the Father. He told His disciples that He would send the Spirit as a Comforter to them after He had ascended to the Father. His Spirit would fill them with power so they could continue His work through the church after He ascended to God the Father in heaven (see John 14:16, 26; Acts 1:8).

Both these promises of the coming of the Spirit—from Joel and Jesus—were fulfilled on the day of Pentecost. The sound of a "rushing mighty wind" and the settling of "cloven tongues as of fire" on each of the apostles left no doubt that they had been filled with the Holy Spirit (see Acts 2:2–3). This gave them confidence and power and turned them into bold witnesses for Jesus Christ.

The Holy Spirit is also the Spirit of promise because of what He provides for believers of all generations. Paul assured the Christians at Ephesus that all believers are "sealed" by the Spirit. This "sealing" is a reference to the process by which documents were authenticated in Bible times. A king would stamp a decree or official proclamation with his royal seal to show that it had been issued under his authority. This order was to be obeyed because it came from the highest authority in the land.

Our sealing by the Holy Spirit at our conversion shows that we belong to Jesus Christ. We have His irrevocable promise that He will abide with us forever—in this life and the life beyond. When the Spirit stamps us with His seal, we are safe and secure in God's love. See also *Assurance of God; Promises of God.*

HOLY WEEK

Believers commemorate the death and resurrection of Christ during the week of the Christian year between Palm Sunday and Easter Sunday. This week is also referred to as "Passion Week," with the word *passion*

A French veteran displays ribbons and medals honoring his service. God expects His people to show Him honor in every area of their lives.

referring to His suffering.

The week before He was executed and resurrected was a busy time in the life of Jesus. It included these events: His triumphal entry into Jerusalem (see John 12:12–19), His celebration of the Memorial Supper with His disciples (see Matthew 26:26–30), His agonizing prayer and arrest in the Garden of Gethsemane (see Luke 22:39–53), His trial before the Jewish Sanhedrin (see Mark 14:53–65), His appearance before Pilate, who pronounced the death sentence against Him (see Luke 23:11–25), His death on the cross (see Matthew 27:50), and His glorious resurrection (see Luke 24:1–12). See also *Easter*; *Resurrection of Christ*.

HONOR

To honor a person is to hold him or her in high esteem and to show him or her great respect. But God alone deserves our highest honor. The Bible is filled with encouragement for believers to honor the Lord. The psalmist prayed, "Let my mouth be filled with thy praise and with thy honour all the day" (Psalm 71:8).

We as believers honor the Lord by expressing our thanks for His blessings (see Ephesians 5:20), singing His praises in worship (see Psalm 118:28), following His will for our lives (see Colossians 1:10), showing kindness to others (see Ephesians 4:32), and pointing others to His light in a dark and sinful world (see Acts 1:8).

HOPE

The world thinks of hope as a feeling that what we want to happen will come to pass. But in the biblical sense, hope is a sure and steady faith in God's promises. Hope does not arise from our desires but from God, who is the source of our hope. The psalmist said of God, "My hope is in you" (Psalm 39:7).

The believer has hope in God's promise of salvation (see 1 Thessalonians 5:8), resurrection (see Acts 26:6–7), and eternal life (see 1 Corinthians 15:19–26). Genuine hope sets Christians apart from unbelievers, who have no hope (see 1 Thessalonians 4:13). See also *Assurance of God*; *Hope of Glory*.

HOPE OF GLORY

The apostle Paul is known as the "apostle to the Gentiles," but he could also be called the "apostle of hope." His writings abound with the theme of the hope that believers have in the promises of Jesus Christ (see sidebar).

In Colossians 1:27 Paul called Jesus the "hope of glory." If we know Christ as our Savior and Lord, we are assured that we will live with Him in His full glory when we reach our heavenly home.

JESUS AS OUR HOPE

- "May the God of hope fill you with all joy and peace as you trust in him, so that you may overflow with hope by the power of the Holy Spirit" (Romans 15:13 NIV).
- "Continue in your faith, established and firm, and do not move from the hope held out in the gospel" (Colossians 1:23 NIV).
- "Having been justified by his grace, we might become heirs having the hope of eternal life" (Titus 3:7 NIV).

To hope in something is to look forward to its fulfillment with confident expectation. Paul also said in this verse that "Christ in you" is our hope of glory. With Jesus as a constant presence in our lives, we are as certain of heaven as if we were already there. See also *Spirit of Glory*.

HOPE OF ISRAEL

See *Creator of Israel*.

HOREB

See *Mount Sinai*.

> A Jewish man prepares to blow a shofar—a ram's horn—near the Western Wall in Jerusalem. Both God the Father and Jesus Christ are referred to as the "horn of salvation" in the Bible.

HORN OF SALVATION

Both God the Father and God the Son are referred to as the "horn of salvation" in the Bible—God in Psalm 18 and Jesus in the Gospel of Luke.

David wrote the eighteenth psalm to express his praise to God for saving him from "all his enemies, and from the hand of Saul" (Psalm 18 title). In David's time the horn of an animal was a symbol of strength. To lift one's horn in arrogance like an ox or a goat was to show pride and power (see Psalm 75:4–5). Thus, God had been a horn of salvation on David's behalf by delivering him from those who were trying to kill him.

This imagery from the Old Testament was picked up in the New Testament and applied to Jesus in a spiritual sense. Zacharias, the father of John the Baptist, declared that God through His Son had "raised up an horn

of salvation for us in the house of his servant David" (Luke 1:69).

This verse is part of the song of praise known as the "Benedictus" that Zacharias sang at the birth of his son John, the forerunner of Jesus (see Luke 1:67–79). An animal horn was used as a container for the oil that was poured on the head of a king in an anointing ceremony (see 1 Samuel 16:13). Thus, Zacharias implied that Jesus was the king of salvation from the kingly line of David. A horn was also considered a symbol of strength (see Psalm 112:9). This imagery as applied to Jesus declared that He would be a powerful Savior.

As the Horn of Salvation, Jesus is the all-sufficient Savior who sprang from the line of David. A trumpet (*shofar*, or ram's horn) in Bible times was made from an animal horn, so we can carry this horn analogy one step further: our role as believers is to "sound the trumpet" about His love and grace to an unbelieving world. See also *Captain of Salvation*; *God of My Salvation*.

HOSANNA

The crowds shouted this triumphal cry as Jesus entered Jerusalem a few days before His crucifixion (see Matthew 21:9, 15). The expression means "save us now." Just a few days later, the fickle crowds were shouting "crucify Him" (Luke 23:21) because Jesus refused to become the military deliverer they wanted Him to be.

HOST OF HEAVEN

God created heavenly beings who are associated with His rule of the universe. These beings ("a multitude of the heavenly host") praised God at the angels' announcement of the birth of Jesus (see Luke 2:13). See also *Lord of Hosts*.

HOSTS, LORD OF

See *Lord of Hosts*.

HOUSEHOLD IDOLS

See *Teraphim*.

HUMANITY OF JESUS

See *Flesh*; *Incarnation of Christ*.

HUMANKIND

Of all the creatures created by God, only humans are said to bear His image (see Genesis 1:27). Although humans were the crown of God's creation, it is well for us to remember that Adam—the first man—was formed from the dust of the earth (see Genesis 2:7). This says very clearly that humans don't have a lot

Dante and Beatrice gaze at the host of heaven, in a Gustave Doré illustration for a nineteenth-century edition of *The Divine Comedy*.

to boast about when it comes to their ancestry.

The Bible declares that we as people are always answerable to our Creator, not the other way around. This is bad news for all earthly rulers—past and present—who try to convince their subjects that they are divine.

Another important truth about humanity is that God created us male and female with equal standing in His sight (see Genesis 1:27). This is the heart of the Bible's teaching about marriage and the family. Man and woman were created for companionship in a monogamous relationship. Through their love and commitment to each other, they are directed by the Lord to "be fruitful, and multiply" and bring children into the world (see Genesis 1:28).

The Lord also created humans with a dual nature—body (material) and spirit (immaterial). The material part of our nature is designed for life in the physical world. But we have a spiritual side that, although invisible, is just as important as the bodies we live in. We as believers have been promised that this part of our selves will live forever. As the apostle Paul expressed it, "We know that if the earthly tent we live in is destroyed, we have a building from God, an eternal house in heaven, not built by human hands" (2 Corinthians 5:1 NIV).

Perhaps the most disturbing truth about humans is that we have been marred with sin because of the sin of the first man, Adam. But God has not left us without hope in this miserable condition. He comes to us in the Person of His Son, Jesus, and redeems us from our slavery to sin. The old hymn "Love Lifted Me" by James Rowe puts it like this:

> I was sinking deep in sin,
> Far from the peaceful shore,
> Very deeply stained within,
> Sinking to rise no more;
> But the Master of the sea
> Heard my despairing cry,
> From the waters lifted me,
> Now safe am I.

See also *Dominion of Man*; *Fall of Man*; *Image of God in Man*.

HUMAN SACRIFICE

The practice of sacrificing children to a pagan god (see 2 Kings 3:26–27) was common among the pagan religions of Bible times, but the custom was specifically prohibited by the Lord (see Deuteronomy 18:10). King Manasseh of Judah was known for his wickedness and idolatry during his long tenure (reigned about 687–642 BC). He sacrificed his own son to the pagan god Molech (see 2 Kings 21:6). See also *Idolatry*.

HUMILITY

Humility is the opposite of arrogance and pride—an attitude that grows out of the recognition that all we are and everything we

---

JESUS TAUGHT AND PRACTICED HUMILITY

- "Whosoever therefore shall humble himself as this little child, the same is greatest in the kingdom of heaven" (Matthew 18:4).
- "Whosoever exalteth himself shall be abased; and he that humbleth himself shall be exalted" (Luke 14:11).
- "Being found in fashion as a man, he [Jesus] humbled himself, and became obedient unto death, even the death of the cross" (Philippians 2:8).

A "sinful woman" shows humility by wetting Jesus' feet with her tears, then wiping them with her hair. The story is found in Luke 7.

192 THE COMPLETE GUIDE TO THE NAMES OF GOD

own are gifts from God (see Romans 12:3; 1 Peter 5:5). The prophet Micah declared that God prefers a spirit of humility in the worshipper more than any outward sacrifice that he might present to the Lord (see Micah 6:8). To have a humble spirit means that we recognize our sin before a holy God (see Isaiah 6:5) and that we submit ourselves to Him and His will for our lives (see Deuteronomy 10:12).

The best example of humility in the Bible is the life of Jesus (see Matthew 11:29).

He urged believers to practice this Christian grace in all their relationships (see Matthew 23:12). See also *Meekness*.

HUSBAND

This name of God appears in connection with the prophet Jeremiah's description of the new covenant that God will make with His people (see Jeremiah 31:31–32). He had led the Israelites out of Egypt and through the wilderness like a loving husband takes care of his family.

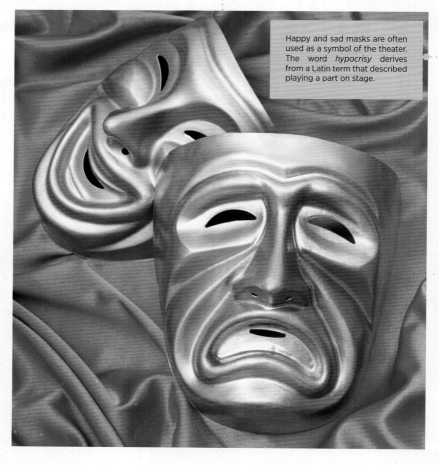

Happy and sad masks are often used as a symbol of the theater. The word *hypocrisy* derives from a Latin term that described playing a part on stage.

But He would provide even more abundantly for His own by sending the Messiah, who would save them from their sins.

The role of a husband involves more than providing for the physical needs of his family. He should also be an encourager, a listener, an emotional support, and a protector for his wife and children. God as a loving husband provides all of these things in abundance for His people. See also *Bridegroom*.

HYPOCRISY

Jesus had no patience with hypocrisy—the sin of pretending to be what one is not. He was particularly critical of the Pharisees for their hypocritical behavior. They made a big show of doing good deeds in order to gain the praise of others. They pretended to be godly and righteous but were actually blind and insensitive to God's truth (see Matthew 23:16). They were critical of the faults of others while ignoring their own (see Matthew 7:1–5).

The opposite of hypocrisy is sincerity and purity of motive. One mark of a true believer is doing the right thing for the right reason and not expecting praise from others in return. "Love must be sincere," the apostle Paul told the Christians at Rome. "Hate what is evil; cling to what is good" (Romans 12:9 NIV). See also *Pharisees*.

I

I AM

This is the name that Jesus called Himself in John 8:58. "I Am" is the equivalent of the name with which God identified Himself to Moses at the burning bush (see *I Am That I Am*). Just like the great I Am of the Old Testament, Jesus claimed to be eternal, timeless, and unchanging. He had always been, and He would always be. In other words, He was of the same divine essence as God the Father.

This claim of divinity was blasphemy to the Jewish religious leaders, so they picked up stones to execute Him—the penalty for such a crime spelled out in the Old Testament law (see Leviticus 24:16). But Jesus' escape proved the claim He was making. He easily avoided their death threat as He slipped miraculously "through the midst of them" (John 8:59). Only when the time was right in accordance with God's plan would He allow Himself to be captured and crucified. See also *I Am That I Am*.

I AM THAT I AM

When God appeared to Moses in a burning bush, Moses wanted to know who was sending him back to Egypt to lead the Israelites

Somewhere in these rugged mountains, God revealed Himself to Moses by the name "I Am That I Am."

out of slavery. He may have been puzzled by the Lord's reply that "I Am That I Am" was behind this plan (see Exodus 3:14; *I Am Who I Am*, NIV).

This name for God is a form of the verb "to be" in the Hebrew language. It expresses His self-existence and the unchangeableness of His character. He transcends the past, the present, and the future. We might express the meaning of this name like this: He has always been, He is, and He will always be.

This is the only place in the Bible where this name appears. But Jehovah or Yahweh, generally rendered as "Lord," is a closely related name that also comes from the Hebrew form of "to be." This name appears hundreds of times throughout the Old Testament. In most translations of the Bible, it appears with a capital *L* followed by smaller capital letters: LORD.

The great I Am never changes; He will never leave us or forsake us. The hymn writer Henry F. Lyte expressed this truth in the form of a prayer:

Change and decay in all around I see;
O Thou who changest not, abide with me!

See also *I Am*; *Immutability of God*.

IDOLATRY

The nation of Israel was surrounded by tribes and nations whose people worshiped gods other than the one true God. Throughout their history the Israelites often fell into the trap of worshiping these pagan deities.

The pagan god mentioned most often in the Bible is Baal, worshiped as the provider of fertility for livestock and crops. While in the wilderness after their escape from Egypt, the Israelites fashioned a golden calf as an object of worship. This was probably an image of the pagan Egyptian fertility god known as Apis.

Most of us never bow down before an idol or a statue that represents a false god. But idolatry is still a problem for us today, just as it was for God's people in Bible times. Any person or thing that we consider more important than God—whether family, career, money, sex, or fame—is a form of idolatry. The first of God's Ten Commandments still speaks to our time: "You shall have no other gods before me" (Exodus 20:3 NIV). See also *Baal*; *High Place*.

IGNORANCE

The dictionary defines *ignorance* as "lack of knowledge and intelligence." Everyone is ignorant about some things. For example, detailed knowledge about the solar system is beyond most of us simply because we have not studied astronomy. But we could overcome this lack of knowledge by doing an extensive study of the subject.

The Bible speaks of ignorance in a spiritual sense. The apostle Paul addressed this issue when he spoke to the philosophers at Athens about their worship of many false gods. "We should not think that the divine being is like gold or silver or stone—an image made by human design and skill," he told them. "In the past God overlooked such ignorance, but now he commands all people everywhere to repent" (Acts 17:29–30 NIV). Paul wanted these philosophers to learn the truth about the supreme God of the universe who had sent His Son, Jesus, to save them from their sins.

The worst form of spiritual ignorance is deliberate rejection of the truth—the refusal to acknowledge God and the evidence about Himself that He has planted in nature and revealed through His Word, the Bible. Paul described people who did this as "darkened in their understanding and separated from the life of God because of the ignorance that is in them due to the hardening of their hearts" (Ephesians 4:18 NIV). This is life's ultimate tragedy. See also *Agnosticism*; *Atheism*.

IMAGE OF GOD IN MAN

The account of the creation in Genesis shows clearly that humans are the most important living things brought into existence by the Lord. Humans were created last, indicating that God meant for this species to rule over His creation (see Genesis 1:26). And even more significant, people are the only living creatures of which it is said, "God created man in his own image" (Genesis 1:27 NIV). What does this "divine image" mean?

Some people speculate that this means that humans have a physical resemblance to God, their Maker. But God is an invisible spirit being (see John 4:24). He does not have bodily features such as hands and feet like people do.

The most likely meaning of our divine image is that we were created with the ability to have a relationship with God. By giving us free will, the Lord left it up to us whether we choose to follow Him or to take another path. We as humans have the ability to reason, think, plan, and make decisions. These are elements of personhood that set us apart as a unique species.

The psalmist realized how fortunate humans are that God created us in His image. He looked around in wonder at the moon and stars and all the other features of the physical universe. Then he asked, "What are mere mortals that you should think about them, human beings that you should care for them? Yet you made them only a little lower than God and crowned them with glory and honor" (Psalm 8:4–5 NLT). See also *Humankind*.

IMAGE OF THE INVISIBLE GOD

See *Express Image of God.*

IMAGERY USED OF GOD

The Bible is filled with figurative language—metaphors, symbols, and images used by biblical writers to communicate divine truth. For example, the psalmist called on the floods, or

---

METAPHORS FOR THE SUPREME GOD

Here are some other interesting metaphors for God that appear in the Bible. They show His power and supremacy in the world He has created.

- He has "measured the waters in the hollow of his hand" (Isaiah 40:12 NIV).
- "Clouds are the dust of his feet" (Nahum 1:3 NIV).
- "He wraps up the waters in his clouds" (Job 26:8 NIV).
- He can "tip over the water jars of the heavens [make it rain]" (Job 38:37 NIV).
- "The LORD rides on a swift cloud" (Isaiah 19:1 NIV).
- "He hurls down his hail like pebbles" (Psalm 147:17 NIV).
- "He soared on the wings of the wind" (2 Samuel 22:11 NIV).
- "He comes down and treads on the heights of the earth" (Micah 1:3 NIV).

rivers and streams, to "clap their hands" in praise to the Lord (see Psalm 98:8). Everyone knows that rivers don't have literal hands to clap. This was just the psalmist's way of calling on the Lord's creation to praise Him for His goodness.

God Himself is often described with figurative language in the Bible. For example, the prophet Isaiah had a vision of the Lord seated on a throne (see Isaiah 6:1). The prophet used this symbol to show His supremacy to all earthly rulers. Seated on their thrones, they ruled over only one nation—a limited part of the earth. But the Lord from His position of ultimate authority, represented by a throne, ruled over the entire world. See also *Anthropomorphism*.

IMMANENCE AND TRANSCENDENCE OF GOD

When theologians speak of God's relationship to the world, they often refer to His immanence (pronounced EM uh nunce) and transcendence (pronounced trans SEND unce). His immanence (from the Latin phrase *in manere*, "to dwell in") means that He dwells within His creation. His transcendence (from two Latin words, *trans*, "across," and *scandare*, "to climb") indicates that He is above and independent of the physical universe.

These may seem like contradictory statements, but both express truths about God that should be kept in balance. He is high and lifted up—beyond our human experience. But at the same time, He is as near to us as the air we breathe. Here is how the prophet Isaiah expressed it: "This is what the high and exalted One says. . .'I live in a high and holy place, but also with the one who is contrite and lowly in spirit'" (Isaiah 57:15 NIV).

God is personal because He lives within us. But He is also the mysterious life force of the universe who is exalted above all creation. He is active in the world, but He is also above and beyond it. When we meditate on these truths, we can exclaim with the psalmist, "LORD, our Lord, how majestic is your name in all the earth!" (Psalm 8:9 NIV).

An unknown fifteenth-century painter portrayed God the Father on a throne (with Jesus and Mary at His side), not unlike Isaiah's vision of God (chapter 6).

IMMANUEL

Seven hundred years before Jesus was born, the prophet Isaiah predicted His coming to earth with these well-known words: "A virgin shall conceive, and bear a son, and shall call his name Immanuel" (Isaiah 7:14). This prophecy was gloriously fulfilled with the birth of Jesus, as described in Matthew's Gospel (see 1:22–23). Matthew added the phrase that gives the meaning of the name Immanuel —"God with us." Most modern translations spell the name as "Emmanuel."

This name was given to Jesus even before He was born by an angel who appeared to Joseph. He needed divine assurance that Mary's pregnancy was an act of the Holy Spirit and that he should proceed to take her as his wife.

The promise of God's presence among His people goes back to Old Testament times. For example, He told Moses, "I will be with you," when He called him to return to Egypt to lead His people out of slavery (see Exodus 3:12 NIV). God called the prophet Jeremiah to the difficult task of delivering a message of judgment to His wayward people. But He promised the prophet, "I am with you and will rescue you" (Jeremiah 1:8 NIV).

King David declared that God's presence would follow him wherever he went: "If I take the wings of the morning, and dwell in the uttermost parts of the sea; even there shall thy hand lead me, and thy right hand shall hold me" (Psalm 139:9–10).

These promises of God's presence with His people reach their peak in His Son, Jesus Christ. He came to earth in the form of the God-man to show that God is for us in our weak, sinful, and helpless condition. As man, He understands our temptations and shortcomings. As God, He can meet all these needs through His love and grace.

Just as Matthew's Gospel begins with the affirmation that God is with us, so it ends with Jesus' promise of His abiding presence: "Surely I am with you always, to the very end of the age" (Matthew 28:20 NIV).

IMMORTALITY

See *Eternal Life.*

IMMORTALITY OF GOD

See *Eternity of God.*

IMMUTABILITY OF GOD

In a world of rapid change, compromise, and political correctness, it's good to know that we can depend on God's immutability (pronounced em MUTE ah BILL ih tee). This big theological term refers to His unchangeable nature. He does not "mutate" from one type of divine being into another. He is constant and dependable—the same yesterday, today, and forever. As the author of the epistle of James put it, He "does not change like shifting shadows" (James 1:17 NIV).

While God is unchanging in His basic nature, this does not mean that He is a static being who is frozen in His tracks and unable to act. When the Israelites failed to serve as a witness to the nations as God desired, He sent His Son, Jesus, to serve as a light to the world. This was a departure from the way He had acted up to that point. But this change grew out of the essence of what He had always been—a loving, benevolent, and merciful God.

The Lord's immutability brings hope to all believers. His grace and forgiveness will give us comfort and joy in every circumstance of life. We can rest in the assurance that He gave the prophet Malachi: "I the LORD do not change" (Malachi 3:6 NIV). See also *I Am That I Am*; *Repentance of God.*

IMPARTIALITY OF GOD

One of the most interesting events in the Bible must have hit the apostle Peter like a

bucket of cold water in the face. He was praying on the roof of a house when God showed him a vision of animals that the apostle considered unclean. He protested with every ounce of his Jewish blood when God told him to slaughter these animals for food. But God replied, "Do not call anything impure that God has made clean" (Acts 10:15 NIV).

A few days later, Peter was persuaded to call on a Gentile named Cornelius—something that a proud Jew like him would not normally do. Peter's agreement to meet this Roman soldier in his house showed that God was breaking down his prejudice toward the Gentiles. "I now realize how true it is that God does not show favoritism," he told Cornelius, "but accepts from every nation the

According to the Law of Moses, pigs—and many other creatures—were forbidden as food to the people of Israel. But Acts 10, the account of the apostle Peter's vision of such animals with the Lord's statement, "Do not call anything impure that God has made clean," proves the "impartiality of God," that He accepts people of all nations.

one who fears him and does what is right" (Acts 10:34–35 NIV).

Peter's statement is the strongest affirmation about God's impartiality in the entire Bible. This apostle and pillar of the church realized that God is concerned about all the people of the world—not just the Jewish race. The Lord has no favored nation, race, or ethnic group today, although He did show favor to the Jews as His chosen people for a time. The door into His kingdom is open to everyone. Once the early church began to act on this insight, there was no way to stop the explosive growth of God's kingdom. See also *Access to God; Gentiles.*

IMPASSIBILITY OF GOD

See *Anthropopathism.*

IMPUTED RIGHTEOUSNESS

The Bible is clear that not one of us is worthy to have fellowship with God because of our sinful nature (see Romans 3:23). Only righteous people—those of high moral character—are able to come into His presence. And the only way to become people like this is to have it transferred to us from some source outside ourselves. This in a nutshell is what the concept of "imputed righteousness" is all about.

God, who is wholly righteous, enabled His Son, Jesus, to avoid all sin and live a righteous and holy life (see Hebrews 4:15). Through His death on the cross, Jesus paid the penalty for our sin. When we accept Jesus as our Lord and Savior, he "imputes" or transfers His righteousness to us, thus bridging the gap that separates us from God.

This may seem like a simplistic explanation for the salvation process. But what does the Bible say? The apostle Paul explained it like this: "God made him who had no sin [Jesus] to be sin for us, so that in him we might become the righteousness of God" (2 Corinthians 5:21 NIV). Sometimes we tend to complicate something that is really very simple and easy to understand. See also *Atonement; Redemption.*

INCARNATION OF CHRIST

The doctrine of the incarnation of Christ affirms that Jesus was born into the world in a human body, although He was also the Son of God. The word *incarnation* comes from a Latin term, *incarnatio*, meaning "taking flesh." As the God-man, Jesus was a unique combination of the human and the divine. In his Gospel the apostle John described Jesus as "the Word. . .made flesh" (John 1:14). See also *Flesh; God-Man.*

THE SOURCE OF OUR RIGHTEOUSNESS

- "There is no one righteous, not even one" (Romans 3:10 NIV).
- "Just as through the disobedience of the one man [Adam] the many were made sinners, so also through the obedience of the one man [Christ] the many will be made righteous" (Romans 5:19 NIV).
- "Not having a righteousness of my own that comes from the law, but that which is through faith in Christ" (Philippians 3:9 NIV).

INCENSE

This sweet perfume was extracted from spices or gums and used in worship ceremonies in Bible times. Incense was burned on the altar of incense in the tabernacle by the presiding priest (see Exodus 30:7–8). The sweet-smelling incense symbolized the prayers of the people, who viewed them as a pleasant aroma offered to the Lord. The gift of frankincense presented to the baby Jesus by the wise men was probably a form of incense (see Matthew 2:11). See also *Altar.*

INCLUSIVENESS OF GOD

See *Impartiality of God.*

INCOMPREHENSIBILITY OF GOD

See *Mystery of God.*

INDEPENDENCE OF GOD

See *Self-Existence of God.*

INFINITY OF GOD

See *Eternity of God.*

INHERITANCE

A gift of property or rights passed from one generation to another is known as an inheritance. In ancient Israel, a father's possessions were passed on to his living sons, with the oldest receiving a double portion (see Deuteronomy 21:17). Esau traded his birthright as the oldest son to his brother Jacob for a bowl of stew (see Genesis 25:29–34).

Believers enjoy a spiritual birthright because they belong to the Lord (see Ephesians 1:13–14). All the redeemed, including Gentiles, become God's adopted children with full inheritance rights (see Galatians 4:5–7). See also *Adoption; Firstbegotten; Heir of All Things.*

Several fragments of biblical manuscripts known as the Dead Sea Scrolls were discovered during the twentieth century at Qumran in southern Israel. In addition to inspiring the Bible when it was first written, God has preserved His Word for future generations.

INIQUITY

This is another word for sin, wickedness, or evil. Jesus taught that evil or iniquity originates in the heart, or from within (see Matthew 23:28). Christ redeems believers from their iniquity, purifies them, and sets them apart for His service (see Titus 2:14). This word for sin appears often in the book of Psalms. One psalmist prayed, "Let not any iniquity have dominion over me" (Psalm 119:133). The word is rendered simply as "sin" by some modern translations. See also *Sin.*

INSPIRATION OF THE BIBLE

When we say that the Bible is inspired, we mean that the Holy Spirit provided supernatural guidance to the people who wrote the books of the Bible. The result of this divine activity is that the Bible is a trustworthy guide for our lives. Although human agents were involved in the recording work, the scriptures are God's Word for us, just as surely as if He had written them down Himself.

The classic passage on the inspiration of the Bible is the apostle Paul's statement to his young coworker, Timothy: "All Scripture is inspired by God and is useful to teach us what is true and to make us realize what is wrong in our lives. It corrects us when we are wrong and teaches us to do what is right" (2 Timothy 3:16 NLT).

Some people believe that God dictated the exact words of the Bible to the human authors who wrote them down. In this view, the writers were nothing more than stenographers who reproduced the divine words. Others believe the writers of scripture were not robots, but they wrote out of their distinctive backgrounds, using words, methods, and styles that were uniquely their own. This second view has much to commend it, since the Bible contains many different types of writing —narrative, history, biography, and poetry. The traits of many different writers are evident in the different books of scripture.

The Gospels of the New Testament are a good example of the interplay between the divine and the human that we see in the Bible. All four of these books focus on the life and ministry of Jesus. But each Gospel writer approached his subject from a little different perspective.

Matthew showed how Jesus was the fulfillment of Old Testament prophecy. Mark described Jesus as a man of action who identified with people through the human side of His divine-human nature. Luke focused on Jesus as the universal Savior for all humankind, including the Gentiles. John wrote his Gospel from a theological perspective, explaining the meaning behind Jesus' words and deeds.

All four of these Gospels were inspired by the Holy Spirit. But each human author was free to present his material in a way that supported his purpose. The result is that we have not one Gospel but four different accounts of the life and ministry of Jesus. It takes all four of these to give us a complete picture of Jesus and His mission of redemption to the world. See also *Bible*; *Synoptic Gospels*.

INTELLIGENCE OF GOD

See *Wisdom of God*.

INTERCESSION

Prayer offered on behalf of others is known as intercession. Christ made intercession for those who were crucifying Him (see Luke 23:34) and for His disciples (see John 17:9–26). Elders of the early church were instructed to pray for the sick (see James 5:14–16).

Paul prayed for Israel to be saved (see Romans 10:1) and for the Colossians to grow spiritually (see Colossians 1:9–12). Christ, our high priest, lives to make intercession for us (see Hebrews 7:25–26). The Holy Spirit helps us intercede for others (see Romans 8:26). See also *Prayer*.

INTERMEDIATE STATE

Some church groups teach that there is an intermediate state to which some believers go between their death and the final resurrection in the end time. This is known as the doctrine of purgatory.

The term comes from the Latin word *purgare*, meaning "to cleanse." In purgatory is where believers who had unforgiven sins when they died are purged and purified for their final destination in heaven. The doctrine is considered important in the Christian traditions that emphasize confession to a priest by believers as the basis for having their sins forgiven.

Most Protestant groups see no need for an intermediate state such as purgatory. They believe confessing their sins directly to the Lord is the only requirement for maintaining a close relationship with Him. At death, they believe their spirits are joined immediately with God in heaven. Their bodies await the bodily resurrection at the second coming of Christ. This view seems to be supported by the apostle Paul in his letter to the Thessalonian believers (see 1 Thessalonians 4:13–17).

INVISIBILITY OF GOD

The Bible is clear that God the Father is a being who exists in the form of immaterial Spirit (see John 4:24). Thus, He is not visible to the human eye. Even Moses, who was confronted by the Lord in a burning bush, was unable to see God as a physical shape or form (see Exodus 3:2).

But just because we can't see God physically doesn't mean He doesn't exist. Moses had faith that the Lord was who He claimed to be—the great I Am—and that He would lead him and the Israelites out of Egyptian slavery. By faith, Moses persevered, following the Lord's guidance as if he were following a figure whom he could see with his eyes (see Hebrews 11:27).

Now, flash forward from Moses' time by more than a thousand years. With the coming of Jesus into the world, there is a sense in which God did finally show Himself—or at least reveal His basic nature in a convincing way. Christ shows us what God is like—a compassionate Father who loves and

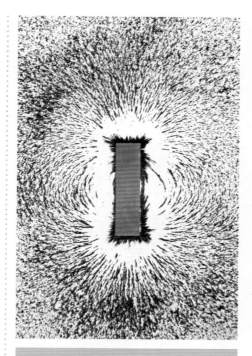

Iron filings align around a bar magnet, showing the normally invisible magnetic field. God is invisible as well—but just as real as magnetic fields, X-rays, air, and other things we can't see.

provides for His children. The apostle John declared, "No one has ever seen God, but the one and only Son, who is himself God and is in closest relationship with the Father, has made him known" (John 1:18 NIV). See also *Express Image of God*.

ISAAC

Abraham and Sarah had a son in their old age (see Genesis 21:1–3), and thus Isaac is one of the forefathers through whom God's chosen people, the Israelites, were descended. Isaac is somewhat overshadowed in the

The prophet Isaiah prepares to write God's message. The statue is at the base of the Column of the Immaculate Conception in central Rome.

Bible by his father, Abraham, and his son Jacob, whose twelve sons became known as the twelve tribes of Israel. But Isaac was a man of faith (see Hebrews 11:9, 20) and a key link in the Israelites' lineage (see Exodus 32:13). In Luke's genealogy of Jesus, he is mentioned as an ancestor of Christ (see Luke 3:34). See also *God of Abraham, Isaac, and Jacob.*

ISAIAH

This Old Testament prophet was known for his prophecies about the coming Messiah—Jesus, the Son of God. Isaiah lived about seven hundred years before the birth of Jesus. But God gave him the ability to foresee the coming of God's special messenger, who would be born of a virgin and would be called Emmanuel, or "God with us" (see Isaiah 7:14).

The prophet's prediction was nothing new to the Jews. For centuries they had been told that God would send such a charismatic personality to His people. But they envisioned this Messiah as a military hero who would deliver the nation from its enemies and restore it to the glory days of the past.

God revealed to Isaiah that the coming Messiah would be totally different than these popular expectations. He would come to earth on a spiritual mission and would deliver God's people through His own suffering and death: "Surely he took up our pain and bore our suffering, yet we considered him punished by God, stricken by him, and afflicted. But he was pierced for our transgressions, he was crushed for our iniquities; the punishment that brought us peace was on him, and by his wounds we are healed. We all, like sheep, have gone astray, each of us has turned to our own way; and the LORD has laid on him the iniquity of us all" (Isaiah 53:4–6 NIV).

This passage from Isaiah is one of the most famous prophecies about the Messiah in the Old Testament. It was fulfilled perfectly by Jesus when He suffered on the cross to bring deliverance from sin to a dark and hopeless world. See also *Prophecies about Christ.*

ISHMAEL

Abraham had a son by Sarah's Egyptian maid, Hagar (see Genesis 16:1–11). After conflicts with Sarah, Hagar fled with Ishmael into the desert, where she was assured by angels that Ishmael would have many descendants (see Genesis 21:8–18). Tradition holds that the Arab peoples are descendants of Ishmael.

ISRAEL

See *Jacob.*

OTHER MESSIANIC PROPHECIES IN ISAIAH

- "A shoot will come up from the stump of Jesse; from his roots a Branch will bear fruit" (Isaiah 11:1 NIV).
- "I lay. . .a precious cornerstone for a sure foundation; the one who relies on it will never be stricken with panic" (Isaiah 28:16 NIV).
- "Nations will come to your light, and kings to the brightness of your dawn" (Isaiah 60:3 NIV).

ISRAELITES

The Lord selected the Israelites to receive His special blessings. They are often referred to as the "children of Israel" or God's "chosen people." Their mission was to proclaim the truths about the one true God to the rest of the world. God promised to bless the Israelites and make their name great. But they in turn were to be a blessing to "all families of the earth" (Genesis 12:3).

God's promise was first issued to Abraham (see Genesis 12:1–3), then passed on through Abraham's son Isaac (see Genesis 22:15–18) and Isaac's son Jacob (see Genesis 28:14). This promise also included God's provision of a land of their own for His people. This came to pass several centuries after Abraham's time when Joshua led the Israelites to occupy the land of Canaan.

Israelites prepare to cross the Red Sea, in one of the many miracles God worked for His chosen people.

Although the Israelites were especially blessed by the Lord, they often repaid His goodness by rebelling against His commands and worshiping false gods. The Lord would punish their sin by sending calamities and troubles to convince them to turn back to Him.

The checkered history of the Israelites is a good picture of the relationship between God and His people in modern times. As believers, we are especially blessed by the Lord with salvation and eternal life. But God wants us to share His blessings with others by helping them find their way into His kingdom. When we sin and tarnish our witness, He patiently calls us back into fellowship with Him. Renewed through repentance and forgiveness, we can continue to be effective witnesses for Him in a dark and sinful world. See also *Jacob*.

Jacob's God-given dream of a ladder to heaven, as envisioned by early nineteenth-century artist William Blake.

J

JACOB

The descendants of Jacob, the grandson of Abraham, became the founders of the twelve tribes of Israel. Thus, Jacob is considered one of the key personalities in the history and development of the Israelites, God's chosen people.

Jacob was the younger (second out of the womb) of twin sons born to Isaac, the son of Abraham (see Genesis 25:24–26). Jacob's twin brother, Esau, should have inherited most of his father's property because of his rights as the firstborn son. But Esau sold this privilege to his brother in a fit of hunger (see Genesis 25:29–34). Later, Jacob cheated Esau out of his father's blessing (see Genesis 27:18–36), and thus became the son of Isaac chosen to receive the covenant promises that God had made to Abraham. The Lord even gave Jacob a new name, Israel, meaning "Prince of God" (see Genesis 32:28–30). This showed that God's promise to bless Abraham's descendants would be realized through Jacob's offspring.

The twelve sons of Jacob were Reuben, Simeon, Judah, Zebulun, Issachar, Dan, Gad, Asher, Naphtali, Benjamin, Joseph, and Levi (see Genesis 49:1–48). The tribe of Levi evolved into the priestly tribe of Israel and did not receive a tribal inheritance like the others did. Joseph's tribeship is represented by his two sons, Ephraim and Manasseh. They are considered the founders of two tribes, thus rounding out the group known as the "twelve tribes of Israel."

Because of Jacob's key position in the lineage of the nation of Israel, he is mentioned many times throughout the Bible. God is often referred to as "the God of Abraham, Isaac, and Jacob" (Exodus 3:15). The psalmist declared that "the God of Jacob is our refuge" (Psalm 46:11). Even Jesus the coming Messiah is referred to as "a Star out of Jacob" (Numbers 24:17). See also *Israelites*.

JAH

Psalm 68:4 is the only place where this name of God appears in the King James Version of the Bible: "Extol him that rideth upon the heavens by his name JAH." Jah (pronounced Yah) is a shortened form of the Hebrew title *Jehovah*, which is rendered as "Lord" in most English translations of the Bible.

The word does appear as part of several biblical compound names. For example, the name Abijah means "whose father is Jehovah." The word *alleluiah* (*hallelujah*, NIV) means "praise the Lord" (Revelation 19:1). See also *Jehovah*.

JEALOUSY OF GOD

Many Bible students are puzzled by the statements in the Bible that God is a "jealous God" (Deuteronomy 4:24). This phrase appears in several other Old Testament passages (see Exodus 20:5; 34:14; Deuteronomy 5:9; 6:15). Jealousy is a sin that believers should avoid. Since God is holy and perfect by nature, how can He be associated with jealousy?

This is one of those cases where a little digging into Hebrew, the original language in which the Old Testament was written, will contribute to our understanding. In the five Old Testament verses cited above, the same Hebrew word (*qanna*) is used to translate the English word *jealousy*. There is no single word in the English language that renders this Hebrew word precisely. So "jealousy" was as close as translators could get to telling us what the original word meant.

An interesting thing about these five Old Testament passages is that they always appear in the context of the Lord's condemnation of false worship, or idolatry. In the first of the Ten Commandments, God told the Israelites

A bronze idol of Baal. The one true God said He was "jealous" in regard to sharing His worship with false gods.

they were to worship Him alone and not to bow down to idols, "for I the LORD your God am a jealous God" (Exodus 20:5 NIV).

Thus, what God is jealous of is what already belongs exclusively to Him—His supremacy that makes Him and Him alone worthy of our worship and praise. The Good News Bible expresses this idea exactly in its rendering of this commandment: "Do not bow down to any idol or worship it, because I am the LORD your God and I tolerate no rivals" (Exodus 20:5 GNT). See also *Idolatry*.

JEHOVAH

The Lord reassured Moses that He would stand with him and give him the strength and power to lead the Israelites out of Egyptian slavery. He told Moses, "I appeared unto Abraham, unto Isaac, and unto Jacob, by the name of God Almighty, but by my name JEHOVAH was I not known to them" (Exodus 6:3). He had already given Moses this promise at the burning bush (see Exodus 3:2, 12). But Moses needed encouragement after Pharaoh rejected his first request to release the Israelites.

God declared to Moses that He was prepared to perform miracles for His people that they had never seen before. As Jehovah, He was the infinite and self-existent God who caused everything to happen and to whom all things must eventually be traced. He would not fail in His determination to bring freedom to His people. When God makes a promise, it's as good as done. See also *I Am That I Am*.

JEHOVAH-JIREH

See *God Will Provide*.

○ GUIDANCE FROM JEHOVAH

In his hymn "Guide Me, O Thou Great Je-hovah," William Williams asked God to provide for him, just as He took care of the Israelites in the wilderness.

Guide me, O Thou great Jehovah,
Pilgrim through this barren land;
I am weak, but Thou art mighty,
Hold me with Thy powerful hand.

JEHOVAH-NISSI

See *Lord Is My Banner*.

JEHOVAH-SHALOM

See *Lord Is Peace*.

JEREMIAH

This major prophet of the Old Testament preached God's message of doom to the nation of Judah for about forty years. The prophet wept openly over the sins of Judah (see Jeremiah 9:1) and declared that the nation would fall to a foreign enemy as punishment for its sin and idolatry (see Jeremiah 16:1–13). This prediction came true when the nation fell to the Babylonians in 587 BC.

But Jeremiah is best known for his prediction that God would establish a new covenant with His people. The Lord's old covenant had failed because of His people's inability to keep the law and measure up to His standard of righteousness. God declared through the prophet that He would "put my law in their minds and write it on their hearts" (Jeremiah 31:33 NIV).

This was the covenant of grace that became the basis of God's relationship with

Often called "the weeping prophet" for his sad writings concerning the destruction of Jerusalem, Jeremiah is depicted in a stained glass window in Cologne, Germany.

man in the person of Jesus Christ. See also *New Covenant*.

JERUSALEM

This city was the religious and political capital of the Jewish people. Situated about fifty miles from the Mediterranean Sea and about twenty miles west of the Jordan River, Jerusalem was known as Salem in Abraham's time (see Genesis 14:18) and as Jebus when the people of Israel entered Canaan, or the promised land (see Joshua 15:8). Jerusalem is considered a holy site by three great world religions—Christianity, Islam, and Judaism.

David captured the city from the Jebusites, renamed it, and turned it into his capital (see 2 Samuel 5:6–9). It was often called the "city of David" (see 2 Chronicles 32:5). Solomon built the magnificent temple in Jerusalem as the center of worship for the Jewish people about 950 BC (see 1 Kings 5:5–8). The city fell to the Babylonians in 587 BC, and its leading citizens were taken away as captives (see Jeremiah 39:1–8).

After the Persians defeated the Babylonians,

King Cyrus of Persia allowed Jewish exiles to return to their homeland and rebuild Jerusalem, including the temple and the city wall (see Ezra 1:1–4).

In New Testament times, Christ wept over the city because of its sin and spiritual indifference (see Luke 19:41–42). He predicted its destruction (see Luke 19:43–44), entered Jerusalem as a reigning spiritual leader (see Matthew 21:9–10), and was crucified on a hill just outside the city wall. As Jesus predicted, Jerusalem was destroyed in AD 70 during a fierce battle between the Roman army and Jewish zealots.

The church was launched in Jerusalem, where it experienced spectacular growth (see Acts 2). The apostle John described the future heavenly city as "New Jerusalem" (see Revelation 21:1–3). See also *New Jerusalem*.

Jesus weeps over Jerusalem, saying, "The days will come upon you when your enemies will build an embankment against you and encircle you and hem you in on every side. They will dash you to the ground, you and the children within your walls. They will not leave one stone on another, because you did not recognize the time of God's coming to you" (Luke 19:43–44 NIV).

JERUSALEM, NEW

See *New Jerusalem*.

JESSE

The father of David and an ancestor of Jesus Christ, Jesse presented his eight sons to the prophet Samuel, who anointed David as the future king of Israel (see 1 Samuel 16:10–13). Jesse is mentioned as the root or shoot that would produce the royal line of David (see Isaiah 11:1, 10; Romans 15:12) and ultimately the Savior (see Matthew 1:5–6). See also *Rod Out of the Stem of Jesse*.

JESUS (His Life)

Jesus was born during the reign of Herod the Great as Roman ruler over Palestine, sometime before 4 BC, the date of Herod's death (see Matthew 2:1). After a public ministry of perhaps three years, He was crucified about AD 30. He preexisted as the eternal Word of God (see John 1:1, 18; 8:58) and participated in the creation of the world (see John 1:3). His advent in human form, including His virgin birth in Bethlehem (see Isaiah 7:14), was foretold in the Old Testament (see Psalm 2:7–8). As the God-man, Jesus was incarnated (given a human body) to reveal God in an understandable way (see John 1:14–18) and "to make reconciliation for the sins of the people" (Hebrews 2:17).

As a boy, Jesus grew physically and advanced in knowledge (see Luke 2:51–52). Yet He had a consciousness of His divine mission (see Luke 2:49). He was baptized by John the Baptist to "fulfill all righteousness" and to identify with humanity (see Matthew 3:15–17). In resisting Satan's temptations at the beginning of His public ministry, the sinless Savior refused to break dependence on the Father and to establish His kingdom in any fashion other than by suffering (see Matthew 4:7–10).

Jesus' public ministry was short and revolutionary (see John 17:4). He came preaching and healing (see Mark 1:38–42), teaching (see Luke 6:6), and seeking the lost (see Luke 19:10). After an early campaign in Judea in southern Palestine, He began a major campaign in the region of Galilee in northern Palestine with Capernaum as His home base. His hometown synagogue in Nazareth rejected Him, but the common people heard Him gladly (see Luke 4:16–32).

Jesus proclaimed a spiritual kingdom that required repentance and faith rather than blind and ritualistic obedience to the law and the legalistic demands of the Pharisees (see Matthew 6:10, 33; Luke 13:3). His later ministry was devoted to training His disciples and preparing them for His death and their witness to others in the Holy Spirit's power (see Luke 24:46–49).

Jesus' actions such as denouncing the Pharisees (see Matthew 23), healing on the

HIS WONDERFUL NAME

Believers never seem to tire of hearing the name of Jesus, according to the hymn "There Is a Name I Love to Hear," written by Frederick Whitfield.

> There is a name I love to hear,
> I love to sing its worth;
> It sounds like music in mine ear,
> The sweetest name on earth.
> Oh, how I love Jesus,
> Oh, how I love Jesus,
> Oh, how I love Jesus,
> Because He first loved me.

Sabbath (see Matthew 12:8–14), and cleansing the temple angered the religious leaders among the Jews and disturbed Roman officials (see Matthew 21:23). His triumphal entry into Jerusalem on a donkey disappointed His followers who wanted an earthly king (see Luke 24:19–21). After observing the Passover with His disciples and instituting the Lord's Supper, He was betrayed into enemy hands (see Luke 22:15–21).

In His trial before Pilate, Jesus acknowledged His kingship but declared His kingdom was "not of this world" (John 18:36). Nevertheless, He was charged with treason and crucified between two thieves (see Luke 23:33). On the third day He arose from the grave, conquering sin and death for believers (see 1 Corinthians 15:57). Jesus ascended to the Father, where He abides with God the Father and intercedes for His believers (see Hebrews 7:25).

Christ will return for righteous judgment

No one really knows what Jesus looked like—but the traditional image is of a long-haired, bearded young man. Jesus was crucified in His early thirties, paying God's price—death—for the sins of the world.

(see Acts 17:31), to raise the dead (see 1 Thessalonians 4:14–17), and to usher in the time when all the people of the world must confess that "Jesus Christ is Lord" (see Philippians 2:9–11). See also *Jesus (His Name)*.

JESUS (His Name)

Jewish custom dictated that a male child be circumcised and named on the eighth day after he was born. Mary and Joseph followed this custom with Jesus (see Luke 2:21). They had been told by an angel even before He was born that His name would be Jesus (see Matthew 1:21). They followed the angel's instruction by giving Him this name.

The name Jesus is the equivalent of the

Old Testament name rendered variously as Jehoshua (see Numbers 13:16), Jeshua (see Ezra 2:2), and Joshua (see Exodus 17:9). It means "Jehovah (or Yahweh) Is Salvation." Thus Jesus' personal name indicated from the very beginning that He was to be God's agent of salvation in a dark and sinful world.

Jesus was actually a common name among the Jewish people when He was born, similar to the popularity of "John" or "Robert" in our society. For example, a believer named Jesus Justus was mentioned by the apostle Paul in his letter to the believers at Colossae (see Colossians 4:11). But the name has become so closely associated with Jesus of Nazareth, the Son of God, that few people are given this name in our time. In the words of Paul, it is the "name . . .above every name" (Philippians 2:9).

The name Jesus appears often by itself in the Gospels (see Matthew 17:18; Mark 14:62; Luke 10:37; John 20:14). But outside the Gospels, it often appears in combination with other names such as "Jesus Christ" (Acts 8:37),

Modern Nazareth is a city of approximately 80,000 people and several high-tech companies, a far cry from the insignificant village of Jesus' day.

"Jesus Christ our Lord" (Romans 6:11), "Lord Jesus" (Colossians 3:17), and "Lord Jesus Christ" (James 2:1). See also *Jesus (His Life)*.

JESUS OF GALILEE/ JESUS OF NAZARETH

In Matthew 26:69 a female servant of the high priest identified Peter as a follower of "Jesus of Galilee." Galilee was one of three provinces, or regions, into which Palestine was divided during New Testament times. This young woman questioned Peter about his association with Jesus because Galilee in northern Palestine was Jesus' home province and the place where He had spent most of His ministry.

Jesus was also referred to during His earthly ministry as "Jesus of Nazareth" because He grew up in this little village located on the southern edge of the province of Galilee (see Luke 2:51). When Nathanael learned that Jesus was from this place, he exclaimed, "Can there any good thing come out of Nazareth?" (John 1:46). He found it hard to believe that a famous prophet and teacher could come from this insignificant "hick town."

But Nathanael changed his mind when he met Jesus in person. When Jesus told him that He knew all about him, Nathanael acknowledged Him as "the Son of God" and "the King of Israel" (John 1:49). He eventually became one of His disciples—the one referred to in the Gospels as Bartholomew (see Mark 3:18).

The significance of these names—Jesus of Galilee and Jesus of Nazareth—is that they attest to the historicity of Jesus Christ. He was not a make-believe figure who emerged from a fiction writer's imagination. He was a real person who grew up in humble circumstances and spent most of His ministry among the common people. Some skeptics may say otherwise, but believers declare that the Gospels are eyewitness accounts of the life of a miracle-working Savior who came from a little village in a backwater province.

If Jesus had been created by a fiction writer, He probably would have been born into society's upper class in the influential city of Jerusalem. He certainly would not have been executed on a Roman cross like a common criminal. See also *Galilee; Nazareth.*

Peter (see Mark 14:33). John was ambitious for position and prestige in Christ's kingdom (see Mark 10:35–37), but he showed a willingness to die for Jesus (see Mark 10:38–39). He was probably the disciple whom Jesus directed to care for His mother while He was dying on the cross (see John 19:26–27).

John was associated with the apostle Peter in bold evangelism in Jerusalem after Jesus' ascension (see Acts 4:13). John left Jerusalem about AD 65 for Ephesus, where he wrote the fourth Gospel and the three epistles of John. He wrote the Revelation while exiled as a political prisoner on the island of Patmos (see Revelation 1:9 –11).

Thousands of people visit the Jordan River each year to be baptized where John baptized his relative, Jesus. John's mother, Elisabeth, was related to Jesus' mother, Mary (see Luke 1:36).

JOHN THE APOSTLE

John was a fisherman from Galilee who became one of the twelve disciples of Jesus (see Matthew 4:21–22). He was described as the disciple "whom Jesus loved" and a member of Christ's inner circle of disciples, which included his brother James, along with Simon

JOHN THE BAPTIST

This prophet of righteousness and preacher of repentance prepared the way for Christ. John's birth, simple lifestyle, and unique role as the Messiah's forerunner was revealed to his father, Zechariah (see Luke 1:13–17), and his mother, Elizabeth, a cousin of Mary—

the earthly mother of Jesus (see Luke 1:5–9, 39–41).

John preached repentance and baptized converts in the Jordan River (see Matthew 3:1–6), reluctantly agreeing to baptize Jesus after proclaiming Him as the "Lamb of God" (see Matthew 3:13–17; John 1:29).

According to the Gospel of John, the preaching of John the Baptist continued for a time after Jesus launched His public ministry (see John 3:22–24). Some of Jesus' first disciples had also been followers of John (see John 1:35–37).

John denounced the hypocrisy of the Pharisees and the immorality and adultery of Herod Antipas, a Roman ruler in Palestine (see Matthew 3:7–8; 14:4). He was executed by Herod at the request of his wife's daughter (see Matthew 14:3–12). John always magnified Jesus rather than himself (see John 3:30), and Jesus commended him highly for his faithfulness (see Luke 7:24–28).

• A WILD MAN IN THE DESERT

John the Baptist lived a plain, simple, solitary life in the desert (see Mark 1:3). He foraged for his food, eating locusts—flying insects similar to grasshoppers—and honey from the nests of bees. His clothes were made from the skin of animals. Today people would probably consider John a hermit or a fanatical wild man.

Why did he live this type of life? Probably to identify with the prophets of Israel's past. It had been more than four hundred years since a prophet had walked among the Jewish people. John wanted to show that the ultimate Prophet—the Messiah who had been promised for centuries—was about to burst upon the scene.

JONAH

This Old Testament prophet was swallowed by a "great fish" while fleeing from God's call to preach to the pagan citizens of Nineveh in Assyria (see Jonah 1:17). After God delivered him from the fish, Jonah did preach to the Ninevites, many of whom turned to the Lord (see Jonah 3:5–10). Jesus compared His coming death and resurrection to God's deliverance of Jonah from the stomach of this fish (see Matthew 12:39–41). See also *Greater Than Jonah/Greater Than Solomon*.

JOSEPH, HUSBAND OF MARY

A descendant of King David (see Matthew 1:20), Joseph was a carpenter by vocation and a righteous man. He took Mary as his wife after an angel explained that Mary had not been unfaithful to him; her pregnancy was a supernatural event brought about by the Holy Spirit (see Matthew 1:19–25).

Joseph was with Mary when Jesus was born in Bethlehem (see Luke 2:16). He took his family to Egypt to escape Herod's wrath, then returned later to Nazareth, where the young Jesus was obedient to His earthly parents (see Matthew 2:13–23; Luke 2:51). Since Joseph does not appear later in the Gospels, it is likely that he died before Jesus launched His public ministry. See also *Son of Joseph*.

JOSEPH OF ARIMATHEA

This member of the Jewish Sanhedrin (see Mark 15:43 NIV) claimed the body of Jesus, prepared it for burial, and laid it in his own new tomb (see John 19:38–41). Where was Joseph when Jesus was dragged before this judicial body for trial? Why did he not step forward in His defense?

We don't know. But we do know that he

While many speak of "Jonah and the whale," the Bible actually says God prepared "a great fish" to swallow the reluctant prophet Jonah.

risked his reputation with that group when he cared for Jesus' body after He died. Even if Joseph was a "secret disciple" of Jesus, his kind act in giving Him a decent burial deserves the thanks of all believers. See also *Nicodemus*.

JOY

Believers experience a feeling of delight because they belong to the Lord. Unlike happiness, which depends on circumstances, true Christian joy is felt by believers even in the midst of trials and tribulations (see 2 Corinthians 6:10). Joy is a result of the indwelling presence of the Holy Spirit (see Galatians 5:22).

Joy is one of the characteristics of authentic worship. The psalmist declared, "Let us sing unto the LORD: Let us make a joyful noise to the rock of our salvation" (Psalm 95:1). See also *Song; Worship of God*.

JUDAH

This son of Jacob was the ancestor of the tribe of Judah, one of the twelve tribes of Israel (see Genesis 29:35). His father, Jacob, bestowed the birthright of Reuben, his oldest son, on Judah, declaring, "The sceptre shall not depart from Judah" (see Genesis 49:10). Judah interceded for his brother Joseph to be sold rather than killed (see Genesis 37:26–27). He is listed as an ancestor of Christ in Matthew's lineage of Jesus (see Matthew 1:2–3) and called "Juda" in Luke's genealogy (see Luke 3:33). See also *Lion of the Tribe of Judah*.

JUDGE

The psalmist declared, "God is the judge: he putteth down one, and setteth up another" (Psalm 75:7). The clear teaching of this verse is that some people are worthy of positions of leadership and authority while others are not. God as Judge has the ability to tell the difference and to elevate one and demote the other.

Right and wrong, good and evil often get so intermingled in this world that even the most discerning people can't tell the difference. But God is the ultimate dispenser of justice. He has the insight to separate the true from the false. He can be trusted to sort things out, reward the deserving, and punish the pretenders.

The Bible is filled with accounts of God's actions as Judge. For example, King Ahab of Israel and his wicked queen, Jezebel, cheated, lied, and enlisted false witnesses to have Naboth killed so they could take his vineyard

The emblem of Jerusalem shows the "lion of the tribe of Judah."

(see 1 Kings 21:1–16). No earthly judge or civil court had the resolve or courage to bring this powerful couple to trial. But God had the last word in the matter.

King Ahab was eventually killed by a stray arrow from an enemy soldier (see 1 Kings 22:34–40). Jezebel was tossed to her death from a window when Jehu took over the kingship (see 2 Kings 9:30–37). These events didn't happen immediately, but God's justice eventually prevailed—and it always does. See also *Justice of God*.

JUDGE OF ALL THE EARTH

This name of God was spoken by Abraham when he talked with the Lord about His decision to destroy the city of Sodom because of its wickedness (see Genesis 18:25). Abraham believed that God was just in all His actions. Surely the "Judge of all the earth" would not destroy the righteous people of Sodom along

Sodom and Gomorrah burn as Lot and his two daughters flee the destruction, but Lot's wife becomes a pillar of salt for looking back. Lot's uncle, Abraham, begged the "Judge of all the earth" to spare wicked Sodom for the sake of only ten righteous people (see Genesis 18). Sadly, God couldn't find that many good people in the city.

with the wicked.

God did follow through on His plan to destroy the city. But He sent an angel to warn the only righteous people in Sodom—Lot and his family—to flee before His judgment fell (see Genesis 19:1, 15–17). This proved that the Lord is fair and equitable in His work in the world as the righteous dispenser of justice.

Two related titles of God that express this same idea are "judge of the earth" (Psalm 94:2) and "Judge of all" (Hebrews 12:23). See also *God of the Whole Earth*; *Justice of God*.

JUDGE OF QUICK AND DEAD

This name of Jesus appears in the sermon that the apostle Peter preached to the Roman centurion Cornelius, a Gentile (see Acts 10:25–43). Peter made it clear to Cornelius that Jesus had been appointed by God the Father as the supreme Judge of all things—the "quick and dead" (v. 42). The NIV renders this title as "judge of the living and the dead."

God's activity as Judge is one of the key themes of the Old Testament (see *Judge* and *Judge of All the Earth*). But after God sent His Son, Jesus, into the world, He established a new way of rendering His judgment. According to the Gospel of John, with the coming of Jesus He "committed all judgment unto the Son" (John 5:22). Jesus is now the agent through whom divine judgment is handed down.

As the Judge of the living and the dead, Jesus is the great dividing line in history. At the great white throne of judgment in the end time, He will send into eternal punishment those who have refused to accept Him as Savior and Lord (see Revelation 20:11–15). Believers will not be involved in this judgment because they have accepted in faith the sacrifice that Jesus has made on their behalf.

But believers will not totally escape divine judgment; they will be subjected to an evaluation known as the judgment seat of Christ. At this judgment the service they have rendered for Jesus Christ will be judged and rewarded accordingly (see sidebar). The exact nature of this judgment and the rewards are unclear. But the fact that we will face this time of accountability before the Lord should motivate us to loyal service in the cause of God's kingdom.

Another name of Jesus that emphasizes His role as Judge is "righteous judge" (2 Timothy 4:8).

JUDGMENT

God executes divine retribution against human activities, especially sin. God's judgment is designed to punish evil (see Exodus 20:5), to correct the misguided (see 2 Samuel 7:14–15), and to prevent His people from wrongdoing (see Luke 13:3–5). His judgment is an expression of His chastening love for believers (see Hebrews 12:5–6). Jesus, God's resurrected Son, has authority to judge all humankind (see John 5:27; Acts 17:31). Believers in Jesus will avoid condemnation and enter eternal life (see John 9:39). See also *Spirit of Judgment/Spirit of Burning*; *Wrath of God*.

PAUL'S TEACHINGS ON THE JUDGMENT SEAT OF CHRIST

- "We must all appear before the judgment seat of Christ, so that each of us may receive what is due us for the things done while in the body, whether good or bad" (2 Corinthians 5:10 NIV).
- "Each of us will give an account of ourselves to God" (Romans 14:12 NIV).
- "Their work will be shown for what it is, because the Day will bring it to light. . . . If what has been built survives, the builder will receive his reward. If it is burned up, the builder will suffer loss but yet will be saved—even though only as one escaping through the flames" (1 Corinthians 3:12–15 NIV).

Angels blow trumpets announcing God's final judgment on humanity (see Revelation 8–9). The painting is from a church in Vienna, Austria.

JUDGMENT DAY

See *Last Judgment.*

JUDGMENT, LAST

See *Last Judgment.*

JUSTICE OF GOD

One of the clearest teachings of the Bible is that God is just; He is fair and impartial in His treatment of all people. God Himself is the source of justice (see Deuteronomy 32:4). In Old Testament times, He was particularly concerned about just treatment of the poor and oppressed, including widows, orphans, and strangers and foreigners in the land of Israel (see Psalms 82:3–4; 146:9; Jeremiah 49:11).

Because God is just, He demands that His people practice justice in all human relationships. The prophet Micah declared that to "do justly" was more important than offering sacrifices and performing other religious rituals (see Micah 6:7–8). See also *Impartiality of God.*

JUSTIFICATION

The act by which God declares a person just or in a right relationship with Him is known as justification (see Romans 5:9). Justification is not accomplished by personal merit or good works (see Galatians 2:16) but by God's grace through our personal faith in Christ (see Ephesians 2:8–9). To be justified is to have peace with God and hope for eternity (see Titus 3:5–7).

The apostle Paul addressed the issue of justification in detail in his epistle to the Romans. The bottom line, he declared, is that believers are "justified freely" by God's grace "through the redemption that is in Christ Jesus" (Romans 3:24). See also *Atonement; Imputed Righteousness; Propitiation for Our Sins.*

JUST MAN

Pontius Pilate, the Roman governor who condemned Jesus to death, received a message from his wife while Jesus was on trial. It had been revealed to her in a dream that Jesus was innocent of the charges against Him, so she tried to get Pilate to release Him. She begged him to "have. . .nothing to do with that just man" (Matthew 27:19).

Pilate also knew that Jesus was not guilty, but he caved in to political pressure from the Jewish religious leaders and pronounced the death penalty against Him. He washed His hands before the crowd and declared, "I am innocent of the blood of this just person" (Matthew 27:24).

The word *just* as applied to Jesus by Pilate and his wife means "innocent." But in other contexts in the New Testament, the names "Just" (Acts 3:14), "Just One" (Acts 7:52; 22:14), and "righteous man" (Luke 23:47) refer to His righteousness and holiness.

Jesus, the sinless and righteous One, was not guilty of any crime or wrongdoing. This makes His death on our behalf all the more meaningful. He willingly laid down His life on the cross as the sacrifice for our sin. See also *Righteous Servant.*

JUST ONE

See *Just Man.*

Pilate washes his hands, a symbolic (and completely ineffective) attempt to avoid blame for condemning Jesus to death. Earlier, Pilate's wife had warned her husband to "have nothing to do with that just man" (Matthew 27:19).

K

KEEPER

The psalmist declared, "The Lord is thy keeper: the Lord is thy shade upon thy right hand" (Psalm 121:5). This is the only place in the Bible where God is referred to as our "keeper."

This name refers to His protection, provision, and watchfulness. The NIV translates the phrase as "The Lord watches over you."

No matter where we are or what we are doing, God has His watchful eye on us. This is both comforting and disturbing. As the writer of Proverbs said, "The eyes of the Lord are in every place, beholding the evil and the good" (Proverbs 15:3). See also *Guide unto Death*.

Jesus hands the "keys of the kingdom of heaven" to Peter, in a mosaic from St. Peter's Basilica in Rome.

KENOSIS

This theological term (pronounced keh NOE sis) relates to the dual nature of Christ—His divinity and His humanity. The term comes from the Greek verb *kenoo*, meaning "to make empty," which occurs in Philippians 2:7: "[Jesus] made himself of no reputation." The NASB renders this phrase as "He emptied himself."

Some liberal scholars have taken this verse to mean that Jesus as God's divine Son put aside or "emptied himself" of certain divine attributes when He was born into the world in human form. According to this kenotic theory, Jesus was first divine with God the Father, then became a man when He came to earth, and then returned to divine status after His resurrection.

The key to interpreting Paul's meaning in Philippians 2:7 is found in the rest of the verse. He went on to say that Jesus "took upon him the form of a servant, and was made in the likeness of men." So Jesus' emptying of Himself refers not to His divine attributes but to His humility and His willingness to become flesh so He could identify fully with human beings. He became God's servant but He never stopped being God's Son. See also *Incarnation of Christ*.

KEYS OF THE KINGDOM

This phrase comes from the words of Jesus to His disciples, "I will give you the keys of the kingdom of heaven" (Matthew 16:19 NIV). This promise of Jesus followed Peter's confession that He was the Messiah, the "Son of the living God" (Matthew 16:16 NIV).

In ancient times a key was a symbol of power and authority. Jesus was using metaphorical language to show that His authority as God's Son was being "handed off" to His twelve disciples. They were to continue, through the Church, the work of redemption that God had sent Him into the world to do. It is still true today that every follower of Jesus is a "keeper of the keys" that He has committed to His Church. See also *Church*; *Head of the Church*; *Priesthood of Believers*.

KINDNESS OF GOD

See *Goodness of God*; *Grace of God*.

KING

Both God the Father and God the Son are referred to as "King" in the Bible. In the Old Testament, the prophet Samuel referred to the Lord by this name when the leaders of Israel requested that he appoint a central political figure to rule over them. It was clear to Samuel that they were choosing poorly—turning away from God as their ruler and king to place their confidence in an earthly king (see 1 Samuel 8:4–10).

After Samuel's time the Lord was spoken of as King many times throughout the history of Israel. Kings of ancient times had unlimited authority. They were answerable to no one, and their word was considered the law of the land. When they died, their sons had the right to succeed them. Thus their influence and power were passed on from generation to generation.

But above these political kings stands the ultimate King, the ruler of the universe. He alone is worthy of our worship and unquestioning obedience.

In the New Testament, Jesus was hailed as King by the crowds when He made His triumphal entry into Jerusalem (see Luke 19:37–38). They had seen His miracles during His public ministry, so they acknowledged Him as the wonder-working Messiah whom God had been promising to send to His people for many centuries.

But in Jesus' time, no king had ruled over the Jews for a period of about five hundred years. They thought their long-promised Messiah would be a powerful king who would restore their nation to its glory days as a political power. When the crowds greeted Jesus as King when He entered Jerusalem, they were thinking of Him in these terms.

Jesus faced this problem throughout His ministry. After the miracle of the feeding of the five thousand, He realized that the crowds "would come and take him by force, to make him a king." He avoided them by slipping away to a secluded spot in a nearby mountain (see John 6:15).

There was nothing Jesus could do to avoid the crowds on the day when He entered Jerusalem. But He rode a donkey, a symbol of humility and peace, rather than a prancing white horse, the steed of choice for military heroes (see Matthew 21:1–5). This showed that He was not a political ruler but a spiritual King—one who had come into the world to conquer sin and death.

KINGDOM OF GOD

This phrase refers to the spiritual reign of God in the hearts of believers (see Luke 17:20–21). This kingdom is partially attained in this life for those who seek God's will. But God's kingdom will be fully established in the world to come (see John 18:36). Jesus preached the "gospel of the kingdom" (Mark 1:14) and taught His disciples to seek His kingdom (see Matthew 6:33) and to pray for its arrival on earth (see Matthew 6:10).

Jesus taught about the kingdom of God in many of His parables. For example, He compared the kingdom to seed scattered on the ground. Some seed will sprout and grow in good soil. But other seed will fall on rocky ground and fail to take root. This shows that the kingdom will flourish in the hearts of some people but will be rejected by others (see Matthew 13:3–8).

Unrepentant sinners cannot inherit the kingdom of God (see Ephesians 5:5). It is reserved for those who repent (see Matthew 3:2) and experience spiritual rebirth (see John 3:3–5). This kingdom is also referred to as the "kingdom of heaven" (Matthew 4:17) and the kingdom of Christ (see Colossians 1:13).

KING ETERNAL, IMMORTAL, INVISIBLE

The apostle Paul referred to the Lord by this name in a beautiful benediction in his first epistle to Timothy: "Unto the King eternal, immortal, invisible, the only wise God, be honour and glory for ever and ever. Amen" (1 Timothy 1:17). The adjectives "eternal, immortal, invisible" express three of God's characteristics, or attributes.

PAY HOMAGE TO THE KING

- "The LORD is King for ever and ever" (Psalm 10:16).
- "The LORD. . .is a great King over all the earth" (Psalm 47:2).
- "Make a joyful noise before the LORD, the King" (Psalm 98:6).
- "Let the children of Zion be joyful in their King" (Psalm 149:2).
- "Then said I, Woe is me! for I am undone; because I am a man of unclean lips, and I dwell in the midst of a people of unclean lips: for mine eyes have seen the King, the LORD of hosts" (Isaiah 6:5).

Residents of Jerusalem spread their coats and tree branches in Jesus' path, hailing Him as king, in a sixteenth-century painting by Pieter Coecke van Aelst.

God is eternal because He has always existed and He always will. Unlike man, who is mortal, He is not subject to sickness and death. And He is invisible because He is a spirit being who exists everywhere at the same time (see John 4:24).

The prophet Jeremiah also referred to God as the "everlasting king" (Jeremiah 10:10). Both he and Paul were familiar with earthly kings who ruled for a few years, then were succeeded by other members of the royal family. Even the long reign of about fifty years achieved by King Manasseh of Judah (see

An artist's conception of the ark of the covenant—perhaps the inspiration for the twenty-fourth psalm, which praises the "King of glory."

2 Kings 21:1) is like the blink of an eye when compared to God's eternal kingship over the nations of the world. See also *King*.

KING OF GLORY

Psalm 24:7–10 is the only place in the Bible where God is called the "King of glory," and the name appears five times in these four verses: "Lift up your heads, O ye gates; and be ye lift up, ye everlasting doors; and the King of glory shall come in. Who is this King of glory? The LORD strong and mighty, the LORD mighty in battle. Lift up your heads, O ye gates; even lift them up, ye everlasting doors; and the King of glory shall come in. Who is this King of glory? The LORD of hosts, he is the King of glory." This is one of

the most beautiful passages in the book of Psalms. The title of the psalm ascribes it to David.

The exuberant joy of this psalm leads some interpreters to speculate that it may have been sung when the ark of the covenant was moved to the city of Jerusalem in David's time. On this occasion David "danced before the LORD" as trumpets sounded and the people shouted with joy (see 2 Samuel 6:14–15).

Two choirs, singing responsively, may have accompanied the ark. One choir sang, "Who is this King of glory?" And the other choir responded by identifying Him as Yahweh, the strong and mighty God of the Israelites.

As the King of Glory, God is worthy of our praise. The psalmist declared, "Not unto us, O LORD, not unto us, but unto thy name give glory" (Psalm 115:1). See also *Glory of God*; *Spirit of Glory*.

KING OF ISRAEL

See *King of the Jews*.

KING OF JACOB

See *Mighty One of Jacob*.

KING OF KINGS

The nineteenth chapter of Revelation describes the return of Christ to earth in the end time when He will triumph over all His enemies. According to verse 16 of this chapter, He will wear a banner across His royal robe. It will be emblazoned with the phrase "KING OF KINGS." This name, emphasizing His supreme rule over all the earth, will be prominently displayed for everyone to see.

In Old Testament times, the title "king of

OUR MATCHLESS KING

The hymn "Crown Him with Many Crowns" by Matthew Bridges and Godfrey Thring praises the Lord Jesus for His role as King of kings in the lives of believers.

Crown Him with many crowns,
The Lamb upon His throne;
Hark! How the heavenly anthem drowns
All music but its own:
Awake, my soul, and sing
Of Him who died for thee,
And hail Him as thy matchless King
Through all eternity.

---

kings" was assigned to a ruler with an empire that covered a wide territory. Often a king of an empire would allow the rulers of conquered nations or tribes to keep their royal titles for political and economic reasons. But it was clear that he as "king of kings" was the undisputed ruler of his vast domain. Thus, the Persian ruler Artaxerxes referred to himself as "king of kings" in a letter that he sent to Jerusalem with Ezra the priest (see Ezra 7:12).

When Jesus returns in glory, He will be the sole ruler of the universe. Meanwhile, He rules over His kingdom known as the Church. If we belong to Him, we are subjects of His kingdom. He should already be King of kings in our lives.

In a passage that looked forward to the birth of the Messiah, the prophet Zechariah called Jesus the "king over all the earth" (Zechariah 14:9). See also *God of the Whole Earth*; *Lord of Lords*; *Offices of Christ*; *Prince of the Kings of the Earth*.

KING OF OLD

See *Ancient of Days.*

KING OF SAINTS

In Revelation 15:3, believers sing two songs—the song of Moses and the song of the Lamb. These songs celebrate redemption and deliverance. Just as Moses' song celebrated deliverance from Egyptian slavery (see Exodus 15:1–19), so the song of the Lamb rejoices in our deliverance from Satan and the bondage of sin and death. Jesus is referred to as "King of saints" in this verse.

Most people think of saints as people who have been beatified and honored by a church body because of their dedicated service to God. But the word *saints* when it appears in the New Testament is a term for believers. Those who have accepted Jesus as Savior and who follow Him as Lord of their lives are saints. Believers as saints make up the Church, the body of Christ.

Thus, Jesus' name as King of saints is

The letters INRI, often seen in artwork of Jesus' cross, are an abbreviation of the Latin phrase *Iesus Nazarenus Rex Iudaerum*, which means "Jesus of Nazareth, King of the Jews." Pilate ordered the message posted on Jesus' cross in three languages (John 19:19–20).

similar to His title "Head of the Church." He watches over His saints and energizes them through His Holy Spirit for the task of carrying out His work in the world. See also *Church*; *Head of the Church*.

KING OF THE JEWS

Pontius Pilate, the Roman official who condemned Jesus to death, asked Him, "Are you the king of the Jews?" Pilate's question and Jesus' name, king of the Jews, appear in all four Gospels (see Matthew 27:11; Mark 15:12; Luke 23:3; John 18:33). The Gospel writers considered this name important because it was the basis of the charge that led to Jesus' execution.

The Jewish religious leaders who turned Jesus over to Pilate were enraged by what they considered His blasphemy, or His claim to be the divine Son of God (see Matthew 26:63–66). But they knew the Romans would never condemn Jesus to death on the basis of their religious laws alone (see John 18:29–32). So they claimed that Jesus was guilty of sedition against the Roman government by claiming to be a king (see Luke 23:2). The implication of this charge is that Jesus was plotting to overthrow Roman rule. This charge was guaranteed to get action from Pilate. One thing his superiors in Rome would not tolerate was unrest or rebellion in the territory over which he ruled.

Jesus never claimed to be a political king. So why didn't He deny that He was the king of the Jews when Pilate asked Him if the charge against Him was true? He refused to answer this question to Pilate's satisfaction because He knew the time for His sacrificial death had arrived. He would allow events to run their course without any intervention on His part because it was His destiny to die on the cross. He would be sacrificed willingly as the king of the Jews in order to provide salvation for the entire world.

Another name of Jesus that is similar to king of the Jews is "King of Israel" (John 1:49; 12:13).

KING OVER ALL THE EARTH

See *King of Kings*.

KNEELING

See *Bowing*.

KNOWLEDGE OF GOD

See *Foreknowledge of God*; *Omniscience of God*.

THE RIGHT TIME FOR REDEMPTION

During His earthly ministry, Jesus was aware that the timing of His death should be in accordance with God's plan. For example, He told His skeptical brothers who wanted Him to declare His purpose openly to others: "My time is not yet here" (John 7:6 NIV). But just a few days before His crucifixion, He told His disciples, "My appointed time is near" (Matthew 26:18 NIV).

Looking back on the cross and Jesus' sacrificial death, the apostle Paul declared, "When the fulness of time was come, God sent forth his Son, made of a woman, made under the law, to redeem them that were under the law, that we might receive the adoption of sons" (Galatians 4:4–5).

In one of the Bible's many ironies, the powerful King of kings, Jesus, is described as a "lamb." One of Jesus' great teachings was that "the last shall be first, and the first last" (Matthew 20:16).

L

LAKE OF FIRE

This word picture of hell, the eternal destiny of all unbelievers in the end time, as a burning lake occurs only in the book of Revelation. This is the place of eternal punishment for all who oppose God, including the beast and the false prophet (see Revelation 19:20), Satan or the devil (see Revelation 20:10), and all people whose names are not written in the book of life (see Revelation 20:15; 21:8).

One of the puzzling things about this lake is that hell, along with death, will also be thrown here, according to the KJV (see Revelation 20:14). If this lake is a metaphor for hell, how can hell be thrown into its own self? A look at a modern English translation solves the problem. The Greek word behind "hell" in this passage is actually retained by the NIV and rendered as "Hades," the realm of the dead. Here the word *hades* is used as a synonym for death, God's final enemy. See also *Hades*; *Hell*; *Second Death*.

LAMB

In the book of Revelation, the apostle John described Jesus as the sacrificial Lamb who laid down His life as redemption for the sins of the world: "Worthy is the Lamb that was slain to receive power, and riches, and wisdom, and strength, and honour, and glory, and blessing" (Revelation 5:12). Notice the things that John declares Jesus the Lamb is worthy to receive.

- *Power.* The Lamb exercises ultimate power over the universe as well as the lives of believers.

- *Riches.* All the material possessions we have accumulated belong to Him.
- *Wisdom.* Jesus is the All-Wise One who grants wisdom to those who follow Him.
- *Strength.* Our physical powers should be dedicated to the service of the Lamb.
- *Honor.* Our behavior as believers should bring honor to the One whom we profess to follow.
- *Glory.* Jesus' glory—His excellence and moral superiority—is magnified when believers are fully devoted to Him and His cause.
- *Blessing.* In this context the word *blessing* means "praise." We should praise the Lamb with our lives as well as our words.

Jesus as the Lamb is one of the major themes of the book of Revelation. As the Lamb, He is worthy to open the scroll that describes God's judgment against the world (see Revelation 5:4; 6:1). The Lamb provides the light for the heavenly city, or New Jerusalem (see Revelation 21:22–23). Those who belong to Jesus have their names written in the Lamb's book of life (see Revelation 21:27). See also *Lamb of God*.

LAMB OF GOD

On two successive days John the Baptist, forerunner of Jesus, referred to Jesus by this name (see John 1:29, 35–36). Of all the names John could have used—King, Messiah, Prophet—he chose to identify Jesus as the "Lamb of God." Lambs were choice young sheep that were used as sacrificial animals in Jewish worship rituals (see Leviticus 14:11–13; 1 Samuel 7:9). Thus, at the very beginning of Jesus' ministry, John realized the sacrificial role He was destined to fill.

The prominence of lambs in the Jewish sacrificial system began with the deliverance of the Israelites from Egyptian slavery, many centuries before Jesus' time. The Lord commanded the people to smear the blood of lambs on the doorposts of their houses. This indicated that they would be passed over when God struck the land with the death of the firstborn (see Exodus 12:21–23). The Jewish festival known as Passover was commemorated from that day on with the eating of unleavened bread and the sacrifice of lambs.

One of the greatest messianic passages of the Old Testament predicted that Jesus would die like a sacrificial lamb. About seven hundred years before Jesus was born, the prophet Isaiah declared of Him, "He was oppressed and afflicted, yet he did not open his mouth; he was led like a lamb to the slaughter, and as a sheep before its shearers is silent, so he did not open his mouth" (Isaiah 53:7 NIV).

On the night before His crucifixion, Jesus picked up on the sacrificial lamb imagery that John the Baptist had used of Him when He began His public ministry. He gathered with His disciples to eat a meal that was part of the observance of the Jewish Passover. But He turned it into a meal that we know as the Memorial Supper, or the Lord's Supper.

Just as the blood of the first Passover lamb had been an agent of deliverance for the Israelites in Egypt, so Jesus' shed blood would provide divine redemption for the entire world. As Jesus passed the cup among His disciples, He told them, "This is my blood of the new testament, which is shed for many for the remission of sins" (Matthew 26:28). See also *Lamb*; *Passover and Feast of Unleavened Bread*.

LAMB SLAIN FROM THE FOUNDATION OF THE WORLD

The affirmation of Revelation 13:8 is not only that Jesus was the Lamb who was sacrificed for our sins but that He was selected for this task before the world was created: "All that dwell upon the earth shall worship him, whose names are not written in the book of life of the Lamb slain from the foundation of the world."

God the Father looked down through the centuries and determined that His Son, Jesus, would die at some time in the future as an atonement for sin. Jesus' death was no accident of history and no afterthought in the mind of God. It was the fulfillment of His eternal plan.

How long did it take for this plan to work itself out? As long as it took. This answer may seem nonsensical and ridiculous, but it's as

SAVED BY THE BLOOD OF THE LAMB OF GOD

- "He did not enter by means of the blood of goats and calves; but he entered the Most Holy Place once for all by his own blood, thus obtaining eternal redemption" (Hebrews 9:12 NIV).
- "It was not with perishable things such as silver or gold that you were redeemed from the empty way of life handed down to you from your ancestors, but with the precious blood of Christ, a lamb without blemish or defect" (1 Peter 1:18–19 NIV).

A Roman soldier nails Jesus to the cross while a centurion looks on. In no way did Jesus' death take God the Father by surprise—Jesus was the "Lamb slain from the foundation of the world."

close as we can get to understanding God and His mysterious ways. The apostle Peter expressed it like this: "One day is with the Lord as a thousand years, and a thousand years as one day" (2 Peter 3:8). See also *Fore-ordained before the Foundation of the World*.

LAND OF PROMISE

See *Canaan*; *Palestine*.

LAST ADAM

The apostle Paul declared in the book of 1 Corinthians, "The first man Adam was made a living soul; the last Adam was made a quickening spirit" (15:45). This is the only place in the Bible where Jesus is called by this name. Paul draws a contrast between Jesus as the "last Adam" and the Adam of the book of Genesis who was the first man created (see Genesis 2:7). This contrast appears at several points throughout the fifteenth chapter of 1 Corinthians.

After God created Adam and placed him in the Garden of Eden, He told him he could eat the fruit from every tree in the garden except one—"the tree of the knowledge of good and evil" (Genesis 2:17). But Adam deliberately disobeyed God and ate the forbidden fruit (see Genesis 3:6). This act of rebellion placed Adam and all his descendants—including everyone born since Adam's time—under the curse of sin and death.

But according to Paul, God had good news for those who were tainted by Adam's sin. He sent another Adam—the last Adam, Jesus Christ—to undo what the first Adam had caused. Paul expressed it like this: "As in Adam all die, even so in Christ shall all be made alive" (1 Corinthians 15:22). The first Adam's legacy of death has been nullified by the last Adam's perfect obedience of God the Father and His sacrificial death on our behalf.

Paul went on in this passage from 1 Corinthians to refer to Jesus as the "second man." Jesus as the second man came from heaven, but Adam was a created being who was formed from the dust of the earth, thus "of the earth, earthy" (1 Corinthians 15:47). See also *Adam*; *Fall of Man*.

LAST JUDGMENT

The Bible speaks clearly about a final or last judgment—a time in the future when God will intervene in history to judge the wicked, reward the righteous, and bring the universe to its appointed conclusion. This judgment is a part of God's purpose for the world (see Acts 17:31). He alone knows when it will happen. Jesus declared that even He did not know the exact time for the last judgment (see Matthew 24:36).

This judgment will be the final or "last" one in a long line of judgments that God has performed in the world. In Old Testament

The rap of a judge's gavel can indicate the conclusion of a court hearing, that a judgment has been rendered. God's "last judgment"—separating believers and unbelievers for eternity—is the ultimate court hearing.

times, He destroyed the wicked and preserved a remnant—Noah and his family—by sending a flood upon the earth (see Genesis 6–8). He also confused the language of the ungodly at the tower of Babel (see Genesis 11:1–9). Pagan nations like the Canaanites and the Egyptians also were subjected to His judgment.

The final judgment is sometimes referred to as the "great white throne" judgment. This term comes from the book of Revelation, where God is depicted as judging the earth while seated on a great white throne (see Revelation 20:11–15).

The last judgment will be universal in scope. All people and nations of the earth—from the beginning to the end of history—will be judged (see Romans 14:10–12). Unbelievers will be condemned to eternal punishment (see Revelation 21:8), while believers will enter into eternal life (see 2 Thessalonians 1:3–10). See also *Eschatology*; *Second Coming of Christ*.

Moses brings the tablets of the law—the Ten Commandments—down from Mount Sinai, in a nineteenth-century engraving by Gustave Doré. The beams of light shining from Moses' head are a reference to Exodus 34:29–30, which says Moses' face "shone" after he met with God.

LAST SUPPER

See *Lord's Supper*.

LAST THINGS

See *Eschatology*.

LAWGIVER

The prophet Isaiah referred to God as "our lawgiver" (Isaiah 33:22). He may have had in mind God's revelation to Moses of His Ten Commandments (see Exodus 20:1–17), a moral code to guide the behavior of His people. God is sovereign over His creation, and He is the source of truth, righteousness, and holiness. He has the right to make the laws and set the standards by which people should live.

Many people have a strictly negative view of God's laws. They think of them only in binding and restrictive terms. But these laws are actually given for our benefit. Following His directives and commands as lawgiver is the key to joy and contentment in this life. The psalmist focused on this positive side of God's laws when he declared, "You [God] are good, and what you do is good; teach me your decrees" (Psalm 119:68 NIV). See also *Judge*.

LAWLESSNESS

See *Sin*.

LAW OF MOSES

This authoritative rule of conduct is spelled out in the Ten Commandments and the Pentateuch—the books of Genesis, Exodus, Leviticus, Numbers, and Deuteronomy. This code was revealed to Moses by the Lord on Mount Sinai (see Deuteronomy 5:1–2). While many of the regulations are ceremonial in nature, the moral law embodied in the Law of Moses is applicable to all generations (see Romans 7:7–12). It was fulfilled by the Gospel and confirmed by Christ (see Matthew 5:17–18).

To the Jewish people of Old Testament times, keeping the Law of Moses was the key to being made acceptable by the Lord. But the apostle Paul declared that law-keeping had been replaced by the covenant of grace. Only through faith in Christ and His sacrificial death were people made righteous in God's sight. He spelled this out clearly in the book

Thin matzo bread, made without yeast (leaven), is eaten by Jewish people as they celebrate the Passover.

of Romans: "Now God has shown us a way to be made right with him without keeping the requirements of the law. . . . We are made right with God by placing our faith in Jesus Christ. And this is true for everyone who believes, no matter who we are" (Romans 3:21–22 NLT). See also *End of the Law*.

LEADER AND COMMANDER

Chapter 55 of Isaiah is one of many messianic passages in his book. Isaiah portrayed the coming Messiah as One who would serve as a "leader and commander" for the people to whom He was being sent by the Lord (see 55:4).

A leader is a person who guides others in the pursuit of a goal. He enlists others to work toward the goal, motivates and inspires them, encourages them through personal example, and keeps them focused on their objective. The title "commander" conjures up a military image. A commander is more directive in his approach to leadership. He knows what has to be done to win a battle, and he marshals his troops to engage the enemy in such a way that victory is assured.

As believers, we have both a leader and a commander in Jesus Christ. His objective is to bring others into His kingdom. Our task is to follow His leadership as we bear witness for Him in the world. As our commander, He has the right to demand our unquestioning obedience. See also *Governor*.

LEAVEN

This fermentation agent is used in making bread. In one of His parables, Jesus compared the kingdom of God with leaven, or yeast, that was mixed with dough to cause bread to rise (see Luke 13:20–21). He was saying that the kingdom of God had a power out of proportion to its size that caused it to permeate and influence all of society. See also *Kingdom of God; Parables of Jesus.*

LENT

The period of about forty days preceding Easter Sunday is known as Lent. Some church groups observe Lent as a time of preparation for the celebration of Jesus' resurrection. Fasting is a part of some Lenten observances. This may be derived from the forty days that Jesus fasted in the wilderness before launching His public ministry (see Matthew 4:1–2). See also *Easter.*

LIFE

We are accustomed to thinking of Jesus in terms of the eternal life that He promises to believers. But in the apostle Paul's letter to the Colossian believers, He described Jesus as the life of believers in the here-and-now. "When Christ, who is our life, shall appear," Paul said, "then shall ye also appear with him in glory" (Colossians 3:4). We don't have to wait until we die to enjoy life with Him. He is our life today—in this present world.

With Jesus as our life, we can live each day with joy in spite of the problems and frustrations that come our way. He is the very essence of the truly good life, and He promises the same to those who follow Him: "I am come that they might have life, and that they might have it more abundantly" (John 10:10).

Other names of Jesus that emphasize the meaningful life He offers believers are "Prince of life" (Acts 3:15) and "Word of life" (1 John 1:1). See also *Resurrection and the Life; Spirit of life.*

WALKING WITH JESUS EVERY DAY

The old gospel hymn "Every Day with Jesus" by Robert C. Loveless expresses the joy of life with Jesus, our life, during every day of our earthly journey.

Every day with Jesus
Is sweeter than the day before,
Every day with Jesus
I love Him more and more;
Jesus saves and keeps me,
And He's the One I'm waiting for;
Every day with Jesus
Is sweeter than the day before.

LIFE-GIVING SPIRIT

See *Quickening Spirit.*

LIGHT

One of the most meaningful names of God in the Bible is "light." This name is applied to both God the Father and God the Son.

In the Old Testament, the psalmist declared, "The Lord is my light and my salvation; whom shall I fear?" (Psalm 27:1). The psalmist knew that after God created the world, the first thing He brought into being was light (see Genesis 1:3–5). Old Testament writers often compared His glory or presence to the light (see Psalm 104:1–2). He led His people in the wilderness during the Exodus with the light from a pillar of fire (see Exodus 13:21).

As the light, God is still a guide for His people. He gives us wisdom and insight to help us make good decisions. In our moments of darkness and discouragement, He gives us hope. He lights up our lives constantly with His love and grace.

God's written Word, the Bible, also shows that light is an appropriate name for Him. He inspired the Bible by divine revelation many centuries ago. Then He worked throughout history to preserve it and pass it down to our generation. His eternal Word still shines like a beacon in a dark and sinful world. As believers, we can declare with the psalmist, "Thy word is a lamp unto my feet, and a light unto my path" (Psalm 119:105).

The psalmist also referred to God as the "sun" (Psalm 84:11), comparing Him to the brightest light in the universe.

In the Gospel of John in the New Testament, Jesus is referred to as the light whom God sent into a world that was stumbling around in the darkness of sin (see John 1:7). Light is one of those things we take for granted until it disappears and the darkness takes over. Most of us know what it's like to grope around in a dark house, bumping against the furniture after the electricity goes out unexpectedly. We are virtually helpless until we locate that candle or flashlight we had placed in a dark closet for just such an emergency.

As the light, Jesus pushes back the darkness and helps us find our way in a chaotic world. He reveals God in all His righteousness, and He bridges the gap that separates sinful humankind from a holy God. He gives us insights from God's written Word, the Bible, that enable us to make wise decisions and live in accordance with His will.

Just as Jesus is the light of our lives, He expects us as believers to reflect His light to others. In His Sermon on the Mount, He called us "the light of the world" (Matthew 5:14). Then He challenged us to "let your light shine before others, that they may see your good deeds and glorify your Father in heaven" (Matthew 5:16 NIV).

The apostle John also referred to Jesus as the "true Light" (John 1:9). See also *Everlasting Light*.

LIGHT OF ISRAEL

This name of God was used by the prophet Isaiah in connection with his prophecy about the nation of Assyria. The Assyrians overran the nation of Israel (northern kingdom) about 722 BC. Isaiah predicted that Assyria would eventually be punished by the Lord for their mistreatment of His people. God—the "light of Israel"—would become a blazing fire that would consume this pagan nation (see Isaiah 10:17). This prophecy was fulfilled about a century after Isaiah's time when Assyria fell to the Babylonians.

These images of light and fire show two different sides of God's nature. It is always better to experience the light of His love than the fire of His wrath. See also *Wrath of God*.

LIGHT OF THE GENTILES

See *Light of the World*.

LIGHT OF THE WORLD

Jesus referred to Himself by this name in a conversation with the Pharisees, His constant critics. They thought He was nothing but a religious quack and a troublemaker. But Jesus claimed to be the Son of God who had been sent on a redemptive mission as the "light of the world" (John 8:12). He also used this name for Himself after restoring the sight of a blind man (see John 9:5).

The Jewish people of Jesus' time—especially the religious leaders like the Pharisees—were filled with religious and national

The word *lamp* (or its plural) occurs forty-four times in the King James Version of the Bible, including Proverbs 6:23: "For the commandment is a lamp; and the law is light."

Physically, the sun is the "light of the world," allowing humans to perceive our surroundings and causing the growth that allows for our life. As the spiritual Light of the World, Jesus performs the same functions.

pride. They realized that God had blessed them as His special people. They thought of His favor as something they deserved because of their moral superiority to the people of other nations. But they forgot that God had blessed them because He wanted them to serve as His witnesses to the rest of the world. Centuries before, God had told their ancestor Abraham, "I will make you into a great nation. . .and all peoples on earth will be blessed through you" (Genesis 12:2–3 NIV).

Jesus was born into the world as a Jew, but His commitment as Savior was to the entire world. This is one reason why He was rejected by the Jewish religious leaders of His time. How could God the Father possibly love the pagan peoples of the world as much as He loved them? They wanted to put limits on God's love and concern.

This problem is still with us today. Some people want to make Jesus into the light of the middle class, or the light of Western society, or the light of the beautiful. But He refuses to be bound by such restrictions. He is also the light of the poor, the light of the Third World, and the light of the unattractive. No matter what your earthly circumstances, He is *your* light.

Another name of Jesus that expresses the same truth as Light of the World is "light of the Gentiles." To the Jews, *Gentiles* was a catch-all term for all non-Jewish peoples. In a famous messianic passage, the prophet Isaiah declared that Jesus would come into the world as a "light of the Gentiles" (Isaiah 42:6). See also *Everlasting Light*; *Gentiles*; *Impartiality of God*.

LION OF THE TRIBE OF JUDAH

This name of Jesus appears in one of the visions of the apostle John in the book of Revelation (see Revelation 5:5). Only Jesus as the "Lion of the tribe of Judah" is worthy to open the scroll that contains God's judgment against the world in the end time. God the Father has delegated to His Son the authority and power to serve as supreme Judge over all things.

The lion, known as the "king of beasts," is legendary for its strength and ferocious nature. Lions do not roam the land of Israel today, but they were common in Bible times. For example, David killed a lion that was threatening his father's sheep (see 1 Samuel 17:37). The judge Samson, one of the super-heroes of the Bible, killed a young lion with his bare hands (see Judges 14:5–6). God the Father also compared His forthcoming judgment against His rebellious people—the nation of Israel (spoken of symbolically as Ephraim) and the nation of Judah—to the fierceness of a lion (see Hosea 5:14).

Jesus as the Lion of the tribe of Judah probably has its origin in the prophecy of Jacob in the book of Genesis. He declared that his son Judah was destined to become the greatest among all his twelve sons whose

LIGHT FOR A DARK WORLD

Jesus is the light for a dark world, according to the hymn "The Light of the World Is Jesus" by Philip P. Bliss.

> The whole world was lost in the
>   darkness of sin,
> The Light of the world is Jesus;
> Like sunshine at noonday His glory
>   shone in,
> The Light of the world is Jesus.
> Come to the Light, 'tis shining for thee;
> Sweetly the Light has dawned upon me,
> Once I was blind, but now I can see:
> The Light of the world is Jesus.

descendants would become the Israelites, God's chosen people. Jacob described Judah symbolically as a lion, or a fearless ruler, who would lead God's people (see Genesis 49:8–12).

This prophecy was fulfilled dramatically throughout the Bible. The tribe of Judah, composed of Judah's descendants, took the lead on the Israelites' trek through the wilderness after they left Egypt (see Numbers 10:14). Moses' census of the people in the wilderness revealed that the tribe of Judah was the largest (see Numbers 1:27; 26:22). King David, the popular ruler of Israel against whom all future kings were measured, was a member of the tribe of Judah, a native of Bethlehem in the territory of Judah (see 1 Samuel 16:1).

Most significantly of all, Jesus the Messiah sprang from the line of Judah. The genealogy of Jesus in the Gospel of Matthew traces His lineage back to Judah (see Matthew 1:2–3;

A "lion of Judah" sculpture in Addis Ababa, Ethiopia. Ethiopian emperors, who claim a descent from Jesus' ancestor King Solomon, have applied the "lion of Judah" title to themselves.

spelled *Judas* in the KJV). Thus Jesus is the Lion of the tribe of Judah who rules among His people as supreme Savior and Lord. See also *Judah*.

LIVING GOD

King Darius of Persia called the Lord by this name when he came to see if Daniel had survived the night he spent among the lions (see Daniel 6:20). Even a pagan king recognized that it would take the "living God" to deliver Daniel from this den of ferocious animals that had been turned into an execution chamber.

God is referred to as the "living" God several times throughout the Bible (see Joshua 3:10; 1 Samuel 17:26; Hebrews 10:31). This title contrasts the one true God—the One who actually exists—with pagan idols that are lifeless counterfeits.

Unlike pagan deities, the living God is capable of acting on behalf of His people. Just as He saved Daniel from the lions, He hears our prayers and stands beside us in our time of need.

LIVING STONE

In 1 Peter 2:4 the apostle Peter compared Jesus to a stone used in the construction of a building. The imagery of a stone is applied to Jesus in other New Testament passages (see *Chief Cornerstone*; *Head of the Corner*). But Peter referred to Jesus here as a "living stone," emphasizing His resurrection from the dead and His close relationship with believers as the living Christ.

Peter went on in the next verse to describe believers as "lively stones" (1 Peter 2:5). Just as Jesus is the living and breathing head of the Church, so believers make up the body of the

Church. Thus the Church is a living organism devoted to the service of Jesus and His kingdom in the time between His ascension to God the Father and His second coming.

Peter summarized the mission of the Church by stating that believers are "a chosen people, a royal priesthood, a holy nation, God's special people, that you may declare the praises of him who called you out of darkness into his wonderful light" (1 Peter 2:9 NIV).

Maybe you never thought about it before, but if you belong to Jesus, you have the Spirit of the Living Stone in your life. We bring honor to Him when we serve as "lively stones" in the world. See also *Spiritual Rock.*

LIVING WATER

This metaphor for salvation and eternal life is what Jesus promised the Samaritan woman who came to draw water from Jacob's Well.

In Revelation 22:17, a "pure river of water of life" originates from the throne of God and the Lamb, Jesus Christ.

"Everyone who drinks this [physical] water will be thirsty again," Jesus told her. "But whoever drinks the water I give them will never thirst" (John 4:13–14 NIV).

The metaphor of Jesus as the living water that quenches our spiritual thirst also occurs in the book of Revelation. In the very last chapter of this final book of the Bible, all people are invited to "take the free gift of the water of life" (Revelation 22:17 NIV).

LOGOS

John the apostle used this Greek term, meaning "word," for Jesus in the prologue to his Gospel (see John 1:1–18). By describing Jesus as the Logos or the Word, John compared

Jesus to the powerful spoken word of God that brought the world into being (see John 1:3). See also *Creation; Word*.

LONGSUFFERING OF GOD

God's longsuffering means that He is patient with sinners; He longs to see them repent and turn to Him for forgiveness and salvation (see Romans 2:4). Other words often used for this divine attribute are forbearance, perseverance, restraint, and steadfastness.

The Lord was patient in His dealings with His people, the Israelites (see Isaiah 48:9). Although they often rebelled against Him, He worked patiently to bring them back into His will (see Exodus 34:6).

Since God is patient with us, His people, we should imitate His longsuffering in our dealings with others. The apostle Paul expressed it like this: "Be ye stedfast, unmoveable, always abounding in the work of the Lord" (1 Corinthians 15:58).

Sundials once tracked the inexorable passage of time without the quick, obvious measurement of seconds and minutes. If God seems slow in His response to the world's evil, it's because of His long-suffering nature—His desire for all people to come to repentance (see 2 Peter 3:9).

LORD

"Lord" is one of the most popular names of Jesus in the New Testament, appearing hundreds of times. But the name, from the Greek word *kurios*, is used in two distinct ways in the New Testament.

In Luke 9:57 the word *Lord* used of Jesus is a term of respect, similar to our use of "mister" or "sir" in modern society. A man approached Jesus and told Him, "Lord, I will follow You wherever You go" (NKJV). This man respected Jesus, but he apparently had no intention of committing his life to Him as his spiritual Lord and Master. He did not reply when Jesus told him about the sacrifice He required of His followers (see Luke 9:58).

Even Jesus' disciples sometimes called Him "Lord" in this polite, respectful sense. For example, He once told a parable about the need for people to wait and watch expectantly for His return. Peter approached Him and asked, "Lord, are you telling this parable to us, or to everyone?" (Luke 12:41 NIV).

As Jesus' earthly ministry unfolded, the polite "Lord" that people used of Him was transformed into a declaration of faith in Him as the divine Son of God the Father. This is the sense in which the apostle Paul called Jesus "Lord" in his first letter to the Christians at Corinth: "Be ye stedfast, unmoveable, always abounding in the work of the Lord" (1 Corinthians 15:58).

After His resurrection and ascension, Jesus became the Lord of history, the Lord of the Church, and the Lord of individual believers. When we declare that "Jesus is Lord," we submit to His lordship and crown Him as the supreme ruler over our lives.

LORD ALMIGHTY

See *Almighty God*.

LORD FROM HEAVEN

The apostle Paul compared Jesus' sinlessness with Adam's sin as the first man: "The first man is of the earth, earthy: the second man is the Lord from heaven" (1 Corinthians 15:47). Adam was a being created from the dust of the earth (see Genesis 3:19). Jesus was not a created being; He had always existed with God the Father. He is the "Lord from heaven."

When Jesus completed His mission on earth as our Redeemer, He returned to His Father in heaven (see Acts 1:9–11). He is seated in heaven at God's right hand (see Colossians 3:1), where He intercedes on our behalf with God the Father (see Romans 8:34).

Just as Jesus came into the world from heaven when the time was right (see Galatians 4:4), so He will return one day to bring the earth as we know it to its conclusion, in accordance with God's plan. As believers, we should be looking forward with watchful readiness to that glorious day (see Matthew 25:13). See also *Heaven; Watchfulness.*

A "family portrait" of the Trinity in heaven, showing a nineteenth-century artist's idea of God the Father (right), Jesus Christ (left), and the Holy Spirit (dove above).

THE ONE FROM HEAVEN

Jesus' coming to earth from heaven the first time as well as His return is celebrated in the hymn "One Day" by J. Wilbur Chapman.

One day when heaven was filled with His praises,
One day when sin was as black as could be,
Jesus came forth to be born of a virgin,
Dwelt among men, my example is He!
Living, He loved me; dying, He saved me;
Buried, He carried my sins far away;
Rising, He justified freely forever:
One day He's coming—O glorious day!

Reenactors hold battle flags during a commemoration of the Battle of Crysler's Farm in Ontario, Canada. The flag would precede its soldiers onto the battlefield—much like God leads His people to victory.

LORD GOD ALMIGHTY

See *Almighty God.*

LORD GOD OF ISRAEL

Zacharias, the father of John the Baptist, used this name for God when he broke out in praise at the news that the Messiah would soon be born: "Blessed be the Lord God of Israel; for he hath visited and redeemed his people" (Luke 1:68). Just as the Lord had blessed His people in the past, He was getting ready to fulfill His promise to send a great deliverer.

But this Messiah was more than a gift to Israel alone. Through Him the entire world would be blessed. We as believers proclaim this truth every year at Christmas when we sing this familiar hymn by Isaac Watts:

> Joy to the world! The Lord is come;
> Let earth receive her King;
> Let every heart prepare Him room,
> And heaven and nature sing.

See also *King of Israel.*

LORD GOD OMNIPOTENT

See *Almighty God.*

LORD IS MY BANNER

Moses gave this name to an altar that he built in the wilderness. The altar memorialized an Israelite victory over the Amalekites because of God's miraculous intervention on their behalf. Most modern translations render the Hebrew words for this name (*Jehovah-nissi*) as "The LORD is my Banner" (Exodus 17:15 NIV).

In Bible times, armies fought under a banner or battle flag that identified their tribe or nation. "The Lord Is My Banner" was Moses' way of saying that the Israelites in the wilderness did not need such a flag. The Lord was the banner under which they fought, and He had given the victory.

In a messianic passage in his book, the prophet Isaiah looked forward to the coming of the Messiah, whom he described as an "ensign," or battle flag (see Isaiah 11:10). See also *Ensign for the Nations.*

This world is anything but peaceful—yet God is called *Jehovah-shalom:* "The Lord Is Peace." True and lasting peace will come in God's perfect time.

LORD IS PEACE

God gave Gideon the task of delivering His people from Midianite raiders who were destroying their crops and stealing their livestock. He assured Gideon of His presence and guidance by burning up a sacrificial offering that Gideon had placed on an altar.

This display frightened Gideon. But God showed him that His intentions were peaceful and that Gideon had nothing to fear. With this assurance, Gideon gave God a special name, *Jehovah-shalom*—translated as "The Lord Is Peace" by modern translations—and also applied this name to the altar Gideon had built (see Judges 6:23–24).

"Peace to you and your house" was a common greeting of Bible times, just as we greet people today with "Good morning" or "How are you?" With this divine name, Gideon expressed his confidence that God intended to bless him and to strengthen him for the task to which he had been called.

God extends this same promise to His people today. The psalmist declared, "The LORD will give strength unto his people; the LORD will bless his people with peace" (Psalm 29:11). See also *Lord of Peace*.

LORD OF HOSTS

Zechariah 8 could be called the "Lord of Hosts" chapter of the Bible, since this divine name appears eighteen times in this chapter. Actually, this name is one of the most popular in the entire Bible. It appears about 250 times, particularly in the prophets and the Psalms.

The compound Hebrew word behind this name is *Yahweh-sabaoth*, "Lord of Hosts." *Sabaoth* means "armies" or "hosts." Thus, one meaning of the name is that God is superior to any human army, no matter its number. The Lord often led His people, the Israelites, to victory over a superior military force (see Judges 7:12–25).

Another possible meaning of Lord of Hosts is that God exercises control over all the hosts of heaven—or the heavenly bodies—including the sun, moon, and stars. The psalmist declared, "Praise ye him, all his hosts. Praise ye him, sun and moon: praise him, all ye stars of light" (Psalm 148:2–3).

The name Lord of Sabaoth appears two times in the King James Version of the Bible (see Romans 9:29; James 5:4). These are rendered as "Lord of Hosts" by modern translations. See also *Host of Heaven*.

LORD OF LORDS

This name in the book of Revelation emphasizes Jesus' supreme authority in the end time when He returns to earth in victory over all His enemies (see Revelation 19:16). He is also called "Lord of lords" in two other places in the New Testament (see 1 Timothy 6:15; Revelation 17:14).

As Lord of lords, Jesus will be superior in power and authority to all the rulers of the earth. Some monarchs of the ancient world were worshiped as divine by their subjects. But only Jesus as Lord of lords is worthy of our worship and total commitment.

Here is how the apostle Paul expressed the meaning of this name in his letter to the believers at Philippi: "God also hath highly exalted him, and given him a name which is above every name: that at the name of Jesus every knee should bow, of things in heaven, and things in earth, and things under the earth; and that every tongue should confess that Jesus Christ is Lord, to the glory of God the Father" (Philippians 2:9–11). See also *King of Kings*.

LORD OF PEACE

As the apostle Paul brought his second letter to the Thessalonian believers to a close, he blessed them with a beautiful benediction: "The Lord of peace himself give you peace always by all means. The Lord be with you all" (2 Thessalonians 3:16). He wanted these Christians, who were going through disagreement and turmoil, to experience the peace that Jesus promises to those who abide in Him.

Promises from the Lord of Peace

- "Peace I leave with you, my peace I give unto you" (John 14:27).
- "Being justified by faith, we have peace with God through our Lord Jesus Christ" (Romans 5:1).
- "He is our peace, who hath. . .broken down the middle wall of partition between us" (Ephesians 2:14).
- "The peace of God, which passeth all understanding, shall keep your hearts and minds through Christ Jesus" (Philippians 4:7).

The dictionary defines peace as "freedom from disquieting or oppressive thoughts or emotions." This definition assumes that peace is the *absence* of elements such as conflict or negative feelings. But we as believers know that peace is actually the *presence* of something. This presence is Jesus Christ, who brings peace and inner tranquility to those who have placed their trust in Him. With Jesus as the Lord of peace in our lives, we can have peace even in the midst of troubling circumstances.

When Jesus was born in Bethlehem, the angels celebrated His arrival by declaring "peace, good will toward men" (Luke 2:14). He also told His disciples on one occasion, "Do not let your hearts be troubled. You believe in God; believe also in me" (John 14:1 NIV). We don't have to go around with a troubled look on our faces if the Lord of peace reigns in our hearts.

The apostle Paul referred to Jesus as "our peace" (Ephesians 2:14). The prophet Isaiah called the coming Messiah "The Prince of Peace" (Isaiah 9:6). See also *Lord Is Peace*.

LORD OF THE DEAD AND LIVING

In Paul's letter to the believers at Rome, he reminded them that "Christ both died, and rose, and revived, that he might be Lord both of the dead and living" (Romans 14:9). Jesus is the Lord of the millions of Christians who have lived in the past and who have now passed on to their reward. He is also the Lord of all believers still living who look forward to eternal life with Him in heaven after their days on earth are over.

Whether we are alive or dead, there is no better place to be than in the hands of our loving Lord. See also *Guide unto Death*; *Judge of Quick and Dead*.

LORD OF THE HARVEST

Matthew 9:38 describes the reaction of Jesus to the crowds in the region of Galilee who came to Him for help. He said to His disciples, "Ask the Lord of the harvest...to send out workers into his harvest field" (NIV). His reputation as a healer and teacher had spread throughout the area. He was moved with compassion when He saw their needs. He longed for more workers to help Him as the Lord of the harvest with the spiritual harvest that pressed in from every side.

Jesus had unlimited power, so why didn't He just take care of all these needs Himself rather than ask His disciples to pray for more workers? Perhaps it was because He knew His time on earth was limited. Even if He healed all the sick and taught all those who flocked after Him, others in the same condition would take their place after He was gone. He needed other committed workers, such as His disciples, who would carry on His work after His death, resurrection, and ascension.

Jesus is still in the harvesting business. His work on earth continues through His Church under the power of the Holy Spirit. He still needs workers to gather the harvest. When we get so concerned about the spiritual needs of others that we begin to pray to the Lord of the harvest for more workers, we might just become the answer to our own prayers. See also *Great Commission of Jesus; Harvest.*

> Jesus' "Lord of the harvest" phrase would have been very descriptive to people accustomed to seeing farmers in their fields, personally involved in bringing the good fruit to harvest.

LORD OF THE SABBATH

The Pharisees criticized Jesus for picking grain on the Sabbath to feed Himself and His hungry disciples. He replied, "The sabbath was made for man, and not man for the sabbath: Therefore the Son of man is Lord also of the sabbath" (Mark 2:27–28). Jesus also claimed to be the Lord of the Sabbath when He was criticized for healing people on this sacred day (see Matthew 12:8–14; Luke 6:5–11).

The original law about Sabbath observance stated simply, "Remember the sabbath day, to keep it holy" (Exodus 20:8). The law went on to restrict people from working on this day—the seventh day of the week, or Saturday—in the Jewish religious system.

Over the years the Pharisees had added all sorts of rules or traditions to this simple law about honoring the Sabbath. For example, one

of these restrictions forbade people from traveling more than about one-half of a mile—or a "sabbath day's journey" (Acts 1:12)—from their homes on this day. These silly rules had reduced the Sabbath from a spiritual principle to little more than an external observance.

When Jesus claimed to be the Lord of the Sabbath, He declared that He would not be bound by the human rules about Sabbath observance that the Pharisees had established. To Him, doing good on the Sabbath by healing people was more important than obeying their ritualistic rules (see Matthew 12:12).

Jesus' claim to be the Lord of the Sabbath also placed Him on the same level as God the Father. It was God who had established the Sabbath (see Genesis 2:2–3). Jesus as the agent of creation (see John 1:1–3) was the authority over the Sabbath. The Creator is always greater than anything He has created. See also *Sabbath*.

In this Byzantine mosaic, Jesus heals a man with a withered hand—on the Sabbath day. His claim to be "Lord also of the Sabbath" infuriated the Pharisees.

LORD OUR RIGHTEOUSNESS

The Lord called Himself by this name when He delivered a disturbing message to His people through the prophet Jeremiah. God would punish His people for their sin and idolatry by allowing the Babylonians to overrun the nation of Judah. But He would preserve a remnant of His people who would remain faithful to Him. He would bless them, allow them to return to their homeland, and give them a special name—"THE LORD OUR RIGHTEOUSNESS" (Jeremiah 23:6).

This name of God emphasizes two of the most important truths of the Bible: (1) God demands righteousness of His people, and (2) we are not able to meet this demand on our own. We must look to Him as the Lord Our Righteousness to provide for us what we cannot attain on our own.

DEPENDING ON THE LORD OUR RIGHTEOUSNESS

- "Hear me when I call, O God of my righteousness" (Psalm 4:1).
- "The LORD. . .shall judge the world with righteousness, and the people with his truth" (Psalm 96:13).
- "I the LORD speak righteousness, I declare things that are right" (Isaiah 45:19).
- "This is the heritage of the servants of the LORD, and their righteousness is of me, saith the LORD" (Isaiah 54:17).

The ultimate fulfillment of this verse did not occur until several centuries after Jeremiah's time. God sent His own Son into the world to pay the price for our sin so we could become justified, or righteous, in His sight. This is strictly a gift of His grace, not something we deserve because we measure up to His demands. The apostle Paul expressed it like this: "God made him who had no sin to be sin for us, so that in him we might become the righteousness of God" (2 Corinthians 5:21 NIV). See also *Righteous*; *Righteous Servant*.

LORD OVER ALL

In Romans 10:12 the apostle Paul declared, "There is no difference between the Jew and the Greek: for the same Lord over all is rich unto all that call upon him." The name of Jesus in this verse—"Lord over all"—may seem to express the same idea as Lord of lords. But there is an important distinction between these two names.

The name Lord of lords refers to Jesus' supreme rule throughout the earth at His second coming. The title "Lord over all" declares that every person, whether Jew or Gentile, is on the same level in relationship to Jesus Christ. Paul made it clear in this verse that Jesus does not have one plan of salvation for the Jewish people and another for Greeks, or non-Jews. Every person comes to salvation by accepting by faith the price He paid on the cross to redeem us from our sin.

A large sculpture of a menorah (a seven-armed lamp stand and symbol of the Jewish people) outside the Israeli parliament building in Jerusalem. Though God chose the Israelites as His "special people," He is "Lord over all"—including the Gentiles.

In New Testament times, the Jews looked upon Greeks, or Gentiles, as pagans who were excluded from God's favor. The learned Greeks, in turn, thought of all people who were not Greek citizens as uncultured barbarians. But Paul declared that Jesus wiped out all such distinctions between people. The ground was level at the foot of the cross. Everyone stood before God as wayward sinners who had no hope except the forgiveness they could experience at the feet of the crucified Savior.

Paul also made it clear in this verse that something is required of sinners who want the salvation that Jesus provides. They must "call upon" Jesus the Son. This involves repenting of their sins, confessing Him as Savior, and committing their lives to His lordship. This is the New Testament equivalent of "calling upon" God the Father that runs like a refrain throughout the Old Testament (see Genesis 12:8; 1 Samuel 12:17; Isaiah 55:6). See also *Gentiles*; *Impartiality of God*.

LORD'S CHRIST

A man named Simeon happened to be in the temple in Jerusalem when the infant Jesus was dedicated to God by Mary and Joseph. The Gospel of Luke tells us that it had been revealed to Simeon by the Holy Spirit "that he should not see death, before he had seen the Lord's Christ" (Luke 2:26). He recognized the young child immediately as the Lord's Christ, the Messiah for whom he had been looking.

The word *Lord's* in this verse refers to God the Father. *Christ* derives from the Greek word *christos*, meaning "anointed." Thus, Simeon recognized Jesus as God's Anointed One, whom the Jewish people had been expecting God to send since Old Testament times.

Even though Jesus was just a little baby in His mother's arms, Simeon realized the moment he saw Him that He was the Messiah. This insight came from the Holy Spirit. So all three Persons of the Godhead—God the Father, God the Son, and God the Holy Spirit—were present at this event. This makes Jesus' dedication at the temple one of the most dramatic passages on the Trinity in the entire New Testament. See also *Christ*; *Trinity*.

LORD'S DAY

Sunday is the first day of the week and the Christian day of worship (see Revelation 1:10). The Jewish day of rest and worship fell on Saturday, the last day of the week. But after Christ's resurrection on the first day of the week, Christians adopted this as their normal day of worship (see Acts 20:7). The Christian

Constantine I, also known as Constantine the Great, made Sunday as the Lord's Day the official policy of the Roman Empire.

custom of Sunday worship was already well established when the Roman emperor Constantine instituted the day as a Christian holiday in AD 321. See also *Sabbath*.

Jesus' "last supper" has been depicted countless times in many art styles. In this image, Jesus and eleven of His disciples are shown with halos. Lacking a halo, and holding a money bag, is Judas Iscariot, who will betray the Lord.

LORD'S PRAYER

Jesus taught this model prayer to His disciples in response to their request, "Lord, teach us to pray" (Luke 11:1). The prayer teaches us to approach God reverently (see Matthew 6:9–10), to ask Him to meet our physical needs on a daily basis (see Matthew 6:11), and to seek His forgiveness and protection (see Matthew 6:12–13).

The conclusion of the prayer acknowledges

that God alone is all powerful and is worthy of all honor and glory. As believers, we should live out this part of the prayer each day by seeking to do His will. See also *Prayer*.

LORD'S SUPPER

Jesus' final meal with His disciples on the night before He was arrested and crucified is known as the Memorial Supper, or the Lord's Supper. He and His disciples were in Jerusalem to celebrate the Jewish Passover. It was customary for the Jewish people during this religious holiday to eat a Passover meal to symbolize God's deliverance of His people from Egyptian slavery (see Exodus 12:12–14). Jesus turned this meal into a supper of remembrance to signify His approaching death.

All four Gospels contain an account of the Lord's Supper (see Matthew 26:26–29; Mark 14:22–25; Luke 22:19–20; John 13:1–17). Jesus made it clear to His disciples when they ate and drank together that the bread and wine symbolized His broken and bleeding body. He also charged them to remember His sacrificial death whenever they celebrated this memorial meal in the future.

The Lord's Supper is still observed as a remembrance of Jesus by church groups all over the world, although in different forms ranging from very informal to highly ritualistic. Some other names by which it is known are Communion, Holy Communion, the Mass, the Eucharist, and the Lord's Table. See also *Sacrament*.

LORD'S TABLE

See *Lord's Supper*.

LORD WHO HEALS

Exodus 15:26 is the only place in the Bible where God is called the "Lord who heals." The Lord used this name to describe Himself after He healed the bitter waters at Marah in the wilderness, making it safe for the Israelites to drink.

The healing power of God is often demonstrated in the Old Testament. For example, He healed Miriam of her leprosy (see Numbers 12:10–16). He healed King Hezekiah of Judah of a mysterious illness (see 2 Kings 20:1–6). He healed people in the wilderness after they were bitten by poisonous snakes (see Numbers 21:5–9).

God is also portrayed in the Old Testament as the healer of the ultimate sickness—sin. The psalmist prayed, "Have mercy on me, LORD; heal me, for I have sinned against you" (Psalm 41:4 NIV). See also *Physician*.

LORD WHO SANCTIFIES

God reminded the Israelites through Moses that the Sabbath was a special day that had been set apart, or sanctified, by Him (see Exodus 31:13). His people were to honor this day by resting from their labors and praising Him through acts of worship.

Just as God set apart the seventh day of the week as a memorial to Him, so He sanctified the Israelites as a nation devoted to Him. As the "Lord who sanctifies," He has the right to demand loyalty and commitment from His people. When He sets us apart for His special use, He also empowers us with the strength and ability to serve as His witnesses in the world. See also *Sanctification*.

LORD WILL PROVIDE

Abraham called God by this name and assigned it to the site where he was told to sacrifice his son Isaac as an offering to the Lord (see Genesis 22:14). This was God's way of testing Abraham's faith and obedience.

When Abraham raised a knife to take Isaac's life, God stopped him. Then Abraham noticed a ram that had been trapped in a nearby thicket. He offered this ram as a sacrifice instead of Isaac. It was clear to him that God had provided this ram for this purpose—thus the name *Jehovah-jireh* or "The LORD Will Provide," as rendered by modern translations.

God still delights in providing for His people. Whatever our needs, He will meet them through His love and grace.

The Lord provided a ram as a sacrifice, after Abraham proved his willingness to offer his son Isaac to God.

LOVE OF GOD

The apostle John tells us in one of his New Testament letters that "God is love" (1 John 4:8). This verse indicates that love is more than one of the divine attributes; God is love itself.

This truth about God was first revealed in the Old Testament when He showered His love upon His special people, the Israelites. Moses reminded these people of God's love for them when they were getting ready to enter the land that God had graciously given them. "The Lord did not. . .choose you because you were more numerous than other peoples, for you were the fewest of all peoples," he told them. "But it was because the Lord loved you and kept the oath he swore to your ancestors that he. . .redeemed you from the land of slavery" (Deuteronomy 7:7–8 NIV).

Since God is eternal—He has always existed—and His very nature is love, this means His love for His people has always been. There has never been a time when He did not love His own. He declared this truth to His people through the prophet Jeremiah: "I have loved you with an everlasting love" (Jeremiah 31:3 NIV). Since His eternity has no end, we can rest assured that His love will abide with us throughout this earthly life and the life beyond.

God's love is more than an abstract concept. It assumed human personality in the person of His own Son, Jesus Christ. The supreme demonstration of God's love was Jesus' death on the cross on our behalf: "This is love: not that we loved God, but that he loved us and sent his Son as an atoning sacrifice for our sins" (1 John 4:10 NIV). See also *Agape*; *Grace of God*.

LOVINGKINDNESS OF GOD

See *Grace of God*.

God's Love in the Book of Romans

- "God's love has been poured out into our hearts through the Holy Spirit" (Romans 5:5 NIV).
- "God demonstrates his own love for us in this: While we were still sinners, Christ died for us" (Romans 5:8 NIV).
- "Neither height nor depth, nor anything else in all creation, will be able to separate us from the love of God that is in Christ Jesus our Lord" (Romans 8:39 NIV).

LUCIFER

This word comes from a passage in the book of Isaiah: "How art thou fallen from heaven, O Lucifer, son of the morning! how art thou cut down to the ground, which didst weaken the nations!" (Isaiah 14:12). The word *Lucifer* means "light-bringer." The NIV translates the word as "morning star."

Most modern interpreters believe the prophet was referring to the fall from power of the king of Babylon, the most powerful ruler of Isaiah's time. But some interpreters once believed that *Lucifer* referred to Satan. According to an ancient Jewish myth, Lucifer was once an angel. He led other angels in heaven to rebel against the Lord, and all of them were cast out of heaven.

These are the so-called "fallen angels" that Jewish scholars cited to explain the origin of evil in the world. But the Bible gives us no smooth and easy explanation for evil and how it came to be. All we know for sure is that much of it is due to human sin, and that God will triumph over all the forces of evil in the end time (see Revelation 19:17–20). See also *Evil*.

The Fall of Lucifer by French engraver Gustave Doré is an illustration for an edition of John Milton's epic poem *Paradise Lost*.

LYRE

See *Harp*.

M

MAGI

See *Wise Men*.

King Saul, with hand to head, is stunned by the news delivered by the spirit of the deceased prophet Samuel: "To morrow shalt thou and thy sons be with me"—meaning, "dead."

MAGIC AND DIVINATION

Magic and divination were prominent in the pagan religious systems of Bible times. But God prohibited the Israelites from participating in these practices. In the book of Deuteronomy, He declared: "There shall not be found among you any one. . .that useth divination, or an observer of times, or an enchanter, or a witch. Or a charmer, or a consulter with familiar spirits, or a wizard, or a necromancer" (Deuteronomy 18:10–11). Eight different types of magic are mentioned in this passage.

Divination. This term refers to attempts to control evil spirits, to penetrate the mysteries of the universe, or to foretell the future by using magical acts, pronouncing superstitious incantations, or interpreting natural signs. Today we refer to such practices as "black magic" or the occult.

Observer of times. The Hebrew word behind "observer of times" is translated by the NIV as one who practices "sorcery." Sorcerers often made their predictions by "reading" the clouds in the sky. The practitioners of this art specialized in distinguishing lucky days from unlucky days and recommending to people the best times to plant crops, make a purchase, take a trip, etc.

Enchanter. The NIV translates the Hebrew word behind "enchanter" as one who "interprets omens." This person predicted the future or told people's fortunes by reading certain signs. One way of doing this was by using a magic cup. The cup of Joseph may have been such a cup (see Genesis 44:2). Another method was to interpret the pattern formed by birds in flight. The art of enchantment is referred to several times in the Old Testament (see Leviticus 19:26; Numbers 23:23; 24:1; 2 Kings 17:17; 21:6; 2 Chronicles 33:6).

Witch. A witch was a person who cast spells or used other supernatural "black magic" tricks to commit evil or wicked acts. The Hebrew word for "witch" or "witchcraft" is used to describe Jezebel and her associates who promoted the worship of the false god Baal throughout the Northern Kingdom during the reign of King Ahab (see 2 Kings 9:22).

Charmer. The Hebrew word behind "charmer" is translated by the NIV as one who "casts spells." It is not clear how a charmer differed from a witch. Some interpreters believe charmers practiced their craft by tying magic knots or using a magic ring.

Consulter with familiar spirits. A practitioner of this form of magic claimed to be able to call up the spirits or ghosts of dead people. They did this at the request of friends or loved ones who sought advice or guidance from the deceased.

King Saul sought out "a woman that hath a familiar spirit" (1 Samuel 28:7) when he wanted to communicate with the prophet Samuel, who had died. This woman was shocked when the spirit of Samuel actually appeared and gave the king some bad news about his forthcoming battle with the Philistines (see 1 Samuel 28:11–19). Her surprise indicates that these consulters with familiar spirits probably used trickery—perhaps ventriloquism—to convince people that they were talking with their departed friends and loved ones.

Wizard. The Hebrew word behind "wizard" means "the knowing one." Thus, a wizard may have been an expert in all the magical tricks associated with sorcery and divination.

Necromancer. The NIV translates the Hebrew word behind "necromancer" as one "who consults the dead." This practitioner of the occult apparently claimed to be able to conjure up the spirits of the dead, just like a consulter with familiar spirits. In addition, necromancers may have used corpses to foretell the future. Some interpreters believe they "read" dead people's bones or veins to determine the future of the survivors of the deceased.

MAGNIFICAT

The virgin Mary's song of praise upon being greeted by her relative Elizabeth a few months before Jesus was born (see Luke 1:46–55) is known as the Magnificat. In Latin this song begins with the word *magnificat,*

Mary's song of praise—the "Magnificat"—appears in several languages on the walls of the Church of the Visitation in Ein Karem, Israel. The site is where tradition says Mary recited her song.

meaning "magnify." Mary began her song by declaring, "My soul doth magnify the Lord." She went on to praise the Lord for remembering "the lowliness of his servant" (NRSV) and for keeping His promise to bless Abraham and his descendants.

Mary's song is similar to the song of Hannah in the Old Testament. Hannah sang praises to God for blessing her with a son after she had been unable to bear children (see 1 Samuel 2:1–10). She gave birth to Samuel, one of the greatest prophets of the Old Testament. See also *Annunciation*; *Mary*.

MAJESTY IN THE HEAVENS

See *Majesty on High*.

MAJESTY ON HIGH

The author of Hebrews said of Jesus, "When he had by himself purged our sins, [he] sat down on the right hand of the Majesty on high" (Hebrews 1:3). This verse refers to the ascension of Jesus. After His resurrection He

spent forty days among His followers. Then He was "taken up" into heaven and "a cloud received him out of their sight" (Acts 1:9). Now in heaven, He is seated at the right hand of God His Father (see Ephesians 1:20; 1 Peter 3:22)—or, as the writer of Hebrews put it, next to the "Majesty on high."

This name of God is a poetic way of referring to His power and glory. He is incomparable in His excellence, magnificence, and splendor. This name appears only here in the Bible. The writer of Hebrews also spoke of God as the "Majesty in the heavens" (Hebrews 8:1). See also *Glory of God*; *Most High*; *Most High God*.

MAKER

Eliphaz the Temanite, one of Job's three friends, used this name for God when he asked Job: "Shall mortal man be more just than God? shall a man be more pure than his maker?" (Job 4:17). Job had accused God of causing his suffering when he, Job, had done nothing wrong. To Eliphaz, a mere mortal

---

GOD'S MAJESTY IN THE PSALMS

- "The voice of the LORD is powerful; the voice of the LORD is full of majesty" (Psalm 29:4).
- "Honour and majesty are before him: strength and beauty are in his sanctuary" (Psalm 96:6).
- "O LORD my God, thou art very great; thou art clothed with honour and majesty" (Psalm 104:1).
- "To make known to the sons of men his mighty acts; and the glorious majesty of his kingdom" (Psalm 145:12).

Made in God's image, humans are able to make things from what God has already created. But He is the ultimate "maker" in the sense of creating from nothing.

such as Job had no right to question the actions of his maker, the Immortal One who did not have to explain His actions to anyone.

God's role as our maker is similar to His acts as our Creator and provider. The psalmist declared, "Know ye that the LORD he is God: it is he that hath made us, and not we ourselves; we are his people, and the sheep of his pasture" (Psalm 100:3). See also *Creator; Potter.*

MAN

See *Humankind.*

MAN APPROVED OF GOD

See *Flesh.*

MAN OF GOD'S RIGHT HAND

In Psalm 80:17 the psalmist asked God the Father to strengthen the One whom He had selected for a special task: "Let thy hand be upon the man of thy right hand, upon the son of man whom thou madest strong for thyself." This "man of God's right hand" refers to Jesus, the Messiah and the agent of God's redemption in the world.

A person who sat at the right side of a king in Bible times was the most important official in the royal court. He was often the second in command who acted as the chief administrator of the king's affairs. Even today, a leader's most important and trusted aide is often referred to as his "right-hand man."

As the man of God's right hand, Jesus came into the world as the dispenser of divine justice and forgiveness. God the Father delegated to Him the task of restoring sinful humankind to fellowship with Him through His death on the cross. When this task was accomplished, the Father summoned His Son back to heaven, where He is seated in the place of authority at His right hand (see Ephesians 1:20).

You've probably heard the old saying, "Don't send a boy to do a man's job." Aren't you glad that Jesus was man enough, and faithful enough, and determined enough, and prayerful enough to accomplish the task that His Father sent Him to do? No person has ever been sent on a more important mission, and He handled it perfectly as the man of God's right hand.

JESUS AT HIS FATHER'S RIGHT HAND

- "Christ Jesus who died. . .is at the right hand of God and is also interceding for us" (Romans 8:34 NIV).
- "Set your hearts on things above, where Christ is, seated at the right hand of God" (Colossians 3:1 NIV).
- "[Christ] has gone into heaven and is at God's right hand—with angels, authorities and powers in submission to him" (1 Peter 3:22 NIV).

MAN OF LAWLESSNESS

See *Satan.*

MAN OF SIN

See *Satan.*

MAN OF SORROWS

This name of Jesus comes from the prophet Isaiah, who said of the coming Messiah: "He is despised and rejected of men; a man of sorrows, and acquainted with grief" (Isaiah

53:3). In our society the word *sorrow* or *sorrows* suggests a state of deep remorse or regret over the loss of something or someone who is highly loved and esteemed. For example, we might say about a couple who have lost a child: "They are still in sorrow a year after the death."

However, when interpreting this name of Jesus in Isaiah's prophecy—"man of sorrows"—an alternative translation to this modern definition might be in order. Perhaps, as the NRSV suggests, Jesus was a man of suffering more than a man of sorrows.

Christ was not a person who was immersed in a state of remorse or regret over a loss that He had experienced. He was an overcomer—a victorious person—in spite of the problems He faced during His earthly ministry. Even His suffering that led to His death on the cross was swallowed up in victory when He drew His last breath and declared, "It is finished" (John 19:30). He had accomplished the purpose for which He had been sent into the world.

There is no doubt that Jesus' suffering on the cross was real. So is the pain that we as believers feel when we are ridiculed for our faith by an unbelieving world. But this should not drive us to sorrow or despair. The man of suffering has already "borne our griefs, and carried our sorrows" (Isaiah 53:4) by dying in our place on the cross. He invites us to cast our cares upon Him during each day of our earthly journey.

Our inspiration for doing so is Jesus Himself, "who for the joy that was set before him endured the cross, despising the shame, and is set down at the right hand of the throne of God" (Hebrews 12:2). See also *Righteous Servant*.

Tears dot the cheeks of Jesus, wearing the crown of thorns, in a fifteenth-century painting by Dieric Bouts.

MAN WHOM GOD ORDAINED

See *Foreordained before the Foundation of the World*.

MARY

A peasant girl from Nazareth named Mary became the earthly mother of Jesus, God's Son. She was engaged to Joseph when an angel informed her that she had been divinely chosen to give birth to the Messiah. When Mary protested that she was a virgin, the angel

Mary may be one of the most depicted women in all forms of art, and rightfully so—she was the mother of the most important Child in human history.

assured her that her conception would come about through the action of the Holy Spirit (see Luke 1:28–37).

After the account of Jesus' birth to Mary and Joseph in the Gospel of Luke, she is mentioned only a few times during Jesus' earthly ministry. Mary witnessed Jesus' first miracle, the turning of water into wine at a wedding feast (see John 2:3). She was present at the cross when Jesus commended her to the care of His disciple John (see John 19:25–27).

Some church groups claim that Mary was a perpetual virgin. But the Gospels make it clear that Jesus had four brothers—technically, half brothers—who were born to Mary and Joseph after the birth of Jesus, their firstborn (see Matthew 13:55–56; Luke 2:7). Many legends about Mary were popularized in the early years of the church, but these are not supported by any factual evidence. See also *Son of Mary*.

MASS

See *Lord's Supper*.

MASTER

This name that Jesus used of Himself appears in the famous "woe" chapter of Matthew's Gospel (chapter 23) in which He condemned the Pharisees. He was particularly critical of their hypocrisy and religious pride. They enjoyed being greeted in the streets with titles that recognized them for their learning and expertise in the Jewish law. But Jesus declared that He as God's Son was the only person who deserved the title of Master. "Neither be ye called masters," He told them, "for one is your Master, even Christ" (Matthew 23:10).

The title Master in this verse is a derivative of a Greek word that means "commander" or "ruler." Modern translations sometimes render this word as "teacher." But Jesus was claiming to be more than a teacher. He made it clear to His disciples and others who were listening that He had the right to serve as the supreme authority in their lives.

In New Testament times, slave owners were sometimes called "masters" (Colossians 4:1), implying their supreme control over every aspect of their slaves' lives. As believers, we are also subject to the will of our Master, the Lord Jesus, who has redeemed us for His service. See also *Good Master; Teacher Come from God*.

MAUNDY THURSDAY

The Thursday of Holy Week is commemorated by many Christian groups with the observance of the Lord's Supper. The term comes from a Latin word meaning "commandment." On the Thursday night just before He was arrested, Jesus instituted the Lord's Supper with His disciples. "A new command I give you," He told them, "love one another. As I have loved you, so you must love one another" (John 13:34 NIV). See also *Easter; Holy Week*.

MEAL OFFERING

See *Sacrificial Offerings.*

MEAT OFFERING

See *Sacrificial Offerings.*

MEDIATOR

A mediator is a person who serves as a "middleman" or "go-between" to bring two opposing parties together. For example, a mediator is often used in labor disputes. Both labor and management leaders agree to abide by the decision of an independent mediator. This avoids the expense and hassle of a lawsuit and brings a quick resolution to the problem.

According to the apostle Paul, Jesus also fills the role of spiritual "mediator" in the world. He is the middleman or go-between who reconciles God to humankind: "There is one God, and one mediator between God and men, the man Christ Jesus" (1 Timothy 2:5).

Humans by nature are sinners. In our sinful state, we are estranged from a holy God, who will not tolerate anything that is unholy or unclean. But Jesus eliminated this gap

US President Jimmy Carter served as a mediator between Egypt and Israel—represented by President Anwar Sadat (left) and Prime Minister Menachem Begin (right)—during the Camp David negotiations of 1978. The accord helped to normalize relations between the two nations.

between God and people by sacrificing His life on the cross for our sins and purchasing our forgiveness. Cleansed of our sin through His blood, we now have fellowship with God the Father. We have been reconciled to God through Jesus' work as our mediator.

Jesus is the perfect mediator between God and humankind because He had both divine and human attributes. As God, He understood what God the Father demanded of people in order to be acceptable in His sight. As a man, He realized the desperate situation of sinful human beings. He was the God-man who was able to bring these two opposites together in a way that brought glory to God and gave us access to His blessings and His eternal presence.

Jesus our mediator also expects His followers to serve as "middlemen" for others in a sinful world. Our job as believers is to point others to Jesus Christ, who wants everyone to enjoy fellowship with God the Father. The apostle Paul expressed it like this: "All things are of God, who hath reconciled us to himself by Jesus Christ, and hath given to us the ministry of reconciliation" (2 Corinthians 5:18). See also *Mediator of the New Testament; Propitiation for Our Sins.*

MEDIATOR OF A BETTER COVENANT

See *Mediator of the New Testament.*

MEDIATOR OF THE NEW TESTAMENT

The writer of Hebrews referred to Jesus as the "mediator of the new testament" (Hebrews 9:15). *Testament* is another word for covenant or agreement. Thus the new testament mentioned here is the new covenant based on the sacrificial death of Christ that God established with His people. Jesus is the one who fulfills the terms of this covenant.

The first covenant of God with His people was formalized in Old Testament times. God agreed to bless the Israelites and serve as their guide and protector if they would follow and worship Him. But the Jewish people broke this covenant time and time again as they fell into rebellion and idolatry.

Finally, God promised through the prophet Jeremiah that He would establish a new covenant with His people. This would be a spiritual covenant written on their hearts rather than a covenant of law (see Jeremiah 31:31–34). This covenant would accomplish for God's people what the old covenant had failed to do—bring them forgiveness and give them a new understanding of God the Father.

On the night before His crucifixion, Jesus declared that He was implementing this new covenant that had been promised by His Father. This covenant would be based on His blood that would be shed to provide redemption and forgiveness of sin for God's people (see Matthew 26:28).

Unlike the old covenant, this new covenant has never been replaced. The mediator of the new covenant has promised that those who belong to Him will enjoy eternal life with Him in heaven. We as believers are willing to bet our lives that He will deliver on His promise.

In the book of Hebrews, Jesus is also called the "mediator of a better covenant" (Hebrews 8:6) and the "surety of a better testament" (Hebrews 7:22). These names express basically the same idea as mediator of the new testament. See also *Covenant of the People*; *Mediator*; *New Covenant*.

MEEKNESS

A spirit of kindness, gentleness, and humility that was commended by Jesus in His Sermon on the Mount: "Blessed are the meek, for they will inherit the earth" (Matthew 5:5 NIV). He modeled this spirit during His earthly ministry (see Matthew 11:29) and taught His followers that true greatness consisted of serving others rather than being served. The apostle Paul cited meekness as one of the fruits of the Spirit (see Galatians 5:22–23). See also *Humility*.

MEGIDDO

See *Armageddon*.

MELCHISEDEC

See *High Priest after the Order of Melchisedec*.

MEMORIAL SUPPER

See *Lord's Supper*.

MERCIFUL AND FAITHFUL HIGH PRIEST

See *Great High Priest*.

MERCY OF GOD

God's mercy is an attribute that is very similar to His grace. But while grace leads Him to forgive the guilty, His mercy is lavished on the poor and helpless. For example, when Joseph arrived in Egypt as a helpless slave, "The LORD was with [him], and shewed him mercy" (Genesis 39:21). Other translations render the Hebrew word behind "mercy" as "kindness" or "compassion."

This attribute of God is mentioned often in the Psalms. When the psalmists thought about their human weakness in comparison to the unlimited strength and compassion of the Lord, they often thanked Him for His mercy (see sidebar).

Jesus told a parable about a traveler who was beaten by thieves and left by the side of the road to die. Two religious professionals saw the man but walked around him and continued on their way. Then a Samaritan—a member of a race of half-breed Jews despised by the pure-blooded Jews—happened by. He stopped and took care of the helpless man. It was clear which one of these three was the traveler's real neighbor: "The one who had

The story of the "good Samaritan" in a relief in a Belgian church. The kindly Samaritan's mercy on a wounded Jew pictures God's goodness to all people.

mercy on him" (Luke 10:37 NIV). See also *Father of Mercies*; *Grace of God*.

GOD'S MERCY IN THE PSALMS

- "Goodness and mercy shall follow me all the days of my life" (Psalm 23:6).
- "Have mercy upon me, O LORD, for I am in trouble" (Psalm 31:9).
- "When I said, My foot slippeth; thy mercy, O LORD, held me up" (Psalm 94:18).
- "Help me, O LORD my God: O save me according to thy mercy" (Psalm 109:26).

MESSENGER OF THE COVENANT

Jesus not only established the new covenant that God had promised for His people (see *Mediator of the New Testament*), but He was also the messenger whom God sent to announce that this new covenant was now a reality. In a famous messianic passage, the prophet Malachi declared that Jesus the Messiah would come as the "messenger of the covenant" (Malachi 3:1).

Throughout the history of Israel, God had sent many agents to deliver His message to His people. The greatest of His messengers were the prophets, who often delivered an unpopular message of divine judgment against the nation's sin and rebellion. But Jesus was the divine messenger who stood out above all the others. He was the messenger of the covenant of grace that God the Father had established with a sinful world.

About seven hundred years before Jesus was born, the prophet Isaiah announced that God the Father would send His servant with a message of joy and comfort for all people. At the beginning of His public ministry, Jesus identified with this prophecy. He stood in the synagogue in His hometown of Nazareth and read these words from Isaiah: "The Spirit of the Lord is on me, because he has anointed me to proclaim good news to the poor. He has sent me to proclaim freedom for the prisoners and recovery of sight for the blind, to set the oppressed free, to proclaim the year of the Lord's favor" (Luke 4:18–19 NIV). Then He declared, "Today this scripture is fulfilled in your hearing" (Luke 4:21 NIV).

For more than three years, Jesus served as the faithful messenger of God's new covenant of grace that He had been sent to establish. Then His earthly ministry ended with His death on the cross and His glorious resurrection. God's plan from the beginning was that His messenger would eventually become the message—the good news about God's love for sinners known as the Gospel. See also *Covenant of the People*.

MESSIAH

One of the most interesting accounts in the New Testament is Jesus' encounter with the Samaritan woman at the well (see John 4:5–26). Jesus stirred her curiosity about the promised Messiah, so she told Him, "I know that Messiah (called Christ) is coming. When he comes, he will explain everything to us" (John 4:25 NIV). Then Jesus told her plainly, "I, the one speaking to you—I am he" (John 4:26 NIV).

The word *Messiah* is rendered by the King James Version as "Messias," the Greek form of the term. *Messias* appears only twice in the KJV—here in John 4:25 and in John 1:41, where Andrew told his brother, Simon Peter, "We have found the Messias." The

Dozens of biblical names and titles apply to Jesus, including "Messiah"—the anointed or chosen one of God.

word *Messiah* appears more often in modern versions of the Bible as a translation of the Greek word *Christos*, meaning "anointed one" (see Matthew 23:10; Mark 9:41; Luke 24:46 NIV).

Jesus discouraged others, even His disciples, from referring to Him by this title (see Matthew 16:20). The Jewish people expected the Messiah to be a political and military deliverer who would throw off the yoke of Rome and restore the fortunes of Israel. Jesus had come into the world as a spiritual Messiah, so He avoided this name because it would lead the people to expect Him to be something He was not.

While the word *Messiah* is rare in the New Testament, the concept appears on almost every page of the New Testament writings. The Greek term *Christos*, rendered as "Christ," means "anointed" or "anointed one"—a word referring to the Messiah or God's chosen one.

When the Messiah is mentioned in the Old Testament, the word itself is seldom used. Usually this leader who was to come is described as a "Prince" (Daniel 8:25), "ruler" (Micah 5:2), or "servant" (Isaiah 53:11). The rare exception is the book of Daniel, which contains a reference to "Messiah the Prince" (Daniel 9:25). See also *Anointed One*; *Chosen of God*; *Messianic Secret of Jesus*.

MESSIANIC PROPHECIES

See *Prophecies about Christ*.

MESSIANIC SECRET OF JESUS

During His ministry Jesus seldom referred to Himself as the Messiah. He even told His disciples not to call Him by this name (see Mark 8:30). His avoidance of the "M-word" is called the "messianic secret."

For hundreds of years the Jewish people had been expecting the Lord to send a Messiah to His people. They thought this ruler would be a military hero who would defeat their enemies and restore the glory of their nation. But Jesus did not fulfill these popular expectations; He came as a spiritual Savior or Messiah whose mission was to deliver the people from their sins. So He deliberately avoided the Messiah label to keep the people from making Him into something He was not. See also *Anointed One*; *Christ*; *Messiah*.

METAPHORS FOR GOD

See *Imagery Used of God*.

MICHAEL

See *Angels*.

MIDDLE WALL OF PARTITION

See *Veil of the Temple*.

MIGHTY GOD

See *Almighty God*.

MIGHTY ONE OF ISRAEL

See *Almighty God*.

MIGHTY ONE OF JACOB

This name of God appears only two times in the Bible, both times in the book of Isaiah (see Isaiah 49:26; 60:16). In these two passages, "Jacob" is a poetic way of referring to the nation of Israel. The descendants of Jacob's twelve sons developed into the twelve tribes of Israel. Jacob himself was also known as "Israel," a name given to him by the Lord after his struggle with God at Peniel (see Genesis 32:28; 35:10).

Three similar divine names that appear in the Old Testament are "God of Jacob" (2 Samuel 23:1), "Holy One of Jacob" (Isaiah 29:23), and "King of Jacob" (Isaiah 41:21). See also *Jacob*; *Star Out of Jacob*.

Jacob wrestles with a mysterious man he later identifies as God. Jacob demands a blessing from the mighty visitor—and gets it (see Genesis 32).

MILLENNIUM

This term applies to the period of one thousand years described in Revelation 20:1–8. Opinions vary on how to interpret this period. Premillennialists expect a literal reign of one thousand years by Christ on earth after His return. Postmillennialists believe that one thousand years of peace will precede Christ's second coming, during which time much of the world will be converted. While believing in the Lord's return, amillennialists view Christ's millennial reign in a spiritual sense. See also *Eschatology*; *Rapture*.

MINISTER OF THE TRUE TABERNACLE

One of the major themes of the book of Hebrews is the supremacy of Christ's priesthood to the Old Testament sacrificial system. In Hebrews 8:1–2 the writer of this book claims that the priesthood established during Aaron's time (see Exodus 40:12–15) was only a shadow of the eternal priesthood provided for believers in heaven. Jesus is the priest of the heavenly sanctuary that God has established for His people; He is the "minister of the true tabernacle."

The most holy place in the Jewish religious system was the holy of holies in the tabernacle or temple. This inner sanctuary represented God's holy and awesome presence. Only the high priest could enter this section of the temple, and he could do so only once a year on the day of atonement. On this special occasion, he offered sacrifice first for his own sins and then for the sins of the people (see Leviticus 16:1–6).

When Jesus died on the cross, the heavy veil or curtain that sealed off this section of the temple was torn from top to bottom (see Matthew 27:50–51). This symbolized that all people now had access to God's presence and forgiveness through the sacrificial death of His Son.

Jesus is now the perfect priest or minister of the true tabernacle in heaven. Here He conducts His ministry of intercession for all believers. "He is able to save completely those who come to God through him," the writer of Hebrews declared, "because he always lives to intercede for them" (Hebrews 7:25 NIV). See *Holy of Holies; Tabernacle.*

MIRACLES

In the biblical sense, a miracle is an event so unexpected and so unbelievable that we attribute it to God and His unlimited power. When we see something like this, we exclaim with the psalmist, "The LORD has done this, and it is marvelous in our eyes" (Psalm 118:23 NIV). One interesting thing about the word *miracle* is that it is used sparingly in the Bible. But other words that mean essentially the same thing appear often. These include "signs" (John 2:11 NIV), "wonders" (Psalm 136:3–4 NIV), and "works" (Psalm 92:5 NIV).

In the Old Testament, God often worked miracles to protect His special people, the Israelites. The ten plagues that He sent upon the Egyptians were supernatural intrusions into the natural order. He used these miracles to convince the pharaoh to release the Israelites from slavery (see Exodus 7–12). While His people were in the wilderness, He provided food and water to keep them alive (see Exodus 16:15–35; 17:1–6).

At a later time in Israel's history, the Lord spoke through miracles to authenticate the mission and message of the prophet Elijah. Divine miracles gave the prophet a victory over the prophets of Baal (see 1 Kings 18:21–39) and sustained him while he was hiding in the wilderness from the wrath of Jezebel (see 1 Kings 18:4–8).

But the greatest miracles in the Bible occurred during the ministry of Jesus (see sidebar). He did not perform His miracles to dazzle the crowds or prove His authority as God's Son. His miracles declared that the kingdom of God had arrived, and it was being fulfilled in His mission of compassion

and redemption. "The blind receive sight," He said, "the lame walk, those who have leprosy are cleansed, the deaf hear, the dead are raised, and the good news is proclaimed to the poor" (Matthew 11:5 NIV).

In addition to His miracles of healing, Jesus also demonstrated through His mighty works that He was Lord over nature (see Mark 4:35–41) and death (see John 11:1–44). His miraculous resurrection after His death on the cross shows that death is not the final word for those who accept Him as Lord and Savior.

Jesus' ministry of miracles continued throughout the early years of the church. The miracles of the apostle Peter were done in the name of Jesus and were demonstrations of God's salvation (see Acts 3:1–16; 9:36–42).

Jesus feeds five thousand men (in addition to women and children) with one boy's lunch of five loaves of bread and two fish.

ALL THE MIRACLES OF JESUS

		Matthew	Mark	Luke	John
1.	Water into wine at Cana				2:1–11
2.	A royal official's son healed at Capernaum				4:46–54
3.	Miraculous catch of fish on Lake Galilee			5:1–11	
4.	A demon-possessed man healed at Capernaum		1:21–26	4:31–35	
5.	Peter's mother-in-law healed at Capernaum	8:14–15	1:29–31	4:38–39	
6.	A leper healed	8:1–4	1:40–45	5:12–16	
7.	A paralyzed man healed at Capernaum	9:1–8	2:1–12	5:17–26	
8.	A lame man healed on the Sabbath at Jerusalem				5:1–15
9.	A man's paralyzed hand healed on the Sabbath	12:9–14	3:1–6	6:6–11	
10.	A centurion's slave healed at Capernaum	8:5–13		7:1–10	
11.	A widow's son raised from the dead at Nain			7:11–17	
12.	A demon-possessed blind man healed	12:22–24			
13.	Stilling of the storm on Lake Galilee	8:18–27	4:35–41	8:22–25	
14.	A wild man among the tombs healed	8:28–34	5:1–20	8:26–39	
15.	Jairus's daughter raised from the dead	9:18–26	5:21–43	8:40–56	
16.	A woman with a hemorrhage healed	9:20–22	5:24–34	8:43–48	
17.	Two blind men healed	9:27–31			
18.	A demon-possessed deaf man healed	9:32–34			
19.	Feeding of the five thousand (Jews)	14:13–21	6:30–44	9:10–17	6:1–15
20.	Walking on the waters of Lake Galilee	14:22–36	6:45–51		6:16–21
21.	The daughter of a Gentile woman healed near Tyre	15:21–28	7:24–30		
22.	A deaf man healed in Gentile territory		7:31–37		
23.	Feeding of the four thousand (Gentiles)	15:29–38	8:1–10		
24.	A blind man healed at Bethsaida		8:22–26		
25.	Transfiguration of Jesus before His disciples	17:1–8	9:2–8	9:28–36	
26.	A demon-possessed boy healed	17:14–21	9:14–29	9:37–42	
27.	Production of a coin for the temple tax at Capernaum	17:24–27			
28.	A man blind from birth healed at Jerusalem				9:1–38
29.	A woman with a crooked back healed			13:10–17	
30.	A man whose body was swollen with fluid healed			14:1–6	
31.	Lazarus raised from the dead at Bethany				11:32–44
32.	Ten lepers healed			17:11–19	
33.	Two blind men/blind Bartimaeus healed at Jericho	20:29–34	10:46–52	18:35–43	
34.	Withering of a fig tree near Jerusalem	21:18–19	11:12–14		
35.	Healing of the ear of Malchus at Jerusalem			22:49–51	
36.	Resurrection of Jesus at Jerusalem	28:1–8	16:1–8	24:1–8	20:1–18
37.	Another miraculous catch of fish at Lake Galilee				21:1–14
38.	Ascension of Jesus to the Father near Jerusalem			24:44–53	

MISSIONS

Jesus made it clear that the process of carrying out His Great Commission to disciple and teach all peoples was one of the purposes of the Church. Even in the Old Testament, Abraham was called to be a blessing to all nations (see Genesis 12:1–3), and Jonah was sent by the Lord to preach to the pagan citizens of Nineveh (see Jonah 1:2). Missions are prompted by God's love (see John 3:16) and humankind's lost condition (see Romans 3:9–23).

Believers are equipped for the task of missions by the Holy Spirit's presence (see Acts 1:8), the Word of God (see Romans 10:14–15), and the power of prayer (see Acts 13:1–4). Christ's followers are to evangelize all nations, baptize believers, and teach His commands (see Matthew 28:19–20). See also *Church*; *Great Commission of Jesus*.

MONOTHEISM

The belief in one—and only one—supreme God is known as monotheism, in contrast to polytheism, or the worship of several gods. This concept was first revealed to God's chosen people, the Israelites. One of their oldest confessions of faith known as the Shema (pronounced shih MAH) declared, "Hear, O Israel: the LORD our God, the LORD is one" (Deuteronomy 6:4 NIV). This was a remarkable insight, since all the nations surrounding Israel worshiped many gods.

This Jewish view of one supreme God was eventually adopted by two other world religions—Christianity and Islam. But of these three, only Christianity declares that God's divine substance is expressed in three different modes—God the Father, God the Son, and God the Holy Spirit. Thus, Christianity is both monotheistic and trinitarian— and it sees no contradiction between these two truths. See also *Polytheism*; *Trinity*.

MOON

This heavenly body or satellite revolves around the earth. It is referred to as the "lesser light" in the account of God's creation of the world (see Genesis 1:16). The Jewish calendar was based on the cycles of the moon. Each new moon marked the beginning of a new month, and its arrival was celebrated with special sacrifices (see Numbers 28:11–15; Psalm 81:3).

To the Israelites the moon and the sun symbolized God's permanence and eternity. The psalmist said of the Lord, "May he endure as long as the sun, as long as the moon, through all generations" (Psalm 72:5 NIV). The moon was worshiped under various names by pagan peoples, but God forbade this practice by His people (see Deuteronomy 4:19). See also *Astrology*; *Stars*; *Sun*.

This photograph shows how the moon only reflects the light of the sun, as the "lesser light" of God's creation in Genesis 1.

MORNING STAR

See *Bright and Morning Star.*

MOSES

This great lawgiver and prophet of Israel led the Israelites out of Egyptian slavery. Moses was recruited by the Lord for this great task when He appeared to Him in a burning bush on Mount Sinai (see Exodus 3:2–3). Moses protested that he was not qualified for the task, but God promised him, "I will be with you" (Exodus 3:12 NIV).

Under Moses' leadership, the Israelites left Egypt after God convinced the Egyptian pharaoh through many signs and wonders to let the people go. Moses led them for forty years through the wilderness toward Canaan, the land that God had promised to Abraham and his descendants.

While in the wilderness, Moses received the Ten Commandments and other parts of the Mosaic Law (see Exodus 20:1–24), exhorted the people to remain faithful to God, built the tabernacle at God's command (see Exodus 36–40), and sent spies to investigate Canaan (see Numbers 13). He impatiently struck a rock to produce water at Kadesh, a sin that led God to deny his entrance into the promised land (see Numbers 20:1–13).

Although he wasn't perfect, Moses is one of the best examples in the Bible of godly leadership. The people were often resentful of his authority. But he refused to allow their stubborn attitude to turn him away from the task that God had called him to do. When the time came for him to step aside, he handed the reins of leadership to his young associate, Joshua, whom he had trained for the job (see Deuteronomy 34:9). The Israelites mourned for thirty days when Moses died (see Deuteronomy 34:8). See

Moses makes a mistake by striking, rather than speaking, to a rock. The people of Israel still get their miraculous water from the rock—but God denies Moses entry into the promised land.

also *Exodus from Egypt; Spirit That Was upon Moses.*

MOST HIGH

This name of God appears in a psalm that David wrote after he was delivered from King Saul and others who were trying to kill him (see 2 Samuel 22:1; Psalm 18). David compared God's ability to save to the power that is unleashed during a severe thunderstorm: "The LORD thundered from heaven, and the most High uttered his voice" (2 Samuel 22:14). To David, the rolling thunder was

OUR VISION OF THE MOST HIGH

An ancient Irish hymn entitled "Be Thou My Vision" declares that God as the Most High should be the inspiration of our lives.

Be thou my vision, O Lord of my heart;
Naught be all else to me, save that
    Thou art:
Thou my best thought, by day or by
    night,
Walking or sleeping, Thy presence my
    light.

like God's voice from heaven.

The book of Psalms refers frequently to God as the "most high" (Psalms 9:2; 73:11; 107:11). The prophet Daniel also used this name (see Daniel 4:24; 7:18). In his long speech in the New Testament, Stephen declared that "the most High dwelleth not in temples made with hands" (Acts 7:48).

There is nothing in this world greater than the Most High. He deserves our deepest loyalty and most fervent praise. See also *Most High God*; *Power of the Highest*.

MOST HIGH GOD

Both Abraham and Melchisedec worshiped and served the same God—the "most high God"—the One in whose name Melchisedec blessed Abraham (see Genesis 14:18–19). This God had given Abraham victory over a coalition of Canaanite kings (see Genesis 14:1–24). To express his thanks to God, Abraham gave Melchisedec a tithe of all his goods.

Most high God is a name for the one true God. He is superior to all the false gods that were worshiped by the pagan peoples of Abraham's time. They had a god for every need and purpose—a god of war, fertility, love, rain, science, literature, truth, etc. But Melchisedec and Abraham worshiped only one God. He was the supreme God of creation who stood above all these "lesser gods" in power and authority.

A lot has changed since the days of Melchisedec and Abraham. But the temptation to worship the lesser gods of the world rather than the one true God of the universe has not. Money, fame, and power are the new gods of our age. But the first of God's Ten Commandments still stands: "You shall have no other gods before me" (Exodus 20:3 NIV). See also *Almighty God*.

MOST UPRIGHT

"The way of the just is uprightness," the prophet Isaiah observed. "Thou, most upright, dost weigh the path of the just" (Isaiah 26:7). This is the only place in the Bible where the divine name "most upright" appears. The NIV renders this name as "Upright One." Isaiah's point is that even the most righteous and upright people are as nothing in comparison to the holiness of the Lord.

Even believers who try to walk the path of righteousness are capable of slipping into sin at any time. But God is not capable of error and wrongdoing. He is the most upright, the one consistent standard by which all human behavior is judged. Isaiah considered this dramatic contrast between the Lord's righteousness and our sin, then declared, "All our righteousnesses are as filthy rags. . .and our iniquities, like the wind, have taken us away" (Isaiah 64:6).

But that is not the end of the story. In spite of our unworthiness, God comes to our rescue through the sacrificial death of His Son: "By grace are ye saved through faith; and that not of yourselves: it is the gift of God: not of works, lest any man should boast" (Ephesians 2:8–9). See also *Holiness of God*; *Holy One*.

MOUNT OF OLIVES

Jesus was betrayed by Judas on the night before His crucifixion on this hill in eastern Jerusalem (see Matthew 26:30). It took its name from the olive groves that grew on the hill. The Garden of Gethsemane, where Jesus agonized in prayer on the night of His arrest, was also located on the Mount of Olives. This peaceful little garden is viewed every year by millions of Holy Land visitors. It sits in the courtyard of a beautiful church known as the Church of All Nations. See also *Garden of Gethsemane*.

Olive trees grow in the Garden of Gethsemane on the Mount of Olives, a place well known to Jesus.

Since the sixth century, an Eastern Orthodox monastery, Saint Catherine's, has resided at the foot of Mount Sinai, a traditional location for the place Moses met with God.

MOUNT SINAI

This mountain peak, also known as Horeb, is where Moses saw the burning bush with God's call to deliver His people (see Exodus 3:1–6). Later it was the site where Moses received the Ten Commandments and other parts of the law from the Lord (see Exodus 19–23).

At Sinai the Lord ordered the people through Moses to keep the covenant He had established with their ancestor Abraham (see Exodus 19:3–6). He showed His power by causing the mountain to shake and covering it with smoke (see Exodus 19:18–19).

The traditional site of Mount Sinai is a peak in the Sinai Peninsula of Egypt known as Jebel Musa ("Mountain of Moses"). At the foot of this mountain sits a Greek Orthodox monastery known as the Monastery of Saint Catherine. It memorializes God's encounter with Moses and the Israelites at this sacred site. See also *Burning Bush*; *Moses*.

MURDERER

See *Satan*.

MUSIC

Music as a form of worship is mentioned throughout the Bible. For example, after the Lord delivered the Israelites from the Egyptian army at the Red Sea, the sister of Moses led the women to give joyful thanks to the Lord: "Miriam. . .took a timbrel in her hand, and all the women followed her, with timbrels and dancing. Miriam sang to them: 'Sing to the LORD, for he is highly exalted. Both horse and driver he has hurled into the sea'" (Exodus 15:20–21 NIV).

The early Christians of the New Testament era also worshiped with music. The

King David is the best known of the Bible's musicians. Much Bible music is a form of worship.

apostle Paul called on the believers at Ephesus to "sing and make music from your heart to the Lord" (Ephesians 5:19 NIV). Fragments of some early Christian hymns even made their way into the New Testament (see 1 Timothy 3:16).

Sometimes our hearts are so filled with thanks to the Lord for His blessings that mere spoken words seem inadequate. That's when music and song come to our rescue. See also *Dancing*; *Worship of God*.

MYSTERY OF GOD

Most of what we know about God has been revealed to us through His creation and the

Bible. By studying His attributes—the qualities of His divine character—we come to understand that God is holy, righteous, merciful, etc. But at the end of the day, what we know about the Lord is like describing how a person looks by examining the tip of his little finger.

As the divine Wholly Other, God exists as Spirit in a dimension outside the realm of our human experience. The only way we know to describe Him is by using images and metaphors that are familiar to us. But He is so much more than the words and figures of speech that come from our mouths.

Perhaps the best example in the Bible of this mysterious side of God's nature is God's reply to Job in the final four chapters of this Old Testament book. For almost forty chapters, Job and his three friends had been debating about the problem of suffering and whether God was the cause of it. Finally, God asked Job, "Who is this that obscures my plans with words without knowledge?" (Job 38:2 NIV). In other words, *"Job, who do you think you are? No one has all the answers about who I am and how I work in the world."*

Then God spends four chapters of the book (see Job 38–41) telling Job about His wondrous and mysterious acts in nature—how He holds the seas back to keep them from flooding the earth (see Job 38:9–11), how the birds soar in the wind (see Job 39:26–28), how He orders the light to appear at the beginning of each new day (see Job 38:12–13).

Chastened by these words from the Lord, Job replies, "Surely I spoke of things I did not understand, things too wonderful for me to know" (Job 42:3 NIV). That's a good attitude for believers to have when we think about the awesome and mysterious God whom we serve. See also *Anthropomorphism*; *Immanence and Transcendence of God*.

PRAISE THE LORD WITH MUSIC

"Praise him with a blast of the ram's horn;
   praise him with the lyre and harp!
Praise him with the tambourine and dancing;
   praise him with strings and flutes!
Praise him with a clash of cymbals;
   praise him with loud clanging cymbals.
Let everything that breathes sing praises to the Lord!" (Psalm 150:3–6 NLT).

When Job complained of the trials in his life, God "defended" Himself by pointing out that His knowledge far surpassed Job's. God used several examples of nature to indicate His power of things mysterious to humans, for example, the sea: "Who shut up the sea behind doors when it burst forth from the womb, when I made the clouds its garment and wrapped it in thick darkness, when I fixed limits for it and set its doors and bars in place, when I said, 'This far you may come and no farther; here is where your proud waves halt'?" (Job 38:8–11 NIV).

The Basilica of the Annunciation is a landmark in modern Nazareth, the town where, two thousand years ago, Jesus grew up.

N

NATIONS

See *Desire of All Nations*; *Ensign for the Nations*.

NATURAL REVELATION

See *Revelation of God*.

NATURE

See *Creation*; *Revelation of God*.

NAZARETH

This obscure town in Galilee was the boyhood home of Jesus (see Mark 1:24). Here is where an angel announced to the virgin Mary that she would give birth to the Messiah (see Luke 1:26–38). It was to Nazareth that the Holy Family returned after their flight into Egypt (see Matthew 2:20–23). Here is where Jesus grew up—from the time when He was a child (see Luke 2:39–40) until the age of about thirty, when He launched His public ministry (see Luke 3:23).

Jesus tried to explain His mission as the Messiah to His friends in the town. But they refused to believe that one of their own could be the Messiah whom God had promised to send to redeem His people (see Luke 4:14–21).

Nazareth was a small village when Jesus lived there, but it has grown into a thriving Arabic population center in modern times. No modern Holy Land tour is complete without a visit to the city. Its main attraction is the Basilica of the Annunciation, a Catholic church built over the reputed site of the angel's announcement to Mary that she would give birth to the Son of God. See also *Annunciation*; *Galilee*; *Jesus of Galilee/Jesus of Nazareth*.

NECROMANCY

See *Magic and Divination*.

NEIGHBOR

In His parable of the good Samaritan, Jesus gave new meaning to the word *neighbor*. The true friend and neighbor of the wounded traveler in this story was not a person who lived nearby but a despised Samaritan who lived quite a distance away. Thus, a neighbor is any fellow human being who is in trouble and could use a helping hand (see Luke 10:30–37).

Jesus also taught that love for others is the supreme example of being a good neighbor. A teacher of the law once asked Him which was the greatest commandment in all of God's laws. Jesus told him that loving God was the highest divine command. But "the second is this," He told the man. "'Love your neighbor as yourself.' There is no commandment greater than these [two]" (Mark 12:31 NIV).

- "You shall not give false testimony against your neighbor" (Deuteronomy 5:20 NIV).
- "Love does no harm to a neighbor. Therefore love is the fulfillment of the law" (Romans 13:10 NIV).
- "Each of you must put off falsehood and speak truthfully to your neighbor, for we are all members of one body" (Ephesians 4:25 NIV).

Jesus announces the "new covenant" during His last supper with the disciples.

NEW ATHEISM

See *Atheism.*

NEW BIRTH

This phrase, meaning a state of regeneration or resurrection from spiritual death (see Romans 6:4–8), comes from Jesus' words to Nicodemus, "You must be born again" (John 3:7 NIV). The Holy Spirit brings regeneration and produces a changed person. This comes about by God's grace through faith in Christ rather than through one's own efforts or good works (see Ephesians 2:8–9). Regeneration, or new birth, helps the believer accept God's offer of salvation and lead a victorious life (see 1 John 5:4–5). See also *Regeneration.*

NEW COVENANT

God expressed His grace to all believers through His final covenant with His people. Prophesied by the prophet Jeremiah (see Jeremiah 31:31–34), the new covenant was symbolized by Jesus when He ate the last supper with His disciples. He called the cup the "new covenant in my blood" (Luke 22:20 NIV). Christ, the mediator of a new and better covenant, assures our eternal inheritance (see Hebrews 8:6; 9:11–15). See also *Covenant*; *Jeremiah*; *Mediator of the New Testament.*

NEW HEAVENS AND NEW EARTH

This phrase refers to the perfected universe that will occur in the end time. The concept comes from the writings of the apostle Peter. At the second coming of Christ, he declared, the present evil age will be replaced by the age to come. The entire universe (heavens and earth) will be remade by the power of

God (see 2 Peter 3:10–13).

A new heavens and new earth are necessary because the old universe has been hopelessly marred by human sin. The physical world must be purified and re-created as a fitting and final dwelling place for the righteous (see Romans 8:19–21). See also *Second Coming of Christ.*

NEW JERUSALEM

This heavenly city of the end time stands in contrast to the sinful city known as "Babylon the great" (Revelation 21:2–22:5). The apostle John identifies this holy, eternal city as the Church, which he refers to as the wife of the lamb. The lamb is Jesus Christ, the founder and sustainer of the Church (see Revelation 21:9).

John declared that this new Jerusalem is not a human creation. It was built by God Himself through the atoning death of His Son (see Revelation 21:2). See also *Body of Christ*; *Church*; *Head of the Church.*

NEW SPIRIT

Just as Jeremiah is known as the prophet of the new covenant (see Jeremiah 31:31–34), Ezekiel might be called the prophet of the "new spirit." This name of the Holy Spirit is unique to him, and he used it three times in his book. In one passage the prophet declared, "I will give you a new heart and put a new spirit in you; I will remove from you your heart of stone, and I will give you a heart of flesh" (Ezekiel 36:26 NIV; see also 11:19; 18:31).

The word *new* does not mean that God would give His people the Holy Spirit for the first time at some time in the future. The Holy Spirit was active with God the Father in the creation and among selected people in Old Testament times (see Genesis 1:2; Numbers 27:18; 1 Samuel 16:13). "New spirit" refers to the spiritual redemption that God would provide for His people through His love and grace. God's Spirit would bind believers to Him in a new covenant sealed with the blood of Jesus Christ. See also *New Covenant.*

NEW TESTAMENT

See *Mediator of the New Testament.*

NICENE CREED

See *Creeds of the Church.*

NICODEMUS

This influential Pharisee came to see Jesus at night because he was curious about His teachings. Jesus impressed upon him the necessity of being born again (see John 3:1–7). Later, Nicodemus cautioned the Jewish officials not to prejudge Jesus (see John 7:50–51). After Jesus was crucified, he and Joseph of Arimathea claimed His body and helped prepare it for burial. Nicodemus may have been an undeclared or secret follower of Jesus. See also *Joseph of Arimathea; New Birth.*

Nicodemus, along with Joseph of Arimathea, removes Jesus' body from the cross. It was to Nicodemus that Jesus first stated the words we know as John 3:16.

O

OATH

In Bible times people often affirmed with oaths that the vows they had made would be kept. This was similar to the pledge a witness makes today in a court of law: "I promise that the testimony I am about to give is the truth." A good example of a biblical oath is the promise Ruth made to her mother-in-law, Naomi: "May the LORD deal with me, be it ever so severely, if even death separates you and me" (Ruth 1:17 NIV).

Taking an oath was considered a serious matter, particularly in Old Testament times. If a person used the Lord's name in an oath, it was considered a sacred promise with serious consequences to follow if the vow was broken (see Judges 11:30–36).

Jesus had no need to use oaths. Since He was God's Son who exemplified the truth, He did not have to guarantee the authority of His teaching with a vow or pledge in His Father's name. He even cautioned His followers against using oaths. "Do not swear by your head, for you cannot make even one hair white or black," He told them. "All you need to say is simply 'Yes' or 'No'; anything beyond this comes from the evil one" (Matthew 5:36–37 NIV).

Christians should be people of such integrity that we don't have to go around guaranteeing what we say with a vow of honesty. This should be evident to others in the way we live.

Jesus wears full kingly attire in this stained glass window from Ireland. "Ruler" is just one of the offices of Christ.

OBSERVER OF TIMES

See *Magic and Divination.*

OFFERINGS

See *Altar; Sacrificial Offerings.*

OFFICES OF CHRIST

Many names or titles are attributed to Christ. But these various names are organized by theologians into the three major roles, or offices, that He filled in His ministry of redemption. These three offices are prophet, priest, and king.

As prophet, Jesus is God's perfect spokesman to the world. He is the last in a long line of prophets whom God sent to reveal His divine character and His will for the human race.

Jesus is also known for His priestly work. Through His atoning death, He became the once-for-all sacrifice for the sins of the world (see Hebrews 9:12).

As king, Jesus is "the ruler of the kings of the earth" (Revelation 1:5 NIV). In the end time, according to the apostle Paul, every

> ## PRAISE FOR THE WORK OF CHRIST
>
> The three offices of Christ are memorialized in "Praise Him! Praise Him!," an old hymn of exuberant praise by Fanny J. Crosby.
>
> Praise Him! Praise Him! Jesus, our
>   blessed Redeemer!
> Heavenly portals loud with hosannas
>   ring!
> Jesus, Saviour, reigneth forever and
>   ever;
> Crown Him! Crown Him! Prophet, and
>   Priest, and King!

knee will bow and every tongue will confess "that Jesus Christ is Lord, to the glory of God the Father" (Philippians 2:11). See also *Great High Priest; Great Prophet; King of Kings.*

OFFSPRING OF DAVID

See *Root and Offspring of David.*

OLD TESTAMENT PROPHECIES

See *Prophecies about Christ.*

OMEGA

See *Alpha and Omega.*

OMNIBENEVOLENCE OF GOD

See *Goodness of God.*

OMNIPOTENCE OF GOD

This attribute of God (pronounced ahm NIP uh tunce) refers to His unlimited and infinite power. The term is derived from two Latin words, *omni* ("all") and *potens* ("power"). Thus, God is all-powerful—the most awesome force in the universe.

The Bible is filled with examples of God's power. He created the universe from nothing by the power of His word (see Genesis 1:1–3). He struck Egypt with ten plagues to convince the pharaoh to release the Israelites from slavery (see Exodus 7–12). He divided the waters of the Jordan River to allow the Israelites to cross over into Canaan (see Joshua 3:14–17). The prophet Jeremiah was familiar with all these mighty acts of the Lord. "Ah, Sovereign LORD," he declared, "you have made the heavens and the earth by your great power and outstretched arm. Nothing is too

The Horsehead Nebula in the constellation Orion, as photographed by NASA's Hubble Space Telescope, hints at God's power, presence, and wisdom. . .as His three great "omnis" describe: omnipotence, omnipresence, and omniscience.

hard for you" (Jeremiah 32:17 NIV).

God's power is underscored by several names attributed to Him in the Bible. He is called the "Almighty God" (Genesis 17:1), the "Lord God omnipotent" (Revelation 19:6), and the "mighty One of Jacob" (Isaiah 49:26). See also *Sovereignty of God*.

OMNIPRESENCE OF GOD

This big word (pronounced AHM knee PREZ unce) refers to one of the classical attributes of God—His universal presence and His ability to be everywhere at the same time. The psalmist declared this truth in these beautiful words: "Whither shall I go from thy spirit? or whither shall I flee from thy presence? If I ascend up into heaven, thou art there: if I make my bed in hell, behold, thou art there. If I take the wings of the morning, and dwell in the uttermost parts of the sea; even there shall thy hand lead me, and thy right hand shall hold me" (Psalm 139:7–10).

God's omnipresence shows that He is not an organic, physical being. He exists as eternal Spirit, and He is not limited by time and space as people are. He fills heaven and earth and everything in between (see Jeremiah 23:23). King Solomon built the temple in Jerusalem as a place where God would make His presence known. When he dedicated the temple with a prayer, Solomon admitted, "Who is able to build a temple for him, since the heavens, even the highest heavens, cannot contain him?" (2 Chronicles 2:6 NIV).

This attribute of God should bring joy to the hearts of all believers. He is always with us, no matter where we are. Through every circumstance of life, His presence is as near as the air we breathe. See also *Immanence and Transcendence of God*.

OMNISCIENCE OF GOD

Theologians refer to the perfect and pervasive knowledge of God as His omniscience (pronounced ahm NISH unce). The term comes from two Latin words, *omnis* ("all") and *sciere* ("to know"). Thus, this attribute of God's divine character allows Him to know everything about the world and its inhabitants.

Perhaps the greatest passage in the Bible that underscores God's omniscience was spoken by the psalmist. "You have searched me, LORD, and you know me. You know when I sit and when I rise; you perceive my thoughts from afar. You discern my going out and my lying down; you are familiar with all my ways. Before a word is on my tongue you, LORD, know it completely" (Psalm 139:1–4 NIV).

God's perfect knowledge is reassuring and disturbing at the same time. When we experience problems, it's comforting to realize that He is aware of what we are going through. We can call on Him in the full confidence that He knows and understands. But He also knows when we behave like spoiled children and fail to follow His will for our

GOD'S OMNISCIENCE IN ACTION

- "The Lord knows all human plans" (Psalm 94:11 NIV).
- "Your ways are in full view of the LORD, and he examines all your paths" (Proverbs 5:21 NIV).
- "Your Father [God] knows what you need before you ask him" (Matthew 6:8 NIV).
- "His eyes watch the nations—let not the rebellious rise up against him" (Psalm 66:7 NIV).

lives. In times like this, knowing that He knows everything about us should drive us to our knees to seek His forgiveness. See also *Foreknowledge of God*; *Spirit of Knowledge and the Fear of the Lord*.

ONE CHOSEN OUT OF THE PEOPLE

Psalm 89 focuses on God's promise to King David that one of David's descendants would always occupy the throne of Israel (see 2 Samuel 7:8–17). Thus the "one chosen out of the people" in verse 19 of this psalm refers to David because he was chosen by the Lord from among the sons of Jesse to replace Saul as king (see 1 Samuel 16:10–13).

But this psalm also looks beyond David's time to its ultimate fulfillment in the Messiah, Jesus Christ. The angel Gabriel made this clear when he appeared to the virgin Mary to tell her that she would give birth to the Messiah, God's chosen one. "He shall be great, and shall be called the Son of the Highest," Gabriel declared, "and the Lord God shall give unto him the throne of his father David" (Luke 1:32).

As the one chosen out of the people, Jesus was not a king in the same sense as David. He did not seek political or military power. His kingship was spiritual in nature. He ushered in the kingdom of God, the dominion over which He reigns with all those who have accepted Him as Lord and Savior.

See also *Chosen One*; *Elect*; *Foreordained before the Foundation of the World*.

ONLY BEGOTTEN OF THE FATHER

See *Only Begotten Son*.

ONLY BEGOTTEN SON

Jesus used this name for Himself in His long discussion with Nicodemus about the meaning of the new birth (see John 3:1–21). A verse from that discussion, John 3:16, is probably the best-known passage in the entire Bible. Most believers can quote it from memory. It has been called "the Gospel in a nutshell" because its twenty-five words tell us so clearly and simply why Jesus came into the world.

The name only begotten Son describes Jesus' special relationship with the Father. He is unique—the one and only of His kind who has ever existed. The fact that He was God's one and only Son makes His role as our Savior all the more significant. God the Father sent the very best when He sent Jesus to die on the cross for our sins.

This name of Jesus appears only in the writings of the apostle John (see John 1:18; 3:18; 1 John 4:9). John in his Gospel also referred to Jesus as the "only begotten of the Father" (John 1:14). See also *Son of God*.

Seeking Godly Wisdom

- "The wisdom of this world is foolishness in God's sight. As it is written: 'He catches the wise in their craftiness'" (1 Corinthians 3:19 NIV).
- "Be very careful, then, how you live—not as unwise but as wise, making the most of every opportunity, because the days are evil" (Ephesians 5:15-16 NIV).
- "Let the message of Christ dwell among you richly as you teach and admonish one another with all wisdom through psalms, hymns, and songs from the Spirit" (Colossians 3:16 NIV).

ONLY WISE GOD

The final two verses of the epistle of Jude form one of the most inspiring benedictions in the New Testament: "Now unto him that is able to keep you from falling, and to present you faultless before the presence of his glory with exceeding joy, to the only wise God our Saviour, be glory and majesty, dominion and power, both now and ever. Amen" (Jude 24–25). Jude wanted his readers to experience the joy of their salvation and to continue to be faithful in their witness to the "only wise God," whom he clearly identified as Jesus their Savior.

This is the only place in the Bible where Jesus is called by this name. The New King James Version translates this phrase as "God our Savior, who alone is wise." Only Jesus Christ has divine wisdom. Worldly wisdom is a poor substitute for the wisdom that God promises to those who follow Him as Savior and Lord.

Jesus the Son and God the Father impart wisdom to believers by several methods—through the Holy Spirit, through the counsel of fellow believers, and through the scriptures, the written Word of God. We will never be as wise as God, who is the fount of all wisdom. But we should be growing in this gift of grace as we walk with Him during our earthly journey. James advised the readers of his epistle: "If any of you lacks wisdom, you should ask God, who gives generously to all without finding fault, and it will be given to you" (James 1:5 NIV).

Another name of Jesus similar in meaning to only wise God is "wisdom of God" (1 Corinthians 1:24). See also *Spirit of Wisdom and Revelation; Wisdom of God.*

ORDINATION

To ordain a person is to set him or her apart for special service to the Lord and His people. In Old Testament times, kings were formally commissioned to their office by having oil poured on their heads (see 1 Samuel 10:1). Aaron and his sons were also set apart as priests to perform sacrifices on behalf of the people (see Exodus 28–29).

Ordination was also practiced in New Testament times. When Jesus began His public ministry, "he ordained twelve, that they should be with him, and that he might send them forth to preach" (Mark 3:14). Jesus had many followers, but He selected these disciples and set them apart for special training. He wanted them to be able to continue His work through the Church after His earthly ministry came to an end. Jesus Himself was sent into the world by the Lord on a special mission. So He is sometimes described as one ordained for ministry by God the Father (see 1 Corinthians 2:7).

Ordination is still practiced by many church groups. Pastors and other leaders are set apart for special service to the church through a ceremony of ordination. See also *Foreordained before the Foundation of the World; One Chosen Out of the People.*

ORIGINAL SIN

This phrase refers to the first recorded sin committed in the Bible—Adam and Eve's disobedience of God's command. It is also referred to as "ancestral sin." Both of them ate a fruit in the Garden of Eden that God had clearly declared off-limits (see Genesis 2:17; 3:6). According to the apostle Paul, this original sin of rebellion against God's authority has infected the entire human race (see Romans 5:12–19). The only answer to this sin problem is acceptance of Jesus Christ, who has purchased our forgiveness through His sacrificial death. See also *Fall of Man*; *Sin*.

OUR PASSOVER

The most important religious celebration among the Israelites was the Passover festival. This religious holiday commemorated the "passing over" of the houses of the Israelites

> The Bible never says that Eve ate an apple. . .but she took fruit from the tree of the knowledge of good and evil, in direct disobedience to God. This was the "original sin."

when God destroyed all the firstborn of the land of Egypt. This occurred as God's final plague against Egypt to convince the pharaoh to release His people from slavery. The Israelites escaped God's judgment by following His command to mark their houses with the blood of sacrificial lambs (see Exodus 12:21–23).

Jesus is "our passover," the apostle Paul declared, because He shed His blood to bring deliverance for God's people, just as the first sacrificial lambs inaugurated the first Passover (see 1 Corinthians 5:7). We remember His sacrifice with reverence every time we partake of Communion, or the Lord's Supper.

The imagery of leaven in connection with Passover also appears in this verse from

1 Corinthians. "Purge out therefore the old leaven," Paul directed the believers at Corinth. *Leaven* is another word for yeast, an ingredient used by the Israelites to cause their bread to rise. They left Egypt in such a hurry on the first Passover that they didn't have time to add leaven to their bread dough (see Exodus 12:34). Whenever they observed this holiday from that day on, they were to eat unleavened bread. This part of Passover was known as the Feast of Unleavened Bread.

Paul referred to believers in this verse as a "new lump" because they were "unleavened." Just as unleavened bread symbolized the Israelites' freedom from Egyptian slavery, so believers are unleavened, or separated from sin and death, by the perfect Passover lamb, Jesus Christ. See also *Lamb of God*; *Passover and Feast of Unleavened Bread*.

OUR PEACE

See *Lord of Peace*.

OVERSEER OF YOUR SOULS

See *Bishop of Your Souls*.

P

PAGAN GODS

See *Idolatry*.

PALESTINE

This territory of the Canaanites became known as the land of the people of Israel. The name Palestine referred originally to the territory of the Philistines, especially the coastal plain south of Mount Carmel. The name was extended during the Christian era to include all of the Holy Land, including both sides of the Jordan River and the Dead Sea region south to Egypt.

After the Canaanites were displaced, the country was called the land of Israel (see 1 Samuel 13:19) and the "land of promise" (Hebrews 11:9). It was considered the promised land because this is the territory that God promised to give to Abraham and his descendants (see Genesis 15:7–16). See also *Canaan; Israelites*.

PALM SUNDAY

See *Triumphal Entry of Jesus*.

PANTHEISM

This term (pronounced PAN thee iz um) comes from two Greek words, *pan*, meaning "all," and *theos*, meaning "God." Thus, pantheism is the theory that God does not exist as a separate being from the universe; that He is actually identical with the physical world. Or, to put it another way, the natural world does not *reflect* God; it *is* God.

Pantheists do believe in one supreme God. But He does not relate to them in a personal way. He is a mystical force in the universe rather than a guide for daily living. They believe creation flows from God, but He does not stand above and apart from His creation. The bottom line of the pantheistic view of God is that He and the universe are one.

By contrast, the biblical view is that God created the universe as a separate entity from Himself. He existed before the physical world, He created it from nothing through His spoken word (see Genesis 1:3), and He is the ruler and controller of His creation (see Jeremiah 51:15). See also *Creation; Self-Existence of God*.

PANTHEON

This word (pronounced PAN thee un) refers to all the gods included in a pagan religious system. Many nations of Bible times were known for their worship of numerous false gods. For

Zeus, portrayed here on a coin, was chief god of the Greek pantheon. In the view of the God of the Bible, worship of these lesser, false gods is idolatry.

example, the Greek and Roman pantheons consisted of gods devoted to war, commerce, science, literature, hunting, and fertility.

The apostle Paul noted monuments commemorating these various gods when he visited the Greek city of Athens. These Athenians were so fearful that they might miss paying homage to one of these gods that they had erected one monument to an "unknown God." Paul used this shrine to remind the citizens of the city that there was only one supreme God of the universe—the one in whom "we live and move and have our being" (Acts 17:28 NIV). This was the God who had sent Jesus into the world as a messenger of salvation for all people.

Most of the people rejected Paul's message, but a few believed and became followers of the Lord (see Acts 17:32–34). This reflects the mixed response that people make to the Gospel, even in our own time. See also *Idolatry.*

PARABLES OF JESUS

Jesus used stories and object lessons drawn from daily life to teach spiritual truths to His hearers. The word *parable* comes from a term that means "comparison" or "a casting alongside." Thus, Jesus in His teaching compared familiar activities such as sowing seed or well-known things such as sheep with the spiritual truths He was trying to get across to His audience. The common people could understand such analogies, so Jesus' parables were one of His most effective teaching methods.

Not every parable of Jesus was an extended story. He also used short parabolic sayings or "one-liners" such as "salt of the earth" and "casting pearls before swine" to communicate spiritual realities. For this reason it is difficult to pin down the exact number of His parables. If all His short similes

In one of Jesus' most famous parables, a kind and generous Samaritan helps a wounded Jew. The story showed how God wants people to treat others, even those of different social classes and ethnicities.

and metaphors are counted as parables, there are as many as fifty in the Gospels. But His major parables, or extended narratives, come to about half that number (see the sidebar "Major Parables of Jesus" on page 302).

Jesus' parables usually grabbed His listeners' attention with a clear, memorable picture of the truth. But sometimes they were difficult to understand. Even His disciples were sometimes puzzled about the meaning of His parables, as they were about the parable of the wheat and the tares, or weeds (see Matthew 13:36). Jesus patiently explained the meaning of the parable to them because they were open-minded and teachable. But His parables sometimes concealed the truth from those who were stubborn, unbelieving, and opposed to His teaching—especially the Pharisees (see Luke 8:9–10). See also *Teacher Come from God.*

PARACLETE

This Greek word for the Holy Spirit expresses the idea of a helper called to one's side. It is translated as "Comforter" in the Gospels (see John 14:16 KJV) and as "advocate" in 1 John 2:1 (KJV). See also *Comforter.*

MAJOR PARABLES OF JESUS

Parable	Matthew	Mark	Luke
1. Lamp on a Lampstand	5:15–16	4:21–22	8:16–17
2. Two Foundations	7:24–27		6:47–49
3. The Sower, or the Soils	13:3–8	4:3–8	8:5–8
4. Wheat and Tares	13:24–30		
5. Good Samaritan			10:30–37
6. Rich Fool			12:13–21
7. Barren Fig Tree			13:6–9
8. Mustard Seed	13:31–32	4:31–32	13:18–19
9. Leaven	13:33		13:20–21
10. Hidden Treasure	13:44		
11. Pearl of Great Price	13:45–46		
12. Fishing Net	13:47–50		
13. Banquet			14:16–24
14. Lost Sheep	18:12–13		15:4–7
15. Lost Coin			15:8–9
16. Prodigal/Lost Son			15:11–32
17. Unjust Steward			16:1–9
18. Rich Man and Lazarus			16:19–31
19. Persistent Widow			18:1–5
20. Proud Pharisee			18:10–14
21. The Pounds			19:11–26
22. Unforgiving Servant	18:23–35		
23. Wages for Vineyard Workers	20:1–16		
24. Two Sons and a Vineyard	21:28–32		
25. Wicked Tenants	21:33–44	12:1–11	20:9–17
26. Wedding Feast	22:1–14		
27. Ten Virgins	25:1–13		
28. Talents	25:14–30		

PARADOX

A paradox exists when two statements or propositions are placed side by side and both are true, but they seem to contradict each other. Anyone who reads the Bible or who studies theology seriously will soon realize that paradox is one of the most common elements of our faith.

For example, we affirm that God is both immanent (nearby) and transcendent (far away) at the same time. He is sovereign or supreme in His rule over the universe. But He also created man with free will and the ability to reject His rule and authority. Both these sets of propositions are true, but they seem to be mutually exclusive.

Paradox is also evident in the life and ministry of Jesus and His continuing work of redemption in the world. He was God's Son, sharing fully in the divine essence of the Father. But He was also fully human, subject to every human emotion and the pain and suffering that led to His death on the cross.

The best we can do with such paradoxical truths as these is to admit the limit of our human understanding. What seems to be impossible from the standpoint of human logic is no problem to God. He is always true to His nature as the all-wise, all-knowing, and all-seeing Lord. It is possible for us to know a few things about Him. But the bottom line is that He is the great "Wholly Other" whose mysteries we cannot fully understand.

This is how the Lord expressed this truth about Himself to the prophet Isaiah: "My thoughts are not your thoughts, neither are your ways my ways" (Isaiah 55:8 NIV). See also *Mystery of God.*

PARDON

See *Forgiveness.*

PARADOXES OF THE GOSPEL

- To be great, we must become servants (see Matthew 20:20-26).
- To save our lives, we must lose them (see Luke 9:24-26).
- To be strong, we must become weak (see 2 Corinthians 12:10).
- To be wise, we must become foolish (see 1 Corinthians 3:18).
- To be exalted, we must become humble (see Matthew 23:12).
- To find rest, we must carry a yoke (see Matthew 11:28-30).

PAROUSIA

This Greek word (pronounced puh ROO see ah), meaning "presence" or "appearance," refers to the return of Christ to earth in the end time. The word does not appear in the New Testament. But theologians often use it to discuss all the events associated with the second coming of Jesus. See also *Second Coming of Christ.*

PARTIALITY

To show favoritism or preference toward some people over others is known as partiality. God's grace and wisdom are available to everyone and free of favoritism or hypocrisy (see James 3:17). Since God loves all people, we as believers should follow His example in our treatment of others. The apostle Paul encouraged Timothy, his young associate in ministry, to practice all the things he had taught him, "without partiality, and to do nothing out of favoritism" (1 Timothy 5:21 NIV). See also *Impartiality of God.*

PASSOVER AND FEAST OF UNLEAVENED BREAD

A Jewish festival that commemorated the Exodus from Egypt (see Joshua 5:10–12), the Passover celebrated how God "passed over" the Hebrew houses in Egypt that were sprinkled with blood while killing the firstborn of the Egyptians on the eve of the Exodus (see Exodus 12). The seven-day Feast of Unleavened Bread recalled the haste with which the slaves left Egypt (see Exodus 12:33–34).

Jesus observed the Passover with His disciples on the night He was betrayed (see Luke 22:15). See also *Lamb of God*; *Our Passover*.

PATIENCE OF GOD

See *Longsuffering of God*.

Jewish people have been honoring God's command to celebrate the Passover for more than three thousand years. Here, sailors aboard the USS *Ashland* consult the Haggadah, the book of readings for the Passover seder.

PATRIARCHS

The founding fathers of the nation of Israel are known as patriarchs. The word is derived from a combination of the Latin term *pater* ("father") with the Greek work *archo* ("to rule"). Thus, a patriarch was a father who ruled over a family or clan.

Fifteen people in the Old Testament are considered the patriarchs of the Israelites: Abraham; his son Isaac; Isaac's son Jacob; and Jacob's twelve sons who became the founders of the twelve tribes of Israel. In the Old Testament, God is often referred to as the "God of Abraham, Isaac, and Jacob"

(Exodus 3:16 NIV). See also *Abraham; Isaac; Israelites; Jacob.*

PAUL THE APOSTLE

This great apostle to the Gentiles was a defender and advocate of the Christian faith in its early years through his thirteen New Testament letters, or epistles. A complex personality, Paul demonstrated both toughness and tenderness in his devotion to Christ. His teachings are both profound and practical (see Philippians 3:7–10).

Paul's Hebrew name was Saul, but his Roman name was Paul (see Acts 13:9). A Roman citizen born at Tarsus in Cilicia (see Acts 22:3), he was a tentmaker by trade—a vocation by which he often supported himself as a minister to the churches that he established (see Acts 18:3).

A strict Pharisee, Paul opposed Christianity in its early years in Jerusalem. He consented to the death of Stephen, the first martyr of the church (see Acts 7:58; 8:1). He was on his way to persecute Christians in the city of Damascus when he was converted to Christianity in his famous "Damascus road" experience (see Acts 9:1–8). From that point on, Paul was zealous for the cause of Christ.

Under the sponsorship of the church at Antioch in Syria, Paul undertook three great missionary journeys to the Roman world, extending westward through Cyprus and Asia Minor into Europe (see Acts 16:9–10). His traveling companions on these tours included Barnabas, John Mark, Timothy, Silas, Titus, and Luke. Along with his successes in making disciples, healing, and planting churches, he suffered a "thorn in the flesh" (see 2 Corinthians 12:7), was frequently arrested, was stoned, and was imprisoned (see Acts 16:22–23).

The Bible gives no physical description of the apostle Paul, but it certainly describes his commitment to God and the Gospel of Jesus Christ. This painting is from a church in Toledo, Spain.

Falsely accused by his enemies, he appealed to the Roman emperor for justice (see Acts 25:10–12). After a hazardous voyage by ship, he spent two years in Rome under house arrest. While guarded by Roman soldiers, he received friends and preached the Gospel (see Acts 28:30–31; Philippians 1:12–14). Most scholars believe he was beheaded in Rome about AD 67 during the reign of the

Roman emperor Nero (see Philippians 2:17; 2 Timothy 4:6–8).

Through his New Testament writings, Paul popularized several theological truths that became the heart of Christian belief for all future generations. These Pauline themes included Jesus as the Messiah, the Son of God; the end of the law as the basis of righteousness; salvation by faith in Jesus Christ and His atoning death; and the Church as the body of Christ that continues God's work of redemption in the world.

PEACE

Peace—harmony and accord brought about by cordial relationships—has its source in God (see Philippians 4:7) through Jesus Christ (see John 14:27) and the Holy Spirit (see Galatians 5:22).

One of the most interesting occurrences of the word *peace* in the Gospels was spoken by Jesus to His disciples soon after His resurrection. He stood among them and said, "Peace be unto you" (John 20:19). These words were the common greeting used by the Jewish people of that day—a wish for their peace, wholeness, and well-being.

When the disciples heard this greeting from Jesus, perhaps they remembered His previous promise to them: "Peace I leave with you, my peace I give unto you: not as the world giveth, give I unto you. Let not your heart be troubled, neither let it be afraid" (John 14:27).

Just as we as believers are assured of God's peace, we are urged to pursue peace and to live peaceably with all people (see 2 Timothy 2:22). See also *God of Peace*; *Lord Is Peace*; *Lord of Peace*.

PEACE OFFERING

See *Sacrificial Offerings*.

PENTECOST

This annual Jewish feast or holy period commemorated the end of the harvest. This feast was also known as the feast of weeks (see Exodus 34:22). The purpose of this feast was to express thanks to God for the crops He had provided. It was sometimes referred to as the day of firstfruits (see Numbers 28:26) because the first loaves of bread made from the wheat harvest were offered to the Lord on that day.

During New Testament times, this holiday was known as Pentecost (from the Greek word *pentekoste*, meaning "fiftieth day") because if fell on the fiftieth day after the Passover celebration. Early Christian believers were gathered in Jerusalem to celebrate Pentecost when they experienced a miraculous outpouring of God's Spirit (see Acts 2:1–4).

Before He ascended into heaven, Jesus told His followers not to leave Jerusalem immediately but to "wait for the gift my Father promised, which you have heard me speak

GOD'S GIFT OF PEACE

- "The Lord blesses his people with peace" (Psalm 29:11 NIV).
- "The punishment that brought us peace was on him [Jesus]" (Isaiah 53:5 NIV).
- "The peace of God, which transcends all understanding, will guard your hearts and your minds in Christ Jesus" (Philippians 4:7 NIV).

about" (Acts 1:4 NIV). After this outpouring of the Holy Spirit, they would be empowered to serve as His witnesses not only in Jerusalem but "in all Judea and Samaria, and to the ends of the earth" (Acts 1:8 NIV). See also *Great Commission of Jesus.*

PEOPLE OF GOD

This phrase was used for the nation of Israel as well as the people of the new covenant, or the Church. The Israelites were called by God as His special people (see Deuteronomy 8:6–9), but all who have accepted Jesus as Lord and Savior are also His people. Peter declared that Gentiles who believed in Jesus as Savior were also part of God's "chosen generation" (1 Peter 2:9). God's people include every kindred, tongue, and nation (see Revelation 7:9). See also *Chosen People; Church.*

PERFECTER OF OUR FAITH

See *Author and Finisher of Our Faith.*

PERFECTION OF GOD

See *Self-Existence of God; Self-Sufficiency of God.*

PERSEVERANCE

Paul counseled persistence, or the ability to endure through difficult circumstances, to the Christians at Corinth. He encouraged them to keep on doing the Lord's work because labor for Him is never in vain (see 1 Corinthians 15:58). Steadfastness in doing good works is one indicator that a believer's faith is genuine (see James 2:14–26). Our persistence in following the Lord also shows our appreciation for His saving grace (see 1 Corinthians 15:57–58).

With the sound of a rushing wind and the appearance of flames of fire above each disciple, God's Holy Spirit initiates the church age at Pentecost.

PERSEVERANCE OF GOD

See *Longsuffering of God.*

PERSONS OF THE TRINITY

See *Trinity.*

PETER THE APOSTLE

Peter, a disciple of Jesus also known as Simon Peter, is often portrayed as a blundering fisherman. But this does not do justice to his rich personality. He was undeniably the most prominent of Jesus' disciples and the one who became the main leader of the church after Jesus' ascension (see Acts 2:14–40).

To Peter also belongs the distinction of being the first to recognize Jesus as the Messiah. When Jesus asked His disciples who He was, Peter replied, "You are the Messiah, the Son of the living God" (Matthew 16:16 NIV). He recognized that Jesus was God's Son who had been sent into the world on a mission of redemption for sinful humanity. Jesus told Peter that His Church would be established through His followers who affirmed the same truth about Him and His mission that Peter had expressed.

Peter swore he would never forsake Christ, but he denied Him three times on the night before His crucifixion (see Matthew 26:69–75). After being forgiven and restored by Jesus, he went on to become a bold spokesman for Christ in the early years of the Christian movement (see Acts 2:14–40). Through God's intervention he overcame his prejudice toward Gentiles and welcomed them into the fellowship of the Church (see Acts 10:34–35).

Peter is a good example of the power of forgiveness and the potential of a life that is totally committed to the Lord and His service. See also *Impartiality of God.*

In one of the Bible's sadder scenes, Peter denies even knowing Jesus. The Lord would soon forgive Peter, who would go on to boldly proclaim the good news of the Gospel—to the point of his own crucifixion, according to early church tradition.

PHARISEES

Members of this Jewish sect insisted on keeping all the oral traditions that had grown up around the Jewish law. During His earthly ministry, Jesus clashed often with the Pharisees because of their hypocrisy and extreme legalism.

The word *Pharisee* means "separated ones." This term may refer to the fact that they separated themselves from the common people. Or it may indicate that they separated themselves for the study and interpretation of the law. To them, the traditional interpretations of the Law of Moses that had been added over several

WOES AGAINST THE PHARISEES

Matthew 23 is often called the "woe chapter" of the New Testament. It contains a series of "woes" or calamities pronounced by Jesus against the Pharisees because of their hypocrisy and self-righteousness.

- "They tie up heavy, cumbersome loads and put them on other people's shoulders" (v. 4 NIV).
- "Everything they do is done for people to see" (v. 5 NIV).
- "You shut the door of the kingdom of heaven in people's faces" (v. 13 NIV).
- "You have neglected the more important matters of the law—justice, mercy, and faithfulness" (v. 23 NIV).
- "You. . .are full of greed and self-indulgence" (v. 25 NIV).
- "You are full of hypocrisy and wickedness" (v. 28 NIV).

centuries were more important than the original law itself. Jesus criticized them for ignoring the commands of God while "holding on to human traditions" (Mark 7:8 NIV).

The Pharisees were threatened by Jesus because He claimed to have religious authority that came directly from God. On one occasion they accused Him of breaking the law against working on the Sabbath by healing a man on that day. Jesus replied, "If any of you has a sheep and it falls into a pit on the Sabbath, will you not take hold of it and lift it out? How much more valuable is a person than a sheep! Therefore it is lawful to do good on the Sabbath" (Matthew 12:11–12 NIV).

Jesus also criticized the Pharisees for their hypocrisy. They pretended to be more zealous in their commitment to the law than any other group in Israel. But Jesus declared that this was nothing but a cover-up for their inner corruption and lack of compassion. "You are like whitewashed tombs, which look beautiful on the outside," he told them, "but on the inside are full of the bones of the dead and everything unclean. In the same way, on the outside you appear to people as righteous but on the inside you are full of hypocrisy and wickedness" (Matthew 23:27–28 NIV). See also *Hypocrisy*; *Sadducees*.

PHYLACTERIES

Phylacteries (pronounced fie LACK tuh rees) were little boxes containing strips of parchment on which portions of the law were written. The Pharisees wore these boxes on their foreheads and hands as a literal obedience of the Lord's command, "Tie them [God's laws] as symbols on your hands, and bind them on your foreheads" (Deuteronomy 6:8 NIV).

The problem with these displays of piety is they were done just for show. Jesus declared that the Pharisees worked hard to observe the externals of religion while omitting "the weightier matters of the law, judgment, mercy, and faith" (Matthew 23:23). See also *Hypocrisy*; *Pharisees*.

A young Jewish man wearing a phylactery prays with a rabbi in Jerusalem.

PHYSICIAN

Jesus did the unthinkable when he called the tax collector Matthew (also known as Levi) as His disciple. The Jews hated tax collectors because they contracted with the Roman government to collect various fees and taxes that the Jews considered unjust. To celebrate his commitment to Christ, Matthew invited his tax collector associates and other friends to a "great feast" (Luke 5:29) for Jesus and His disciples.

The scribes and Pharisees were horrified that Jesus and His disciples would associate with such sinful people. But Jesus replied to their criticisms, "They that are whole need not a physician; but they that are sick" (Luke 5:31). He had been sent to people such as these. They needed a Savior and deliverer. He was the physician who could heal them of their desperate sickness known as sin.

Jesus' role as physician is one of the most prominent in the Gospels. Most of His miracles were performed for people who were suffering from various physical problems—blindness, deafness, leprosy, and possession by evil spirits. But in many of these miracles, He went beyond healing the body to healing the soul and the spirit through forgiveness of sin. For example, after healing a paralyzed man, He told him, "Take heart, son; your sins are forgiven" (Matthew 9:2 NIV).

Jesus the physician is still in the healing business. He offers hope to the discouraged, His abiding presence to the lonely, comfort to the grieving, and peace to the conflicted. But most of all, He brings deliverance from the most serious problems of the human race—sin and death.

We as believers don't need an appointment to see Jesus. He is always near, according to an old hymn by William Hunter entitled "The Great Physician."

> The great Physician now is near,
> The sympathizing Jesus;
> He speaks the drooping heart to cheer,
> Oh, hear the voice of Jesus.
> Sweetest note in seraph song,
> Sweetest name on mortal tongue;
> Sweetest carol ever sung,

Jesus, blessed Jesus.

See also *Lord Who Heals*.

PILLAR OF FIRE AND CLOUD

This visible sign of God's presence guided the Israelites in the wilderness after they left Egypt (see Exodus 14:24). This phenomenon apparently existed as a cloud during the day and took the form of a fire at night to protect the people and serve as a guiding light. In the Bible both clouds and fire are associated with God's power and presence.

In the New Testament, Jesus identified Himself as the "light of the world" (John 8:12). With this metaphor, He challenged the people to pay allegiance to Him just as they had followed this mysterious light in the wilderness. See also *Cloud*; *Fire*; *Light of the World*.

PIONEER OF OUR FAITH

See *Author and Finisher of Our Faith*.

PLANT OF RENOWN

The Lord gave the Israelites an interesting message through the prophet Ezekiel: "I will raise up for them a plant of renown, and they shall be no more consumed with hunger in the land, neither bear the shame of the heathen any more" (Ezekiel 34:29).

Is this verse a description of the coming Messiah or a reference to the fertility of the renewed land of Israel? The KJV and NRSV translations treat the verse messianically, while the NASB and NIV render it as a reference to Israel ("land renowned for its crops," NIV).

The context of this verse provides

God's presence looked something like this as He led His people out of slavery in Egypt. God gave the Israelites a "pillar of a cloud" in the daytime, and a "pillar of fire" at night.

support for the messianic interpretation. The entire thirty-fourth chapter of Ezekiel describes how God the Father will send a shepherd, His servant David, to feed His flock (see Ezekiel 34:23). As the plant of renown, this servant from David's line will provide God's people with all the food they need so "they shall be no more consumed with hunger."

This title of Jesus is similar in meaning to His description of Himself as "bread" (John 6). He is the spiritual sustenance that believers need to keep their faith healthy and in tune with His will for their lives. See also *Bread.*

PNEUMATOLOGY

See *Holy Spirit.*

POLYTHEISM

In contrast to monotheism, which emphasized devotion to the one and only true God, polytheism is the practice of worshiping many gods. The nations surrounding Israel worshiped multiple gods, a practice that led to immorality (see 2 Kings 23:13–14), prostitution (see Numbers 25:1–9), and child sacrifice (see Jeremiah 7:29–34).

The first two of the Ten Commandments make it clear that devotion to the one and only supreme God was not to be mixed with worship of any other false or pagan god (see Exodus 20:3–5). See also *Monotheism.*

A shanty town in Guatemala. God has always called on His people to show special concern for the poor and weak of society.

POOR

In Bible times the people most in need of financial aid were widows, orphans, the handicapped who were forced to beg for a living, and strangers and aliens in the land. God had a special concern for people like this who were down on their luck. He directed His people, the Israelites, to take care of them: "There will always be poor people in the land. Therefore I command you to be openhanded toward your fellow Israelites who are poor and needy in your land" (Deuteronomy 15:11 NIV).

Jesus also demonstrated God's concern for the poor (see Luke 6:20). He commended a poor widow for her sacrificial gift in the temple (see Luke 21:2–4). He had compassion on people with physical disabilities and restored several of them to health (see Mark 8:22–23). The followers of Jesus should continue His emphasis on support for the poor of the world.

○ OPPRESSION OF THE POOR

The prophet Amos cited a case of oppression of the poor by the wealthy of his time. He condemned the rich for using "garments taken in pledge" in their worship at pagan shrines (see Amos 2:8 NIV).

By law, if a poor man put up his outer robe as security for a loan, the garment had to be returned to him by sundown so he could use it for a blanket (see Deuteronomy 24:12–13). But the rich were ignoring this law and even using the robes they had taken from the poor as blankets on which they could kneel down to worship in pagan temples.

PORTION

The word *portion* appears often in the Bible in connection with inheritance rights. For example, each of the twelve tribes of Israel received a portion of the land of Canaan as an inheritance that the Lord had promised (see Joshua 19:9). By law, the firstborn son in a family received a double portion of his father's estate as an inheritance (see Deuteronomy 21:17). In Jesus' parable of the prodigal son, the youngest son asked his father for his portion or share of the estate ahead of time (see Luke 15:12).

The psalmist probably had this inheritance imagery in mind when he called God his "portion" (Psalm 119:57). The Lord was his spiritual heritage, passed down to him by godly people of past generations. Unlike an earthly inheritance that can be squandered, this is an inheritance that will last forever.

But comparing God to a legacy from the past has its limits. Truths about God can be passed on from generation to generation, but personal faith cannot. Parents can and should teach their offspring about God, but it is up to each child to accept this heritage through his or her own personal choice.

Two other names of God that describe Him as a portion are "portion in the land of the living" (Psalm 142:5) and "portion of mine inheritance" (Psalm 16:5). See also *Inheritance.*

PORTION IN THE LAND OF THE LIVING

See *Portion.*

PORTION OF MINE INHERITANCE

See *Portion.*

The Bible describes God as a potter who can make—or remake—His product however He chooses.

POSSESSION BY DEMONS

See *Demonic Possession*.

POSSESSOR OF HEAVEN AND EARTH

See *God of the Whole Earth*.

POTENTATE

See *Blessed and Only Potentate*.

POTTER

The prophet Isaiah longed for the wayward people of Judah to follow the Lord. If they became pliable clay in His hands, they would be shaped into beautiful vessels who would glorify His name: "O LORD, thou art our father," he prayed. "We are the clay, and thou our potter; and we all are the work of thy hand" (Isaiah 64:8).

God as the master potter is a graphic image that appears often throughout the Bible. For example, while the prophet Jeremiah looked on, a potter ruined a vase he was working on and had to start over again with the same lump of clay. Jeremiah compared the nation of Judah to this pottery reshaping process. Shape up, he declared, or you will be reshaped by the Lord's discipline (see Jeremiah 18:1–9).

The hymn writer Adelaide A. Pollard expressed this truth in a positive way:

> Have Thine own way, Lord! Have Thine own way!
> Thou art the Potter, I am the clay.
> Mould me and make me after Thy will,
> While I am waiting, yielded and still.

See also *Creator*; *Maker*.

POWER OF GOD

In 1 Corinthians 1:23–25 the apostle Paul admitted that many people were skeptical of a crucified Savior. If Jesus was such a great person, they reasoned, why did He wind up being executed on a Roman cross like a common criminal? To them His crucifixion was a sign of weakness, not a demonstration of strength.

On the contrary, Paul pointed out, Christ showed great power in His crucifixion. He was the very "power of God" (v. 24) whom the Father sent to atone for the sins of the world through His death. The death of One on behalf of the many showed the extent of this divine power.

Jesus' power was demonstrated many times during His earthly ministry. He stilled a storm and calmed the waters on the Sea of Galilee (see Mark 4:37–39). He cast demons out of a demented man (see Luke 4:31–35). He raised His friend Lazarus from the dead (see John 11:43–44). But He refused to come down from the cross and save Himself, although the crowd taunted Him to do so (see Matthew 27:39–43).

This is a good example of power under

CHRIST AS THE POWER OF GOD

- "Your faith should not stand in the wisdom of men, but in the power of God" (1 Corinthians 2:5).
- "Though he was crucified through weakness, yet he liveth by the power of God" (2 Corinthians 13:4).
- "Be strong in the Lord, and in the power of his might" (Ephesians 6:10).
- "Be thou partaker of the afflictions of the gospel according to the power of God" (2 Timothy 1:8).

control. Jesus could have called legions of angels to come to His rescue (see Matthew 26:53). But this would have nullified the purpose for which God the Father had sent Him into the world. His divine power was never greater than when He refused to use it. See also *Christ Crucified*.

POWER OF THE HIGHEST

The angel Gabriel spoke these words of assurance to Mary, the mother of Jesus: "The power of the Highest shall overshadow thee: therefore also that holy thing which shall be born of thee shall be called the Son of God" (Luke 1:35). Mary would give birth to the Son of God, although she was a virgin. His conception would occur through the action of the Holy Spirit, whom Gabriel called the "power of the Highest."

No other word describes the work of God's Spirit as well as "power." Throughout the Bible this is the dominant feature of His miraculous work. For example, Saul as the first king of Israel learned firsthand about the overwhelming power of the Holy Spirit. Insanely jealous of David, he sent several assassins to kill him. But the Spirit of God came upon them, causing then to utter prophecies instead of carrying out the king's orders.

Finally, Saul himself went to murder David, but the same thing happened to him (see 1 Samuel 19:19–24). He fell into a prophetic trance, and the people asked, "Is Saul also among the prophets?" (v. 24). King Saul was the most powerful man in Israel, but he was no match for the Holy Spirit and His power. God's Spirit protected David, who had been selected by the Lord to succeed Saul as king.

In the New Testament, when Jesus prepared to ascend to His Father, He told His disciples, "You will receive power when the Holy Spirit comes on you; and you will be my witnesses in Jerusalem, and in all Judea and Samaria, and to the ends of the earth" (Acts 1:8 NIV).

As Jesus promised, the Holy Spirit did empower His disciples and other early believers to carry out the Great Commission. The initial outpouring of the Holy Spirit occurred on the day of Pentecost. This transformed His followers into bold witnesses for Jesus. Their zeal in preaching the Gospel is described throughout the book of Acts. From the Jews to the Samaritans to the Gentiles, the good news about Jesus spread like a roaring forest fire until it reached the very center of the Roman Empire, the capital city of Rome (see Acts 28:14–31).

NO BABBLING ALLOWED

In His teachings on prayer in His Sermon on the Mount, Jesus told His followers, "Do not keep on babbling like pagans, for they think they will be heard because of their many words" (Matthew 6:7 NIV).

The word translated as "babbling" in this passage means to speak without thinking. Pagan people of the ancient world called on their gods by repeating stock phrases and legalistic formulas over and over again. In their contest with the prophet Elijah on Mount Carmel, for example, the prophets of Baal called out "from morning even until noon, saying, O Baal, hear us" (1 Kings 18:26).

What a contrast this is to Jesus' approach to prayer. He taught His disciples to place their daily needs before the Lord with confidence. Prayer is not heaping up meaningless words but sincere communication with our heavenly Father.

But the Holy Spirit has not restricted His work to that long-ago time. He is still at work in the modern world through those who follow Jesus as Lord and Savior. God the Father will do His work through us as believers: "'Not by might nor by power, but by my Spirit,' says the LORD Almighty" (Zechariah 4:6 NIV). See also *Church*; *Gospel*.

PRAISE OF GOD

See *Worship of God*.

PRAYER

Prayer is one of those things that most of us take for granted. But just think what a great privilege it is. God wants us as unworthy human beings to commune with Him—the supreme ruler of the universe. He has promised to hear our prayers when they are offered in faith and humility. The apostle Peter put it like this: "The eyes of the Lord are on the righteous and his ears are

A woman prays at the Western (or "Wailing") Wall in Jerusalem, the remains of the original Jewish temple. The wall is a special place for Jewish prayers—but God's people can pray to Him anywhere, anytime.

attentive to their prayer" (1 Peter 3:12 NIV).

Most of us think of prayer as asking God for His blessings and benefits. This is a form of prayer known as petition, bringing our personal requests before the Lord. But there is so much more to prayer than this. In our prayers, we should offer our adoration to God simply because He is and He deserves our highest praise. Thanksgiving is also a vital part of prayer. God should receive our thanks for specific ways in which He has blessed our lives.

No prayer to God is complete without the confession of our sins and our humble plea for his forgiveness. King David modeled this element of prayer after His sin of adultery with Bathsheba. "Have mercy on me, O God," he prayed. "Wash away all my iniquity and cleanse me from my sin" (Psalm 51:1–2 NIV).

Perhaps the most neglected dimension of prayer is intercession. When we pray for others and intercede on their behalf before the Lord, we are practicing the unselfish servanthood that Jesus commended for all believers (see Matthew 20:27).

Jesus prayed often to His heavenly Father and also taught us how to pray in His model prayer, often referred to as the Lord's Prayer (see Matthew 6:9–13). But he also warned us against some false forms of prayer. We should not pray just to impress people, and we should not just mouth a bunch of pious words that don't come from the heart (see Matthew 6:7). See also *Lord's Prayer*; *Worship of God*.

PRECIOUS CORNERSTONE

See *Chief Cornerstone*.

PREDESTINATION

This theological concept refers to God's knowledge in advance of who will accept His gift of salvation. Since God is all-knowing, or omniscient, He knows all things—even our choices long before we make them. Therefore, He knows who will become believers and who will refuse to become part of His kingdom.

But God's foreknowledge of what will happen does not mean that He will predestinate some people to be saved and others to be eternally lost. This depends on whether people exercise the free will He has given them and respond in faith to His generous gift. His eternal purpose is that all people will come to know Jesus Christ as Savior and Lord (see 1 Timothy 2:4). See also *Divine Election*; *Foreknowledge of God*; *Free Will of Man*.

PREEXISTENCE OF JESUS

See *Beginning of the Creation of God*.

PRESENCE OF GOD

See *Angel of His Presence*; *Face of God*.

PRIDE

This feeling of arrogance because of one's accomplishments or status in life is the very opposite of humility, or putting others before oneself. Excessive pride is a serious sin because it attributes to oneself the glory and honor that belong to God alone.

Jesus told a parable about a self-righteous Pharisee and a penitent tax collector to emphasize the problem of pride. Both men went to the temple to pray. The proud Pharisee thanked God that he was not a sinner like other people. But the humble tax collector prayed, "God, have mercy on me, a sinner" (Luke 18:13 NIV).

Jesus made it clear which of these two men found favor in God's sight. The humble tax collector "went home justified before God." Jesus noted, "For all those who exalt themselves will be humbled, and those who humble themselves will be exalted" (Luke 18:14 NIV). See also *Humility*.

PRIEST FOREVER

See *Great High Priest*.

PRIESTHOOD OF BELIEVERS

This doctrine is sometimes referred to as the "universal priesthood." In essence, it means that people do not have to go through a human priest in order to reach the Lord. Every believer has direct access to God because of

the atoning sacrifice of Christ.

The concept of the priesthood of all believers was popularized by Martin Luther, the spearhead of the Protestant Reformation of the 1500s. He based the doctrine on two verses from the writings of the apostle Peter: "As you come to him, the living Stone—rejected by humans but chosen by God and precious to him—you also, like living stones, are being built into a spiritual house to be a holy priesthood" (1 Peter 2:4–5 NIV).

Other passages in the Bible support the doctrine of universal priesthood. For example, when Jesus died on the cross, the veil in the temple was split in two from top to bottom. This showed that the gap between Jews and Gentiles was now removed and that all people could come into God's presence

A statue of the Protestant reformer Martin Luther, who more than anyone popularized the concept of the "priesthood of believers."

(see Matthew 27:50–51).

The Bible is also clear that Christ is the only authorized mediator between God and man (see Ephesians 3:11–12). Therefore, we can come boldly and directly to Him (see Hebrews 4:15–16). This doctrine also emphasizes the ministry responsibility of all believers. As priests of God, we should reach out to others in a spirit of love (see Galatians 3:28). See also *Access to God*; *Mediator*; *Veil of the Temple*.

PRIESTHOOD OF CHRIST

See *Great High Priest; Offices of Christ.*

PRIESTS

Religious leaders made sacrificial offerings on behalf of the people. The priesthood originated with Aaron, and his descendants were sanctified to the office (see Exodus 29:9, 44). Jesus, our faultless high priest, paid for our sins once and for all by sacrificing Himself on the cross (see Hebrews 7:27).

According to the author of the book of Hebrews, earthly priests die and are succeeded by others who serve only for a limited time. But Jesus has "a permanent priesthood. Therefore he is able to save completely those who come to God through him, because he always lives to intercede for them" (Hebrews 7:24–25 NIV). See also *Aaron; Great High Priest; High Priest.*

PRINCE

The apostle Peter used this title for Jesus in a sermon before the Jewish Sanhedrin. He and the other apostles had just been released miraculously from prison by an angel after they were arrested for preaching about Jesus. Peter declared in his sermon that the Jewish religious leaders were guilty of crucifying Jesus, the "Prince" whom God the Father had sent into the world (see Acts 5:30–31).

Prince is a title with at least three different meanings in the Bible. Peter could have had any one or all of these in mind when he referred to Jesus as a Prince.

1. A prince was the son of a king. If a king had several sons, his oldest was generally the one who succeeded his father on the throne. Perhaps Peter had Jesus as God's Son in mind when he called him a Prince.

2. *Prince* is a generic term often used in the Bible for a leader or ruler. For example, when Moses tried to stop a fight between two Israelites, one of them asked him, "Who made thee a prince and a judge over us?" (Exodus 2:14). When Peter called Jesus a Prince, he may have been saying that Jesus had been exalted by God to serve as a ruler over His people.

3. Sometimes the word *prince* is used as a synonym for "king" (see 1 Kings 11:34). By saying that Jesus was a Prince, Peter could have implied that He was the one and only sovereign ruler over God's people.

What Peter said about Jesus as a Prince boils down to this: He is the one and only Son of God appointed by the Father to rule over His people like a good king, administering justice and righteousness in His name. See also *Prince of Princes; Prince of the Kings of the Earth.*

ANOTHER PRINCE

Jesus is the Prince over God's kingdom. But He recognized there is another prince—Satan—who tries to undermine His work. He referred to Satan several times as "the prince of this world" (John 12:31; 14:30; 16:11). The apostle Paul also called Satan "the prince of the power of the air" (Ephesians 2:2).

PRINCE OF LIFE

See *Life.*

PRINCE OF PEACE

See *Lord of Peace.*

PRINCE OF PRINCES

The prophet Daniel foresaw the coming of an evil power that would stand against the Lord: "He will destroy many and take his stand against the Prince of princes. Yet he will be destroyed, but not by human power" (Daniel 8:25 NIV).

This verse was fulfilled in Jewish history, but it also awaits its ultimate fulfillment in the end time. It refers in the short term to Antiochus IV, Epiphanes, an evil Greek ruler who persecuted the Jews. As a long-range prophecy, it refers to the Antichrist, or beast, of the last days who is described in the book of Revelation (see Revelation 19:20).

Antiochus tried to force the Jewish people to adopt Greek culture, even going so far as to erect an altar to the pagan Greek god Zeus in the temple. His atrocities led to rebellion by the Jews under the leadership of the Maccabees during the period between the Old and New Testaments. Antiochus died in disgrace following his defeat by these Jewish zealots.

The ultimate earthly evil force will be the Antichrist, who stands against Christ, His Church, and their influence for good in the world. But this evil person will be overcome by Christ (see Revelation 14:9–11; 19:20), just as Antiochus met defeat in his time. No earthly power is able to stand against the Prince of princes. See also *Prince*; *Prince of the Kings of the Earth.*

PRINCE OF THE KINGS OF THE EARTH

The apostle John addressed the book of Revelation to the seven churches of Asia Minor whose members were undergoing persecution by the Roman authorities. John wanted these believers to understand that he was not writing under his own authority but under the command and direction of Jesus Christ, the "prince of the kings of the earth" (Revelation 1:4–5).

On display in a German museum, a bust of Antiochus IV, Epiphanes, one of the Bible's evil "prince of princes."

Earthly rulers like the emperors of the Roman Empire would come and go. But Jesus was an eternal King, not a temporary monarch who would rule for a few years, then be replaced by another. He stands above and beyond all the kings of the earth.

Other titles of Jesus that are similar in meaning to this title are "King of Kings" (Revelation 19:16) and "king over all the earth" (Zechariah 14:9). If Jesus is the world's supreme King, there is no doubt that He has the right to reign over His Church and in the lives of those who claim Him as their Savior and Lord. See also *King of Kings*; *Prince of Princes*.

PRINCE OF THE POWER OF THE AIR

See *Satan*.

PRINCE OF THIS WORLD

See *Satan*.

RESTING IN GOD'S PROMISE

The old hymn "I Know Whom I Have Believed" by Daniel Webster Whittle is a song of faith and confidence. We can rest assured that the Lord will keep His promise of eternal life for all believers.

I know not why God's wondrous grace
To me He hath made known,
Nor why, unworthy, Christ in love
Redeemed me for His own.
But I know whom I have believed,
And am persuaded that He is able
To keep that which I have committed
Unto Him against that day.

PROGRESSIVE REVELATION

See *Revelation of God*.

PROMISED LAND

See *Canaan*; *Palestine*.

PROMISES OF GOD

Making promises is dangerous because we can't see into the future. Circumstances we can't foresee often arise, making it impossible for us to keep the promises we have made to others.

But God, who knows all things, can make promises without worrying about what the future holds. The Bible is filled with promises He has made to those who acknowledge His lordship and follow His will. In Old Testament times, He made a threefold promise to His special people, the Israelites. He would be their God (see Deuteronomy 26:17), they would be His people (see Deuteronomy 7:6), and He would make His presence felt among them (see Deuteronomy 20:1).

Along with these divine promises, He also pledged that He would give His people a land of their own (see Genesis 15:7). All of this happened just as He promised, although the Israelites were sometimes undeserving of His blessings.

God also promised to send a Messiah to serve as a spiritual deliverer for His people (see Isaiah 9:6). This promise was fulfilled when He sent His own Son, Jesus, into the world (see John 3:16). Jesus also brought with him many more divine promises—forgiveness of sins (see 1 John 1:9), our future resurrection (see 1 Corinthians 15:20–24), and eternal life with God the Father and Jesus the Son (see John 10:28–29).

The apostle Paul viewed Jesus as the

God promises Abraham offspring "as the stars of heaven" (Genesis 22:17), a vow that came true with the ongoing nation of Israel.

fulfillment of God's promise to His people in Old Testament times. "If you belong to Christ," he told the Galatian believers, "then you are Abraham's seed, and heirs according to the promise" (Galatians 3:29 NIV). See also *Assurance of God; Holy Spirit of Promise; Hope.*

PROPHECIES ABOUT CHRIST

For many centuries the prophets of the Old Testament had been predicting that God would send the Messiah to serve as a deliverer for His people. These prophecies were fulfilled by Jesus.

In His hometown of Nazareth at the beginning of His ministry, Jesus read from one of these familiar prophecies written by Isaiah several centuries before. It was clear to the people that He was identifying Himself as the Messiah whom the prophet had written about: "The Spirit of the Lord is on me, because he has anointed me to proclaim good news to the poor. He has sent me to proclaim freedom for the prisoners and recovery of sight for the blind, to set the oppressed free" (Luke 4:18 NIV).

Scores of other messianic prophecies are recorded in the Old Testament. Here is a list of the major ones, along with their fulfillment in the New Testament.

PROPHET MIGHTY IN DEED AND WORD

See *Great Prophet.*

Prophecies About Christ		Old Testament Passage	New Testament Fulfillment
1.	Born in Bethlehem	Micah 5:2	Luke 2:4–6
2.	Born of a virgin	Isaiah 7:14	Luke 2:7
3.	Meekness and humility	Isaiah 42:2	Matthew 12:15–19
4.	Ministry in Galilee	Isaiah 9:1–2	Matthew 4:12–28
5.	Prophet like Moses	Deuteronomy 18:15–18	Acts 3:20–22
6.	Son of God	Proverbs 30:4	Luke 1:32–35
7.	Worker of miracles	Isaiah 35:5–6	John 11:47
8.	Savior of Gentiles	Isaiah 42:1	Acts 10:45–47
9.	Anointed with the Spirit	Isaiah 42:1	John 3:34
10.	Suffering for others	Isaiah 53:4–12	Matthew 20:28
11.	Mocked by enemies	Psalm 22:7–8	Matthew 27:28–30
12.	Buried with rich	Isaiah 53:9	Matthew 27:57–60
13.	Resurrected from death	Psalm 16:10	Luke 24:5–9
14.	Ascension to the Father	Psalm 68:18	Acts 1:9
15.	At God's right hand	Psalm 110:1	Hebrews 1:3
16.	Universal rule	Daniel 7:14	Philippians 2:9–11

PROPHET OF NAZARETH OF GALILEE

See *Great Prophet.*

PROPHETS

These inspired messengers were called by God to declare His will and spoke by His authority. They emphasized that they spoke for the Lord by declaring, "Thus saith the LORD" (Jeremiah 28:16; *This is what the LORD says*, NIV).

Jesus was the last in a long line of prophets whom God sent to His people across many centuries. He Himself claimed to be a prophet (see Luke 13:33). He was the ultimate spokesman for the Lord, since He came into the world as God's own Son. See also *Great Prophet*; *Offices of Christ*; *Spirit of Prophecy.*

PROPITIATION FOR OUR SINS

The apostle John declared in one of his letters: "Herein is love, not that we loved God, but that he loved us, and sent his Son to be the propitiation for our sins" (1 John 4:10).

The word *propitiation* comes from the old English word *propitiate*, meaning "to appease" or "to satisfy." Thus, John says in this verse that God the Father sent His Son, Jesus, to serve as the satisfaction for our sins. This word is the key to one of the classical theories of the atonement, or the sacrificial death of Jesus. Another word that is used for this concept is *expiation.*

According to this view, God is a holy God who cannot tolerate sin. This puts us as humans in a dilemma because we are not capable of living a sinless life, no matter how hard we try. To make matters worse, God is also a just God who—in order to be true to His nature—must punish sin wherever He

A statue of the prophet Daniel at an Austrian church. Prophets carried God's message to the world—though the words on this scroll are an abbreviated paraphrase of King Darius's statement after Daniel survived a night in the lions' den: "He is the living God, who worketh signs and wonders in earth."

finds it. So our sin separates us from God and makes us liable to His punishment. *Hopeless* is the only word that adequately describes this situation.

But, according to the apostle John, God loved us too much to allow us to continue in this dilemma. He sent His Son, Jesus, to die to pay the penalty that He demanded from us because of our sin. Jesus was the sacrifice that covered over or atoned for our sin and restored the broken relationship between a holy God and sinful people.

Propitiation is not a word that most of us drop into a casual conversation. Most people would not understand it. But aren't you glad that God knows the term and that Jesus lived out its meaning through His life and death?

We as believers can celebrate because Jesus came into the world to propitiate. See also *Atonement*; *Mediator*; *Reconciliation*.

Jesus as Our Propitiation/Ransom

Another New Testament term that means basically the same thing as *propitiation* is *ransom*. In the Old Testament, this described the price that was paid to purchase a person's freedom from slavery or punishment. In the New Testament, Jesus applied this word to Himself when He declared, "The Son of man came not to be ministered unto, but to minister, and to give his life a ransom for many" (Mark 10:45).

PROTOEVANGELIUM

See *Seed of the Woman*.

PROVIDENCE OF GOD

The dictionary defines *providence* as "divine guidance or care." As a Christian doctrine, the word refers to God's guidance of human acts or historical events to bring about His purpose. God has given us the freedom to make our own choices. But even when we act contrary to His will, He can use circumstances growing out of that bad choice to bring about His purpose.

One of the best biblical examples of the Lord's providence at work is the account of Joseph and his brothers in the book of Genesis. In a fit of jealousy, his brothers sold him into slavery in Egypt. This was clearly an act of sin on their part. But God, through a series of timely events, brought good out of this bad situation.

Joseph eventually became a high official in the Egyptian government (see Genesis 41:41). When he was finally reunited with his brothers, he forgave them for their injustice against him. Then he made arrangements for his entire family to come to Egypt to escape a severe famine in their homeland. With the eyes of faith, he could see how the Lord had worked behind the scenes to preserve his family.

"God sent me ahead of you. . .to save your lives by a great deliverance," he told his brothers. "So, then, it was not you who sent me here, but God" (Genesis 45:7–8 NIV). See also *Divine Election*; *Foreknowledge of God*; *Free Will of Man*.

King David sings psalms of worship in a seventeenth-century painting by Jan de Bray. David authored many of the psalms, though others are attributed to Solomon, Moses, and lesser Bible characters.

PSALMS, BOOK OF

This poetic book of the Old Testament is filled with hymns of praise and prayers of thanksgiving to God. Its title is derived from a Greek word that implies that these psalms were to be sung to the accompaniment of a musical instrument. King David of Judah wrote many of these psalms (see titles of Psalms 54, 59, 65). But many other unknown writers contributed to this book, which was probably compiled across many centuries of biblical history.

Generations of believers have found the psalms to be a rich source of devotional inspiration, with their emphasis on the goodness, stability, power, and faithfulness of God. See also *Worship of God.*

PUBLICANS

Publicans, or tax collectors, were hated and looked upon as traitors by their fellow Jewish citizens (see Matthew 5:46) because they purchased the right to collect taxes in a specific area of Israel for the Roman government. The best-known publican in the Bible is Matthew, whom Jesus called away from his tax-collecting booth to become one of His disciples (see Matthew 9:9). See also *Friend of Publicans and Sinners.*

PURGATORY

See *Intermediate State.*

PURIFICATION

The Law of Moses in the Old Testament prescribed purification, ceremonial or spiritual cleansing, rites for people who had been defiled by touching a corpse, by contact with bodily discharges, by childbirth, and by

leprosy (see Leviticus 14–15). The mother of Jesus offered turtledoves and pigeons as a sacrifice in her ceremonial cleansing (see Luke 2:21–24). See also *Ceremonial Washing.*

Matthew holds a quill pen in the stained-glass window of a French chapel. In his first life as a publican, he would have used the pen to record tax payments. After meeting Jesus, he would write the first Gospel.

Jesus as "rabbi" (or teacher) in a nineteenth-century engraving of the Sermon on the Mount.

QR

QUICKENING SPIRIT

This title of Jesus appears in connection with His name as the "last Adam" (1 Corinthians 15:45). Adam's disobedience of God brought sin and death into the world. But Jesus' perfect obedience nullified the divine curse against Adam and brought the possibility of eternal life to humankind. As the "quickening spirit" (*life-giving spirit*, NIV), Jesus offers eternal life to all who accept Him as Savior and Lord. See also *Last Adam*.

RABBI/RABBONI

When Nicodemus came to talk with Jesus, he complimented Him by saying, "Rabbi, we know that you are a teacher who has come from God. For no one could perform the signs you are doing if God were not with him" (John 3:2 NIV). In modern society "rabbi" is the official title of the leader of a Jewish congregation. It is similar to the title "reverend" for a Protestant minister or "father" for a Catholic priest.

But in Jesus' time, the word *rabbi* was a term of respect meaning "teacher" or "master." Nicodemus wanted to learn more about this Jewish teacher and miracle worker who was impressing the crowds in the region of Galilee.

In John 20:16 Mary Magdalene's recognition of Jesus as "rabboni" paid homage to Him as her master. After His resurrection she recognized Him as such when He called her by name. *Rabboni* is the Aramaic form of *rabbi*. Aramaic was the common language spoken in Israel during New Testament times.

Whether we call Jesus rabbi or rabboni, the meaning is the same: He is our master teacher and guide who deserves our utmost respect and loyalty. See also *Good Master*; *Master*; *Teacher Come from God*.

RADIANCE OF GOD'S GLORY

See *Brightness of God's Glory*.

RANSOM

See *Propitiation for Our Sins*.

RAPTURE

This word refers to God's deliverance of the Church and all believers out of the world in the end time. The doctrine is based on the apostle Paul's description of this event in connection with the second coming of Christ: "The dead in Christ will rise first. After that, we who are still alive and are left will be caught up together with them in the clouds to meet the Lord in the air" (1 Thessalonians 4:16–17 NIV).

Bible interpreters disagree on the exact timing of the rapture. Some believe it will occur before the second coming of Christ and the great tribulation that will strike the earth. Others believe it will happen at the same time as Jesus' return. See also *Great Tribulation*; *Second Coming of Christ*.

READY FOR CHRIST'S RETURN

See *Watchfulness*.

RECONCILIATION

The basic meaning of this theological term is "to exchange." Thus, reconciliation is the process by which our separation from God is exchanged for a relationship of peace and fellowship.

This exchange is possible because of Christ's sacrifice on our behalf. Our sin barred us from fellowship with a holy God. But His Son's atoning death paid the penalty demanded by our sin and allowed us into God's presence. This process of reconciliation came about through the Lord's initiative. As the apostle Paul expressed it, "All this is from God, who reconciled us to himself through Christ" (2 Corinthians 5:18 NIV).

Just as we as believers have been reconciled to God, we are to be ambassadors of reconciliation for others (see 2 Corinthians 5:18–20). See also *Mediator*.

JESUS' MINISTRY OF RECONCILIATION

* "It behoved him [Jesus] to be made like unto his brethren, that he might. . . make reconciliation for the sins of the people" (Hebrews 2:17).
* "When we were enemies, we were reconciled to God by the death of his Son" (Romans 5:10).
* "God was in Christ, reconciling the world unto himself" (2 Corinthians 5:19).

REDEEMER

This divine name is used for both God the Father and God the Son. In the Old Testament, the name reflects the concept of the kinsman-redeemer. In the close-knit families and clans of Bible times, the nearest relative of a family member in trouble was expected to come to that person's rescue.

For example, if an impoverished relative

Countless portraits of Jesus have been painted over the centuries. This one, by the sixteenth-century Italian Titian, is entitled *Christ the Redeemer*.

had been forced to sell himself into slavery, his next of kin would buy or "redeem" his freedom. If a person lost his property to a debtor, his kinsman-redeemer was responsible for buying it back and restoring it to this family member. This is exactly what happened in the book of Ruth. Boaz, a kinsman of Naomi's deceased husband, Elimelech, bought back the property Elimelech had lost and restored it to Naomi (see Ruth 4:1–9).

The prophet Isaiah declared that God is the ultimate Redeemer who will come to the rescue of His people (see Isaiah 54:8). In another passage in his book, the prophet Isaiah also referred to the Lord as the "Redeemer of Israel" (Isaiah 49:7). We can rest assured that no trouble that we experience is so deep that it is beyond the Redeemer's reach.

The prophet Isaiah also referred to the

coming Messiah as a Redeemer for God's people (see Isaiah 59:20). But He was to be a Redeemer of a different type. Jesus Christ the Redeemer would free God's people from their bondage to sin and death. He would do so by dying on the cross for our benefit. The purchase price that He would pay for our salvation was none other than His own precious blood.

The patriarch Job, like Isaiah, also received a glimpse of this Redeemer of the future. Out of his suffering and despair he declared, "I know that my redeemer liveth, and that he shall stand at the latter day upon the earth" (Job 19:25).

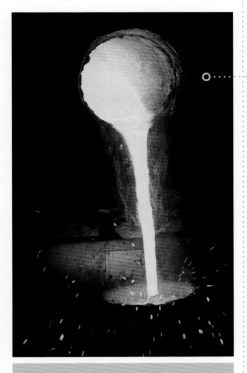

Molten metal is poured into a casting mold. The "refiner's fire" helps remove impurities from the raw material.

What Isaiah and Job only hoped for has now come to pass. We can rejoice with the apostle John because "the blood of Jesus Christ. . .cleanseth us from all sin" (1 John 1:7). See also *Redemption*; *Salvation*.

REDEMPTION

The process of buying back property that had been forfeited because of indebtedness or of buying back a person who had been sold into slavery (see Exodus 6:6) is known as redemption. This idea describes perfectly the work of Christ, who "bought us back" from sin and death through His atonement on the cross as our Redeemer (see Matthew 20:28). See also *Atonement*; *Redeemer*.

REFINER'S FIRE

This name of Jesus appears in the final chapter of the Old Testament. The prophet Malachi compared the coming Messiah to the hot fire that metalworkers of Bible times used to purify ore such as silver: "Who may abide the day of his coming? and who shall stand when he appeareth? for he is like a refiner's fire" (Malachi 3:2). The ore was heated in a pot until it turned to liquid and the dross or waste material rose to the surface. Then the metalworker used a ladle to skim off the dross, leaving the pure and uncontaminated silver.

This image of the Messiah must have been a surprise to the Jewish people of Malachi's time. They expected the Messiah to come as a conquering hero who would restore Israel to its glory days as a political kingdom. But the prophet informed them that the Messiah would come in judgment against Israel because of its sin and rebellion.

The name Refiner's Fire emphasizes Jesus' role as judge. His second coming will bring judgment against all who have refused to accept Him as Savior and Lord (see 2 Peter 2:9). See also *Judge of Quick and Dead*; *Wall of Fire*.

REFLECTION OF GOD'S GLORY

See *Brightness of God's Glory*.

REFUGE

Moses called God by this name as the Israelites were getting ready to enter the promised land. He reminded the people to follow the Lord as they occupied the land because He alone was a dependable source of refuge and protection. "The eternal God is thy refuge," he told them, "and underneath are the everlasting arms" (Deuteronomy 33:27).

After they settled in Canaan, the Israelites designated certain population centers as cities of refuge (see Numbers 35:6–7; Joshua 20:7–9). An Israelite who killed another person accidentally could flee to one of these cities to escape the dead man's family who were seeking revenge. His safety was guaranteed by the elders of the city while the circumstances surrounding the death were under investigation.

With God as our refuge, we have nothing to fear from those who seek to do us harm. Even in death, there is no safer place to be than in the arms of the everlasting God.

Another name of God that expresses basically the same idea as refuge is "shelter" (Psalm 61:3). See also *Fortress*; *Hiding Place*.

SAFE IN THE ARMS OF THE LORD

The phrase "everlasting arms" in Deuteronomy 33:27 has been immortalized in the hymn "Leaning on the Everlasting Arms," written by Elisha A. Hoffman. Generations of believers have been inspired by this grand old hymn.

What a fellowship, what a joy divine,
Leaning on the everlasting arms;
What a blessedness, what a peace is mine,
Leaning on the everlasting arms.
Leaning, leaning,
Safe and secure from all alarms;
Leaning, leaning,
Leaning on the everlasting arms.

REGENERATION

The process of regeneration occurs when the Holy Spirit changes a person's spiritual nature, enabling him or her to respond to God in faith. Regeneration is strictly an act of God. The human will has no part in this divine activity.

The apostle Paul explained the need for regeneration when he told the believers at Ephesus, "You were dead in your transgressions and sins" (Ephesians 2:1 NIV). In their natural sinful state, they were unable to respond to the Lord. But God, Paul went on to say, made them "alive with Christ" (Ephesians 2:5 NIV). This regeneration or rebirth of their nature made them capable of responding to God's offer of salvation through the death of His Son (see Ephesians 2:5–6).

The Bible uses several different words and phrases to describe the concept of regeneration. These include "renewed," "reborn," and "born of God." Jesus had this concept in mind when He told Nicodemus, "No one can see the kingdom of God unless they are born again" (John 3:3 NIV). He went on to identify the Holy Spirit as the agent of this supernatural work of God (see John 3:8). See also *New Birth*.

REMISSION OF SINS

This phrase appears several times in the New Testament, particularly in the Gospel of Luke and the book of Acts. For example, in his sermon to the crowds on the day of Pentecost, the apostle Peter declared, "Repent, and be baptized. . .in the name of Jesus Christ for the remission of sins" (Acts 2:38).

Remission is a form of the word *remit*, which means "to release" or "to relax." Most modern translations render the phrase as "forgiveness of sins." See also *Forgiveness*.

REMNANT

This small group of God's people remained loyal to Him, in spite of the sin and idolatry among the rest of the population. Moses was the first person in the Bible to speak of the remnant. He predicted that the Israelites, God's special people, would be scattered among the nations (see Deuteronomy 28:62–68). But God would eventually bring back a righteous remnant of His people to resettle their homeland (see Deuteronomy 30:1–10).

The prophets of the Old Testament picked up this remnant theme and declared that Israel would be punished for its unfaithfulness (see Isaiah 1:9). But a righteous remnant of His people would be preserved (see Isaiah 10:20–22).

In the New Testament, the apostle Paul expanded on this remnant theme. The new faithful remnant, according to him, was the Church founded by Jesus when the nation of Israel failed to bring other nations to the Lord. God continues to work in the world today through His faithful remnant, the Church (see Romans 11:5). See also *Church*.

Repentance is like a U-turn when we realize we're on the wrong path—the path that leads us away from God.

REPENTANCE

True repentance is a profound sorrow for one's sin, a turning away from it, and a turning to God for forgiveness and restoration. Repentance is necessary for salvation (see Luke 13:5) and for believers when they yield to temptation and fall into sin (see Revelation 3:19).

The best example of repentance in the Old Testament is that of King David. After he committed adultery with Bathsheba, he prayed to the Lord, "Wash away all my iniquity and cleanse me from my sin. . . . Create in me a pure heart, O God, and renew a steadfast spirit within me" (Psalm 51:2, 10 NIV).

In the New Testament, John the Baptist called on people to "repent. . .for the kingdom of heaven is at hand" (Matthew 3:2). Jesus continued John's emphasis on repentance as the first step for those who wanted to enter His kingdom (see Mark 1:15). To the scribes and Pharisees who criticized Him for associating with sinners, He replied, "I came not to call the righteous, but sinners to repentance" (Luke 5:32).

Repentance is a gift of God's eternal love (see Romans 2:4) that brings us into fellowship with Him and keeps us there, even

when we wander from His will. We have this promise from the Lord through the words of the apostle John: "If we confess our sins, he is faithful and just and will forgive us our sins and purify us from all unrighteousness" (1 John 1:9 NIV). See also *Repentance of God*.

REPENTANCE OF GOD

Some Bible students are confused by the statements about the "repentance" of God in the King James Version. For example, the Lord declared to the nations through the prophet Jeremiah: "If that nation, against whom I have pronounced, turn from their evil, I will repent of the evil that I thought to do unto them" (Jeremiah 18:8). Since God is wholly righteous, how can the Bible speak of His repentance? Doesn't His perfect nature mean that He has no sin of which to repent?

This puzzle is solved when we remember that the basic meaning of the word *repentance*

Mary and Martha react to the raising of Lazarus in a painting by Vincent van Gogh. Jesus had shortly before told Martha that He is "the resurrection, and the life."

is "to change." Here is how the NIV renders the passage: "If that nation I warned repents of its evil, then I will relent and not inflict on it the disaster I had planned." Notice the NIV's distinction between *repent* ("turn from sin") and *relent* ("change one's mind"). God doesn't repent but He does relent.

Thus, the message of this passage is that God's blessings depend on our actions. He will either bless us or punish us, depending on whether we follow or reject His will. See also *Repentance; Immutability of God*.

RESTRAINT OF GOD

See *Longsuffering of God.*

RESURRECTION AND THE LIFE

Jesus used this name for Himself in His conversation with Martha, the sister of Lazarus. She was disappointed that Jesus had not arrived at their home in Bethany before Lazarus died. She knew Jesus could perform miracles of healing, so she scolded Him, "Lord. . .if you had been here, my brother would not have died" (John 11:21 NIV). Jesus told her, "I am the resurrection and the life. The one who believes in me will live, even though they die; and whoever lives by believing in me will never die" (John 11:25–26 NIV).

Jesus' double-edged reply to Martha made it clear that He was the master of the living and the dead. He was capable at any time of raising Lazarus as well as any others who had died. At the same time, He could guarantee eternal life for the living. In this sense, those who believed in Him would never die. This included Martha, as well as all believers of the future.

Then Jesus proceeded to deliver on His promise. He stood before the burial chamber where the body of Lazarus had been placed. Then, just as God the Father created the world with the words of His mouth (see Genesis 1:1–31), Jesus the Son brought His friend back to life with the simple verbal command, "Lazarus, come out" (John 11:43 NIV).

Note the things that are missing from this account: no incantations over the body, no lightning flash from heaven, no magical tricks to dazzle the crowd. Just three simple words from Jesus—and Lazarus walked out of the tomb. You don't have to be a genius to figure out that a person of such sensitivity and power is worthy of our loyalty and devotion. Jesus alone has the keys to life and death. See also *Life; Spirit of Life.*

RESURRECTION OF CHRIST

Jesus returned to physical life following His death. His resurrection was foretold in the Psalms (see Psalm 16:10–11) and by the prophets (see Isaiah 53:10–12), announced by Christ Himself (see Mark 9:9–10), and proclaimed by the apostles (see Acts 2:32; 3:15). It validates our faith and witness

APPEARANCES OF JESUS AFTER HIS RESURRECTION

- To Mary Magdalene at the empty tomb (see Mark 16:9).
- To other women at the empty tomb (see Matthew 28:1–10).
- To two followers on their way to Emmaus (see Luke 24:13–32).
- To Peter, apparently in Jerusalem (see Luke 24:33–35).
- To ten of His disciples in Jerusalem, Thomas absent (see John 20:19–25).
- To the eleven disciples in Jerusalem, Thomas present (see John 20:26–29).
- To His disciples at the Sea of Galilee (see John 21:1–14).
- To His disciples at His ascension near Jerusalem (see Luke 24:44–53).
- To five hundred followers (see 1 Corinthians 15:6).
- To James and all the apostles (see 1 Corinthians 15:7).
- To the apostle Paul (see 1 Corinthians 15:8).

(see 1 Corinthians 15:14–15), assures believers of our own bodily resurrection (see 1 Corinthians 15:18–20), emphasizes our final victory over sin and death (see 1 Corinthians 15:17, 26, 54, 57), and inspires faithfulness in Christian service (see 1 Corinthians 15:58).

Jesus spent forty days among His followers after He was resurrected and before His ascension to the Father. He used this time to show proofs that He was alive and to give them further instructions about the witness they were to bear through the Church (see Acts 1:1–8). Several post-resurrection appearances of Jesus are recorded in the New Testament (see sidebar on page 335). See also *Resurrection and the Life*.

REVELATION OF GOD

How do we as earthbound beings come to know God, who is beyond our human experience? This is possible because of something known as God's revelation. He has taken the initiative to make Himself known to us. Without this action on His part, we would not be able to know anything about Him and His divine nature.

One dimension of the revelation of God is general or natural revelation. We know about God through our observation of the natural world that He has created. The beauty and complexity of nature tell us that He is all-powerful and that He has put order and design into His creation (see Job 37:14–19).

Another way that God has revealed Himself is through special or supernatural revelation. His interaction with His special people, the Israelites, is a good example of this type of revelation. He appeared to Moses in a burning bush (see Exodus 3:1–3), making it known that He was a God of compassion who wanted to relieve the suffering of His people. His deliverance of the Ten Commandments to Moses revealed that He was a holy and righteous God who demanded that His people live up to His standards (see Exodus 20:1–18).

The best example of God's special revelation is the Bible. It contains a record of His acts in history and His guidelines for daily living. Through reading the Bible, we come to understand what He is like and how He wants us to act.

Theologians also speak of God's progressive revelation. Throughout history He has revealed Himself to different generations of people, in accordance with their ability to understand His nature and His will. For example, in Old Testament times, people presented sacrificial animals to atone for their sin. But in the fullness of time, God sent His Son to serve as the once-for-all sacrifice for sin.

God doesn't change, but He does accommodate Himself to changing conditions. The writer of the book of Hebrews talked about the old, outmoded method of dealing with sin and compared it to the new. "He [God] sets aside the first to establish the second," he declared. "And by that will, we have been made holy through the sacrifice of the body of Jesus Christ once for all" (Hebrews 10:9–10 NIV). See also *Divine Accommodation*; *Spirit of Wisdom and Revelation*.

REVENGE

Many people retaliate or attempt to "get even" with others for their wrongful actions, but Jesus rebuked His disciples for a vengeful spirit (see Luke 9:54–56) and commanded them to have a forgiving heart (see Matthew 5:38–44). He commanded us to love our enemies and show mercy toward others (see

Luke 6:35–38). Vengeance is to be exacted only by God (see Proverbs 20:22), who alone is impartial in His judgment and just in His treatment of all people. See also *Forgiveness*.

Worshippers quietly hold candles during a church service in Tblisi, Georgia. The prophet Habakkuk said silence was an appropriate response before God.

REVERENCE FOR GOD

This feeling of deep respect and awe that people are to show toward God is often referred to in the Bible as "fear of God," as in this verse: "The fear of the Lord is true wisdom" (Job 28:28 NLT). The opposite of reverence for God is blasphemy—or disrespect and contempt for His name and the denial that He exists or is involved in His creation.

One of the classic Bible passages on respect and reverence for God comes from the little-known prophet Habakkuk: "The Lord is in his holy temple; let all the earth keep silence before him" (Habakkuk 2:20). See also *Blasphemy*.

RIGHTEOUS

The word *righteous* is used in combination with other words in the Bible to express several different names for Jesus—for example, "righteous Branch" (Jeremiah 23:5), "righteous judge" (2 Timothy 4:8), and "righteous servant" (Isaiah 53:11). But 1 John 2:1 is the only place in the King James Version where Jesus is called "the righteous"—period: "If any man sin, we have an advocate with the Father, Jesus Christ the righteous" (1 John 2:1). The

NIV renders this name as "Righteous One."

Jesus can be called the "righteous" or the "Righteous One" because He is the only person who has ever lived who achieved perfect righteousness. Although He was capable of doing wrong because of the human side of His nature, He never gave in to temptation and stumbled into sin.

He was tempted by Satan at the beginning of His ministry to establish an earthly kingdom and to use His powers for His own self-interests. But He resisted all of these temptations (see Luke 4:1–13). In the Garden of Gethsemane on the night before His crucifixion, He admitted that "the flesh is weak" (Matthew 26:41). In an agonizing prayer, He asked God to deliver Him from the suffering of the cross, if possible. But He finally yielded His will to His Father's purpose and plan (see Matthew 26:37–42).

Because Jesus is righteousness personified, He calls us, His followers, to a life of righteousness. We will never achieve perfection and a sinless existence in this life, but we ought to be growing in that direction. He has promised to guide us along this journey. "The eyes of the Lord are over the righteous," the apostle Peter declared, "and his ears are open unto their prayers" (1 Peter 3:12). See also *Righteous Servant*; *Branch of Righteousness*.

RIGHTEOUS BRANCH

See *Branch of Righteousness*.

RIGHTEOUS JUDGE

See *Judge of Quick and Dead*.

RIGHTEOUS MAN

See *Just Man*.

RIGHTEOUSNESS OF GOD

This attribute of God signifies His holiness, moral purity, justice, and acts of goodness. Only God is righteous (see Psalm 119:137). His laws and judgments are righteous (see Psalm 19:9), and He alone can credit righteousness to people (see Romans 10:9–10).

The apostle Paul wrote extensively about God and His righteousness. His righteousness was revealed perfectly in the life and ministry of His Son, Jesus: "He made Him who knew no sin to be sin on our behalf, so that we might become the righteousness of God in Him" (2 Corinthians 5:21 NASB).

As believers, Christians are encouraged to pursue the interests of God's righteous kingdom (see Matthew 6:33). See also *Holiness of God*; *Imputed Righteousness*; *Lord Our Righteousness*.

RIGHTEOUS SERVANT

The theme of service and servanthood runs throughout the scriptures. For example, several different people in the Bible are referred to as a "servant of God" or "God's servant" because of the loyal service they rendered for the Lord (see sidebar). But Jesus is the only person who deserves to be called God's "Righteous Servant." He was the holy and righteous One whom the Father sent on a mission of redemption for the entire world.

This name of Jesus appears in one of the famous Servant Songs of the prophet Isaiah (see Isaiah 42:1–4; 49:1–6; 50:4–9; 52:13–53:12). This Servant, the Messiah, would undergo great suffering while carrying out His mission. But it would be for a divine purpose. His suffering and death would provide a means of deliverance for the human race that was trapped in sin.

Jesus identified Himself specifically as the Suffering Servant from God the Father whom Isaiah predicted. At the beginning of His public ministry, He quoted Isaiah's first Servant Song (see Isaiah 42:1–4; Matthew 12:18–21). His words implied that the mission of God's Suffering Servant was being fulfilled through His teaching and healing ministry.

Jesus saw His work as that of a humble servant. On one occasion His disciples began to argue over who would occupy the places of honor at His side in His future glory. He gently reminded them: "Whoever wants to be first must be slave of all. For even the Son of Man did not come to be served, but to serve, and to give His life as a ransom for many" (Mark 10:44–45 NIV).

Today the servant work of Jesus continues through His Church. We who belong to Him are automatically in the serving business. The apostle Paul declared that we as believers should think of ourselves as "a living sacrifice, holy, acceptable unto God, which is your reasonable service" (Romans 12:1). See also *Branch of Righteousness*.

RIGHT HAND OF GOD

See *Man of God's Right Hand.*

ROCK

First Samuel 2:2 is part of Hannah's prayer of dedication when she brought her son, Samuel, to Eli the priest. God had answered her prayer for a son, and she followed through on her promise to devote him to the Lord. She had found the Lord to be the "rock," the strong and dependable One who answers the prayers of His people.

The word *rock* when used of God refers not to a small stone but to a massive outcropping of rock, such as that on a mountainside. These huge formations are common throughout the land of Israel. These types of rocks remain fixed in place from one generation to the next, just as God is the eternal, unmovable One who is not subject to the ravages of time.

Other names of God that describe Him as the rock or the stone are "Rock of Israel" (2 Samuel 23:3), "rock of my refuge" (Psalm 94:22), "rock of my salvation" (2 Samuel 22:47), and "rock of my strength" (Psalm 62:7). See also *Eternity of God*; *Immutability of God*; *Spiritual Rock.*

A GALLERY OF GOD'S SERVANTS

The two people in the Bible who are most often called "servant of God" are Moses (see Exodus 14:31; Deuteronomy 34:5; Revelation 15:3) and David (see 2 Samuel 3:18; Psalm 89:3). But the title is also applied to several other famous and not-so-famous Bible personalities, including the following.

- Abraham (see Genesis 26:24).
- Ahijah (see 1 Kings 14:18).
- Caleb (see Numbers 14:24).
- Daniel (see Daniel 9:17).
- Elijah (see 2 Kings 9:36).
- Isaiah (see Isaiah 20:3).
- Job (see Job 1:8).
- Joshua (see Joshua 24:29).
- Samuel (see 1 Samuel 3:9–10).
- Solomon (see 1 Kings 1:26).
- Zerubbabel (see Haggai 2:23).

The Rock of Gibraltar, off the southwestern tip of Europe, is often used as a symbol of strength. But God as "Rock" is the One who put the Rock of Gibraltar in its place!

ROD OUT OF THE STEM OF JESSE

In one of his predictions about the coming Messiah, the prophet Isaiah declared, "There shall come forth a rod out of the stem of Jesse, and a Branch shall grow out of his roots" (Isaiah 11:1). We are accustomed to associations of the Messiah with King David. But in this passage, Isaiah traced the Messiah back to one generation before David—to his father, Jesse.

Two passages in the Bible tell us all we know about Jesse. His father was Obed, the son of Boaz and Ruth. Thus, Jesse was of mixed blood, since Ruth was a Moabite and Boaz was a Jew (see Ruth 1:4; 4:13–22). Jesse had eight sons, including David. One of the most beautiful stories in the Bible is how God through the prophet Samuel turned down all of Jesse's older sons for the kingship of Israel in favor of David, Jesse's youngest son. David had to be called in from the fields where he was watching his father's sheep to be presented for Samuel's review (1 Samuel 16:1–13).

Why did Isaiah compare the coming Messiah to a rod, or shoot, from the stem, or stump, of Jesse? Perhaps to remind us that the Messiah sprang from a family of mixed Jewish and Gentile blood, signifying that He would be a deliverer for all people, not just the Jews. Isaiah also predicted that the nation of Judah would fall to a foreign power, thus bringing to an end the dynasty of David. But from the stump of this fallen tree God would bring new life—the Messiah, who would reign in a spiritual sense over God's people.

Isaiah also described the coming Messiah as a "root of Jesse" (Isaiah 11:10). This name expresses the same idea as rod out of the stem of Jesse. See also *Jesse*.

ROOT AND OFFSPRING OF DAVID

Jesus used this name for Himself in the closing verses of the final chapter of the last book of the Bible (see Revelation 22:16). It's as if He used His last opportunity to tell the world who He is and what His life and ministry are all about.

Notice the dual focus of this name—the "root" of David and the "offspring" of David. It summarizes His existence as the God-man, the One who is both fully human and fully divine.

Since Jesus is the divine Son who served as the agent of creation (see *Beginning of the Creation of God*), He is David's creator, or root. But because He came to earth in human form, He is also David's descendant, or offspring—the Messiah from the line of David who reigns over the spiritual kingdom that He came to establish. Thus Jesus is both superior to David and the rightful heir to his throne. See also *Son of David*.

ROOT OF JESSE

See *Rod Out of the Stem of Jesse*.

RULER IN ISRAEL

See *Governor*.

RUTH

This Moabite woman remained loyal to her Jewish mother-in-law, Naomi, after the death of their husbands. Ruth moved with Naomi to Bethlehem (see Ruth 1:16–19), where she gleaned grain in the fields of Boaz. She eventually married Boaz and became an ancestor of David and Jesus (see Ruth 4:9–22). Ruth, a Gentile, is included in the earthly genealogy of Jesus (see Matthew 1:5). This shows that Jesus came into the world as a Savior for all people—Gentiles as well as Jews. See also *Gentiles*; *Impartiality of God*.

Ruth clings to her mother-in-law, Naomi, while Ruth's sister-in-law, Orpah, turns to leave. Ruth, a non-Jew, would become an ancestor of Jesus Christ, Savior of the world.

God's concern over His people's rest was so strong He made the Sabbath part of His Ten Commandments.

S

SABAOTH

The apostle James declared of the poor, "The cries of them which have reaped are entered into the ears of the Lord of sabaoth" (James 5:4). The word *sabaoth* means "hosts." Thus, James is speaking of the Lord of hosts. While this title for God appears frequently in the Old Testament, this is one of only two places where it occurs in the New Testament (see also Romans 9:29).

This verse describes God as hearing the cries of the poor who are being oppressed by the rich. The Lord of all the hosts of heaven and earth is on the side of the poor. He will render justice on their behalf (see James 5:5–6). See also *Lord of Hosts*; *Poor*.

SABBATH

The Jewish day of worship and rest was established when God rested after the six days of creation (see Genesis 2:1–3). The fourth of the Ten Commandments called for the Sabbath to be observed and "kept holy" (see Exodus 20:8). The Pharisees placed restrictions on Sabbath observance that prohibited acts of mercy or necessity (see Mark 2:23–24). But Jesus declared that "the sabbath was made for man and not man for the sabbath" (Mark 2:27–28).

The Old Testament Sabbath fell on the seventh day of the week, or our Saturday. Most Christian groups observe Sunday as the day of worship because of Christ's resurrection on the first day of the week (see 1 Corinthians 16:2). See also *Lord's Day*; *Lord of the Sabbath*.

SACRAMENT

A ritual or religious act that serves as a channel of God's grace is known as a sacrament. Roman Catholics and most Greek Orthodox churches observe seven sacraments: (1) baptism; (2) confirmation (consecration of a baptized person for a fuller endowment of the Holy Spirit); (3) eucharist (mass or the Lord's Supper); (4) penance (confession of sins to a priest); (5) marriage; (6) extreme unction (anointing of a sick or dying person); and (7) holy orders (conferring of authority on the vocational ministers of the church).

Most Protestant groups observe only two such rituals—baptism and the Lord's Supper—and even these are called "ordinances" by most evangelical groups (see Matthew 3:13–15). See also *Baptism*; *Lord's Supper*.

SACRIFICE

See *Altar*; *Sacrificial Offerings*.

A palm dove, common to Israel. God's rules allowed people to sacrifice doves if they couldn't afford a lamb, and fine flour if they couldn't afford doves (see Leviticus 5).

SACRIFICIAL OFFERINGS

In Old Testament times, the Israelites brought offerings to the Lord. These were sacrificed at the altar on their behalf by the priests of the nation. The people believed these sacrifices would atone for their sins and restore fellowship with God. Several different types of offerings are mentioned in the Bible.

Burnt offering. The burnt offering featured the burning of a sacrificial animal on the altar in the tabernacle or temple (see Exodus 40:6). The animal was left on the fire until it was totally consumed. Thus, it is sometimes referred to as the "whole" burnt offering (see Deuteronomy 33:10; Psalm 51:19). In some of the other offerings involving a sacrificial animal, the meat was removed from the fire before it was consumed and was eaten by the priests and their families. The purpose of the burnt offering is not stated in the Bible. Many interpreters believe it symbolized the dedication of the Israelites to the Lord after His forgiveness and restoration.

Drink offering. This was an offering of fine wine, usually given in connection with another sacrifice, such as a burnt offering (see Numbers 29:11–18).

Meat offering. Just as the name implies, this was a complete meal offered to God (see Leviticus 6:14). Some versions of the Bible render this as "cereal offering," "grain offering," or "meal offering." This sacrifice was presented to atone for sin.

Peace offering. In this offering, a slaughtered animal was presented to the Lord, along with the firstfruits of the harvest (see Leviticus 17:5–6). It apparently symbolized His forgiveness and acceptance. Other names for this sacrifice were "heave offering," "thank offering," and "wave offering."

Sin offering. This sacrifice, consisting of a slaughtered animal, was required if a person had committed a sin for which restitution or repayment was not possible (see Leviticus 6:25). This was also referred to as a "guilt offering."

Trespass offering. If a person had committed sin or wrongdoing for which restitution could be made, he brought this offering to the priest (see Leviticus 14:12). The trespass offering required a person to bring an animal for sacrifice.

With the coming of God's Son, Jesus Christ, and His atoning death, the need for these Old Testament sacrifices no longer exists. The author of the book of Hebrews declared: "The blood of goats and bulls. . . sprinkled on those who are ceremonially unclean sanctify them so that they are outwardly clean. How much more, then, will the blood of Christ, who through the eternal Spirit offered himself unblemished to God, cleanse our consciences from acts that lead to death, so that we may serve the living God!" (Hebrews 9:13–14 NIV). See also *Altar.*

SADDUCEES

This priestly aristocratic party of New Testament times rejected the oral traditions of the Jewish faith. On this point they disagreed with the Pharisees, who considered the traditions that surrounded the law almost as important as the law itself. To the Sadducees, only the original teachings of the Pentateuch (the first five books of the Old Testament) were authoritative.

Many of the Sadducees were wealthy by New Testament standards. Because of their privileged position, they urged the people to cooperate with the Roman authorities who ruled over their country. The Sadducees considered any challenge to the establishment as a threat to their security.

Jesus clashed with the Sadducees on one occasion when they asked him about marriage and the resurrection. He warned His disciples to avoid their teachings (see Matthew 16:1–12). See also *Pharisees.*

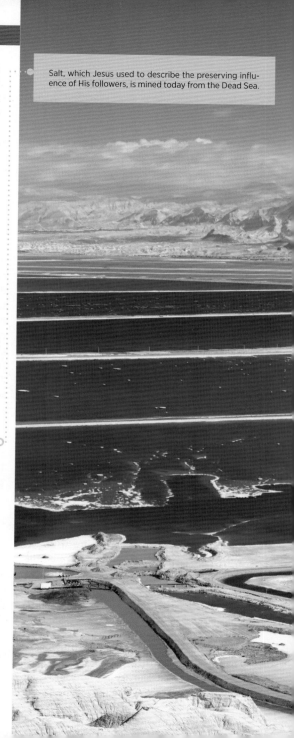

Salt, which Jesus used to describe the preserving influence of His followers, is mined today from the Dead Sea.

SAINTS

We are accustomed to thinking of saints as believers honored by a church organization for their extreme devotion to God—for example, Saint Augustine or Saint Theresa. But the word is often used in the New Testament for common, everyday believers—all those who have accepted Jesus as their Savior and have committed their lives to Him.

The apostle Paul was particularly fond of using the word *saints* in this way. For example, he told the believers at Rome that he was on his way to Jerusalem "to minister unto the saints" (Romans 15:25). He also spoke of the wonders of the Gospel of grace that had been "made manifest to his saints" (Colossians 1:26).

So according to Paul, Christians don't have to wait for centuries to be recognized for their saintly way of life or their contribution to the Church. If you are a believer in Christ, you are automatically a saint. See also *King of Saints*.

SALT

In Bible times just as today, salt was used to season and preserve food. It was a valuable commodity in a society in which refrigeration and cold storage did not exist. Jesus used the imagery of salt to describe His followers. If they did not demonstrate their distinctive purity and holiness as His people, they would have no influence in the world. Believers have no higher calling than to serve as the "salt of the earth" in a sinful and decadent culture (see Matthew 5:13). See also *Sermon on the Mount*.

SALVATION

This total work of God in delivering us from sin and reconciling us to Himself is

God's gift, and it is available to all who trust in Jesus, God's Son, as their Lord and Savior (see Ephesians 2:8).

Salvation has several different dimensions. See *Atonement; Conversion; Imputed Righteousness; New Birth; Reconciliation; Redemption; Regeneration; Repentance; Sanctification.*

Several different divine names also portray God as the author of salvation. See *Captain of Salvation; God of My Salvation; Horn of Salvation; Redeemer.*

THE THREE TENSES OF SALVATION

1. Past. We have been saved because of our faith in Christ and His atoning death (see Acts 16:31).
2. Present. We are in the process of being saved from sin's power (see Philippians 2:12).
3. Future. We will be saved in the end time from the very presence of sin (see Romans 13:11).

SAMARITANS

These former full-blooded Jews had corrupted their bloodline by intermarrying with pagans and foreigners. Most Jews despised the Samaritans, even refusing to travel through the region where they lived.

But Jesus harbored no such prejudice toward the Samaritans. He talked with a Samaritan woman at a well outside her village and offered her "living water" during one of His trips through their territory. In His parable of the good Samaritan, he told about a kind Samaritan traveler who came to the aid of a wounded man, even when his fellow Jewish citizens refused to get involved (see Luke 10:25–37).

These encounters show that Jesus' love is broad enough to include even the outcasts of society. He is the universal Savior. See also *Gentiles; Impartiality of God.*

SANCTIFICATION

This is the process of consecrating or setting something apart for holy purposes. In the Old Testament, priests, Levites, and each family's firstborn child were consecrated to the Lord. In the New Testament, sanctification was regarded as a work of grace following conversion (see Philippians 1:6). God calls all believers to holiness and sanctification (see 1 Thessalonians 4:3, 7). Those sanctified are committed to God's truth and serve as witnesses to His power and grace in the world (see Romans 6:11–13).

Sanctification is a process that continues throughout our lives as believers (see Hebrews 10:14). It will be completed only when we are "made perfect" in the presence of the Lord in heaven (see Hebrews 12:23). See also *Consecration; Lord Who Sanctifies.*

SANHEDRIN

Jesus was arrested on a charge of blasphemy by this high court of the Jewish nation (see John 18:19–21). This body did not have the authority to put Jesus to death. So it brought Jesus before Pilate, the Roman procurator, for sentencing (see Mark 15:1). In the King James Version, this group is referred to as the "council" (Luke 22:66; Acts 5:34). See also *Trials of Jesus.*

The Samaritans, despised by the Jews of Jesus' time, continue as a people group today. Here, a Samaritan priest holds a Torah scroll on the biblical Mount Gerizim.

SATAN

As the superhuman enemy of God, Satan is an evil being who works tirelessly to oppose His work in the world. Man's first encounter with Satan occurred in the Garden of Eden. Appearing in the form of a snake, he persuaded Adam and Eve to eat the fruit that God had declared off-limits to the couple. This act brought sin into the perfect world that God had created (see Genesis 3:6).

Ever since this first appearance in the Bible, Satan has continued his opposition to God and His people. Through temptation, he leads people into sin and rebellion against the Lord. He even tempted Jesus to turn away from His mission of redemption for which God the Father had sent His Son into the world. But Jesus overcame Satan's seductions

(see Luke 4:5–8) and stayed on track all the way to the cross. His atoning death and bodily resurrection brought a glorious victory over the power of Satan and the forces of evil and death (see 1 Peter 3:18, 22).

The major weapon in Satan's arsenal is deception. He tries to convince us that sin is no big deal or that we deserve the good things of life, even if we have to lie and steal to get them. He is an expert at stretching the truth and convincing us that a good result can be obtained by doing wrong (see 2 Corinthians 11:13–15). But Jesus was fully aware of Satan's tricks. He called him the "wicked one" and warned against his tactics (see Matthew

13:19, 38). The apostle Paul also referred to Satan's "signs and lying wonders" (2 Thessalonians 2:9).

Satan's influence is a powerful force in our world today. But this will not go on forever. He will be defeated after Jesus' second coming. He and his evil agents will be cast into the lake of fire, where they will be "tormented day and night for ever and ever" (Revelation 20:10). See also *Antichrist; Evil.*

OTHER NAMES AND TITLES FOR SATAN

- Accuser of our brethren (see Revelation 12:10).
- Beelzebub (see Matthew 12:24).
- Belial (see 2 Corinthians 6:15).
- Deceiver (see Revelation 20:10).
- Father of lies (see John 8:44).
- Man of sin (see 2 Thessalonians 2:3).
- Murderer (see John 8:44).
- Prince of the power of the air (see Ephesians 2:2).
- Prince of this world (see John 16:11).
- Son of perdition (see John 17:12).
- Tempter (see Matthew 4:3).

SAVIOUR

The name *Saviour* is applied to both God the Father and God the Son in the Bible. In the Old Testament, the Lord assured His people through the prophet Isaiah, "There is no God else beside me; a just God and a Saviour" (Isaiah 45:21). God wanted His people to remember that He as their Saviour was the only true God. He demanded their loyalty and obedience.

The word *Saviour* when used of God in the Old Testament usually refers to physical deliverance. The supreme example of this was God's rescue of the Israelites from Egyptian slavery through the Exodus. Acting as a Savior, or deliverer, He sent plagues against the Egyptians until the pharaoh gave in and let His people leave the country.

Not until the New Testament does God's role as a Savior reach its full flower. An angel told shepherds in the fields outside Bethlehem on the day Jesus was born: "I bring you good tidings of great joy, which shall be to all people. For unto you is born this day in the city of David a Saviour, which is Christ the Lord" (Luke 2:10–11). The shepherds were awestruck and excited by the news that this newborn baby was to be a Savior for God's people (see Luke 2:8–15).

In Bible times any person who rescued others from danger was called a savior or deliverer. For example, the judges of Israel whom God raised up to deliver His people from oppression by their enemies were called "saviours" (Nehemiah 9:27). But the only true Saviors in a spiritual sense are God the Father and God the Son.

The name that Mary and Joseph gave their firstborn Son expresses His work as Savior. *Jesus* means "God Is Salvation." From the very beginning it was clear that His purpose was to do for us what we could not do for ourselves—deliver us from bondage to sin and death.

The phrase "all people" in the message of the angels to the shepherds shows that Jesus was God's gift to the entire world. The universal nature of Christ's redemptive work is expressed by two other Savior titles in the New Testament—"Saviour of all men" (1 Timothy 4:10) and "Saviour of the world" (1 John 4:14). See also *Saviour of the Body.*

SAVIOUR OF ALL MEN

See *Saviour*.

SAVIOUR OF THE BODY

The apostle Paul told the believers at Ephesus, "The husband is the head of the wife, even as Christ is the head of the Church: and he is the saviour of the body" (Ephesians 5:23). The context of this verse makes it clear that he was not referring to a human body but to the Church as the body of Christ. Paul went on in verse 25 to say, "Husbands, love your wives, even as Christ also loved the church, and gave himself for it."

Christ is the head of the Church, and the Church that He founded is so closely related to Him that it is referred to as His body several times in the New Testament (see 1 Corinthians 12:27; Ephesians 1:22–23; Colossians 1:18). Thus, the Church is not a building or a lifeless institution but a living organism, dedicated to advancing the cause of the kingdom of God in the world.

Christ not only died for us as believers, but He also sacrificed Himself for His Church. We

FOUNDED ON HIS LIFE

"The Church's One Foundation," a hymn by Samuel J. Stone, describes the ultimate sacrifice that Jesus made for His church.

The church's one foundation
Is Jesus Christ her Lord;
She is His new creation,
By spirit and the Word:
From heaven He came and sought her
To be His holy bride,
With His own blood He bought her,
And for her life He died.

bring honor and glory to Him when we work through His Church to serve as witnesses of His love and grace to others. See also *Body of Christ*; *Church*; *Head of the Church*.

SAVIOUR OF THE WORLD

See *Saviour*.

SCAPEGOAT

Once a year, on the day of atonement, the high priest of Israel made atonement for the sins of the entire nation. This ceremony included the offering of two goats as sacrifices to atone for the Israelites' sins. One goat was selected by the casting of lots to serve as the blood sacrifice (see Leviticus 16:8–22). The other goat, known as the scapegoat, was kept alive so it could be carried away into the wilderness. This action symbolized the forgiveness and removal of the sins of the nation.

The original meaning of the term *scapegoat* was "far removed." This goat is a fitting symbol of Christ (see Isaiah 53:6), who takes our sins "far away" through His atoning death on our behalf. See also *Atonement*.

SCEPTRE OUT OF ISRAEL

Balaam, a pagan magician, was hired by the king of Moab to pronounce a curse against the Israelites. But Balaam was led by the Lord to bless the Israelites instead. He even prophesied that a strong leader would rise up to crush the Moabites: "There shall come a Star out of Jacob, and a Sceptre shall rise out of Israel, and shall smite the corners of Moab" (Numbers 24:17).

This verse is also considered a prophecy with a long-range fulfillment, referring to Jesus as the Savior-Messiah whom God would

send to deliver His people.

A scepter was a short staff, similar to a walking stick, that symbolized the power and authority of a king. In the book of Esther, King Ahasuerus of Persia extended his royal scepter for Queen Esther to touch (see Esther 5:2–3). This gave her permission to come into his presence and present her request to the king.

The imagery of a royal scepter as applied to Jesus symbolizes His power, authority, and universal dominion. In the book of Hebrews, God the Father declares to Jesus the Son, "Your throne. . .will last for ever and ever; a scepter of justice will be the scepter of your kingdom" (Hebrews 1:8 NIV). See also *Consolation of Israel; Glory of Israel; Light of Israel*.

SCRIBES

The scribes and Pharisees are often mentioned together in the Gospels as if they were united in their opposition to Jesus (see Matthew 15:1; John 8:3; *teachers of the law*, NIV).

The office of scribe developed in Old Testament times when they were charged with the responsibility of copying the scriptures. Laboriously copying a sacred document by hand was the only way to reproduce and pass on God's commands in written form.

By New Testament times, scribes had assumed the task of interpreting and teaching God's law as well as copying it. This is why they are mentioned often with Pharisees as those who opposed Jesus. Both were committed to preserving the traditions that had grown up around the written law. They considered these additions as binding as the original law itself.

Jesus criticized these "sacred traditions," broke many of them Himself during His teaching and healing ministry, and insisted they were not as authoritative as God's law in its original form (see Mark 7:1–5). See also *Pharisees*.

A modern scribe copies the Torah, the first five books of the Bible. In Jesus' time, the scribes also interpreted and taught the scripture.

SEA OF GALILEE

See *Galilee*.

SECOND ADVENT

See *Second Coming of Christ*.

SECOND COMING OF CHRIST

At the end of the present age, Christ will return to the earth to render judgment and bring His redemptive plan to conclusion.

During His earthly ministry, Jesus promised His followers that He would return to earth after His death, resurrection, and ascension to the Father (see John 14:3). But He also indicated that the time of His second coming was uncertain (see Matthew 25:13). This called for them to live in a state of watchful readiness. He could return at any time, perhaps when they least expected it (see Luke 21:34–36).

Our task as believers is not to spend our days trying to figure out the exact time of Jesus' second coming. We should be carrying out His Great Commission and sharing the Gospel with others until He returns (see Acts 1:8–11). See also *Watchfulness*.

SECOND DEATH

This phrase refers to spiritual death, final death, or eternal separation from God—the fate of those who refuse to accept Christ as Savior and Lord (see Revelation 21:8). Writing in the book of Revelation, the apostle John declared, "The lake of fire is the second death" (Revelation 20:14 NIV). Thus, "second death" and "lake of fire" appear to be figurative ways of referring to hell, or the eternal punishment of unbelievers. See also *Death*; *Hell*; *Lake of Fire*.

SECURITY OF THE BELIEVER

See *Assurance of God*.

SEED OF DAVID

See *Son of David*.

SEED OF THE WOMAN

God the Father said to the serpent, Satan, in the Garden of Eden: "I will put enmity between thee and the woman, and between thy seed and her seed; it shall bruise thy head, and thou shalt bruise his heel" (Genesis 3:15). This conversation occurred after Satan had persuaded Adam and Eve to eat the forbidden fruit, in direct disobedience of God's command. This verse is known as the *proto-evangelium*, a Latin term meaning "the first Gospel."

It is called "the first Gospel" because it

contains the first prediction in the Bible of the coming of Christ into the world. Jesus is depicted as the "seed of the woman," Eve. He will wage war against Satan's forces. Satan will manage to bruise His heel—a reference to the forces that executed Jesus on the cross. But Jesus will rise triumphantly from the dead and deal a crushing blow to Satan's head. In the end time, Jesus will win the final and ultimate victory over Satan and cast him into the lake of fire (see Revelation 20:10).

The name "seed of the woman" may be a subtle reference to the virgin birth of Jesus. He was conceived in Mary's womb by the Holy Spirit, not by a human father. She was told by the angel Gabriel, "The Holy Spirit will come on you, and the power of the Most High will overshadow you. So the holy one to be born will be called the Son of God" (Luke 1:35 NIV). See also *Annunciation*.

Jesus was the "seed of the woman" in the sense that there was no earthly father involved in His conception.

SELF-CONTROL

Living a self-controlled life means mastering one's personal desires and passions. Other words in the Bible that mean essentially the same thing are "sober" (1 Peter 4:7), "temperate" (Titus 1:8), and "discipline" (Job 36:10). The apostle Paul listed self-control, or temperance, as a work of the Holy Spirit in the lives of believers (see Galatians 5:22–23). See also *Fruit of the Spirit*.

SELF-DENIAL

See *Discipleship*.

SELF-DISCLOSURE OF GOD

See *Revelation of God*.

SELF-EXISTENCE OF GOD

One question that most children ask sooner or later is "Where did God come from?" Their little minds have grasped the reality that they are created beings who came into the world through the actions of their parents. Their inquisitive minds lead them to believe that God must have been caused by something.

The best answer we have for this question is "Nothing caused God; He has always existed." Theologians call this doctrinal truth the aseity of God. *Aseity* is a Latin word that means "from oneself." Thus, God derives His existence from within Himself. He is self-originated. He does not owe His existence to anyone, anything, or any elemental force outside Himself. He is the Self-Existent One.

One of the classic passages in the Bible that expresses this truth about the Lord was spoken by the prophet Isaiah. The prophet asked the people of Judah, "Whom did the LORD consult to enlighten him, and who

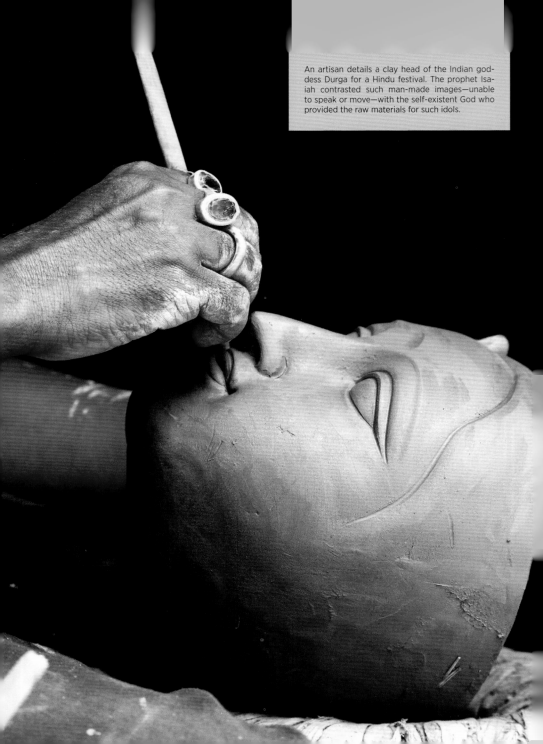

An artisan details a clay head of the Indian goddess Durga for a Hindu festival. The prophet Isaiah contrasted such man-made images—unable to speak or move—with the self-existent God who provided the raw materials for such idols.

taught him the right way? Who was it that taught him knowledge or showed him the path of understanding?" (Isaiah 40:14 NIV).

The answer to Isaiah's question is obvious. No one has served as God's counselor, taught Him knowledge, or given Him understanding. These abilities are part of His nature as the eternal God who has always existed. Isaiah was shocked that the people of his nation had forsaken this awesome God and fallen into worship of dumb idols—statues of wood or stone that had to be created by human hands.

God's self-existence is considered by many theologians to be His foundational characteristic, or attribute. It is precisely because He is independent from everything that exists that He is all-powerful and all-knowing and that He exists from eternity as the supreme Creator and ruler of the universe.

God's self-existence was evident to His Son, Jesus. When He was criticized for healing a lame man on the Sabbath, He replied, "As the Father has life in himself, so he has granted the Son also to have life in himself" (John 5:26 NIV).

This is one of the strongest statements about the nature of Jesus in the Gospels. Just as God has existed from eternity as a noncreated being, so has His Son, Jesus. He did come into the world as a man at a specific point in time—a doctrine known as the incarnation. But there was never a time when He did not exist with the Father, even before the world was created. See also *Omnipotence of God*; *Self-Sufficiency of God*.

SELF-RIGHTEOUSNESS

See *Pride*.

THE SELF-EXISTENT JESUS

The Gospel of John expressed Jesus' self-existence and His oneness with the Father like this: "In the beginning was the Word, and the Word was with God, and the Word was God. The same was in the beginning with God. All things were made by him; and without him was not any thing made that was made" (John 1:1–3).

SELF-SUFFICIENCY OF GOD

This attribute of God is similar to His self-existence (see above)—but with a slight difference. His self-sufficiency means that He needs nothing; He has everything He needs for a perfect existence. The apostle Paul expressed this truth perfectly in his dialogue with the philosophers of Athens. The Lord, he declared, "is not served by human hands, as if he needed anything" (Acts 17:25 NIV).

In our service to God, we should remember that God does not need our offerings, our time, our praise, or our devotion in order to complete something that is lacking in His nature. He does *desire* these things from us, but He will not be diminished if we refuse to honor Him with these gifts. The bottom line is that we need God, but He can get along quite well without us. See also *Self-Existence of God*.

SEPARATENESS OF GOD

See *Pantheism*.

SERAPHIM

See *Angels*; *Cherubim*.

SERMON ON THE MOUNT

Jesus' most famous sermon is a long monologue in which He instructed His disciples on how to live as citizens of the kingdom of God. It is called the Sermon on the Mount because Jesus' taught these principles to His disciples from a mountainside (see Matthew 5:1). This spot is marked today by a beautiful little chapel known as the Chapel of the Beatitudes.

Here's a thumbnail summary of the ten major principles that Jesus taught in the Sermon on the Mount.

1. *The Beatitudes.* Those who live as

Artist Carl Heinrich Bloch painted this classic scene of Jesus' Sermon on the Mount in the 1800s.

citizens of God's kingdom will be richly rewarded (see Matthew 5:3–12).

2. *Salt and light.* Our Christian influence matters in a wicked world (see Matthew 5:13–16).

3. *Genuine righteousness.* Believers are called to live by the deeper meaning of God's law (see Matthew 5:17–48).

4. *How to avoid hypocrisy.* Our giving, praying, and fasting should issue from the right motives (see Matthew 6:1–18).

5. *First things first.* Putting God's kingdom ahead of everything else frees us from anxiety over lesser matters (see Matthew 6:19–34).

6. *Leave the judging to God.* Believers should avoid judging people in a harsh and thoughtless manner (see Matthew 7:1–6).

7. *Genuine prayer.* How to claim the privileges and blessings of prayer (see Matthew 7:7–12).

8. *The two ways.* Choose the narrow way that leads to life rather than the broad way that leads to destruction (see Matthew 7:13–14).

9. *Bearing good fruit.* We will be known and judged by our fruits or deeds (see Matthew 7:15–20).

10. *Action, not talk.* Obeying God matters more than mouthing words about our commitment to Him and His will (see Matthew 7:21–29). See also *Beatitudes*.

SERPENT

Satan in the form of a serpent, or snake, tempted Adam and Eve to disobey God and to sin in the Garden of Eden (see Genesis 3:1–5). Moses raised the image of a serpent on a pole to heal the people who had been bitten by poisonous snakes. This symbolized Jesus' future sacrificial death to deliver people from their sin (see John 3:14–15). See also *Satan*.

SERVANT OF THE LORD

See *Righteous Servant*.

SEVEN SPIRITS

The apostle John greeted the seven churches of Asia Minor with these words: "Grace be unto you, and peace, from him which is, and which was, and which is to come; and from the seven Spirits which are before his throne" (Revelation 1:4). This reference to the Holy Spirit as "seven Spirits" is puzzling to many Bible students.

We know from the apostle Paul's writings that the Holy Spirit is one. He declared to the believers at Corinth, "By one Spirit are we all baptized into one body" (1 Corinthians 12:13). So how could the apostle John claim that the Holy Spirit is seven in number?

The best explanation is that John used the number seven to emphasize the fullness and completeness of the Holy Spirit. Seven was considered the perfect number in Bible times, and it appears often throughout the Bible to symbolize wholeness and perfection (see Deuteronomy 16:15; Matthew 18:21–22). John used the number in this sense many times throughout Revelation: seven candlesticks (see 1:12), seven stars (see 1:16), seven seals (see 5:1), seven horns (see 5:6), and seven eyes (see 5:6).

SHADDAI

This is a transliterated Hebrew name for God. With its preceding article *el* (el Shaddai), it is translated in most English versions of the Bible as "the Almighty" or "Almighty God."

It refers to His unlimited power and His self-sufficient nature. See also *Almighty God*; *Omnipotence of God*; *Self-Sufficiency of God*.

SHADE

The psalmist said of God, "The LORD is thy shade upon thy right hand" (Psalm 121:5). This unusual name for God was probably inspired by the hot, dry climate of the land of Israel. To the psalmist, God was his figurative "shade" under whom he could rest from the oppressive heat during the hottest part of the day. He also described God as his cooling-off place "upon [his] right hand." The right hand was considered the place of favor and honor. Thus, to experience the Lord as his shade on the right was to be doubly refreshed and blessed.

The prophet Micah also used this imagery of a shade tree to refer to the comfort of God's people after the coming of the Messiah. "They shall sit every man under his vine and under his fig tree; and none shall make them afraid" (Micah 4:4). With Jesus as our protector and refuge, we have nothing to fear from those who would do us harm.

Are you overworked, overheated, frustrated, confused, or confounded? Maybe it's time you took a refreshing break by sitting down under the ultimate shade. See also *Dwelling Place*.

SHELTER

See *Refuge*.

SHEMA

See *Monotheism*.

A solitary tree in the Omani desert provides a small amount of shade for Bedouins. The Bible describes God as a refreshing shade for His people.

SHEOL

This Hebrew word (pronounced SHE ole) refers to a gloomy region where the spirits of people went after they died. The word is translated by the King James Version as "hell" (2 Samuel 22:6) or "grave" (Psalm 49:15). The New International Version renders *sheol* as "grave," "place of the dead," or "gates of death."

Some passages in the Old Testament describe sheol as a place inhabited by both the righteous and unrighteous (see Isaiah 38:10). But other passages indicate that the righteous will avoid sheol because of their commitment to the Lord (see Psalm 49:15). These discrepancies show that the Israelites of Old Testament times did not have a fully developed concept of the afterlife. This awaited the coming of Jesus and His teachings on eternal life for believers and eternal punishment for unbelievers. See also *Hell*.

SHEPHERD

This name of God is a favorite of Bible students, perhaps because it occurs in one of the most familiar passages in God's Word—the Twenty-Third Psalm. This psalm has been called the "shepherd psalm" because of its beautiful description of the Lord as the shepherd of His people: "The LORD is my shepherd; I shall not want" (Psalm 23:1).

David wrote this psalm in his latter years as he reflected on the Lord and how He had led him throughout his life. Like a shepherd who leads his sheep to green pastures and peaceful streams for food and water, the Lord had supplied David's needs. From his humble beginnings as a shepherd boy to the throne of Israel, God had walked with David and blessed him with more than he deserved. David was confident that He would continue

> ## THE LORD AS OUR SHEPHERD
>
> - "He [God] brought his people out [of Egypt] like a flock; he led them like sheep through the wilderness" (Psalm 78:52 NIV).
> - "The LORD is God. . . . We are his people, the sheep of his pasture" (Psalm 100:3 NIV)
> - "He [God] tends his flock like a shepherd; he gathers the lambs in his arms" (Isaiah 40:11 NIV).

to sustain him, even as he walked "through the valley of the shadow of death" (Psalm 23:4).

Like David, all of us need the divine shepherd, who will guide us throughout this life and beyond. Another name of God that uses shepherd imagery is "Shepherd of Israel" (Psalm 80:1). See also *Good Shepherd*.

SHEPHERD OF ISRAEL

See *Shepherd*.

SHEPHERD OF YOUR SOULS

See *Good Shepherd*.

SHIELD

This divine name comes from one of the psalms of David in which he prayed for protection from his enemies. He used military terminology to characterize God as his "shield" who would surround him and absorb the blows of those who were on the attack (see Psalm 5:12).

The Hebrew word behind "shield" in this

verse refers to the large full-body shield that warriors crouched behind. This protected them from arrows being shot by archers from a distance. A smaller version of the shield was known as a buckler. It was worn on the arm to protect soldiers in hand-to-hand combat.

As our shield, God provides maximum protection. He literally surrounds us with His watchful care. See also *Buckler.*

SHILOH

In his old age, the patriarch Jacob pronounced his blessings on his twelve sons, whose descendants would become the twelve tribes of Israel. He had a special message for Judah, the tribe destined to produce the rulers of Israel: "The sceptre shall not depart from Judah, nor

Soldiers of Egyptian pharaoh Hatshepsut carry both spears for offense and shields for defense. God is a protective shield to all who believe in Him.

a lawgiver from between his feet, until Shiloh come; and unto him shall the gathering of the people be" (Genesis 49:10).

Shiloh is a Hebrew word meaning "the one to whom it belongs." Thus, Jacob was saying that Judah would wield the royal scepter of leadership in Israel until the one to whom the scepter belonged arrived on the scene. This is a veiled reference to the coming Messiah.

Jesus is the One to whom all authority and power belong because God has delegated His jurisdiction over His people to His Son.

Jesus is also deserving of all power because He rules in justice and righteousness. Just a little power can go to an earthly ruler's head, but Jesus will never use His power for anything but the good of His Church and those who devote their lives to Him and His service.

No matter what happens to us in this life, we can rest safe and secure in the arms of Shiloh—the One who holds the whole world in His hands. See also *Sceptre Out of Israel*.

SIGNAL FOR THE NATIONS

See *Ensign for the Nations*.

SIGNS AND WONDERS

See *Miracles*.

SIN

Sin occurs when people rebel against God, ignore His commands, and surrender to the power of evil rather than His will. Sin was introduced into the human race when Adam and Eve disobeyed God in the Garden of Eden (see Genesis 3:6). No one can claim with a straight face that he or she is free of sin. The apostle Paul declared, "All have sinned and fall short of the glory of God" (Romans 3:23 NIV).

One of the most graphic images for sin in the Bible comes from a Greek word that means "to miss the mark." The word is usually translated simply as "sin," but behind it is a truth that all of us know very well. When we sin, we miss the mark that God has intended for our lives.

The Bible has a rich vocabulary for the concept of sin. It is described as "disobedience" (Romans 5:19), "iniquity" (Isaiah 33:24), "transgression," or the breaking of God's laws (Matthew 15:3), and "wickedness"

(Job 4:8). Satan, the tempter, is a master at leading us into sin.

Sin is not only doing what is wrong. We also sin when we fail to do what we know is right. This is sometimes referred to as a sin of omission: "If anyone, then, knows the good they ought to do and doesn't do it, it is sin for them" (James 4:17 NIV). The Bible also makes a distinction between *sin* and *sins*. "Sin" refers to our corrupt nature, while "sins" refers to wrong deeds or actions. Christ died for both our evil nature and our evil acts.

The consequence of sin is spiritual death, but God's gift to us is forgiveness of our sins and eternal life through Jesus Christ (see Romans 6:23). See also *Evil*; *Satan*.

SINAI

See *Mount Sinai*.

SIN OFFERING

See *Sacrificial Offerings*.

SION

See *Zion*.

SOBER

See *Self-Control*.

SOLOMON

David's son and successor as king of Israel (reigned c. 970–930 BC), Solomon was known for his great riches, and he brought fame and glory to the nation of Judah. But Jesus claimed that His authority and power were "greater than Solomon" (see Matthew 12:42). See also *Greater Than Jonah/Greater Than Solomon*.

Using a dartboard as a visual aid, the literal truth of sin—missing the mark—is almost humorous. But sin is a deadly serious issue in God's eyes, requiring a deadly serious answer: the crucifixion of Jesus Christ.

SONG

The twelfth chapter of Isaiah is one of the shortest in his book. But it is unapologetically joyful as the prophet thought about the Lord whom he served: "The LORD JEHOVAH

Solomon uses his God-given wisdom to decide which of two women is the actual mother of a disputed baby. Read the entire story in 1 Kings 3.

is my strength and my song" (Isaiah 12:2). In addition to this verse, which describes God as his "song," every one of its verses expresses this theme of praise and celebration.

God's people have a lot to sing about. He has provided for our salvation through His Son. He sustains us every day with His love and grace. He has promised eternal life with Him in heaven after we depart this earthly life. As our song, He deserves to be praised with our songs of joy. See also *Music*; *Worship of God*.

JOY IN THE OTHER VERSES OF ISAIAH 12

- "O LORD, I will praise thee" (v. 1).
- "With joy shall ye draw water out of the wells of salvation" (v. 3).
- "Praise the LORD" (v. 4).
- "Sing unto the LORD" (v. 5).
- "Cry out and shout" (v. 6).

SON OF ABRAHAM

This name of Jesus is cited in the very first verse of the New Testament (see Matthew 1:1). Abraham was the father of the Jewish people, the Israelites. Many centuries before Jesus' time, God called Abraham to leave his home and family in Mesopotamia and move to the land of Canaan. Here God would begin to build a nation that would be His exclusive possession. He promised Abraham, "I will bless those who bless you, and whoever curses you I will curse; and all peoples on earth will be blessed through you" (Genesis 12:3 NIV).

As the "son of Abraham," Jesus is the fulfillment of this promise, or covenant, that God made with Abraham. In His human lineage and by His nationality, Jesus was a Jew—the people whom God promised to bless above all the nations of the earth.

But God never intended for His promise of blessing to apply only to the Jewish people. He wanted all peoples on earth to be brought to Him through the influence of Abraham's offspring. When the Jews forgot this part of the covenant, He sent His Son, Jesus, to remind them that He had placed no limits on His love and grace. Jesus as the son of Abraham fulfilled God's redemptive plan by coming as a Savior for the entire world. See also *Abraham*.

SON OF DAVID

Perhaps it is not accidental that the very first verse of the New Testament refers to Jesus as the "son of David" (Matthew 1:1). As David's son, He ties together the Old and New Testaments. The genealogies of Jesus in the Gospels of Matthew and Luke make the point that Jesus in His human lineage was descended from David (see Matthew 1:6; Luke 3:31). Thus, Jesus fulfilled God's promise to

The literal son of Abraham—Isaac—is nearly sacrificed by his father, obeying God's command. God sends an angel to stop the test, and Isaac grows up to continue the family line that will include the ultimate "son of Abraham," Jesus Christ.

David that one of David's descendants would always reign over His people (see 2 Samuel 7:1–16; Psalm 132:11–12).

During Jesus' earthly ministry, the crowds and individuals whom He healed often called Him the "son of David" (Matthew 9:27; Mark 10:47; Luke 18:38). But Jesus never used this name for Himself. He may have avoided it because it tended to feed the expectation of the Jewish people that the Messiah would come as a political conqueror, not a spiritual Savior.

Another name of Jesus similar in meaning to son of David is "seed [or offspring] of David" (2 Timothy 2:8). See also *David*.

SON OF GOD

A Roman military officer known as a centurion presided over the execution of Jesus. He was awestruck by the earthquake and other miraculous signs that accompanied Jesus' death (see Matthew 27:50–53). Looking at Jesus on the cross and His calmness in the face of death, he declared that He was none other than the "Son of God" (Matthew 27:54). Ironically, this pagan solider affirmed what the Jewish religious leaders refused to believe.

Son of God as a name or title for Jesus appears many times throughout the New Testament (see Matthew 14:33; Acts 9:20; Romans 1:4). It emphasizes His divine nature and shows that He came to earth under the authority of God the Father on a mission of redemption.

This name also highlights His close, personal relationship with God. He knew God like no other person has ever known Him, and He addressed Him often in His prayers as "Father" (John 17:1–26). He taught His disciples in His model prayer to approach God in the same way: "Our Father which art in heaven" (Matthew 6:9).

In Bible times a son was expected to honor and obey his parents (see Exodus 20:12; Ephesians 6:1). Jesus as God's Son was perfectly obedient to the Father. He refused to be sidetracked from the mission on which He was sent into the world. His last words from the cross were "It is finished" (John 19:30). This was not the whimper of a dying man but a declaration of victory over the forces of sin and death. He had accomplished the work that His Father commissioned Him to do. See also *Only Begotten Son*.

SON OF JOSEPH

After Jesus miraculously fed five thousand people (see John 6:2–11), He claimed to be the spiritual bread that had come down from heaven (see John 6:32–33). But the Jewish religious leaders rejected His claim. They attempted to discredit Him in the eyes of the crowd by pointing out that they knew His parents: "Is not this Jesus, the son of Joseph, whose father and mother we know?" (John

In a seventeenth-century painting by Bartolomé Esteban Perez Murillo, God the Father looks down over His Son, Jesus, whom the Jewish leaders called "the son of Joseph."

6:42). To them He was only the "son of Joseph," not a special messenger from God.

Jesus was the son of Joseph, but not in the sense that these religious leaders had in mind. Jesus had no human father; He was conceived in his mother's womb by the Holy Spirit (see Luke 1:35). Technically, He was Joseph's stepson or his adopted son.

The Gospel records tell us very little about Joseph. But the few facts we do have make it clear that he was a person of sterling character. He and Mary were engaged to be married when he learned that she was pregnant. He prepared to break the engagement. But an angel assured him that Mary had not been unfaithful to him and that her baby was of divine origin. To Joseph's credit, he believed this explanation—one that must have seemed like a fairy tale—and took Mary as his wife (see Matthew 1:19–24).

Jesus grew up in Nazareth like any normal Jewish boy. Apparently he learned the trade of carpentry and woodworking from his stepfather, Joseph. Mark 6:3 refers to an event soon after Jesus launched His public ministry. In this verse Jesus is called a carpenter and His mother, Mary, and four brothers are mentioned. But nothing is said about Joseph.

This has led to speculation that Joseph may have died during Jesus' growing-up years. If this is true, Jesus as Mary's firstborn son may have assumed responsibility for His family's welfare from an early age. See also *Joseph, Husband of Mary*.

SON OF MAN

A man approached Jesus and promised to become His disciple. But Jesus told him, "Foxes have dens, and birds have nests, but the Son of Man has no place to lay his head" (Luke 9:58 NIV). He wanted this would-be follower to know that serving Him would require sacrifice.

"Son of Man" is the name that Jesus used most often when referring to Himself. This title was probably inspired by Daniel's prophecy of God's messenger who would come on a mission of redemption (see Daniel 7:13–14). The name appears in the New Testament almost one hundred times, most of these on the lips of Jesus in the Gospel narratives. A careful study of these occurrences reveals that He used this title in three different ways.

1. Sometimes He used Son of Man in a general way, almost as a substitute for the first-person pronoun "I." A good example of this usage is Jesus' response in the verse from Luke above.

2. When Jesus predicted His suffering and death, He often spoke of Himself as the Son of Man. For example, He warned His disciples, "The Son of man must suffer many things, and be rejected of the elders and chief priests and scribes, and be slain, and be raised the third day" (Luke 9:22).

3. With this name or title, Jesus often referred to Himself as a person of exceptional authority and power. He made it clear that He was not acting on His own but under the authority of God the Father. When the Pharisees criticized Him for healing on the Sabbath, He told them, "The Son of man is Lord also of the sabbath" (Mark 2:28).

Now we know *how* Jesus used the title. But the *why* is not as easy to explain. Perhaps He wanted to show His total identification with humankind. The Son of Man came to earth as a man—our brother and fellow sufferer—to deliver us from our bondage to sin. See also *Flesh*; *Incarnation of Christ*.

SON OF MARY

Mark 6:3 is the only place in the New Testament where this name of Jesus appears. It was spoken by the citizens of Nazareth, Jesus' hometown ("Is not this the carpenter, the son of Mary?"). They could not believe that the boy who had grown up in their midst could be the Messiah and great prophet sent from God. They knew Him only as a carpenter who happened to be the "son of Mary."

Son of Mary as a title for Jesus is unusual because a man in Bible times was usually identified by His father's name (for example, "Isaiah the son of Amoz," Isaiah 1:1). Jesus' designation as the son of Mary in this verse lends support to the view that His father,

Mary grieves at the foot of the cross of her Son, Jesus, while the apostle John—appointed by Jesus to care for Mary—waits nearby.

Joseph, had died while Jesus was a boy (see *Son of Joseph*).

Mary knew from the very beginning that the baby Jesus who was conceived in her womb by the Holy Spirit was God's special gift to the world (see Luke 1:26–38). But she apparently brought Him up like any normal boy (see Luke 2:51–52). Mark 6:3 shows that she had other sons and daughters who were born by natural means after Jesus' miraculous conception. But Jesus as her firstborn son must have had a special place in her heart.

She knew about His special powers because she told the servants at a wedding feast where the wine ran out, "Do whatever he tells you" (John 2:5 NIV). Jesus responded to her confidence in Him by turning water into wine—His first miracle as reported in John's Gospel.

Did Mary realize that her firstborn son was destined to be executed like a common criminal? We don't know, but the Bible does tell us that she was at the execution site when He was nailed to the cross. One of the last things Jesus did before He died was to make arrangements for the welfare of His mother.

With the words "Here is your mother," He instructed His disciple John to take care of her. John reported in his own Gospel, "From that time on, this disciple took her into his home" (John 19:27 NIV). See also *Mary*.

SON OF PERDITION

See *Satan*.

SON OVER HIS OWN HOUSE

One purpose of the book of Hebrews was to show that Jesus Christ is superior to the religious laws and regulations and the sacrificial system of the Old Testament. Hebrews

---

MARY AND THE MANGER

The Christmas hymn "Gentle Mary Laid Her Child" by Joseph Simpson Cook reminds us that the Savior of humankind came into the world like an ordinary baby with a human mother.

Gentle Mary laid her Child
Lowly in a manger;
There He lay, the undefiled,
To the world a stranger:
Such a Babe in such a place,
Can He be the Savior?
Ask the saved of all the race
Who have found His favor.

3:5–6 is part of an argument by the writer of the book that Jesus is superior to Moses, the great deliverer and lawgiver of God's people in Old Testament times.

Moses was faithful in his house, or the household of God's people of faith. But he was nothing more than a servant in this house. But Jesus was a "son over his own house" (v. 6), or the Church that He founded by His sacrificial death. Since a son who ruled *over* a household is superior to a servant *in* that house, this means that Jesus is superior to Moses.

These verses refer to a time in the wilderness when Moses' brother, Aaron, and Moses' sister, Miriam, questioned his leadership over the people of Israel. God put an end to their rebellion by pointing out that Moses was His true prophet "who is faithful in all mine house" (Numbers 12:7).

But no matter how faithful Moses had been to God, Jesus was even more so. He was God's own Son who gave His life to set people free from their bondage to sin. All

The spirit of adoption allows followers of Christ to call God "Daddy."

believers are blessed by the faithfulness He demonstrated to God's redemptive plan. See also *Head of the Church*.

SONS OF GOD

See *Children of God*.

SORCERY

See *Magic and Divination*.

SOVEREIGNTY OF GOD

This theological phrase expresses the truth that God is the all-powerful ruler of the universe. God's creation of man and the world implies His continuing rule and sovereignty (see Genesis 1:1; Psalm 8:1–5). His supreme authority is also expressed by several of His titles that refer to His universal power and dominion. See also *Almighty God*; *God of the Whole Earth*; *Omnipotence of God*.

SPECIAL REVELATION

See *Revelation of God*.

SPIRIT OF ADOPTION

In Romans 8:15 the apostle Paul compared the situation of people before they become believers to the new status they enjoy after their conversion: "Ye have not received the spirit of bondage again to fear; but ye have received the Spirit of adoption, whereby we cry, Abba, Father." Their old lives are comparable to that of slaves in bondage with no rights or privileges. But after coming to new life in Christ, they have all the advantages of sonship as a child of God the Father.

Paul used the concept of adoption to emphasize our new status with God. We were once children of sin, but God delivered us from our bondage and adopted us as His own. So close is our relationship to God as our adoptive Father that we can call Him "Abba," an Aramaic word equivalent to our modern "Daddy" or "Papa."

The Holy Spirit as the Spirit of adoption has a vital role in this adoption process. His presence in our lives assures us that we belong to God. His Spirit will never let us forget that we enjoy a position of dignity and honor in the family of God the Father and Jesus the Son. See also *Abba, Father*; *Adoption*.

SPIRIT OF CHRIST

The King James Version of Romans 8:9 is made even more impressive by a modern translation. The New International Version renders it like this: "You, however, are not in the realm of the flesh but are in the realm of the Spirit, if indeed the Spirit of God lives in you. And if anyone does not have the Spirit of Christ, they do not belong to Christ."

The first dramatic truth emphasized by this verse is that the Holy Spirit is both the Spirit of God and the Spirit of Christ. This is a bold affirmation that Jesus was one with the Father but separate from Him at the same time. Our minds have a hard time taking in this concept, but this is the clear teaching of the Bible.

The apostle Paul also declared in this verse that the Holy Spirit is a gift of God's grace that transforms believers when they accept Jesus as Savior and Lord. Paul even went so far as to say that the presence of the Holy Spirit in our lives is proof of our salvation, showing that we "belong to Christ."

This name for the Holy Spirit—Spirit of Christ—also shows that He was closely

connected with Jesus' earthly ministry and that He continues to empower the Church to continue Jesus' work in our time. The Holy Spirit enabled the prophets to foresee the coming of Jesus into the world (see 1 Peter 1:10–11). The Spirit unites the Church, Jesus' body, to Him as the head of the Church (see 1 Corinthians 12:12–13). The Holy Spirit causes us as believers to grow more and more like the Lord whom we serve (see 2 Corinthians 3:18).

Two similar names that Paul used for the Holy Spirit are "Spirit of his [God's] Son" (Galatians 4:6) and "Spirit of Jesus Christ" (Philippians 1:19).

SPIRIT OF COUNSEL AND MIGHT

The prophet Isaiah looked more than six hundred years into the future and predicted

Parents, teachers, and coaches can give wise advice—but only God's Spirit offers both "counsel and might."

the coming of the Messiah (see Isaiah 11:2). This great leader among God's people would be filled with God's Spirit, whom the prophet referred to as the "spirit of counsel and might."

All of us have known people who love to give us their advice and counsel—at no charge! And we know others who are people of action. But how many people do you know who can tell you what to do and then fill you with the strength to accomplish their own advice? People like this are a rarity, but Isaiah declared that work like this is just a routine "day at the office" for the Holy Spirit.

The Holy Spirit knows what we as believers

should do to bring our lives into line with God's will. He warns us about the dangers of temptation. But He also gives us the strength to resist temptation. When we do stumble and fall, He assures us of our restored relationship with God when we confess our sins before God the Father and Jesus the Son.

Counsel *and* might. This unusual combination of skills is just one more proof of God's love for His people. See also *Counsellor*.

SPIRIT OF FAITH

Second Corinthians 4:13 is the only place in the New Testament where the Holy Spirit is called the "spirit of faith." It is no accident that it appears in the writings of the apostle Paul, who had more to say about faith than any other New Testament writer (see sidebar).

To understand this verse from 2 Corinthians, we need to consider Paul's famous statement about the centrality of faith in the book of Ephesians: "By grace are ye saved through faith; and that not of yourselves: it is the gift of God: not of works, lest any man should boast" (Ephesians 2:8–9).

Notice that Paul did not say in this verse that we are saved *by* faith, but *through* faith. It is Christ's sacrifice on the cross that saves; we claim this sacrifice for ourselves by placing our faith in Him as our Savior and Lord. Faith is our human response to His sacrifice that we must exercise before we can experience forgiveness for our sins and find new life in Jesus Christ.

If human faith is an essential element of the salvation process, how do we have such faith? Paul's answer is that saving faith is a work of the Holy Spirit—the spirit of faith. He alone can convict us of sin and lead us to declare our faith in Jesus Christ as our Savior. Without the movement of the Holy

---

PAUL: THE APOSTLE OF FAITH

- "Therefore being justified by faith, we have peace with God through our Lord Jesus Christ" (Romans 5:1).
- "I am crucified with Christ: nevertheless I live; yet not I, but Christ liveth in me: and the life which I now live in the flesh I live by the faith of the Son of God, who loved me, and gave himself for me" (Galatians 2:20).
- "I have fought a good fight, I have finished my course, I have kept the faith" (2 Timothy 4:7).

Spirit to kindle faith in our hearts and minds, we would remain hopelessly lost in our sin. See also *Faith*; *Faithful and True*.

SPIRIT OF GLORY

The apostle Peter encouraged believers who were being persecuted for their faith with these words: "If ye be reproached for the name of Christ, happy are ye; for the spirit of glory and of God resteth upon you" (1 Peter 4:14).

The apostle may have been thinking back to the time when Jesus told His disciples what to do when they were persecuted for following Him. They were to "take no thought how or what ye shall speak: for it shall be given you in that same hour what ye shall speak. For it is not ye that speak, but the Spirit of your Father which speaketh in you" (Matthew 10:19–20).

In effect, Jesus told His followers not to retaliate against or resist their persecutors but to trust the Holy Spirit—the "spirit of glory"—to take care of them and give them the words to say in rebuttal. The same Spirit that guided Him throughout His ministry would also abide with them, strengthening them to serve as His bold witnesses.

The spirit of glory does not desert us during our times of persecution. He honors us for our sacrificial suffering in God's service, just as He glorified Jesus by raising Him from the dead (see 1 Peter 3:18). See also *Father of Glory*; *Glory of God*.

SPIRIT OF GOD

When Jesus was baptized by John the Baptist at the beginning of His public ministry, "he saw the Spirit of God descending like a dove, and lighting upon him" (Matthew 3:16–17). This event is reported by all three Synoptic

The Holy Spirit, depicted as a dove in a church's stained-glass window.

Gospels (see also Mark 1:9–11; Luke 3:21–22).

But Matthew's Gospel is the only one of the three that calls the Holy Spirit who descended upon Jesus the "Spirit of God." This is a common name for the Spirit in the Old Testament (see 1 Samuel 11:6; Job 33:4), but it appears only a few times in the New Testament (see Romans 8:9; 1 Corinthians 2:11).

Perhaps Matthew used this name for the Holy Spirit because he wanted to emphasize that Jesus was empowered directly by God Himself when He sent His Spirit upon His Son. Matthew's Gospel is also known for its portrayal of Jesus as the fulfillment of Old Testament prophecy. And the coming of the Spirit upon Jesus at His baptism fulfilled Isaiah's prophecy about the Messiah that "the spirit of the LORD shall rest upon him" (Isaiah 11:2).

One of the most interesting things about this passage is Matthew's description of God's Holy Spirit "descending like a dove" and lighting on Jesus. As a spirit being, the Holy Spirit is invisible. The only other time in the Bible when the Spirit appeared in visible form was on the day of Pentecost. He appeared to the apostles as "cloven tongues like as of fire" and settled on "each of them" (Acts 2:3).

Was the visible appearance of the Holy Spirit at Jesus' baptism God's way of assuring Jesus of His power and presence? Possibly. But Jesus had been conscious of His unique mission from an early age (see Luke 2:48–50).

Did the Holy Spirit actually look like a dove, or was Matthew using symbolic language? Matthew says the Spirit descended "like a dove," but Luke's account says the Spirit came down "in a bodily shape like a dove upon him" (Luke 3:22). Many modern churches must believe that the Holy Spirit appeared as a literal dove, since their baptistries feature the figure of a dove hovering over the baptismal waters.

Maybe we're trying a little too hard to make sense of the details in this passage and missing the real message that Matthew was trying to get across. Here's the double-edged bottom line: (1) God was pleased to send His Son into the world as His personal representative on a mission of redemption. (2) This mission was so important that He empowered Jesus with His own Spirit for the task.

SPIRIT OF GOD'S SON

See *Spirit of Christ.*

SPIRIT OF GRACE AND SUPPLICATIONS

The prophet Zechariah looked into the future to the coming of the Messiah, the one "whom they pierced"—a clear reference to the crucifixion of Jesus. Along with the Messiah, God the Father would also send the Holy Spirit, whom Zechariah described as the "spirit of grace and of supplications" (Zechariah 12:10).

The Holy Spirit is the spirit of grace because He convicts people of their sin and leads them to place their faith in Jesus Christ (see John 16:8–11). No one can earn God's grace or purchase His indwelling Spirit. He gives His grace and His Spirit generously to those who confess His Son, Jesus, as Savior and Lord.

Supplication, or confession, is a distinct form of prayer in which a person is keenly aware of his or her sin and cries out to God for forgiveness. Jesus commended the unrighteous publican or tax collector because he prayed, "God be merciful to me a sinner" (Luke 18:13). The Holy Spirit is the spirit of

Fire can be terrifying, and it is an apt metaphor for God's judgment.

supplications because He leads us to drop our self-righteous pride and throw ourselves upon the mercy and grace of God for forgiveness and restoration. See also *Grace of God*; *Prayer*.

SPIRIT OF JESUS CHRIST

See *Spirit of Christ*.

SPIRIT OF JUDGMENT/ SPIRIT OF BURNING

Isaiah 4:4 emphasizes the Holy Spirit's work as judge. His twin titles—"spirit of judgment" and "spirit of burning"—show that He is active with God the Father and Jesus the Son in exercising divine judgment against sin and rebellion. Isaiah referred to the Spirit's judgment against the sinful nation of Judah, but the three Persons of the Trinity have the authority to exercise judgment against sin wherever it is found.

The name spirit of burning depicts divine judgment as a fire. Most of us think of fire in negative terms because of the destruction it can cause. But fire can also purify, as it does when ore is heated to separate useless dross from a precious metal such as silver. We as believers should pray for the spirit of burning to convict us of our sin, refine our lives, and shape us into instruments of usefulness in God's service.

These names of the Holy Spirit are similar to names by which God the Father and Jesus the Son are known. God is called a "consuming fire" (Hebrews 12:29), and Jesus is described as a "refiner's fire" (Malachi 3:2). See also *Fire*.

SPIRIT OF KNOWLEDGE AND THE FEAR OF THE LORD

These two names of the Holy Spirit are among six that the prophet Isaiah cited in just one verse (see Isaiah 11:2). This in itself is unusual. But another striking feature of the verse is that the prophet grouped these names together into three sets of two names each. Perhaps he thought of these sets of two as names that were closely related to each other.

So how do the "spirit of knowledge" and the "spirit of the fear of the LORD" relate? Isaiah may have had in mind a well-known verse from the book of Proverbs: "The fear of the LORD is the beginning of knowledge" (Proverbs 1:7 NIV). In the Bible "fear of the Lord" means respect or reverence for God. So this proverb declares that a healthy respect for God is the most important attitude for a person to have as he accumulates the knowledge he needs in order to be happy and successful in life.

Through His Spirit, God plants in our hearts a reverence for Him that leads us to honor the Lord in our lives. This is the foundation on which we build knowledge and understanding through the continuing influence of His Spirit.

This is what happened with the prophet Daniel in the Old Testament. When he was a young man, he was taken into captivity after his native Judah fell to the Babylonian army. Trained for service as an administrator in the Babylonian government, he managed to remain faithful to God while rendering service to a pagan king. Even his captors recognized that "an excellent spirit, and knowledge, and understanding. . .were found in the same Daniel" (Daniel 5:12). See also *Reverence for God*.

SPIRIT OF LIFE

In Romans 8:2 the apostle Paul declared, "The law of the Spirit of life in Christ Jesus hath made me free from the law of sin and death." This statement reminds us of another of his famous declarations about the Holy Spirit: "Where the Spirit of the Lord is, there is liberty" (2 Corinthians 3:17). By the law of the "Spirit of life" in Romans, Paul means the principle by which the Holy Spirit operates.

Life in the Spirit gives us the power to live free from the law, or principle, of sin and death. This does not mean that believers will never experience death, because physical death is the lot of every human being. Paul means that those who have accepted Jesus Christ as Savior and Lord are no longer in bondage to sin and death. Just as Jesus defeated death, He has promised that all believers will enjoy eternal life with Him.

As the Spirit of life, the Holy Spirit shares a name with Jesus, who is called the "resurrection and the life" (John 11:25 NIV). Those who have Jesus and the Holy Spirit in their lives are not held hostage by the threat of death. See also *Life*; *Resurrection and the Life*.

The spirit of prophecy tells John what to write in what we know as the last book of the Bible, Revelation.

LIFE FOR THE CHURCH

In his hymn "O Spirit of the Living God," Henry H. Tweedy prayed that the Holy Spirit would continue to empower the Church for its work in the world.

O Spirit of the living God,
Thou light and fire divine,
Descend upon Thy church once more
And make it truly Thine.
Fill it with love and joy and power,
With righteousness and peace;
Till Christ shall dwell in human hearts
And sin and sorrow cease.

SPIRIT OF PROPHECY

The apostle John, author of the book of Revelation, fell in awe before an angel at the throne of God. The angel told John not to worship him but to worship God and His Son, Jesus Christ. The angel went on to identify the Holy Spirit who bore witness of Jesus as the "spirit of prophecy" (Revelation 19:10).

The coming Messiah was often spoken of by the prophets of the Old Testament. This insight did not come to them through the power of their intellect but by direct revelation of God through the agency of His Holy Spirit (see 2 Peter 1:21).

These inspired prophecies were not

restricted to the Old Testament. When Simeon saw the infant Jesus in the temple, He declared that He was the long-awaited Messiah whom God had finally sent to His people. This truth was revealed to Simeon by the Holy Spirit (see Luke 2:25–27). See also *Prophecies about Christ*.

SPIRIT OF TRUTH

Jesus told His disciples that He would not always be with them in bodily form. But He promised to send the Holy Spirit to serve as their comforter and guide. "When he, the Spirit of truth, is come," He said, "he will guide you into all truth" (John 16:13).

One dimension of truth is "in accordance with fact." In other words, do the facts support a specific statement or claim, proving it to be true? But the word *truth* can also refer to something that is enduring or authentic, in contrast to something that does not last or is artificial or of little value.

The second meaning of truth is what Jesus had in mind when He spoke of the Holy Spirit as the "Spirit of truth." His disciples would discover that the Spirit was enduring and dependable. He would never leave them or forsake them. When all else crumbled and faded away, the Spirit would continue to empower their lives.

In John 15 Jesus told His disciples that the Spirit of truth would also help them bear witness of Him "because ye have been with me from the beginning" (John 15:27). The memory of Jesus' physical presence would eventually grow dim in their minds. But the Holy Spirit would help them recall His life and teachings and pass these truths on to others. This is exactly what happened in the book of Acts as the apostles bore witness about Jesus to people who had not seen Him in the flesh.

But even the disciples would not live forever. To preserve a record of Jesus' life, they recorded, under the inspiration of the Holy Spirit, what they remembered about Him. They also repeated these stories to other early believers, who faithfully wrote down these eyewitness accounts. These records were passed on to future generations through the written Gospels of the New Testament. All of us as believers are beneficiaries of their faithful witness.

Jesus was right. The Spirit of truth is eternal. He is still revealing the truth about Jesus almost two thousand years after His death, resurrection, and ascension. Though we have never seen Jesus in the physical sense, we feel His presence through the work of His Spirit. See also *Faithful and True Witness*; *Truth*.

SPIRIT OF UNDERSTANDING

See *Spirit of Wisdom and Revelation*.

SPIRIT OF WISDOM AND REVELATION

The apostle Paul expressed this beautiful prayer for the believers at Ephesus: "That the God of our Lord Jesus Christ, the Father of glory, may give unto you the spirit of wisdom and revelation in the knowledge of him" (Ephesians 1:17). This name of the Holy Spirit is striking because of its combination of three important ingredients of the spiritual life—revelation, knowledge, and wisdom.

Revelation is the process by which God makes Himself known to man. Our human minds would know nothing about God unless He had chosen to reveal Himself to us. He has done this supremely through the written scriptures.

The writings that make up the Bible were

revealed by God. But He inspired human beings through the activity of His Spirit to understand these divine messages and to write them down. "No prophecy of Scripture came about by the prophet's own interpretation," the apostle Peter declared. "Prophecy never had its origin in the human will, but prophets, though human, spoke from God as they were carried along by the Holy Spirit" (2 Peter 1:20–21 NIV).

Through the inspired scriptures we gain knowledge about God—His nature as Creator, sustainer, and redeemer. But the Spirit teaches us more than factual information about God. We come to know Him in a personal sense as the God who loved us enough to send His own Son, Jesus Christ, to save us from our sins.

Finally, wisdom is one of the ministries of the Holy Spirit in our lives. Wisdom is the ability to apply the facts to practical situations. Knowing the truth and applying and living the truth are two different things. The Holy Spirit gives us the wisdom to honor God by the way we live out our faith in the real world.

Another name of the Holy Spirit that is similar to spirit of wisdom and revelation is "spirit of wisdom and understanding" (Isaiah 11:2). In addition to inspiring human beings to write down God's revelation in the Bible, the Holy Spirit works with us as we read these writings. He opens our understanding so we can comprehend and apply God's message to our lives. With the Holy Spirit as our helper and guide, the Bible is always as fresh and up-to-date as a live broadcast of a breaking news event on local TV. See also *Wisdom of God*; *Revelation of God*.

SPIRITS IN PRISON

See *Descent into Prison by Jesus*.

SPIRIT THAT WAS UPON MOSES

During the Exodus from Egypt, the Israelites often frustrated Moses, their leader who had been selected by the Lord. Finally, Moses grew tired of their constant bickering and the burden of solo leadership. He needed others to help him with the task of hearing complaints and settling disputes. "I am not able to bear all this people alone," he told the Lord, "because it is too heavy for me" (Numbers 11:14).

God responded by instructing Moses to select seventy elders with leadership skills from among the tribal leaders of the people. Then He empowered them for their assignment as Moses' assistants by filling them with the "spirit that was upon him [Moses]" (Numbers 11:25). The same Spirit of God who enabled Moses to bear the responsibility of leadership among God's people would strengthen them for their work under Moses' supervision.

This account shows that leadership and the Holy Spirit go together like a portrait in a picture frame. God never selects a person for a job without giving him the power through His Spirit to accomplish the task He has called him to do. The Bible is filled with examples of people whom God filled with His Spirit after calling them to serve as leaders of His people (see Numbers 27:18–21).

If God has called you to some important leadership task, you can rest assured that His Spirit will make you equal to the challenge. See also *Moses*.

SPIRITUAL GIFTS

The Holy Spirit bestows talents and abilities upon believers for the growth and edification of fellow believers and the Church. The apostle Paul identified several of these gifts in his

God places His Spirit on the special leaders He calls—from Moses down through the present day. In this photo, evangelist Billy Graham preaches in Flushing, New York, in 2005.

letters to the believers at Rome and Corinth. Gifts listed in Romans are preaching, serving, teaching, encouraging, giving, leading, and helping others (see Romans 12:6–8). Gifts listed in 1 Corinthians are wisdom, knowledge, faith, healing, miracles, prophecy, discernment of spirits, tongues, and interpretation of tongues (see 1 Corinthians 12:8–11).

In another section of 1 Corinthians known as the "Love Chapter of the New Testament," Paul declared that love for others is the supreme spiritual gift (see 1 Corinthians 13:1–15).

THE SUPREMACY OF LOVE

"If I could speak all the languages of earth and of angels, but didn't love others, I would only be a noisy gong or a clanging cymbal. . . . If I gave everything I have to the poor and even sacrificed my body, I could boast about it; but if I didn't love others, I would have gained nothing.

"Love is patient and kind. Love is not jealous or boastful or proud or rude. It does not demand its own way. It is not irritable, and it keeps no record of being wronged. It does not rejoice about injustice but rejoices whenever the truth wins out. Love never gives up, never loses faith, is always hopeful, and endures through every circumstance. . . .

"Three things will last forever—faith, hope, and love—and the greatest of these is love" (1 Corinthians 13:1, 3–7, 13 NLT).

SPIRITUAL ROCK

The apostle Paul reached back into Jewish history to create this unusual name for Jesus: "All our fathers were under the cloud, and all passed through the sea. . .and did all drink the same spiritual drink: for they drank of that spiritual Rock that followed them: and that Rock was Christ" (1 Corinthians 10:1, 3–4).

These verses reminded the Jewish people of their wilderness wandering years after their deliverance from slavery in Egypt. God guided them with a cloud, signifying His presence (see Exodus 13:21). He also gave them safe passage through the Red Sea with the Egyptian army in hot pursuit (see Exodus 14:21–27).

In the dry and barren wilderness, God also provided water for His people. It gushed from a rock when Moses struck it with his staff at God's command (see Numbers 20:8–11). Paul picked up on the rock imagery from this wilderness experience and described Jesus as the "spiritual Rock" who meets the needs of God's people. Just as the rock in the desert was the source of water for the Israelites, Christ guides and protects those who place their trust in Him.

Was Jesus actually present with the Israelites in the wilderness? Paul declared that Christ, their spiritual Rock, "followed them." Was Paul speaking metaphorically? We can't say for sure. We know that Jesus existed with God the Father from eternity before the world was created (see John 1:1–3). He came to earth in human form many centuries after the Israelites left Egypt. But He had the power to assume any form He desired at any time.

Maybe it's best to leave this argument to the theologians and scholars. But one thing we can say for sure is that Jesus is a modern-day spiritual Rock who quenches our thirst and provides strength and stability for daily living. That's all we as believers really need to know. See also *Living Stone.*

STAR OUT OF JACOB

This is a name assigned to the coming Messiah by Balaam, a pagan magician who blessed the

Israelites (see *Sceptre Out of Israel*). The Messiah would be a "Star out of Jacob" who would rule over His people with great power and authority (see Numbers 24:17).

The nation of Israel is sometimes referred to in the Bible as "Jacob" because it sprang from the twelve sons, or tribes, of the patriarch Jacob. A star was considered the symbol of an exceptional king. For example, Joseph had a dream in which the sun and moon and eleven stars bowed down to him (see Genesis 37:9). The eleven stars symbolized his brothers, who did eventually fall on their faces before him. This happened several years after this dream when Joseph became a high official in Egypt (see Genesis 43:26; 44:14).

The word *star* is tossed around loosely in our time. We have rock stars, movie stars, and superstars in every sport from badminton to wrestling. But the name of Jesus will live on long after all these pseudo-stars have disappeared. His eternal reign as the Star out of Jacob is assured by none other than God the Father: "And the seventh angel sounded;

Moses strikes the rock, producing water, in a stained-glass window in Brussels, Belgium. The apostle Paul used this event to coin a title for Jesus: "spiritual Rock."

and there were great voices in heaven, saying, The kingdoms of this world are become the kingdoms of our Lord, and of his Christ; and he shall reign for ever and ever" (Revelation 11:15). See also *Mighty One of Jacob*.

STARS

The people of the ancient world regarded all heavenly bodies as stars, except the sun and moon (see Genesis 1:16). The stars were considered a mark of God's creative power (see Psalm 19:1). The word *stars* is also used in the Bible as a figure of speech for angels (see Job 38:7).

The most notable star in the Bible is the one that appeared in the sky to signal the birth of Jesus. Wise men from the East, probably astrologers, saw this star and came to pay homage to the newborn Jesus in Bethlehem (see Matthew 2:1–2). See also *Moon*; *Sun*.

LEANING ON GOD'S STRENGTH

- "Those who hope in the LORD will renew their strength. They will soar on wings like eagles; they will run and not grow weary, they will walk and not be faint" (Isaiah 40:31 NIV).
- "The Sovereign LORD is my strength; he makes my feet like the feet of a deer, he enables me to tread on the heights" (Habakkuk 3:19 NIV).
- "God is our refuge and strength, an ever-present help in trouble" (Psalm 46:1 NIV).

STEADFASTNESS OF GOD

See *Longsuffering of God.*

STEM OF JESSE

See *Rod Out of the Stem of Jesse.*

STONE

See *Living Stone.*

STRENGTH

Moses led the Israelites to sing a song of praise to the Lord after He rescued them from the pursuing army of Pharaoh at the Red Sea. "The LORD is my strength and song," he sang,

Modern art depicts an ancient event: God's parting of the Red Sea to allow the Israelites to escape Egypt. Moses then led the people in a song about God's strength.

"and he is become my salvation. . .my father's God, and I will exalt him" (Exodus 15:2). This verse belongs to a passage known as the song of Moses (see Exodus 15:1–19).

The people had witnessed the awesome power of the Lord as He divided the waters of the sea to give them safe passage. Even before this event, He had plagued the Egyptians again and again until Pharaoh allowed the Israelites to leave the country. No wonder Moses referred to this wonder-working God as his "strength."

There is no shortage of power in the God we serve. And He invites us to partake of His strength in our times of need. See also *Power of God; Power of the Highest.*

STRONG TOWER

"The name of the LORD is a strong tower," the author of Proverbs said. "The righteous runneth into it, and is safe" (Proverbs 18:10). Towers were massive stone structures built above the defensive walls of ancient cities. From these elevated positions, defenders could shoot arrows or hurl stones on the enemy forces outside the wall. These towers also served as a final line of defense if the invading army should succeed in breaking through the wall or battering down the city gate.

The writer of Proverbs knew that the Lord was as dependable as one of these defensive towers. His righteous followers can seek safety and security in Him. This imagery also appears in the Psalms, where God is referred to as a "high tower" (Psalms 18:2; 144:2). See also *Fortress*.

SUN

The Lord created this heavenly body to bring life-giving heat and light to Earth (see Matthew 5:45). The people of many ancient cultures were so impressed with the sun and its permanence that they made it an object of worship. But this form of idolatry was strictly forbidden by the Lord (see Deuteronomy 4:19). He brought the sun into being, and no created thing is worthy of our worship. See also *Dayspring from on High*; *Moon*.

This close-up view of the sun, through NASA's Extreme Ultraviolet Imaging Telescope, shows wild activity of which early people were unaware. Sadly, many worshiped the created sun rather than its Creator.

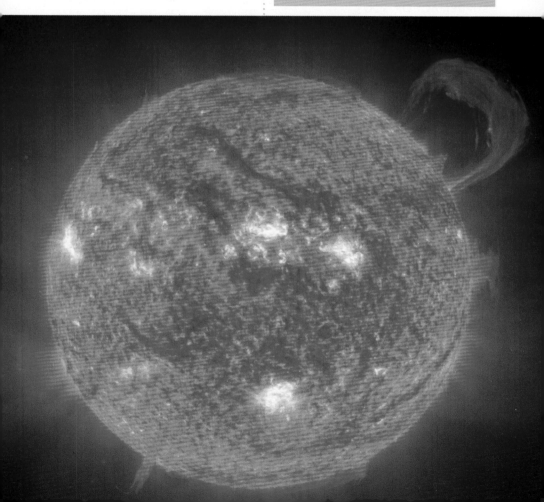

SUN OF RIGHTEOUSNESS

See *Dayspring from on High.*

SUPERNATURAL REVELATION

See *Revelation of God.*

SUPPLICATION

See *Spirit of Grace and Supplications.*

SUPREMACY OF GOD

See *Almighty God; Sovereignty of God.*

SURE FOUNDATION

See *Foundation.*

SURETY OF A BETTER TESTAMENT

See *Mediator of the New Testament.*

SYNOPTIC GOSPELS

This term comes from the Greek word *synopsis,* meaning "to see together." The Gospels of Matthew, Mark, and Luke are called the Synoptic Gospels because of their similarity. They report many of the same events from the life of Jesus, using a similar chronology. Sometimes their accounts of an event follow one another almost word-for-word.

Scholars believe the Gospel of Mark was written first, and that Matthew and Luke followed Mark's pattern, even including some material from Mark almost verbatim. But both Matthew and Luke do contain information not found in Mark or any other Gospel. For example, only Luke tells us about the birth of Jesus in Bethlehem (Luke 2:1–7). And Matthew alone reports Jesus' parable of the unforgiving servant (Matthew 18:23–35).

The Gospel of John is not considered a Synoptic Gospel because it is so different from Matthew, Mark, and Luke in the way it treats the life and ministry of Jesus. For example, it does not contain a single major parable of Jesus. Many of the miracles of Jesus reported by the three Synoptic Gospels do not appear in John. Instead of focusing exclusively on the major events in Jesus' life, John goes behind the scenes to give us the theological meaning of many of these happenings. See also *Inspiration of the Bible.*

Jacob Jordaens' seventeenth-century portrait *The Four Evangelists*. Matthew, Mark, and Luke wrote the synoptic Gospels, meaning their account of Christ's life and ministry "see together." John's Gospel stands separately.

T

TABERNACLE

This tent or portable sanctuary was built in the wilderness at God's command as a place of worship for the Israelites (see Exodus 40:2–8). It was also called the tent of meeting because it was considered a place of encounter between God and His people. The tabernacle foreshadowed Christ's incarnation when "the Word was made flesh, and dwelt among us" (John 1:14). Solomon's temple built in Jerusalem eventually replaced the tabernacle as the central place of worship for the Jewish people. See also *Minister of the True Tabernacle*; *Temple*.

A model of the Old Testament tabernacle, in the Timna valley of Israel. The ancient Israelites worshiped God at this portable sanctuary.

TAX COLLECTORS

See *Publicans*.

TEACHER COME FROM GOD

This name of Jesus was spoken by Nicodemus, a wealthy and respected Pharisee who wanted to learn more about Jesus and His teachings. He had probably heard about Jesus from others in the region of Galilee. To his credit, Nicodemus did not judge Jesus based on hearsay. He sought to talk with Him face-to-face before deciding what to make of this teacher and miracle worker from Nazareth (see John 3:2).

The Gospels contain many references to Jesus' ministry as a teacher. In this role He communicated God's message to individuals like Nicodemus as well as large groups of people (see Mark 4:1). He was also a patient teacher with His disciples, who were slow to understand His mission of redemptive suffering (see Luke 24:45–47).

Jesus was an effective "teacher come from God" because of His teaching style. He did not focus on abstract theories but

on down-to-earth truths that the common people could understand. He used familiar objects from everyday life—birds, flowers, sheep, salt, bread, water, light—to connect with the life experiences of His audience. He told stories, or parables, to illustrate divine truths He wanted the people to understand and act upon.

But the most impressive thing about Jesus' teaching is that it was stamped with the power of God the Father. Jesus did not quote learned rabbis from the past to authenticate His words, as was the custom among the religious teachers of His day. He made it clear that He spoke under direct commission from God Himself. The people were "amazed at his teaching, because his words had authority" (Luke 4:32 NIV). See also *Master*; *Parables of Jesus*; *Rabbi/Rabboni*.

SUBJECTS OF JESUS' TEACHINGS

- Eternal life (see Mark 10:28–30; John 7:37–38).
- Faith (see Matthew 14:27, 31; Luke 17:6, 19).
- Forgiveness (see Mark 11:25–26; Luke 17:3–4).
- Holiness (see Matthew 5:8; Luke 1:74–75).
- Kingdom of God (see Matthew 13:11–50; Luke 22:29–30).
- Love (see Matthew 18:15; John 13:34–35).
- Money (see Mark 12:43–44; John 6:27).
- Prayer (see Matthew 6:9–13; John 14:13–14).
- Service (see Matthew 20:28; Luke 22:27).
- Wisdom (see Mark 4:12; John 6:45).

TEACHERS OF THE LAW

See *Scribes*.

TEMPERANCE

See *Self-Control*.

TEMPLE

This was the central place of worship for the Jewish people. Three separate temples were built on the same site in Jerusalem. The first was Solomon's temple, built about 960 BC. This temple was destroyed by the Babylonian army when they overran the city of Jerusalem in 586 BC. A second temple was built in 515 BC by Jews who returned to Jerusalem after the exile among the Babylonians and Persians.

About 500 years later, the Roman governor Herod the Great enlarged and remodeled this second temple into a more ornate structure. This building was destroyed by the Roman army in AD 70, never to be rebuilt. The only part of "Herod's temple" that remains is the foundation, known as the Temple Mount or the Western Wall. But the Jews still consider this a sacred site. They gather here for prayer and meditation, often stuffing written prayers into the crevices of this massive wall. Most modern tours of the Holy Land include a visit to this place of prayer.

The Jews believed that God's presence inhabited the temple. Even Jesus referred to it as "the house of God" (Matthew 12:4). But the Church that He established was destined to surpass the temple in importance and scope. The Church includes people of all nations and races, not just the Jews. It is the new temple of God in which the Spirit of God dwells. And since believers are part of His Church, His Spirit dwells in us as well. The apostle Paul reminded the Christians at Corinth, "Don't you know that you your- selves are God's temple and that God's Spirit dwells in your midst?" (1 Corinthians 3:16 NIV). See also *Church*; *Veil of the Temple.*

A model of the second temple in Jerusalem, on display at the Israel Museum.

TEMPTATIONS OF JESUS

The first temptations of Jesus occurred at the beginning of His public ministry. He was led by the Spirit of God into the wilderness, where He fasted and prayed. While He was alone and hungry, Satan tempted Him to turn stones into bread to meet His physical needs (see Matthew 4:2–3). Then Satan tried to convince Him to prove His divine power by jumping off the highest point of the temple to dazzle the crowds (see Matthew 4:5–7). Another temptation was to use His power to become a military leader and conquer the world for His own glory (see Matthew 4:8–9).

But Jesus resisted all of Satan's tricks. He would not be turned aside from His spiritual mission as God's Son to become an atoning sacrifice for sin.

After He had fasted for forty days, Jesus was "an hungred," in the terminology of the King James Version. At this point, Satan arrived to suggest Jesus turn the stones of the wilderness into bread. Jesus turned away the temptation by quoting from the book of Deuteronomy.

As His earthly ministry was drawing to a close, Jesus faced the greatest temptation of His life—to save Himself from suffering on the cross and His certain death. In the Garden of Gethsemane, He agonized in prayer over what to do, finally yielding to His Father's will. "Not my will," He prayed, "but yours be done" (Luke 22:42 NIV).

The temptations of Jesus are a good example of the human and divine dimensions of His nature. He was human enough to be tempted just as we are. But He had the divine power to resist sin and to follow His destiny all the way to the cross. As the writer of Hebrews put it: "We have one who has been tempted in every way, just as we are—yet he did not sin" (Hebrews 4:15 NIV). See also *Garden of Gethsemane*.

If you look closely at the east façade of the US Supreme Court building, you'll find Moses, holding the tablets of the Ten Commandments.

TEMPTER

See *Satan*.

TEN COMMANDMENTS

These ethical commands were given by the Lord to Moses on Mount Sinai. Also called the Decalogue, the Ten Commandments summarize the basic moral laws of the Old Testament that are still considered authoritative in our own time.

Four of these commandments deal with our responsibilities to God: (1) recognize the Lord alone as God, (2) have nothing to do with pagan gods, (3) do not misuse the Lord's name, and (4) sanctify the Sabbath day (see Exodus 20:1–11).

The last six commandments deal with our obligations to other people: (5) honor your father and mother, (6) do not murder, (7) do not commit adultery, (8) do not steal, (9) do not bear false witness against others, and (10) do not desire anything that belongs to your neighbor (see Exodus 20:12–17).

Jesus summed up these commandments in two great principles—supreme love for God and loving our neighbors as ourselves (see Matthew 22:37–40). See also *Law of Moses*.

TENT OF MEETING

See *Tabernacle*.

TERAPHIM

This Hebrew word (pronounced TEHR uh feem) refers to miniature images of false gods. These idols may have been carried from place to place or kept in private homes. When Rachel left her home in Mesopotamia to go to Canaan with Jacob, she carried her father's "images" (see Genesis 31:19). The Hebrew word behind "images" in this verse is *teraphim*. The term is rendered as "household idols" in some translations.

The worship of teraphim was a form of idolatry included in God's condemnation of

false worship in the Ten Commandments (see Exodus 20:1–5). See also *Idolatry*.

The tetragrammaton, a shortened form of the name of God, decorating a church in Vienna, Austria.

TETRAGRAMMATON

This word (pronounced TET ruh GRAM uh ton) is from a Greek term that means "four letters." It refers to the form in which one of the names of God was written in the Hebrew scrolls of the Old Testament. The English equivalent of this name in Hebrew is YHWH, thus the "four letters."

This name of God was a form of "to be" in the Hebrew language. The Jews believed this name was too sacred to be pronounced or read aloud. So they cloaked the name by putting it in a form that could not be spoken. The only way to pronounce it in English is to add vowels to the four consonants, like this: YaHWeH. This gives us the English term *Yahweh*.

In most English versions of the Bible, this divine name is rendered simply as "Lord." But it usually appears in large and small capital letters (Lord) to distinguish it from other names of God that appear in the Old Testament. See also *I Am That I Am*; *Yahweh*.

THANK OFFERING

See *Sacrificial Offerings*.

THANKSGIVING

By offering thanks we express our gratitude to God for His blessings. The psalmist praised the Lord for His goodness and mercy (see Psalm 116:12–19). Our Christian inheritance of salvation and eternal life should inspire our thanksgiving to God (see Colossians 1:12). The apostle Paul encouraged believers to live each day in a spirit of thanksgiving to the Lord: "Sing and make music from your heart to the Lord, always giving thanks to God the Father for everything" (Ephesians 5:19–20 NIV). See also *Prayer*; *Worship of God*.

THEOLOGY

This word comes from two Greek words: *theos*, meaning "God," and *logos*, meaning "study" or "word." Thus, theology is the study of God. Theologians who devote their lives to this discipline probe into such deep subjects as the nature of God, His creation, and His purpose for humankind and the world. You will find these subjects discussed in this book—but in a user-friendly style without the theological jargon.

Some people believe that theology is a futile pursuit because God is a divine, mysterious being who is totally beyond our human understanding. But God has chosen to reveal Himself to us through the truths that inspired writers have recorded for us in the Bible. We *can* know the things about God that really matter. The bottom line is that He sent His Son, Jesus, as the mediator who brings us into a personal relationship with the Father through faith and our commitment to His will for our lives. See also *Doctrine*; *Trinity*.

THEOPHANY

This term (pronounced thee AHF uh nee) is derived from two Greek words, *theos*, meaning "God," and *phaino*, meaning "to appear." Thus, it refers to a "God appearance," or a visible manifestation of God's presence. Theophanies are rare, appearing only in the Old Testament. Perhaps the best-known biblical theophany is God's appearance to Moses in the form of a burning bush.

Other theophanies in the Old Testament include the angel who struggled with Jacob at Peniel (see Genesis 32:24–30), the pillar of fire and cloud that God used to guide the Israelites during the Exodus from Egypt (see Exodus 14:24), the fire and smoke that covered Mount Sinai (see Exodus 19:18), and the prophet Isaiah's vision of God in the temple (see Isaiah 6:1–5). See also *Burning Bush*; *Pillar of Fire and Cloud*.

An eighteenth-century artist tried to capture the impressive nature of Solomon's throne as described in 1 Kings 10. The Bible uses the idea of a throne to signify God's power and authority.

THRONE

Kings sat on these ornate chairs to symbolize their authority. King Solomon's throne was decorated with ivory and gold. Beside it sat statues of lions to show his undisputed royalty and power. On the steps that the king had to climb to get to his seat of power were twelve more lions—one on each side of the six steps. No wonder the writer of 1 Kings added this observation about Solomon's throne: "Nothing like it had ever been made for any other kingdom" (1 Kings 10:20 NIV).

But Solomon's throne is like a common chair in comparison to the throne occupied by the Lord. The biblical writers often used the imagery of God on His throne to signify His unlimited power and authority. For example, the prophet Isaiah declared that heaven was God's throne and earth was His footstool (see Isaiah 66:1). This metaphor showed clearly that God ruled over every part of the universe. In the New Testament, Jesus is said to be sitting "at the right hand of the throne of God" (Hebrews 12:2 NIV), serving side by side with the Father as judge and ruler of the world.

This throne imagery comes to fruition in the book of Revelation. In the apostle John's vision of heaven, he saw the Lord sitting on a throne (see Revelation 4:2–3). From this throne He will preside in the end time over the defeat of the forces of evil (see Revelation 20:9–10). Unbelievers will also be judged from His seat of authority that John described as the "great white throne" (see Revelation 20:11–15). See also *Imagery Used of God*.

TIME AND GOD

We humans are very conscious of time. We gauge our lives by the clock and the need to get certain things done in an allotted amount of time. We are also very aware of the aging process and the approaching end of our time on earth.

But God is very different from people in this regard. He is not bound by the constraints of time. As a being who has existed from eternity—before time began—He is the Lord over time itself. He stands above time, watching over His universe and bringing it to its appointed conclusion—whether that be tomorrow, a thousand weeks from now, or a million years in the future.

God is never in a hurry, because He has all the time He needs to accomplish His purpose for His creation. He must surely smile to Himself when He sees the inhabitants of His earth scurrying around in a frenzy, trying to get another job done before the sun goes down or the clock strikes five to end the workday. This thought about God and His mastery of time may have been what the apostle Peter had in mind when he wrote, "Do not forget this one thing, dear friends: With the Lord a day is like a thousand years, and a thousand years are like a day" (2 Peter 3:8 NIV). See also *Eternity of God*.

TOWER

See *Strong Tower*.

GOD ON HIS THRONE

- "God reigns over the nations; God is seated on his holy throne" (Psalm 47:8 NIV).
- "You, LORD, reign forever; your throne endures from generation to generation" (Lamentations 5:19 NIV).
- "When the Son of Man comes in his glory, and all the angels with him, he will sit on his glorious throne" (Matthew 25:31 NIV).

TRANSCENDENCE OF GOD

See *Immanence and Transcendence of God.*

Peter, James, and John cringe in fear as Jesus is "transfigured" (changed) before their eyes. Flanking Jesus are the Old Testament figures Moses and Elijah.

TRANSFIGURATION OF JESUS

This radical transformation in the Savior's appearance glorified God. Accompanied by His disciples Peter, James, and John, Jesus went to a mountain at night to pray. Moses and Elijah appeared and discussed Jesus' death, emphasizing Jesus as the fulfillment of the law and the prophets. Shining with God's glory from within, Christ was overshadowed by a cloud as a voice declared, "This is my Son. . . . Listen to Him!" (Matthew 17:5 NIV).

These experiences affirmed Christ's divinity and mission and helped prepare Jesus and His disciples for the events leading to His death. See also *Glory of God.*

TRANSGRESSION

This word, which refers to a violation of God's law that was considered a serious sin, occurs mostly in the Old Testament, particularly in the wisdom writings—Job, Psalms, and Proverbs. Job asked the Lord to reveal to him "my transgression and my sin" (Job 13:23). He wondered what divine law he had broken that might explain his severe suffering.

The Hebrew word behind "transgression" is sometimes rendered by modern translations as "offense," "unfaithfulness," or "rebellion." See also *Sin.*

TREE OF KNOWLEDGE OF GOOD AND EVIL

The fruit of this tree in the Garden of Eden was declared off-limits by the Lord (see Genesis 2:9–17). The tree symbolized the sovereignty of God—His right as the ruler of creation to set limits on human behavior. After Adam and Eve disobeyed God and ate the forbidden fruit, they were banished from the garden and became subject to hard labor and death (see Genesis 3:3–24). See also *Fall of Man; Tree of Life.*

TREE OF LIFE

The fruit of this tree in the Garden of Eden would bring eternal life if eaten (see Genesis 3:22). After Adam and Eve sinned and ate from the forbidden tree, they no longer had access to the tree of life. From that time on, the sin of Adam and Eve condemned humankind to a life of shame, guilt, and death. But this changed with the coming of Christ. He was the "second Adam" who canceled the effects of the "first Adam's" sin. This He accomplished by offering eternal life to humankind through His atoning death. See also *Tree of Knowledge of Good and Evil*; *Last Adam*.

God sent an angel to the Garden of Eden to keep Adam and Eve from the tree of life. It was a consequence of their sin of disobedience in eating from the tree of the knowledge of good and evil.

TRESPASS

See *Sin*.

TRESPASS OFFERING

See *Sacrificial Offerings*.

TRIALS OF JESUS

This series of trials or appearances of Jesus before Jewish and Roman authorities ended with His death. A careful study of the four Gospels reveals six different phases in these trials. Here's a brief summary of these appearances.

Before the Jewish Religious Leaders
- Preliminary hearing before Annas, father-in-law of the high priest Caiaphas (see John 18:12–24).
- Hearing before Caiaphas the high priest and other leaders (see Matthew 26:57–67; Mark 14:53–65).
- Official trial and condemnation before the full Sanhedrin (see Matthew 27:1–2; Mark 15:1; Luke 22:66–71).

Before the Roman Authorities
- First appearance before Pilate, Roman governor of Judea (see Matthew 27:11–14; Mark 15:2–5; Luke 23:1–5; John 18:28–37).
- Hearing before Herod Antipas, Roman governor of Galilee and Perea (see Luke 23:6–12).
- Second appearance before Pilate, who pronounced the death sentence (see Matthew 27:15–26; Mark 15:6–15; Luke 23:13–25; John 18:38–19:16).

See also *Sanhedrin*.

TRIBE OF JUDAH

See *Lion of the Tribe of Judah*.

TRIBULATION

See *Great Tribulation*.

TRIED STONE

See *Chief Cornerstone*.

TRINITY

The doctrine of the Trinity is perhaps the most distinctive teaching of the Christian faith. Christians believe, along with Jews and Muslims, that there is one—and only one—supreme God of the universe. But only Christianity affirms that God makes Himself known in three separate but related realities—God the Father, God the Son, and God the Holy Spirit.

How can God be one but three at the same time? This doesn't make sense to our logical minds. But believers insist that this doctrine is not only Bible-based but also proven through our practical experience.

In the Old Testament, God often worked through His Spirit. At the creation, His Spirit hovered over the waters (see Genesis 1:2). The Spirit of God in man brings wisdom and understanding (see Job 32:8). God promised that His Spirit would rest upon the Messiah,

There's no easy way to describe the Trinity, but some use the example of water. Though water is one substance, it can appear in three distinct forms: liquid, solid (ice), and gas (vapor).

whom He would send into the world (see Isaiah 11:2).

When Jesus launched His public ministry, the Trinity was evident in His work. For example, He subjected Himself to baptism at the hands of John the Baptist, His forerunner. As He came out of the water, "he saw the spirit of God descending like a dove and alighting on him. And a voice from heaven said, 'This is my Son, whom I love; with him I am well pleased'" (Matthew 3:16–17 NIV). Here we see all three Persons of the Trinity at work—God the Father, God the Son, and God the Holy Spirit.

Our experience as recipients of salvation also confirms the reality of the Trinity. God's love for sinful humankind motivated Him to send His Son, Jesus, as an atoning sacrifice. Jesus was obedient to His Father's will and died on the cross for us (see John

People spread palm branches and cloaks on the road before Jesus, shouting "Hosanna" ("Save") during the Lord's triumphal entry into Jerusalem.

3:16). Through the work of God's Spirit, we are convicted of our sin and moved to repent and accept God's generous gift (see Galatians 4:6). See also *Eternal Spirit*; *Everlasting Father*; *Monotheism*.

TRIUMPHAL ENTRY OF JESUS

Jesus entered Jerusalem on the Sunday before His crucifixion the following Friday. He was greeted with shouts of joy from the crowds, who were looking for an earthly king. With His entry, Jesus acknowledged He was the promised Messiah—but a spiritual deliverer rather than a conquering military hero (see Matthew 21:1–11). This event is observed by believers every year on Palm Sunday, the Sunday before Easter. See also *Easter*; *Holy Week*.

TRUE GOD

See *God (name of Jesus)*.

TRUE LIGHT

See *Light*; *Light of the World*.

TRUE TABERNACLE

See *Minister of the True Tabernacle*.

TRUE VINE

See *Vine*.

TRUE WITNESS

See *Faithful and True Witness*; *Witness*.

"Some trust in chariots and some in horses," wrote David in Psalm 20:7, "but we trust in the name of the LORD our God" (NIV).

TRUST

We put our confidence in the people or things that we trust. In Old Testament times, the prophets often criticized the Israelites because they put their trust in military might rather than in the power of the Lord (see Isaiah 36:9). God's name and His Word are worthy of our trust (see Psalms 33:21; 119:42). Christ warned that people may deceive and be unworthy of trust (see Matthew 10:17–21), but we may place ultimate trust and confidence in Him (see John 6:35–37). See also *Assurance of God*; *Faith*.

TRUTH

Jesus used this name for Himself in a conversation with His disciple Thomas. He told Thomas, "I am the way, the truth, and the life: no man cometh unto the Father, but by me" (John 14:6). This is the only place in the New Testament where Jesus is referred to by this name.

We usually use the word *truth* in referring to our words or speech. For example, we might pay a compliment to a friend by saying, "She always tells the truth." This use of the word certainly applies to Jesus. He always spoke the truth to His disciples and to others, even when they had a hard time accepting it. This was especially the case with His statements about His coming death (see Matthew 16:21–22).

But beyond speaking the truth, Jesus acted out the truth in His life and ministry. And even more importantly, He *was* and *is* the truth because He is the ultimate reality in the universe. This is the sense in which Jesus referred to Himself as the truth in His conversation with Thomas.

We live in a world in which it is sometimes hard to nail down the truth. Our materialistic society tries to convince us that money and possessions are the essence of truth and the way to the good life. Some people say learning or knowledge is the ticket to the truth. Others believe that we all must find truth for ourselves by constructing it from our own life experiences. What is truth for one person may not be truth for another, these people say, because there is no such thing as absolute truth.

These modern theories remind us of Pilate, the Roman governor who pronounced the death sentence against Jesus. When Jesus told him that He had come into the world to "testify to the truth" (John 18:37 NIV), Pilate asked sarcastically, "What is truth?" (John 18:38). The truth stood so close to Pilate that he could touch it, but he missed it because of his unbelief.

What a tragedy! And what an accurate picture of a sinful and unbelieving world—the arena into which we as believers are sent to bear witness of the truth (see Mark 16:15). See also *Spirit of Truth*.

TRUTHFULNESS OF GOD

We live in a world in which deception and half-truths abound. Businesses make false claims about their products and services. Investment hucksters cheat the elderly out of their retirement savings. Athletes take performance-enhancing drugs to give themselves an edge over their competitors. In a society like this, it's tempting to give in to despair and determine to trust no one.

But there is one being, our Creator, in whom we can place our ultimate trust. God is the source of all truth, and He always deals with us in truth and integrity. He never makes any false claims that He cannot live up to. This attribute of the divine character is sometimes referred to as the veracity of God.

Moses discovered that God was dependable and trustworthy as He led the Israelites in the wilderness under God's direction. The Lord had promised Moses that He

JESUS AS THE TRUTH

- "Those who were in the boat worshiped him [Jesus], saying, 'Truly you are the Son of God'" (Matthew 14:33 NIV).
- "You will know the truth, and the truth will set you free" (John 8:32 NIV).
- "When he, the Spirit of truth, comes, he will guide you into all the truth" (John 16:13 NIV).

would go with him and help him bear up under this difficult task (see Exodus 3:12). Just before the Israelites reached the land of Canaan, Moses sang a song of thanksgiving to this God of truth, who always keeps His promises. "He is the Rock, his works are perfect, and all his ways are just," he sang. "A faithful God who does no wrong, upright and just is he" (Deuteronomy 32:4 NIV). See also *Spirit of Truth*.

When Jesus prayed for His disciples, He asked the Father to "Sanctify them by the truth." Then Jesus proclaimed, "Your word is truth" (John 17:17)

Jesus spoke His harshest words against people like the Pharisees, whose hard-hearted unbelief prevented them from acknowledging Him as Lord.

U

UMPIRE

See *Daysman*.

UNBELIEF

Many people refuse to believe in God and to acknowledge His works (see John 16:9). Jesus knew about unbelief. He met it in his own hometown, Nazareth. The people here had known Him as a boy, so they assumed He was nobody special. He left them with their skeptical attitudes and went to other places where people were more open to His message (Matthew 13:54–58).

Unbelief is caused by Satan's power (see John 8:43–47), an evil heart (see Hebrews 3:12), and self-glorification and pride (see John 5:44). Those who refuse to believe and reject the Gospel are in turn rejected by God (see John 8:24). See also *Agnosticism*; *Atheism*.

UNCLEAN

See *Ceremonial Washing*.

UNCLEAN SPIRITS

See *Demons*.

UNIVERSALISM

This belief suggests that all people are covered by the salvation of Christ, even those who never make a personal profession of faith in Him as Lord and Savior. Universalists emphasize the love of God and deny that there will be a final judgment or an eternal punishment for unbelievers. Most universalists are also known as "free thinkers" who teach that man is inherently good and that Jesus was a great teacher but was not divine.

UNIVERSAL PRIESTHOOD

See *Priesthood of Believers*.

UNKNOWN GOD

See *Pantheon*.

UNPARDONABLE SIN

This is the sin of blasphemy against the Holy Spirit, or attributing the work of Christ to Satan, as the critics of Jesus did. They accused Him of casting demons out of people "by the prince of demons" (Mark 3:22 NIV). Many interpreters believe this sin consists of decisively and finally rejecting the testimony of the Holy Spirit about Christ's person and work and the invitation to confess Jesus as Savior and Lord. Perhaps the ultimate blasphemy is to pretend to serve Christ while actually doing the work of Satan, or influencing others to do the same. See also *Blasphemy*.

UNSPEAKABLE GIFT

See *Gift of God*.

UPRIGHT ONE

See *Most Upright*.

V

VEIL OF THE TEMPLE

According to the Gospel of Matthew, when Jesus died on the cross, the veil (*curtain*, NIV) in the temple was "torn in two from top to bottom" (Matthew 27:51 NIV). This was a curtain or drape that divided the temple into two separate sections—one for Jews and the other for Gentiles, or non-Jews. Gentiles were not allowed to go beyond this curtain into the Jewish section.

The tearing of this barrier showed that Jesus' death was a universal sacrifice. His atonement brought reconciliation and peace to people of all races and nationalities. The apostle Paul picked up on this description of the curtain from Matthew's Gospel and used it to emphasize the inclusion of the Gentiles in God's plan of redemption. "He [Jesus] is our peace," Paul declared, "who hath made both one, and hath broken down the middle wall of partition between us" (Ephesians 2:14). See also *Gentiles; Impartiality of God.*

VENGEANCE

See *Revenge.*

VERACITY OF GOD

See *Truthfulness of God.*

Jesus is the vine, His followers the branches, and our spiritual growth—which comes through Him—the fruit (John 15:5).

VINE

Jesus spoke of Himself by this name during the last supper that He ate with His disciples. "I am the vine; you are the branches," He told them. "If you remain in me and I in you, you will bear much fruit; apart from me you can do nothing" (John 15:5 NIV). He knew they would need to be firmly attached to Him as the "vine" in order to weather the crisis of His forthcoming execution and death.

The imagery that Jesus used was that of a grapevine. This domestic vine had one main stem with several smaller shoots or runners branching off in all directions. These smaller branches owed their lives to this main stem. They could not live apart from the big vine that was rooted in the ground. In the same way, Jesus' disciples were to stay attached to Him as their Lord and Savior. He as the vine would sustain and nourish them so they would bear "much fruit" in the days ahead.

The fruit that Jesus mentioned probably referred to the witness that they would bear for Him after His resurrection and ascension to God the Father. Most of these disciples, His "branches," did abandon Him when He was arrested and executed on the cross (see Matthew 26:56). But after His resurrection, they regained their courage and continued the work that Jesus had trained them to do (see Acts 1:13–14; 2:42–43).

In the Old Testament, the nation of Israel was often referred to as a vine (see Psalm 80:8; Isaiah 5:2). But the people fell into sin and idolatry, becoming an empty vine that bore no fruit for the Lord (see Hosea 10:1). Jesus, therefore, has become the "true vine" (John 15:1) whom God has sent to bring salvation to His people.

VIRGIN BIRTH OF JESUS

Jesus was miraculously conceived by the Holy Spirit and born to the virgin Mary. This event was foretold by the prophet Isaiah (see Isaiah 7:14) and revealed to Mary by an angel (see Luke 1:26–33).

This miracle was just as puzzling for Mary as it is for most of us today. But God did not give her—or us—a medical explanation. In some strange and mysterious way, God would "overshadow" Mary by His Spirit to bring about a miraculous conception. Once formed in Mary's womb, Jesus was born through the natural biological process that brings children into the world.

Thus, from the beginning Jesus had two natures. His divine nature as God's Son was joined with a human nature, in Mary's womb, by a direct act of the author of all creation. God is not limited in His work by our human understanding. See also *Advent*; *Incarnation of Christ*.

VISIONS

See *Dreams and Visions*.

VOW

See *Oath*.

Five watchful virgins meet the bridegroom—Jesus, in this nineteenth-century painting—while five foolish virgins, who'd slept and allowed their lamp oil to run dry, are left out of the celebration.

WALKING WITH GOD

See *Discipleship.*

WALL OF FIRE

The prophet Zechariah used this name for God to describe the Lord's protection of the city of Jerusalem after the exile (see Zechariah 2:5). The city's defensive walls had been destroyed by the Babylonians several decades before. This meant the Jewish exiles who returned to Jerusalem were in a precarious position. But God promised to protect them by becoming a "wall of fire" around the city.

Fire is often associated in the Bible with God's presence and protection. For example, He used a pillar of fire at night to guide His people on their journey through the wilderness (see Exodus 13:21). The prophet Zechariah was assuring the citizens of Jerusalem that they could depend on the Lord's protective presence at this dangerous point in their lives. See also *Fire; Pillar of Fire and Cloud; Refiner's Fire.*

THE WALL OF FIRE STILL BURNS

"The Lily of the Valley," an old hymn by Charles W. Fry, assures us that God continues to guide and protect His people.

> He will never, never leave me, nor yet forsake me here,
> While I live by faith and do His blessed will;
> A wall of fire about me, I've nothing now to fear,
> With His manna He my hungry soul shall fill.

WATCHFULNESS

This attitude of expectant readiness for the return of Christ should characterize all believers. Jesus told a parable about a wedding and ten wise and foolish virgins to emphasize this truth. The virgins in His parable were probably friends of the bride who were supposed to join the wedding procession at some point as it passed by.

Since the wedding was at night, all ten girls carried tiny oil-burning lamps to light the path as they walked with the rest of the wedding party. The wise virgins carried an extra supply of oil for their lamps, but the foolish virgins did not. When the wedding procession was delayed, the lamps of the foolish virgins ran out of oil, and they were unable to join in the celebration of this joyous occasion (see Matthew 25:1–10).

Jesus' message in this parable is clear: be prepared. The second coming of Christ can happen at any moment, and we need to be ready at all times. See also *Second Coming of Christ.*

WATER

See *Living Water.*

WAVE OFFERING

See *Sacrificial Offerings.*

WAY

John 14:5–6 is one of only three places in the Gospels where Jesus' disciple Thomas is mentioned beyond a mere listing of the Twelve (see John 11:16; 20:24–29). The context of these two verses shows that Thomas was puzzled by Jesus' statement that He would leave His disciples soon after His death, resurrection, and ascension (see John 14:1–4).

Thomas wanted to know how he and the other disciples could find their way to Jesus after He left. Jesus replied in spiritual terms, assuring him that He was the only "way" to their eternal reward: "I am the way and the truth and the life. No one comes to the Father except through me" (John 14:6 NIV). Thomas didn't need to know all the details about this destination or how to get there.

This conversation between Jesus and Thomas has a valuable lesson for modern believers. Sometimes our curiosity about heaven takes our eyes off the One who has promised to take us there. We wonder where heaven will be. What will our resurrected bodies look like? Will we know our family members and friends? Will heaven's streets be paved with literal gold?

The truth is that we don't know the answers to any of these questions. But we do have a grasp of the most important thing: Jesus is the only way to that wonderful place. He knows the way there, and we know Him as the way. So we can relax, put away our road maps, and leave the driving to Him. See also *Guide unto Death; Heaven.*

WESTERN WALL

See *Temple.*

WHITE THRONE JUDGMENT

See *Last Judgment.*

WICKEDNESSS

See *Sin.*

WICKED ONE

See *Satan.*

WILLING SPIRIT

See *Free Spirit*.

WIND

In the Bible the Holy Spirit is often compared to the wind. Jesus told Nicodemus that no one can see the wind; yet we feel the effects of the wind when it is blowing (see John 3:8). This is a reflection of how the Holy Spirit works. God's Spirit is not visible to us, but we know that He works in our hearts to convict us of sin and bring us closer to Him. When the Holy Spirit empowered believers on the day of Pentecost, this mysterious, invisible force

made a sound "like the blowing of a violent wind" (Acts 2:2 NIV). See also *Breath of the Almighty*; *Free Spirit*; *Holy Spirit of Promise*.

WISDOM OF GOD

God's wisdom is often spoken of in the Bible in connection with His creation of the physical world. The complexity of the universe—its immense size, numerous living things, and the complexity of its operation—led the writer of Proverbs to exclaim, "By wisdom the LORD laid the earth's foundations, by understanding he set the heavens in place" (Proverbs 3:19 NIV).

Though the wind is invisible, its effects can be seen—as is the case with the Holy Spirit, often compared to the wind.

The classic definition of wisdom is the ability to apply knowledge or facts to practical situations. This definition is appropriate when applied to God and His creation. He not only knew how to create the various parts of the universe, but He was also wise enough to fit them all together into a harmonious whole for the benefit of earth's creatures.

This is one meaning of the six days of creation in the book of Genesis (see Genesis 1). The Lord did not create by accident or happenstance. He followed an orderly plan in the creation process.

Wisdom is not something that God hoards just for Himself. He wants to share it with humans, the crown of His creation. He did so with the prophet Daniel. This wisdom enabled Daniel to interpret the dream of the king of Babylon (see Daniel 4:18–27). Even this pagan ruler recognized that the prophet had "insight, intelligence and outstanding wisdom" (Daniel 5:14 NIV). When appropriated and used, godly wisdom will always serve as a positive witness in an ungodly world. See also *Only Wise God; Spirit of Wisdom and Revelation.*

WISE GOD

See *Only Wise God.*

WISE MEN

After Jesus was born in Bethlehem, several wise men (*magi,* NIV) came from a country in the faraway East to present gifts to the newborn king (see Matthew 2:1–3). These men were members of a priestly caste who practiced the art of astrology. They believed the sun, moon, and stars gave off periodic signs that foretold future events and the destiny of individuals and nations. They probably came from the territory of ancient Babylonia, since this nation had a prominent class of magicians who read the signs of the stars (see Isaiah 47:13).

This verse shows that Jesus' birth had worldwide implications. Although born a Jew in Jewish territory, He was worshiped from the very beginning by other nations—represented by these pagan magicians—as one who was destined to become a universal King. See also *Astrology.*

WITCHCRAFT

See *Magic and Divination.*

WITNESS

See *Faithful and True Witness.*

God's Wisdom in His Son, Jesus

- "We preach Christ crucified: a stumbling block to Jews and foolishness to Gentiles, but to those whom God has called, both Jews and Greeks, Christ the power of God and the wisdom of God" (1 Corinthians 1:23–24 NIV).
- "We declare God's wisdom, a mystery that has been hidden and that God destined for our glory before time began. None of the rulers of this age understood it, for if they had, they would not have crucified the Lord of glory" (1 Corinthians 2:7–8 NIV).

The Bible doesn't say how many wise men visited young Jesus, but traditionally, the number is three—perhaps because they brought three gifts.

WIZARD

See *Magic and Divination*.

WONDERFUL COUNSELLOR

See *Counsellor*.

WONDERS

See *Miracles*.

WORD

The prologue of John's Gospel (see John 1:1–18) focuses on Jesus as the eternal Word who existed with God the Father before the creation of the world. John declared of Jesus, "In the beginning was the Word, and the Word was with God, and the Word was God" (John 1:1).

This verse is an obvious reference to the first three words of the first book of the Bible—Genesis 1:1. Just as God was "in the beginning" (Genesis 1:1), so Jesus existed "in the beginning" (John 1:1) as the eternal Word. This Word, who assumed human form to make His dwelling among human beings on earth (John 1:14), is comparable to the words that God used to speak the universe into being (Genesis 1:3).

Words are the primary units of language that enable humans to communicate with one another. In the same way, Jesus reveals the will and mind of God the Father to earthbound mortals.

The description of Jesus as the Word

Word is a word with multiple meanings in scripture. It can describe a specific message from God, the entire collection of letters we call the Bible, and Jesus Himself.

is unique to the apostle John's writings. In his first epistle, John declared, "There are three that bear record in heaven, the Father, the Word, and the Holy Ghost: and these three are one" (1 John 5:7). This leaves little doubt that John thought of Jesus as the Word who was the second Person of the Trinity.

John continued this imagery in the book of Revelation. He described Jesus as victorious over all His enemies in the end time: "He is dressed in a robe dipped in blood, and his name is the Word of God" (Revelation 19:13 NIV). See also *Logos*.

WORD OF GOD

See *Bible*.

WORD OF LIFE

See *Life*.

WORKS OF GOD

God's deeds or mighty acts are often referred to as His "works." For example, the psalmist declared, "How great are your works, LORD, how profound your thoughts!" (Psalm 92:5 NIV). The theme of praising God for His works appears throughout the Psalms. His works that deserve our praise include creation and the natural world (see Psalm 104:24–25), His provision for our needs (see Psalm 107:8–9), and His teachings (see Psalm 119:27).

In other places in the Bible, additional works of the Lord are cited. These include His providence (see Genesis 50:18–20), His judgment (see Habakkuk 1:5), and His redemptive acts (see Psalm 31:5).

Jesus, God's Son, came into the world to do the work of redemption that was dear to the heart of His Father. "As long as it is day, we must do the works of him who sent me," He told His disciples. "Night is coming, when no one can work" (John 9:4 NIV). Jesus knew that His earthly ministry would last only about three years. He used His time wisely, training His disciples to continue His work after His earthly ministry came to an end. His divine good news, the Gospel, is still changing lives through the action of the Holy Spirit and the ministry of the Church. See also *Miracles*.

WORKS OF MAN

See *Good Works*.

WORSHIP OF GOD

The word *worship* comes from the old English word *worthship*, referring to someone or something that is worthy of our honor and devotion. Thus, the truth that drives our worship is that only the one supreme God of the universe is worthy of our reverence and commitment. Anything short of this is idolatry.

Authentic worship has several elements. The first is adoration or praise. Whether we worship God in private or in public, we should come before Him with joyful praise for His goodness and mercy. Along with the psalmist, we should declare in His presence, "From the rising of the sun to the place where it sets, the name of the LORD is to be praised" (Psalm 113:3 NIV).

Another element of worship is thanksgiving. When we offer our thanks to God for His goodness, we admit that we are not self-sufficient, that we need His constant guidance and presence. The apostle Paul encouraged the Philippian Christians to present their requests to God in an attitude of thanksgiving (see Philippians 4:6).

Worship is not complete until we have recognized God's holiness, compared His righteousness with our sin, and confessed our shortcomings to Him. Then we can claim this promise from the apostle John: "If we confess our sins, he is faithful and just and will forgive us our sins and purify us from all unrighteousness" (1 John 1:9 NIV). See also *Music*; *Psalms, Book of*; *Song*.

WRATH OF GOD

Some people are uncomfortable with the idea of the wrath of God. But the Bible presents a clear picture of this doctrine. His wrath is not an irrational fit of anger but His calm and calculated response to the problem of human sin.

In the Old Testament, God's people, the Israelites, often refused to obey His commands. In response to their waywardness, His wrath often "waxed hot" (Exodus 22:24) or was "kindled" (Numbers 11:33) against them. The purpose of His indignation was to turn them from their sinful ways back to obedience of Him as the one true God. The prophets often spoke of God's wrath being directed against His people because of their worship of false gods (see Jeremiah 44:8).

In the New Testament, the wrath of God is often connected with His future judgment. For example, the apostle Paul spoke of a day of wrath to come that would condemn unbelievers. But believers would be delivered from this judgment of the Lord (see Ephesians 2:2–5).

The Bible is clear that all people are sinners (see Romans 3:23). Thus, everyone deserves God's wrath, or judgment, against sin. But the Gospel's good news is that we can

> ### BOW DOWN AND WORSHIP THE LORD
>
> - "Worship the LORD in the splendor of his holiness" (1 Chronicles 16:29 NIV).
> - "Come, let us bow down in worship, let us kneel before the LORD our maker" (Psalm 95:6 NIV).
> - "We [wise men from the East] saw his [Jesus'] star when it rose and have come to worship him" (Matthew 2:2 NIV).

be delivered from His wrath through faith in Jesus and His atoning death (see Romans 3:24–25).

God's wrath is also referred to in the Bible and in various English translations as His "anger" (Exodus 4:14), "fury" (Isaiah 51:17), "hot displeasure" (Deuteronomy 9:19), "indignation" (Psalm 102:10), and "burning . . .anger" (Isaiah 30:27). See also *Judgment*; *Last Judgment*.

For some people, destructive tornadoes picture God's wrath. The Bible shows His anger in both floods and flames—but also His mercy through Jesus Christ.

YZ

YAHWEH

The Hebrew spelling of one of the major names for God in the Old Testament, translated in most English Bibles as "Lord" (in large and small capital letters: LORD) or "Jehovah." But one modern translation, the Holman Christian Standard Bible, renders this divine name as "Yahweh." A form of the Hebrew verb "to be," this name emphasizes God's eternity. See also *Eternity of God; I Am That I Am; Tetragrammaton.*

The Western Wall, a remnant of Solomon's temple, an area known as "Zion" since Bible times.

ZION

This hill was the site of an ancient fortress of the Jebusites before it was captured by David and is one of the hills on which Jerusalem was built. In Solomon's time this section of Jerusalem was extended to include the temple area. Sometimes all of Jerusalem is referred to as "Zion." The psalmist declared, "The Lord is great in Zion; and he is high above all the people" (Psalm 99:2). In some passages in the KJV, Zion is spelled as "Sion" (see Psalm 65:1). See also *Jerusalem*.

INDEX OF SCRIPTURES QUOTED

Proverbs

Isaiah

Jeremiah

ART CREDITS